12420236   2.50

THOMAS DE QUINCEY

Thomas De Quincey (1785-1859), oil painting of 1845 by Sir John Watson Gordon. Reproduced with permission of the National Portrait Gallery, London.

Thomas De Quincey
Bicentenary Studies

EDITED AND WITH AN INTRODUCTION BY
Robert Lance Snyder

UNIVERSITY OF OKLAHOMA PRESS : NORMAN AND LONDON

Library of Congress Cataloging-in-Publication Data
Main entry under title:

Thomas De Quincey: Bicentenary studies.

   Papers from the Annual Convention of 1981 of the Modern Language Association, New York, N.Y.
   Includes bibliographies and index.
   1. De Quincey, Thomas, 1785–1859—Criticism and interpretation—Congresses. I. Snyder, Robert Lance, 1944– . II. Modern Language Association of America. Meeting (1981: New York, N.Y.)
PR4537.T48   1985   828'.809   85-40487
ISBN 0-8061-1849-0 (alk. paper)

The paper in this book meets the guidelines for permanence and durability of the Committee on Production Guidelines for Book Longevity of the Council on Library Resources, Inc.

Copyright © 1985 by the University of Oklahoma Press, Norman, Publishing Division of the University. Manufactured in the U.S.A. First edition.

FOR CAROL AND JONATHAN

Contents

Editor's Preface   xi
Texts and Abbreviations   xv
Editor's Introduction   xvii

1. Thomas De Quincey and the Fall of Literature
   E. Michael Thron   3
2. De Quincey's Icons of Apocalypse: Some Romantic Analogues
   V. A. De Luca   20
3. "In a Stranger's Ear": De Quincey's Polite Magazine Context
   John C. Whale   35
4. "The True Hero of the Tale": De Quincey's *Confessions* and Affective Autobiographical Theory
   Michael Cochise Young   54
5. De Quincey's Retrospective Optics: Analogues of Intoxication in the Opium-Eater's "Nursery Experiences"
   Martin Bock   72
6. Thomas De Quincey and Sigmund Freud: Sons, Fathers, Dreamers—Precursors of Psychoanalytic Developmental Psychology
   Charles L. Proudfit   88
7. The Dark Interpreter and the Palimpsest of Violence: De Quincey and the Unconscious
   Robert M. Maniquis   109

8. The Artist as Murderer: De Quincey's Essay "On Murder Considered as One of the Fine Arts"
   A. S. Plumtree — 140

9. De Quincey and the Dark Sublime: The Wordsworth-Coleridge Ethos
   John Beer — 164

10. Grazing the Brink: De Quincey's Ironies
    John E. Jordan — 199

11. Innocence and Revenge: The Problem of De Quincey's Fiction
    Grevel Lindop — 213

12. De Quincey as Gothic Parasite: The Dynamic of Supplementarity
    Jan B. Gordon — 239

13. Nexus in De Quincey's Theory of Language
    Frederick Burwick — 263

14. "Booked for Utter Perplexity" on De Quincey's English Mail-Coach
    Arden Reed — 279

15. Confession, Digression, Gravitation: Thomas De Quincey's German Connection
    Joel D. Black — 308

16. "The Loom of *Palingenesis*": De Quincey's Cosmology in "System of the Heavens"
    Robert Lance Snyder — 338

The Contributors — 361

Index — 365

Illustrations

Thomas De Quincey, oil painting by Sir John Watson Gordon — Frontispiece

Thomas De Quincey, charcoal and pastel sketch by Thomas Hood — Page xviii

Thomas De Quincey, daguerreotype photograph — xxii

Editor's Preface

This book is the outgrowth of a colloquium which I organized for the Annual Convention of 1981 of the Modern Language Association. Three of the chapters—those by Frederick Burwick, V. A. De Luca, and Arden Reed—stemmed from papers delivered at that session; the others have been selected from responses to an open invitation for submissions published in *PMLA, Studies in Romanticism,* and the *Wordsworth Circle.* In editing the volume, I owe an incalculable debt of gratitude to its contributors, from whom I have learned more about De Quincey than I would have thought possible. Their careful research and critical insight have stimulated me to reconsider what, to borrow his own terminology, might be called the "organology" of De Quincey's oeuvre. Whorled and digressive as the individual parts of that structure are, they seem to me now to constitute a pattern of epigenesis that sheds considerable light on a frequently neglected dimension of Romantic aesthetics. To say only this much, of course, is simply to record a personal judgment, but it is yet one which I must acknowledge in this context.

More specific kinds of indebtedness are easier to state than to repay. I particularly wish to thank John Beer, V. A. De Luca, John E. Jordan, and J. Hillis Miller, all of whom graciously consented to serve as editorial consultants for the project. Their detailed and perspicacious comments on papers which I forwarded for review were consistently exemplary of the gentle but discriminating art of humane scholarship. For whatever weaknesses remain in the contents of this book I alone accept full responsibility. In this connection I would be remiss not to express heartfelt appreciation as well to my colleagues J. P. Telotte, of Georgia Institute of Technology, and J. Stephen Russell, of Hofstra University, who, besides reading several of the essays submitted, were unfailing sources of support and encouragement when my energies as an editor periodically ebbed. I am also grateful to the National Portrait Gallery, in London, and the Trustees of Dove Cottage, in Grasmere, for their permission to use, respectively, Sir John Watson Gordon's painting of De Quincey of 1845 and the daguerreotype print of De Quincey of 1850 as illustrations. To Frederick Burwick, finally, I am deeply obliged for his kindness in sending me a photograph of Thomas Hood's previously unpublished sketch of De Quincey of 1821, a work among the papers of Taylor and Hessey that passed into the collection of Marquess Crewe and that later was discovered by Alvin Whitley. Such an unsolicited favor is but another mark that I have encountered of the truly collaborative interest in the writer whom this book commemorates.

Several other individuals have contributed significantly to the transformation of an inchoate idea into a finished reality. A. D. Van Nostrand, Head of the Department of English in Georgia Tech, played an indispensable role in securing from the College of Sciences and Liberal Studies a generous grant-in-aid that supported publication of the work. I am even more indebted to him for allowing me released time from teaching duties to complete the undertaking. I am also grateful to John N. Drayton, Editor-in-Chief of the University of Oklahoma Press, for being so receptive to the project's merits when I first submitted a prospectus to him. Jeffrey Plank assisted with the typing of the manuscript in its final stages; without his help I could not have managed as smoothly the necessary evil of deadlines. And, in closing, my colleagues in the School of Humanities in Seattle Pacific University, especially Jean Allen Hanawalt, have contributed much through their friendship while I was completing work on this book and acclimatizing to the Pacific Northwest.

My most abiding and least measurable debt of all is indicated in the book's dedication. Without the love of my wife and son I would be far less able either to pursue or to enjoy the labors of scholarship. My thanks to them goes beyond words.

ROBERT LANCE SNYDER

Seattle, Washington

Texts and Abbreviations

All quotations from De Quincey except those specifically noted below or in the notes are taken from *The Collected Writings of Thomas De Quincey*, ed. David Masson, 14 vols. (Edinburgh: Adam and Charles Black, 1896–97). Citations from this standard edition are designated parenthetically in the text by volume and page number (e.g., 1:42). Quotations from the following works, either by or about De Quincey, are identified in the text by the appropriate abbreviation and page number (e.g., C, p. 13).

C   *Confessions of an English Opium-Eater and Suspiria de Profundis* (Boston: Ticknor, Reed, and Fields, 1852). This volume reprints the original version of the *Confessions* of 1821–22.

D   *A Diary of Thomas De Quincey, 1803*, ed. Horace A. Eaton (London: Noel Douglas, n.d.).

Hogg   *De Quincey and His Friends: Personal Recollections, Souvenirs and Anecdotes of Thomas De Quincey, His Friends and Associates*, ed. James Hogg (London: Sampson Low, Marston, 1895).

Japp   *De Quincey Memorials*, ed. Alexander H. Japp, 2 vols. (New York: United States Book Co., 1891).

Page   *Thomas De Quincey: His Life and Writings, with Unpublished Correspondence*, ed. H. A. Page (pseud. Alexander H. Japp), 2 vols. (London: John Hogg; New York: Scribner, Armstrong, 1877).

PW   *The Posthumous Works of Thomas De Quincey,* ed. Alexander H. Japp, 2 vols. (London: William Heinemann, 1891).

SP   *Confessions of an English Opium-Eater and Suspiria de Profundis* (Boston: Ticknor, Reed, and Fields, 1852). This volume contains the first reprint of the original *Blackwood's Edinburgh Magazine* series of the *Suspiria* that appeared in the March–July 1845 numbers.

Biblical quotations are from either the Authorized (King James) Version (AV) or the Revised Version (RV) and designated as such.

Editor's Introduction

Throughout his life Thomas De Quincey was haunted by suspicions of some inveterate discontinuity, randomness, or errancy in the order of things. Embarking on his literary career late, at age thirty-six, with the serial publication of *Confessions of an English Opium-Eater*, he first delineated what was to become a characteristic obsession in terms of a personal failure. He had planned, we are there told, to devote his entire life to the construction of an encyclopedic work to be titled, after an unfinished treatise by Spinoza, *De emendatione humani intellectus*, only to see his aspirations petrify into "a memorial . . . of hopes defeated, of baffled efforts, of materials uselessly accumulated, of foundations laid that were never to support a superstructure" (*C*, p. 105). A similar fate befell another of his projects at the time when, spurred on by his reading of David Ricardo, he drafted a modestly ambitious commentary on political economy but found any further creativity subverted by his yielding to "the Circean spells of opium" (*C*, p. 108).

More than thirty years after recording these abortive ventures, he articulated, now in ontological terms, a wider view of the abiding mystery for him of coherence and connection. "Man is doubtless *one* by some subtle *nexus*," he wrote in his *Autobiographic Sketches*, "some system of links, that we cannot perceive, extending from the new-born infant to the superannuated dotard: but, as regards many affections and passions incident to his nature at different stages, he is *not* one, but an intermitting creature, ending and beginning anew" (1:43). In adapting this passage from his earlier *Suspiria de Profundis*, De Quincey interpolated the description of man as being "but an intermitting

Thomas De Quincey (1821), charcoal and pastel sketch by Thomas Hood. Courtesy of Lady Margaret Crewe. Photograph obtained by Professor Alvin Whitley, University of Wisconsin. Reproduced with the kind permission of Professor Frederick Burwick, University of California.

creature," as though six years before his death he were reformulating philosophically what he already knew firsthand all too well, namely, the fragmented, broken, seemingly disjointed nature of his experience. The pattern of De Quincey's life, of course, more than warranted such an outlook. As several of the following essays emphasize, the outward circumstances of his career were indeed chaotic, a fact which helped shape his frequently proclaimed image of himself as a pariah and which inclined him to construe a prevenient state of spiritual harmony that was ruptured repeatedly by the "infinite iteration" of the "aboriginal fall" (13:304). Preeminently intellectual and scholarly, he yet was forced to mortgage his talents to the periodical press to maintain a meager livelihood. Such exigencies, coupled with "the oppression of inexpiable guilt" (3:446) over his opium addiction, occasionally led him to the brink of despair. Thus, in one of his darkest confessions, he outlined a nightmarish vision that aptly summarizes his frustrations as a writer:

In parts and fractions eternal creations are carried on, but the nexus is wanting, and life and the central principle which should bind together all the parts at the centre, with all its radiations to the circumference, are wanting. Infinite incoherence, ropes of sand, gloomy incapacity of vital pervasion by some one plastic principle, that is the hideous incubus upon my mind always. [Page, 1:325]

Without denying this clearly haunted side of De Quincey's consciousness, however, we must be wary of letting it dominate or, worse, predetermine our estimate of his actual achievement. Too often critical response to his writing has succumbed to the fallacy of identifying his dramatic personae or self-projections with the man himself, of naïvely assuming that a single and generally sensational stereotype is an accurate representation of his abilities as a writer. At one extreme, for example, De Quincey has been made to share the predicament of that tortured Piranesi who, in the Opium-Eater's famous dream, endlessly gropes his way up interminable staircases in some cosmic or Kafkaesque prison (see 3:438–39). At another extreme, modeled on a far different tableau, he has been reduced to that self-disparaging, though ironic, caricature in the *Confessions* portraying him comfortably ensconced in his Grasmere cottage with a decanter of laudanum and a book of German metaphysics near to hand (see 3:410). Both vignettes give us a truncated view of De Quincey, the first suggesting traits of unremitting but foredoomed energy and the second a habitual but self-indulgent indolence. What each preconception leaves out of account is the intricate combination of disparate qualities, of "infinite activities, infinite repose" (3:395), that makes De Quincey's best works a graphic illustration in prose of the synthesizing Romantic imagination. We need, in short, by resisting formulaic images of the man, to recognize the extraordinary subtlety and versatility of his mind, that intelligence which Coleridge in his letters hailed as "at once systematic and labyrinthine."

The task is admittedly complicated by the mixed nature of De Quincey's canon. In addition to such "impassioned" and autobiographical works as the *Confessions, Suspiria de Profundis,* and *The English Mail-Coach,* the plethoric diversity of his essays on subjects literary, cultural, philosophic, political, and historical renders him difficult to categorize except by recourse, as V. A. De Luca has observed, to the dodge of consigning him to the amorphous realm of "nonfictional prose." And what cannot be subsumed under a conventional taxonomy tends to be ignored, sometimes dismissed, as merely marginal or idiosyncratic. Add to this the common inference that widely heterogeneous concerns in an author bespeak an unfocused sense of purpose, and the groundwork for neglect is firmly established. To be sure, not all the productions of this singular polymath come up to a uniform level of interest or expectation, but collectively they reveal a writer who can be admired for the integrity of what he did accomplish amid the most pressing distractions.

That integrity, I would submit, can best be measured in terms of De Quincey's responsiveness to the tensions of his life and age. Although besieged by debilitating self-doubt and inclined to striking defensive poses, he yet struggled with his personal anxieties, fears, and frustrations in ways that often help illuminate larger complexities of the early nineteenth century in England. As an ardent admirer of Wordsworth, for instance, he cherished the construct of "some far halcyon time" (*PW*, 1:16) that antedates and counterbalances the archetypal fall into self-consciousness; growing up fifteen years later than his mentor, however, De Quincey confronted a different array of challenges and was honest enough to admit their profoundly unsettling impact on him. "Even the character of your own absolute experience," he remarked, "past and gone, which (if anything in this world) you might surely answer for as sealed and settled for ever—even this you must submit to hold in suspense, as a thing conditional and contingent upon what is yet to come" (3:314–15). His awareness of such radical provisionality, moreover, was inseparable from the rapid acceleration of social change which he witnessed. In 1845, reacting to the "gathering agitation of our present English life" wrought by the development of railways, electricity, and the steam engine, he voiced alarm that "this colossal pace of advance" threatened a collapse of the spirit "towards the vortex of the merely human" (*SP*, p. 148). His responses as a writer to these tensions reflect another kind of integrity as well. The same impulse that prompted the autobiographical De Quincey to trace the "heraldries" of memory also motivated the discursive essayist to survey the various crosscurrents of his milieu: it was the overriding need to decipher the mystery of his experience, to uncover within it some underlying design, to locate a center that would hold. Gifted, as he liked to claim, with "a logical instinct for feeling in a moment the secret analogies or parallelisms that connected things else apparently remote" (3:332), he was a subtly self-effacing author whose works virtually *are* his life. In that congruence, that commensurate relation, can be found a reliable index of both his achievement and his contemporaneity.

Viewed in this light, De Quincey emerges as a key transitional figure who cannot be comprehended by reductive stereotypes of him as beleaguered journalist or complacent drug addict. If Robert Martin Adams is correct in classifying him among the "equivocal Romantics," it is equally true that De Quincey is an

Thomas De Quincey (1850), daguerreotype photograph. Reproduced with the kind permission of the Trustees of Dove Cottage, Wordsworth Museum, Grasmere.

ambiguous Victorian who, while proleptically foreshadowing issues associated with subsequent writers, at the same time encapsulates and reenacts the legacy of his immediate forebearers. He is, simply stated, an anomaly. But he is also one whose literary corpus comprises an elaborate, strangely protean mosaic that constantly tests our static conceptions of the man, the period, and generic boundaries—and therein lies his unique importance. Virginia Woolf, herself adept in the art of juggled perspectives, hints at what this quality entails in noting that De Quincey "shifted the value of familiar things." More so than with many less syncretic authors, therefore, our understanding of him must hinge on an unbiased and close scrutiny of his texts. There we may further discover, as another of his readers, Jorge Luis Borges, might say, that in exploring the hieroglyphics of his mind De Quincey inscribes the outline of his own identity.

Two pictorial representations can perhaps provide a preliminary frame of reference for a reassessment of his works. Unlike Sir John Watson Gordon's painting (frontispiece), which presents a stiffly formal image of De Quincey, two portraits included here depict more intimate, though contrasting, likenesses. The first is a hitherto unpublished sketch by Thomas Hood, probably executed in 1821, that shows in soft profile the gentleman-scholar who awoke to sudden anonymous fame as "the Opium-Eater," a designation by which he remained known to the public for the next three decades. This is the man who, alert to the demands of social propriety, began his career by apologizing, half-ingenuously, for "obtruding on our notice his moral ulcers, or scars" (*C*, p. vii). However, the relaxed features and curiously detached look of the individual in Hood's portrait also suggest the ambivalence of one who, in the same prefatory address, insisted that his "self-accusation does not amount to a confession of guilt" and then exonerated himself from any lingering imputation of blame on the grounds that his "life has been, on the whole, the life of a philosopher" (*C*, p. ix). The daguerreotype of 1850, on the other hand, projects anything but a serenely contemplative De Quincey. This is the man who, having endured great personal hardship during the preceding thirty years, has come to know fully the important but painful truth that "far more of our deepest thoughts and feelings pass to us ... as *involutes* (if I may coin that word) in compound experiences incapable of being disentangled, than ever reach us *directly,* and in their own abstract shapes" (*SP,* p. 173). The toll of a lifetime devoted to penetrating the obscurities of "our fantastic existence" (12:158) can be gauged from the haggard face and flat stare of the eyes in the photograph. Yet this is also the De Quincey who realized that "either the human being must suffer and struggle as the price of a more searching vision, or his gaze must be shallow, and without intellectual revelation" (*SP,* p. 259). Both images together compass the odyssey of his commitment as a writer, and both adumbrate something of the integrity that guided it from within.

If the essays here assembled do not examine all the facets of De Quincey's artistry in prose, neither do they offer a merely impressionistic overview of his place in nineteenth-century literary history. Instead they demonstrate, from a variety of critical perspectives, scholarly abilities that De Quincy himself highly esteemed: "gifts of interpretation applied to what is dark, of analysis applied to what is logically perplexed, of expansion applied to what is condensed, of practical improvement applied to what might else be overlooked as purely speculative" (3:291n.). To the extent that in exercising such gifts these bicentenary studies lay the foundation for a fresh recognition of De Quincey's achievement, the purpose of the collection will be fulfilled.

THOMAS DE QUINCEY

1

Thomas De Quincey and the Fall of Literature

E. MICHAEL THRON

Thomas De Quincey can be of great use to us today. The current debates about the definition and influence of what we academics have called Literature test any of us when we approach authors who, traditionally, have been on the borders of the canon.[1] De Quincey has been used variously as an observer of his times, as a commentator upon Coleridge, Wordsworth, Keats, and minor figures of the Romantic movement, as a prose stylist in his own right, and as a minor figure himself not worth too much critical effort. In this chapter I highlight several prominent, current arguments that promote De Quincey and place the assumptions that ground those arguments next to a differing view of his place in our thinking about Literature.

To begin, the best contemporary critics of De Quincey retain the more traditional forms of appreciation and analysis. For example, V. A. De Luca declares that "[De Quincey] is one of the last writers upon whom the tradition of the apocalyptic vision maintains its hold more or less in traditional form, one of the first in whom the spiritual journey of the self assumes its familiar modern guise."[2] These comments and those like them see De Quincey as a voyager into the Self, even as the creator of the modern Self, and they depend most often on the autobiographical works from *Confessions of an English Opium-Eater* through *Autobiographic Sketches* and *Suspiria de Profundis*.

Another approach, which initially seems a contradiction of this search for the modern Self, is the perspicacious monograph by Robert M. Maniquis entitled "Lonely Empires: Personal and Public Visions of Thomas De Quincey."[3] Maniquis is one of the few critics who not only has read De Quincey's journalism and scholarly reviews but also believes that we may read those works as counterparts of De Quincey's "impassioned prose" (1:14). In other words, in his public voice De Quincey was searching for the same thing recorded in his private voice: the salvation of the individual from determinism. Maniquis says that "we can read his journalistic pieces on the Roman Empire just as we read *The English Mail-Coach,* for the Opium-Eater's history and his dreams are only versions of one consistent kind of writing in which the pariah is saving himself. He is blind to the way he uses historical order to cleanse his stains away."[4] History and David Ricardo's theory of rents are the "inside out" of the damning personal dream. In short, if De Quincey's visions in prose will not give us a unity, as in De Luca's study, his personality will; and the public and the personal, the political and the self, are one. In this form of criticism De Quincey becomes a prototype of Romanticism's "endeavour to discover transcendence in experience"[5] and is typical of Romanticism. We have him, through theory, under control and useful for any discussion of Literature as a reflection of that tradition.

There are other ways to view the man and his works, of course. Albert Goldman's useful book *The Mine and the Mint* contains seeds of another approach. After an exhaustive journey through De Quincey's borrowings and plagiarisms, Goldman concludes that "instead then of regarding De Quincey, by turns, as a scholar, an historian, an authority on economics, or a novelist, one would do better to treat him for the most part as a very able literary journalist, the sort of writer who takes each assignment as it comes and treats it as best he can with the materials at his disposal."[6] This is a cold judgment, certainly, that we should soften with the tone of Edward Sackville-West's *A Flame in Sunlight* and the accuracy of Grevel Lindop's recent biography, where he sees a De Quincey who "wanted credit for what he might have done rather than for what he did."[7] Goldman's work has not received much critical notice because the material reads like a doctoral thesis that is presented as biographically interesting but not as a threat to the works we usually find worthy of critical attention. Goldman's labors, however, can be seen as the groundwork necessary for a new theoretical beginning in our thinking about De Quincey. De Quincey, after all, was a journalist before he became part of the canon of English Literature.

Another necessary concept for a new beginning is contained in Alvin B. Kernan's clear and direct essay "The Idea of Literature" and his subsequent work on the rise and fall of Literature.[8] Kernan traces the idea and value of literature qua Literature from the latter half of the eighteenth century to its canonization in English curricula across America. He sees the idea of Literature developing over that time period as an organic opposite to a scheduled industrial society; or, as he puts it, "A machine invariably turns out quantities of identical, mass-produced goods, but a work of literature is defined as the rare and absolutely unique product of unpredictable genius."[9] For Kernan literature is "an artificial, changing social creation, responding and adjusting to such changes as the printing press, new forms of patronage, [and] the growth of democratic societies,"[10] that meets a human need. He attacks Northrop Frye's conception of a Platonic form residing behind the social construct and, in so doing, attacks the concept of the Romantic imagination. If the modern institutionalization of literature in Literature-as-Romantic-Idealism is under attack, we need either to defend it as such or to readjust our thinking about the works we have valued using that assumption.

If we see the recent criticism of De Quincey that I initially outlined as supporting and promoting De Quincey as part of this Romantic, and now institutionalized, view of Literature, the struggle to wedge him in between, say, Lamb and Hazlitt on one side and Keats and Shelley on the other is some task indeed. But if we take Kernan's description as an accurate reflection of what is going on around us right now (that is, the organic, unique, and artist-as-genius interpretation of Literature as falling apart) and Goldman's careful undermining of the uniqueness and originality of most of De Quincey's work as accurate as well, we should readjust our thinking on De Quincey. If we combine the views of Kernan and Goldman, we should begin with De Quincey dwelling in that limbo between literature as mass-produced goods and Literature as the product of the imaginative genius.

To begin our readjustment, we should draw attention away from what De Quincey wrote to how he wrote because, by his own admission, his circumstances forced his authorship and often determined his style. Although his early ambitions, rather than practice, were well within the course of a Romantic literary career (poetry, romances, historical commentary),[11] his pose in his first major work, the *Confessions,* is one of the author in spite of himself:

> I trust that it will prove not merely an interesting record, but, in a considerable degree, useful and instructive. In *that* hope it is that I have drawn it up; and *that* must be my apology for breaking through that delicate and honourable reserve which, for the most part, restrains us from the public exposure of our own errors and infirmities. [3:209]

Throughout his career he never gave up this pose of the gentleman-scholar who writes to inform, instruct, and uplift his readers. Even when confessing his opium habits and darkest dreams, he does so as the experimenter; his body, mind, and spirit are objects of his own instruction: "I was the idol; I was the priest; I was worshipped; I was sacrificed" (3:442). Whether this is a sensational pose, conscious or unconscious, or an accurate reflection of what he was is complicated by his continuous need for money. After his early London experiences, the return to Oxford, and his subsequent flight, his penury would drive him to the editorship of the *Westmoreland Gazette,* to a promise of essays for William Blackwood, and finally to Taylor and Hessey, publishers of the *London Magazine,* where "the terms they held out to contributors were ultra-munificent," and "seeing that money was just then of necessity, the one sole object to which I looked in the cultivation of literature—naturally enough ... I offered my earliest paper" (3:127–28).[12]

This continuous struggle between the gentleman-scholar and the journalist that is apparent in the details of his life became the frame or container for his work, just as the fact of his opium addiction was his notorious by-line. His lifework dealt in literary gossip, reluctant self-revelation, scholarly journalism, a Gothic tale or two, and, common to all those genres, the possibility of discovering the sublime within the confines of one human life.[13] And that common ground of the sublime is why most still value him and find him of continued interest.

Yet De Quincey's fame rests not on works we consider unified, and hence organic Literature, but on works that were never completed to his or our satisfaction. *Confessions of an English Opium-Eater*, as first published serially in the *London Magazine* (1821), was to have a third part, and his revised edition of 1856 is bloated and still incomplete. *The English Mail-Coach* was to be part of the never-completed *Suspiria de Profundis;* "Murder Considered as One of the Fine Arts" began as a satire based upon Swift's *A Modest Proposal* (1729) and was finally revised and "completed" years later with, of all things, a postscript. "On the Knocking at the Gate in *Macbeth*" was one of the "Notes from the Pocket-Book of a Late Opium-Eater," written to capitalize on his new-won fame of 1821. In fact the work he is remembered by depends upon anticipated fulfillment; he has a habit of seldom finishing anything despite his enormous productivity. But his best work is not a Romantic aesthetic of organic fragmentation (finding the world in a grain of sand); rather, it is part of a life lived through and within the incomplete—an incompleteness that dwelled in the way he had to live, not in the way he chose to live. He worked within a system of literary journalism that demanded his life in pieces, and on that base we should begin our understanding of him.[14]

I am proposing that we begin not with an organic definition of Literature or with the sublime dream visions of De Quincey but instead with the routines and mores of his life. He had to write to live: any theory of literature developed from that premise would be skeptical, but not cynical, and would begin its arguments with De Quincey's career as a periodical journalist rather than with his accomplishments in scholarship or Literature. Such a view would accept the weaknesses of so much of his work as part of the cost of his trade and not as failures of the spirit; it would see his finest work as Journalism, not as Literature; it would free him from the onus of failure when placed beside a Keats or Shelley. He was standing in a different place from that of the poets, and one theory based on the poet-as-genius will not cover the pantheon of poets and essayists. But De Quincey is very useful for this view because he reported his journey; he saw himself as the object and the subject, as the observed and the observer, in one—as the "idol" and the "priest." It follows that if he converted his daily struggle into his writing, with or without opium, the fragmentation of the way he had to work would shape his prose. This transparency between the demands of the periodical press and his prose becomes as much a subject for De Quincey as anything else he experienced.

In the *Confessions* of 1821-22 he tells us how he transfers a mundane image into his dreams:

That, as the creative state of the eye increased, a sympathy seemed to arise between the waking and the dreaming states of the brain in one point,—that whatsoever I happened to call up and to trace by a voluntary act upon the darkness was very apt to transfer itself to my dreams. [*C*, p. 110]

If we couple this ability to transfer waking images into dreams with the other effects of his opium addiction (the deep-seated anxiety, the swelling of space and time, the revival of the minutest incidents of childhood), we might construct a dream structure that *resolves* the incompleteness of his daily life; and most critics have taken this approach. In this view the dream visions become the completion of this experience of the incomplete. In organic theories of Literature the explanations, digressions, and stylistic dodges surrounding the dream visions are preparations for the sublime resolutions contained within the visions, and they should be, as Wordsworth said of his sublime visions in *The Prelude* (1850), like "angels stopped upon the wing."[15] If they are not, they are unforgivable flaws.

One of the better essays arguing that the dream visions do resolve the necessities of De Quincey's life is Roger J. Porter's "The Demon Past: De Quincey and the Autobiographer's Dilemma." His argument matches De Luca's unity of prose with a unity of intention and personality: "The autobiography is so largely predicated on dreams because the dream is, for De Quincey, the act which completes the tendency of earlier experience."[16] Porter grounds this assertion on Northrop Frye's concept of the "creative world . . . deep within,"[17] which is the basis of the established definition of Literature as the expression of that unified world. In this view the painful journey within to find the self is the journey of ancient myth. It produces the salvation of the individual from a disjunctive and meaningless yet scheduled world brought on by social, technological, and political modernity. Predictably, Porter ends his essay with De Quincey and Keats, in the same sentence, believing in the "strength of art."

The commentators sympathetic to this view begin with that "strength of art" and transform De Quincey's life accordingly; even Maniquis's idea of De Quincey's public voice becomes intelligible through an examination of the internal journey. The drive for a unified, psychological interpretation is so great in contemporary criticism of De Quincey that it ignores 80 per cent of what he wrote; in short, we find those works which fit our desire for unity, and, when even those fail us, we discover his personality and his Unconscious, and they turn out to be ours as well through the assumption that the Unconscious is real and universal.

We depend so much on De Quincey's dreams and visions as unifiers of his work and personality because that view provides us with a secure reading within our assumptions about Romantic Literature. He provides us with a noble escape from the mechanical world and within that escape a definition and example of Literature as power. De Quincey gives us the place where the sublime infuses our experience. We read De Quincey and confirm our own place in the world, and it becomes as hard to see past him as it is to see past our own minds. If we accept my argument that De Quincey provides us with a view of how we have created our own assumptions about Literature, we should look at those methods to see our own. In short, we could use De Quincey for an understanding of the creation of our own blindness. To do so, we must assume that he is, as Marlow would say of Lord Jim, "one of us." We must take on

his assumptions so that we may find our own limitations.
    First, we should not ignore what he so clearly flees: the utilitarianism of the nineteenth century. If Literature was created as a mighty opposite to the world, however, we should not dismiss that world in an abstraction like "utilitarianism" or "industrialization." De Quincey's aversion to his world was specific and direct. He clearly tells us what he flees in his "Introductory Notice" to *Suspiria de Profundis,* one of his best of many good-byes to his century:

Already, in this year 1845, what by the procession through fifty years of mighty revolutions amongst the kingdoms of the earth, what by the continual development of vast physical agencies,—steam in all its applications, light getting under harness as a slave for man, powers from heaven descending upon education and accelerations of the press, powers from hell (as it might seem, but these also celestial) coming round upon artillery and the forces of destruction,—the eye of the calmest observer is troubled; the brain is haunted as if by some jealousy of ghostly beings moving amongst us; and it becomes too evident that, unless this colossal pace of advance can be retarded (a thing not to be expected), or, which is happily more probable, can be met by counter forces of corresponding magnitude, forces in the direction of religion or profound philosophy, that shall radiate centrifugally against this storm of life so perilously centripetal towards the vortex of the merely human, left to itself, the natural tendency of so chaotic a tumult must be to evil; for some minds to lunacy, for others to a reägency of fleshly torpor. [*SP,* p. 148]

The gathering agitation, as he describes it, resides in the "vast physical agencies" rather than in the political forces of his time. The England of 1845 dances to the pounding of the steam engine and printing press, not the harmonies of a political philosophy or poetic line.
    We who are so used to technological progress sometimes forget the changes in these "vast physical agencies" during De Quincey's lifetime. When De Quincey first published his *Confessions* in 1821, there were less than 100 miles of railroad track in England and the "loco-motive" traveled fifteen to twenty miles an hour at best, a speed so unusual that early riders were terrified.

By 1854 there were nearly 9,000 miles of track, George Stephenson was boasting that 400 miles per hour might be the limit of human endurance riding the railroad, and Isambard Kingdom Brunel boasted of traveling 90 miles per hour on his Great Western Railroad.[18] The "light getting under harness" mentioned by De Quincey reflects the sudden expansion of studios in England under Louis Jacques Mandé Daguerre's patent during the 1840s. The daguerreotype needed exposures of twenty seconds in 1841, ten seconds in 1842, and five seconds by 1851.[19] Artillery and other "forces of destruction" were undergoing rapid improvement with the continued development of the bursting shell by Henry Shrapnel, the invention of the needle gun by the Prussians, the new accuracy of fire resulting from the rifling of cannon, and the promise of more and more rapid-fire weapons after Samuel Colt's first patent in 1835.[20]

These changes both fascinated and appalled De Quincey. In the chapter "Travelling" of his *Autobiographic Sketches,* he outlines the change in traveling speed by coach of 5 miles per hour to the locomotive's speed of 50 miles per hour by the time of his middle age. He even blesses such progress with the word "organic": "Then first [after the complete development of roads and railroads] will be seen a political system truly *organic—i.e.,* in which each acts upon all, and all react upon each: and a new earth will arise from the indirect agency of this merely physical revolution" (1:271).

The efficiency of railroads and the speed of the electric telegraph that promised, for De Quincey at least, an organic and recognizable public body brought a false surface of cause and effect to anyone living through such changes. We think that because a plane leaves Chicago at 8:00 A.M. there is an inevitable connection between that leaving and its arriving in Denver at 9:30 A.M. The distance and time in between are a surface of causes and effects that is taken for granted; the time in between excludes, for the traveler, such mundane concerns as the working of the engines, the pilot's skill, and the cabin pressure. De Quincey discovers in opium a medium to transfix that schedule, stop it even when it predicts motion and distance, and draw the images of everyday travel onto the stage of his dreaming mind to connect with his "memorials," as he calls them, of the past. It is as if the time and distance between were stilled in reverie and all became a sublime digression from the scheduled life. As De Quincey travels or writes a perfunctory essay or recounts the events of his life, he drops away from the obvious linearity of the form, the surface if you will of travel or printing. He avoids the necessarily linear in two ways: first, by procrastinating in his personal life and on the page, and, second, by discovering the dreams that coincide with that procrastination. By reporting those dreams, he infuses the surface of his life and his prose with mystery and depth. The dreams give his life and his prose significance if not meaning. They turn his prose into Literature and his life into that of the Poet; and opium is the catalyst for his dreams. Opium becomes the elixir of Literature and the creator of the cathedral of significance that enshrines his discovery of the Romantic Self. De Quincey, then, provides us with a record of the creation of the Self and its now common link with the creation of Literature. In so doing he deliberately argues against the professional bases of his life as a journalist.

From this flight and subsequent discovery of the Self and Literature, we may construct an axiom for De Quincey's life: as his public world became more graphic, useful, scheduled, and predictable, his inner world became more metaphoric, useless, and spiritually powerful. If we take that movement from the outside to the inside as good, as a movement toward the well of truth and Literature, we have returned to Kernan's discussion of the definition of Literature as organic and opposed to the mechanistic world of the nineteenth century, and that is the very definition under attack in our time. As we attack that definition, we eliminate, supposedly, the value of Romanticism.

To show how De Quincey reports the creation of Self and Literature, I use a familiar example from "On the Knocking at the Gate in *Macbeth*" in an unfamiliar way. The essay originally appeared as one of the "Notes from the Pocket-Book of a Late Opium-Eater" in the *London Magazine* for October 1823. He begins casually enough with a personal observation: "From my boyish days I had always felt a great perplexity on one point in *Macbeth*"; but within three sentences we read, "Here I pause for one moment, to exhort the reader" (10:389), and we have a long paragraph explaining why the faculty of understanding cannot capture the feeling of the knocking at the gate. He returns but quickly digresses again, explaining the Williams murders (which became the basis for the postscript to "Murder Considered as One of the Fine Arts") as an example of another nearly contemporary and real knocking at the gate. We must sympathize, says De Quincey, with the murderer, not the murdered, and we are lectured once more in a footnote on the meaning of "sympathy." The "Note," even in so short a space, has placed so many obstacles in our way that we wonder when and where we will get the explanation of the knocking. Of course, if we can believe him, De Quincey has been waiting since boyhood.

His style to this point has been conversational and pedantic (in a charming way) and a suspenseful conspiracy against a quick reading expected from a "Note." Because there are so many diversions in such a short space, it is easy to see his misdirections, but when he finally discusses the knocking at the gate, the page opens, and a smooth flight is before us:

Here, as I have said, the retiring of the human heart and the entrance of the fiendish heart was to be expressed and made sensible. *Another world has stept in;* and the murderers are taken out of the region of human things, human purposes, human desires. They are transfigured: Lady Macbeth is "unsexed"; Macbeth has forgot that he was born of woman; both are conformed to the image of devils; and the world of devils is suddenly revealed. But how shall this be conveyed and made palpable? In order that a new world may step in, this world must for a time disappear. The murderers and the murder must be insulated—*cut off by an immeasurable gulf from the ordinary tide and succession of human affairs*—locked up and sequestered in some deep recess; we must be made sensible that the world of ordinary life is suddenly arrested, laid asleep, tranced, racked into a dread armistice; time must be annihilated, relation to things without abolished; and all must pass self-withdrawn into a deep syncope and suspension of earthly passion. Hence it is that, when the deed is done, when *the work of darkness is perfect,* then the world of darkness passes away like a pageantry in the clouds: the knocking at the gate is heard, and it makes known audibly that the reaction has commenced; the human has made its reflux upon the fiendish; the pulses of life are beginning to beat again; and *the re-establishment of the goings-on of the world in which we live first makes us profoundly sensible of the awful parenthesis that had suspended them.* [10:393]

I have italicized parts of this remarkable passage to emphasize how clearly De Quincey establishes the contrast of the secret, guilty, and sublime world of the murderers to the "ordinary tide and succession of human affairs." The ordinary world is successive, mundane, and bustling; the world of murder is dark, perfect, a timeless and "awful parenthesis." The power within that awful parenthesis brings significance to the ordinary just as Literature does.[21]

In this fragment we have a miniature pattern of the significant works of Thomas De Quincey. Within the secret of his awful parenthesis there is a murderer, a profound and unspeakable guilt building upon the death of his sister, for which he blames himself. We can multiply these parentheses of guilt easily: the vision of sudden death in *The English Mail-Coach,* the body of his sister in "The Affliction of Childhood," the loss of Ann of Oxford Street and the crocodile dream in the *Confessions,* the specter of the Brocken in *Suspiria de Profundis,* the knocking at the door in the postscript to "Murder Considered as One of the Fine Arts," and even the last battle in the historical essay "The Revolt of the Tartars." His impassioned prose becomes the supersaturated solution for the visions within the parentheses, and his style signals the change from the previous amusements and understandings of the journalist-scholar. The inside and outside of the parenthesis are clearly related by a transfer of style and purpose. His disgust and hatred for the process of writing,[22] the very fact of his labor that is reflected in his continuous digressions, footnotes, and conversational delays, are transferred to the guilt of his luxuriant wanderings and digressions within his dreams. This revulsion toward his life as lived becomes the profound guilt of his dreams and the basis of his creation of the significant Self. His task becomes ennobled and worthy of a poet searching for the answers to significant questions. It is *Literature*.

Again in his "Introductory Notice" to *Suspiria de Profundis* he tells us what he is doing. Through opium he recovered his childhood and the "worlds of death and darkness which never again closed, and through which it might be said that I ascended and descended at will" (*SP*, p. 155). His childhood is the substance of his dreams, and the opium expands the solitude necessary for those dreams and provides space for the "awful parenthesis" of his solitude as well. De Quincey creates the dream within the rush and hurry of the world of "steam in all its applications, light getting under harness as a slave for man, powers from heaven descending upon education and accelerations of the press" (*SP*, p. 148). The opium brings the grandeur of solitude discovered in his remembrance of childhood and regains for him the profound significance that was lost to a scheduled world that dissipates thought and feeling. The opium provides the parenthesis itself within which De Quincey hides from modern machines and society and within which De Quincey creates Literature.

But even then he could not escape. The harassment and anxiety of his daily life follow him into these dream parentheses, not as substance but as structure. In *Suspiria de Profundis* he answers a fictional "cynical reader" (*SP*, p. 156) who often objects to all those wanderings by telling several anecdotes that explain the structure of his style. First is the fellow who wants to take the shortest road to see the beauties of the Lake District. De Quincey replies, " 'Might it not be as well to ask after the most beautiful road, rather than the shortest?' " (*SP*, p. 157). Then comes the important caduceus metaphor where the opium becomes the withered shaft, and the dreams become the flowing plants luxuriantly wrapped around it. Both examples emphasize the digressive and opulent nature of the dreams, a structural transference of the digressions and avoidances of his other prose and of his life. After several other examples he combines all the images in an impassioned explanation for our amusement and understanding to end his "Introductory Notice": "The true object in my 'Opium Confessions' is not the naked physiological theme... but those wandering musical variations upon the theme,—those parasitical thoughts, feelings, digressions, which climb up with bells and blossoms round about the arid stock; ramble away from it at times with perhaps too rank a luxuriance" (*SP,* pp. 158–59). The very structure of escape and wandering resides within his dreams, assuring him of a journey without end. Motion is retained by the dreams, and the only stillness is in the dreamer and observer; and that stillness is the stillness not of understanding but of the Opium-Eater: "For it seemed to me as if then first I stood at a distance, and aloof from the uproar of life; as if the tumult, the fever, and the strife, were suspended; a respite granted from the secret burdens of the heart; a sabbath of repose; a resting from human labors" (*C,* p. 81).

Because De Quincey was so transparent about everything that affected him, he is an excellent guide to this interpretation of his own work. In a sense he gives us Literature and its criticism all in one, and this makes him very useful for us today because we are questioning Literature itself. Laurence Stapleton in *The Elected Circle* has a clever answer to these problems of the definition and value of Literature in De Quincey's work. Stapleton locates the value and significance outside the dream visions, calling them "mere experiment" and overheated rhetoric, and within De Quincey's own explanations of those visions. "What De Quincey says *about* dreaming and the value of it," contends this critic, "is always more convincing than the specimens that he gives of it, however useful they might be to a psychologist."[23] The autobiographical and experiential material leading to the dream visions is more valuable because it is not fictional (though it might contain lies) yet retains a narrative form. The dream visions are collections of images going nowhere—a fictionality without narrative, a form reached again only much later by Virginia Woolf in *Jacob's Room* (1922) and *The Waves* (1931).[24] As my previous argument suggests, I could not agree with such a conclusion because the walls between the dream visions and the narrative are really quite permeable, and one side forms the structural base of the other side. But I find a very interesting point in Stapleton's essay. De Quincey's creation of a form that is dependent upon narrative but is not fictional could be De Quincey's greatest help for us now. If Stapleton is right that "De Quincey evolves an appropriate form in which he is able simultaneously to narrate, to interpret and to intensify"[25] and that he escapes the limitations of Literature (that is, its opposition to our own social and technological world), then De Quincey might be one who could help us through these debates.

Returning to Kernan's argument that Literature is an institution dependent upon the "anti-mechanical: the natural, the organic, the intrinsic, the spontaneous, the human and humane"[26] and that that antimechanical institution has depended upon fictionality as its sine qua non, it follows that in De Quincey we have a writer who shows us how Literature is created from a form that is not Literature at all. The form he had to use because of his poverty, his opium, and his gentleman-scholar's ambitions never allowed him to complete his plans as either a scholar or a man of Literature. He, more than almost any other memorable writer of his age, had to confront the press for what it was, and he created with his "brain, so time-shattered," works of "significancy and value" (5:304). In my opinion not only did he "enlarge the capacity of prose"[27] as Stapleton claims—this is not a matter of disembodied style—but also he is the lens through which we see the interaction of social and technological forces within an extremely sensitive and perceptive mind. His works are silent, printed testimony of that struggle, and they are of use to contemporary literature as we experience the contentions of our own time. He could not complete his planned escape into Romantic Literature, and he had the courage to record his failure. De Quincey reminds us that we too cannot escape but that a literature that is an intrinsic part of our private and public lives may be possible.

NOTES

1. For full coverage of the recent debates see "Professing Literature: A Symposium on the Study of English," [*London*] *Times Literary Supplement*, 10 December 1982, pp. 1355-63; and the special issue devoted to "The Politics of Interpretation" in *Critical Inquiry* 9 (September 1982).

2. V. A. De Luca, *Thomas De Quincey: The Prose of Vision* (Toronto: University of Toronto Press, 1980), p. 150.
3. Robert M. Maniquis, "Lonely Empires: Personal and Public Visions of Thomas De Quincey," in *Literary Monographs*, vol. 8, ed. Eric Rothstein and Joseph Anthony Wittreich, Jr. (Madison: University of Wisconsin Press, 1976), pp. 47–127.
4. Maniquis, "Lonely Empires," p. 88.
5. De Luca, *Thomas De Quincey*, p. 148.
6. Albert Goldman, *The Mine and the Mint: Sources for the Writings of Thomas De Quincey* (Carbondale: Southern Illinois University Press, 1965), p. 160.
7. Edward Sackville-West, *A Flame in Sunlight: The Life and Work of Thomas De Quincey*, ed. John E. Jordan (1936; London: Bodley Head, 1974); Grevel Lindop, *The Opium-Eater: A Life of Thomas De Quincey* (London: J. M. Dent, 1981), p. 268.
8. Alvin B. Kernan, "The Idea of Literature," *New Literary History* 5 (1973): 31–40; Alvin B. Kernan, *The Imaginary Library: An Essay on Literature and Society* (Princeton, N.J.: Princeton University Press, 1982). For an excellent analysis of the particularities of Kernan's sketch of the developing idea of Literature, see also John Gross, *The Rise and Fall of the Man of Letters: A Study of the Idiosyncratic and the Humane in Modern Literature* (New York: Macmillan, 1969).
9. Kernan, "The Idea of Literature," p. 33.
10. Kernan, *The Imaginary Library*, p. 25.
11. De Quincey's youthful plans, as revealed in his diary entry for 26 May 1803, included such projected works as "Yermak the Rebel, a Drama," "A Pathetic Tale, of Which a Black Man Is the Hero," "A Life of Julius Caesar," and "An Essay on Poetry" (see *D*, p. 181).
12. For details see Horace Ainsworth Eaton, *Thomas De Quincey: A Biography* (London: Oxford University Press, 1936), pp. 226–91.
13. On the last point J. Hillis Miller's chapter on De Quincey in *The Disappearance of God: Five Nineteenth-Century Writers* (1963; reprint, Cambridge, Mass.: Harvard University Press, Belknap Press, 1975), pp. 17–80, remains the classic work.
14. In this paragraph and my later discussion of "On the Knocking at the Gate in *Macbeth*" I have adapted and expanded ideas first formulated in my article "A New Introduction for Thomas De Quincey," *Prairie Schooner* 55 (1981): esp. pp. 219–23.
15. William Wordsworth, *The Prelude: 1799, 1805, 1850*, ed. Jonathan Wordsworth, M. H. Abrams, and Stephen Gill (New York: Norton, 1979), 14.98 (1850).
16. Roger J. Porter, "The Demon Past: De Quincey and the Autobiographer's Dilemma," *Studies in English Literature, 1500–1900* 20 (1980): 605.
17. Northrop Frye, "The Drunken Boat: The Revolutionary Element in Romanticism," in Northrop Frye, ed., *Romanticism Reconsidered: English*

Institute Essays, 1962 (New York: Columbia University Press, 1963), p. 16.

18. See Francis D. Klingender, *Art and the Industrial Revolution*, ed. and rev. Arthur Elton (London: Evelyn, Adams and Mackay, 1968), pp. 139, 126.

19. See B. E. C. Howarth-Loomes, *Victorian Photography: An Introduction for Collectors and Connoisseurs* (New York: St. Martin's Press, 1974), p. 21.

20. See W. Y. Carman, *A History of Firearms: From Earliest Times to 1914* (New York: St. Martin's Press, 1955), pp. 52, 121, 144, 172. Material in this and the following paragraph also appears in my essay "Speed, Steam, Self, and Thomas De Quincey," in Norman A. Anderson and Margene E. Weiss, eds., *Interspace and the Inward Sphere: Essays on Romantic and Victorian Self* (Macomb, Ill.: Western Illinois University, 1978), pp. 51–52.

21. For a similar analysis of this passage see De Luca, *Thomas De Quincey*, pp. 42–43.

22. In a letter of 1844 to Mary Russell Mitford, for example, De Quincey remarks: "Whatever I may have been writing is suddenly wrapt . . . in one sheet of consuming fire. . . . I cannot endure to look at it: and I sweep it away into vast piles of unfinished letters or inchoate pages begun and interrupted under circumstances the same in kind" (as cited in Eaton, *Thomas De Quincey*, p. 418). This disgust was not a single occurrence but a recurring pattern.

23. Laurence Stapleton, *The Elected Circle: Studies in the Art of Prose* (Princeton, N.J.: Princeton University Press, 1973), pp. 138–39.

24. John Lent, in "Thomas De Quincey, Subjectivity, and Modern Literature: A Consideration of the Release of Vision in *Confessions of an English Opium-Eater* and *Suspiria de Profundis*," *Sphinx* 9 (1979): 36–58, develops fully this connection between De Quincey's prose poetry and modern Literature, using John E. Jordan's connection, in *Thomas De Quincey, Literary Critic: His Method and Achievement* (Berkeley and Los Angeles: University of California Press, 1952), of De Quincey's theories to Wordsworth's as a basis of the argument. According to this view De Quincey is the precursor of the Literature of Modernism. I would say certainly, but in the impassioned prose only.

25. Stapleton, *The Elected Circle*, p. 165.

26. Kernan, *The Imaginary Library*, p. 27.

27. Stapleton, *The Elected Circle*, p. 133.

2

De Quincey's Icons of Apocalypse: Some Romantic Analogues

V. A. DE LUCA

Two images dominate the long apocalyptic dream vision that concludes De Quincey's *The English Mail-Coach:* a chariot of power and a temple of deliverance, the first ensconced in the second. Here is the most illustrative passage:

> Two hours after midnight we approached a mighty Minster. Its gates, which rose to the clouds, were closed. But, when the dreadful word that rode before us reached them with its golden light, silently they moved back upon their hinges; and at a flying gallop our equipage entered the grand aisle of the cathedral. Headlong was our pace; and at every altar, in the little chapels and oratories to the right hand and left of our course, the lamps, dying or sickening, kindled anew in sympathy with the secret word that was flying past. Forty leagues we might have run in the cathedral, and as yet no strength of morning light had reached us, when before us we saw the aerial galleries of organ and choir. Every pinnacle of the fretwork, every station of advantage amongst the traceries, was crested by white-robed choristers that sang deliverance; that wept no more tears, as once their fathers had wept; but at intervals that sang together to the generations, saying,
>
> > "Chant the deliverer's praise in every tongue,"
>
> and receiving answers from afar,
>
> > "Such as once in heaven and earth were sung."
>
> And of their chanting was no end; of our headlong pace was neither pause nor slackening. [13:322-23]

The temple is enormous, a "mighty Minster"; it is complex in its many "chapels and oratories," in its "traceries" and "fretwork," in its choir of the living and a necropolis of the dead; it is lofty in its architecture, with "aerial galleries," and "pinnacle[s]" and "gates" that "[rise] to the clouds." The chariot, only superficially disguised as a mail-coach, is compact, linear, horizontal in its thrust. It distributes, "like the opening of apocalyptic vials" (13:272), news of the Lord's victories; but it can also distribute death through the blind force of its motion, as it presently threatens to do in the dream vision itself. The temple and the chariot are complementary images—one static and the other dynamic, one enclosing and the other penetrating, one all form and the other all motion. They are icons of the apocalypse, of the power and the beauty of the Godhead revealed, of death, resurrection, horror, and joy, the Four Last Things.

De Quincey is fascinated with these images. His writings are filled with fantasies of celestial architecture, "cities and temples, beyond the art of Phidias and Praxiteles, beyond the splendours of Babylon and Hekatómpylos" (3:395). He dreams of "the domes and cupolas of a great city ... caught perhaps in childhood from some picture of Jerusalem" (3:445), and he tells us of the visions of his Spanish Military Nun, who saw "the interlacings of boughs overhead forming a dome that seemed like the dome of a cathedral. She saw, through the fretwork of the foliage, another dome, far beyond the dome of an evening sky, the dome of some heavenly cathedral" (13:204). De Quincey even devotes a climactic spot in *Confessions of an English Opium-Eater* to such visions, quoting a Wordsworthian rendering of evening clouds as a vision of the New Jerusalem:

> Fabric it seemed of diamond and of gold,
> With alabaster domes and silver spires,
> And blazing terrace upon terrace, high
> Uplifted.
>
> [*The Excursion*, 2.839–42; De Quincey, 3:440]

Images of precipitous speed are similarly abundant in De Quincey's writings—hurricanes in the air, rushing vehicles on land, irresistible columns of water—and, in one extraordinary vision, "a vault seemed to open in the zenith of the far blue sky, a shaft which ran up forever. I, in spirit, rose as if on billows that also ran up the shaft forever; and the billows seemed to pursue the throne of God; but *that* also ran before us and fled away continually" (*SP*, p. 176).

A speeding throne is a kind of chariot; indeed, it is as close as De Quincey gets to the Merkabah of Hebrew prophecy and Kabbalist tradition, God's "throne-in-motion," as Harold Bloom has called it.[1] *The English Mail-Coach* provides a feast of such biblical echoes, and when De Quincey exclaims of the coach, "What a thundering of wheels!—what a trampling of hoofs!— what a sounding of trumpets!" (13:294), the apocalyptic resonances are hard to miss—particularly since he himself attaches to the mail-coach the term "apocalyptic" and an insistently messianic purpose:

The mail-coach it was that distributed over the face of the land, like the opening of apocalyptic vials, the heart-shaking news of Trafalgar, of Salamanca, of Vittoria, of Waterloo. These were the harvests that, in the grandeur of their reaping, redeemed the tears and blood in which they had been sown. [13:272]

To explore the extent of these resonances would require a commentary on the whole of *The English Mail-Coach*.[2] Here I am more interested in De Quincey's response to these traditional apocalyptic icons as it relates to the responses we find in his Romantic contemporaries, in particular Blake, Shelley, and Keats. On crucial occasions each of the writers borrows from Ezekiel, the first of the prophets to establish the images of the chariot and the temple as representations of divine power and sacred form. Visions of these apocalyptic forms bracket Ezekiel's prophecy at the beginning and the end like bookends:

As for the likeness of the living creatures, their appearance was like burning coals of fire, like the appearance of torches; it went up and down among the living creatures: and the fire was bright, and out of the fire went forth lightning. And the living creatures ran and returned as the appearance of a flash of lightning. Now as I beheld the living creatures, behold one wheel upon the earth beside the living creatures, for each of the four faces thereof. The appearance of the wheels and their work was like unto the colour of a beryl: and they four had one likeness: and their appearance and their work was as it were a wheel within a wheel. When they went, they went upon their four sides: they turned not when they went. [Ezek. 1:13-17, RV]

And the glory of the Lord came into the house [i.e., temple] by the way of the gate whose prospect is toward the east. And the spirit took me up, and brought me into the inner court; and behold, the glory of the Lord filled the house. And I heard one speaking unto me out of the house; and a man stood by me. And he said unto me, Son of man, *this is* the place of my throne, and the place of the soles of my feet, where I will dwell in the midst of the children of Israel for ever. [Ezek. 43:4-7, RV]

The fourfold attributes of the chariot and its living creatures, after an intervening stretch of tumultuous historical prophecy, eventually locate themselves tangibly and permanently in the final eight chapters of architectural specifications for the four-gated temple of the New Jerusalem.

When these images descend to the Romantic period, they appear most conspicuously in Blake, particularly in his late poem *Jerusalem*. The city of Golgonooza in that poem is, as Blake himself acknowledges, a free-form version of Ezekiel's temple:

Fourfold the Sons of Los in their division: and fourfold,
The great City of Golgonooza: fourfold toward the north
And toward the south fourfold, & fourfold toward the
    east & west
Each within other toward the four points: that toward
Eden, and that toward the World of Generation,
And that toward Beulah, and that toward Ulro:
Ulro is the space of the terrible starry wheels of Albions
    sons:
But that toward Eden is walled up, till time of renovation:
Yet it is perfect in its building, ornaments & perfection.[3]

Similarly, at the end of the poem the chariot of the Almighty appears:

The Four Living Creatures Chariots of Humanity Divine
    Incomprehensible
In beautiful Paradises expand These are the Four Rivers
    of Paradise

And the Four Faces of Humanity fronting the Four
    Cardinal Points
Of Heaven going forward forward irresistible from
    Eternity to Eternity.⁴

Blake works two essential changes on his source in Ezekiel. For one thing, he reverses the order in which the apocalyptic icons are presented to us. The temple vision that forms the climax of Ezekiel's prophecy is moved to chapter 1, while the chariot vision that opens the Book of Ezekiel becomes the climactic vision of the finale of *Jerusalem*. The second change is that Blake places *man himself* in the chariot of power: it is the chariot of "Humanity Divine." Ezekiel's chariot belongs to the order of divine things, his temple to the order of history, or, rather, of historical possibility. He wishes to bind the divine power to an earthly place and to a human ritual.⁵ But for Blake the city of Golgonooza is a contingent structure, a work of art that will serve until time is finished, and at that point fourfold order and energy shall flow from the intellect of risen humanity, free from the need for mediating structures.

In his attachment to traditional biblical imagery and to a Protestant strain of prophecy regarding man's redemption, De Quincey reveals his affinities to the sensibility that produced Blake's vision and, in a more muted way, the prophetic strains in Wordsworth and Coleridge. Like Ezekiel, De Quincey is concerned with the fulfillment of God's promise within history, and *The English Mail-Coach* is essentially about the emergence of England as the Kingdom of the Just on earth,⁶ or, as he says in another and earlier essay, "England, as the centre of this great resurrection; centre for the power; centre, most of all, for the moral principle at work" (3:62). Thus it is significant that he too begins with an overture that enumerates the attributes of the coach—the "glory of motion," the "animal beauty and power," a "central intellect," an "awful *political* mission" (13:271, 272)— and that he ends with a vision of a "mighty" cathedral filled with fugal music and choral hymns. Like Blake, De Quincey insists on including the chariot in the final vision as well, leading all of risen humanity in procession: "The quick and the dead that sang together to God, . . . all the hosts of jubilation, like armies that ride in pursuit, moved with one step, . . . as brothers we moved together" (13:326).

At the same time there is a disquieting alteration of Ezekiel's vision and a contraction of the possibilities of freedom offered by Blake. Insofar as De Quincey's dream cathedral represents a vision of an ultimate order, on earth or in heaven, it is an order from which humanity can never liberate itself; no matter how swiftly the coach speeds, no matter how far it travels—forty leagues, seventy leagues—it remains inside the cathedral, and indeed the dream spends itself before the outer limits of the structure are even glimpsed. Yet the situation can be posed in just the opposite perspective. Recall that, if Ezekiel presents a vision of a divine chariot, it is to vouchsafe the possibility of an earthly temple in time to come. De Quincey presents us with a prosaic material chariot, a mail-coach, but the great cathedral rises only in dreams. Motion and power are given material embodiment, form and beauty only spectral presence; the chariot is historical, the promise of order a figment of sleep.

As we try to grasp the totality of his vision, these equivocal perspectives induce a certain disequilibrium, a vertigo, effects that De Quincey specializes in. Form oppresses, proliferates, is inescapable, or else it becomes unsteady, shimmers, dissolves, offers no resistance to the onslaught of material power. We become lost in paradoxes. In De Quincey's works there is a tendency for the House of God, the Heavenly Temple, to turn into an astronomical wilderness, where forms appear to exist only to mock the possibility of human freedom. Thus it is in the scientific version of the Heavenly City, the vision of interstellar space in the essay "System of the Heavens" (1846):

> Without measure were the architraves, past number were the archways, beyond memory the gates. Within were stairs that scaled the eternities above, that descended to the eternities below: above was below, below was above, to the man stripped of gravitating body: depth was swallowed up in height insurmountable, height was swallowed up in depth unfathomable. [8:34]

We are not far in such visions from the reduplicating architecture and infinite regresses of the dream visions of Piranesi in the *Confessions,* which J. Hillis Miller has explicated so well,[7] structures that are, of course, explicitly labeled "Prisons."

And at the same time that form attenuates, loses centering, and yet imprisons, power compacts itself into a moving solid, the battering ram of "Death the crowned phantom, with all the equipage of his terrors" (13:318), or into what De Quincey calls in his novella "The Household Wreck" the "mighty Juggernaut of social life, moving onwards with its everlasting thunders, paus[ing] not for a moment to spare, to pity, to look aside, but rush[ing] forward for ever, impassive as the marble in the quarry, caring not for whom it destroys" (12:159–60). Or else power liquefies into forms like the Bore in the second version of the *Confessions,* a "mighty refluent wash... leaving memorials, by sight and by sound, of its victorious power" (3:307). Equivocal at best in dreams, the icons of apocalypse tend to horrify in their material incarnations, which is why De Quincey tends to look for the fulfillment of history not in history itself but in dreams about history. Even in dreams one takes one's chances, but at least the possibility of redemptive harmonies remains open there.

Thus we see everywhere in De Quincey's treatment of the images of the chariot and temple signs of a breakdown of the prophetic integrations that these images represent for the biblical apocalyptic writer and for Blake. Each image appears to contain stresses tugging in opposite directions, toward order and chaos, vitality and destruction, and, what is more, both images tend to pull away from one another. In Blake and Ezekiel chariot and temple share in each other's attributes. Their chariots are notable for radial symmetry and geometrical perfection, and their temples for the presence of a heroic vitality, but the best De Quincey can do in his "Dream-Fugue" to unify the images is to send his chariot galloping through the cathedral. Yet even so the one remains all blundering force, the other all nervous geometry.

What these equivocations and instabilities signify, I think, is a radical doubt in De Quincey's mind that power can be yoked to the idea of order to fulfill a humanistic prophecy and, with the doubt, a knowledge that either element alone will surely fail to suffice. In this respect De Quincey is closer to the second generation of the Romantics than he is to Blake and Wordsworth, poets who never doubted the immediacy of prophetic possibility. In poets like Shelley and Keats an equivocal stance similar to De Quincey's is apparent along with a similar fascination for the apocalyptic emblems themselves. Shelley, for instance, is deeply attracted to Ezekiel's image of the chariot, as Harold Bloom taught us long ago in *Shelley's Mythmaking*.[8] It provides, for example, the model for this cynosure vision in act 4 of *Prometheus Unbound*, revealing the Chariot of the Spirit of the Earth:

> A sphere, which is as many thousand spheres,
> Solid as chrystal, yet through all its mass
> Flow, as through empty space, music and light:
> Ten thousand orbs involving and involved,
> Purple and azure, white and green and golden,
> Sphere within sphere, and every space between
> Peopled with unimaginable shapes
> Such as ghosts dream dwell in the lampless deep
> Yet each intertranspicuous, and they whirl
> Over each other with a thousand motions
> Upon a thousand sightless axles spinning
> And with the force of self-destroying swiftness,
> Intensely, slowly, solemnly roll on—
> Kindling with mingled sounds, and many tones,
> Intelligible words and music wild.[9]

In this vision of the postmillennial earth one is reminded of De Quincey's postal service, which "spoke as by some mighty orchestra, where a thousand instruments, all disregarding each other, and so far in danger of discord, yet all obedient as slaves to the supreme *baton* of some great leader, terminate in a perfection of harmony" (13:272). Likewise, Shelley's vision combines dynamic motion with spatial complexity and musically reconciled harmonies.

Ever restless, however, Shelley gets no closer than this to an apocalyptic temple vision with its geometrical perfections. Though the sphere is orbicular and balanced, it rolls on relentlessly; there is no center to this redeemed cosmos, and its only constancy is that of change. Thus we see how far Shelley's millennial vision is from that of Ezekiel, who looked forward to a permanent structure that would enshrine the law, a structure whose very name would *locate* divinity: "And the name of the city from that day shall be, The Lord is there" (Ezek. 48:35, RV). If motion is privileged over form in Shelley's imagination, then it is likely that his sense of the chariot is prone to decay, like De Quincey's, into merely those things that motion on its own can offer: change and destruction.

A strain of this sense enters *Prometheus Unbound* in the figure of Demogorgon, whose chariot, despite its saving purpose, resembles that of "Death the crowned phantom" in *The English Mail-Coach.* "The coursers fly / Terrified," Panthea says; "watch its path among the stars / Blackening the night."[10] And in Shelley's final apocalyptic poem a death called Life, accompanied by a cluster of chariot images that ironically echo Ezekiel, sweeps away the notion that power in this world, the thrust of history, the "mighty Juggernaut of social life" as De Quincey calls it, can bring us to redemption:

> So came a chariot on the silent storm
> Of its own rushing splendour, and a Shape
> So sate within as one whom years deform
>
> Beneath a dusky hood and double cape
>   Crouching within the shadow of a tomb,
> And o'er what seemed the head a cloud like crape
>
> Was bent, a dun and faint etherial gloom
> Tempering the light; upon the chariot's beam
>   A Janus-visaged Shadow did assume
>
> The guidance of that wonder-winged team.
>   The Shapes which drew it in thick lightnings
> Were lost: I heard alone on the air's soft stream
>
>   The music of their ever moving wings.
> All the four faces of that charioteer
>   Had their eyes banded . . . little profit brings

> Speed in the van and blindness in the rear,
>   Nor then avail the beams that quench the Sun
> Or that these banded eyes could pierce the sphere
>
>   Of all that is, has been, or will be done.—
> So ill was the car guided, but it past
>   With solemn speed majestically on.[11]

Everything in what we possess of *The Triumph of Life* suggests that there is no power other than this hooded Death,[12] a suggestion we also find in De Quincey, who relegates his cathedrals of salvation only to dreams.

There is yet another great dream cathedral in Romantic literature, and it too represents a form of ultimate imagining, a crown of vision for its creator, like the "Dream-Fugue" for De Quincey and the chariot of Life for Shelley. Keats has the imagination of stasis, as Shelley has of motion, and it is interesting that in his own great unfinished dream vision, *The Fall of Hyperion,* he should focus on the more static of the apocalyptic icons, the temple. Yet, like Shelley's chariot, this temple too is darkened—darkened and deadly to most mortals:

> I look'd around upon the carved sides
> Of an old sanctuary with roof august,
> Builded so high, it seem'd that filmed clouds
> Might spread beneath, as o'er the stars of heaven;
> So old the place was, I remembered none
> The like upon the earth; what I had seen
> Of grey cathedrals, buttress'd walls, rent towers,
> The superannuations of sunk realms,
> Or nature's rocks toil'd hard in waves and winds,
> Seem'd but the faulture of decrepit things
> To that eternal domed monument.
> . . . .
>   Turning from these with awe, once more I rais'd
> My eyes to fathom the space every way;
> The embossed roof, the silent massy range
> Of columns north and south, ending in mist
> Of nothing, then to eastward, where black gates
> Were shut against the sunrise evermore.
> Then to the west I look'd, and saw far off

> An image, huge of feature as a cloud,
> At level of whose feet an altar slept,
> To be approach'd on either side by steps,
> And marble balustrade, and patient travail
> To count with toil the innumerable degrees.[13]

In this vision we find many of the familiar attributes from descriptions of the apocalyptic temple—vastness, architectural complexity, an insistence upon the orientation of the four compass points—but with many ironic revisions. Keats's temple is not new as the Temple is new, or as the heavenly Jerusalem is New, but older than nature; not finite in its bounds but trailing off in two directions in a repetitive indefiniteness; not open to a redeemed community through four gates but, with its one gate barred, blocking out the dawn; not signifying "The Lord is there" but, rather, commemorating the memory of a God that has fallen, for this is the temple of Saturn, consigned to the fossil heap of historical change.

For all its counterpointing of traditional apocalyptic conventions, Keats's temple presents some interesting affinities to De Quincey's dream cathedral. Although De Quincy is more traditional in keeping the gate of his temple open and the location of his altar at the east end, he joins Keats as the only other major Romantic writer to locate a life-or-death race against time inside a visionary temple. Although it is highly improbable that De Quincey knew the manuscript of *The Fall of Hyperion* (it was not published until 1856-57), a comparison of the two visions yields a telling play of contrasts within similarities. The naves of these temples are unsafe: in De Quincey's dream what should be a mansion of deliverance turns into a speedway for death-dealing engines. On its "arrow-like flight of the illimitable central aisle," the coach plunges toward "a female child, that rode in a carriage as frail as flowers.... Face to face she rode, as if danger there were none" (13:324). In Keats's vision the floor itself is lethal:

> "If thou canst not ascend
> These steps, die on that marble where thou art.
> Thy flesh, near cousin to the common dust,

> Will parch for lack of nutriment—thy bones
> Will wither in few years, and vanish so
> That not the quickest eye could find a grain
> Of what thou now art on that pavement cold.
> The sands of thy short life are spent this hour,
> And no hand in the universe can turn
> Thy hour glass, if these gummed leaves be burnt
> Ere thou canst mount up these immortal steps."
> I heard, I look'd: two senses both at once
> So fine, so subtle, felt the tyranny
> Of that fierce threat, and the hard task proposed.[14]

De Quincey's victim lingers in the aisle sweetly unaware of impending doom; Keats's victim races with the knowledge that his own life is at stake. Speed for Keats then is a mode of self-rescue; for De Quincey it is the agency of destruction itself. But for both writers the altar is the only safe place to be. We need to see what this altar represents.

If Shelley subverts the apocalyptic image of divine power by suggesting that it is only Life, Keats subverts the apocalyptic image of a Heavenly Mansion-to-Come by suggesting that it is only the Memory of loss. Such memory is lethal (if Saturn can die, so can you—and soon) unless it is eternalized in form—that is, unless one can lodge oneself on its very altar as votive priest. De Quincey, as usual, is more equivocal than either Keats or Shelley, though these poets are equivocal enough. He has the imagination both of stasis and of motion and introduces Shelley's chariot into Keats's temple but backs away from the darkest designations that the young dead poets who preceded him in such visions bestowed on their creations. De Quincey's chariot destroys but calls itself the agent of a superintendent order; his temple is too vast to measure and is manifestly unprotecting but calls itself our promised home. De Quincey compounds the separate menaces presented in the alternative visions of Keats and Shelley and pronounces them both good.

Is this merely timidity, the qualms of orthodoxy,[15] or is it an overdetermined mode of irony? I suggest that it is neither and that the good that De Quincey finds in these visions is ultimately of a different sort from that promised by humanistic prophecy. When all things cancel each other out, when doubt and faith exchange identities, when order dwarfs power and power ravages order, then we are in a world of images where external signification is emptied and the signifiers as signifiers obtrude themselves on our awareness. But what can they then signify except the texts out of which they are composed? Anyone familiar with De Quincey's work knows that the prose structure becomes more self-advertising as the images become more visionary; he strives for a convergence of images and words so pressured that what is apprehended in the reason as language is heard in the imagination as musical notes. De Quincey's apocalypse is one that displays the artist as master of woven contraries artfully integrated out of the muddle of faith and hope, doubt and despair, that the world of experience provides him.

If this is a paltry or at most a second-best consolation, our comparisons should indicate that such a drift in signification is evident in all Romantic versions of the icons of apocalypse. It is not a new notion that aesthetic signification in the Romantic period tends to pour into images that religious signification has vacated, that Keats's temple, for example, is an all-but-transparent allegory of this shift. Writers who make the shift—and this applies to De Quincey in particular—presumably do so as a strategy to deal with their genuine anxieties about material necessity and historical change. They acknowledge these forces by endowing them with apocalyptic status and then cunningly circumscribe them in images that stress their own artifice. But we do well to remind ourselves that even in a poet of such firm prophetic faith as Blake the fourfold city of Golgonooza signifies, on one level at least, Blake's own art and that the Jerusalem where all human forms are to be identified is the name of a poem. We note also that in Shelley's most millennially hopeful work the sphere of earth's chariot with its "force of self-destroying swiftness" is a perfect mirror of Shelley's own verse.[16] In such a context it is little wonder that the "fugue" in De Quincey's "Dream-Fugue" leaps to prominence. Tennyson's Camelot, the city "'built / To music, therefore never built at all, / And therefore built for ever,'"[17] is not far off, while Yeats's Byzantium, the "artifice of eternity,"[18] waits in the wings.

De Quincey's work is part of the process that turns High Romantic humanism—the apocalyptic image as prophetic of redemptive human change—into Modernism—the glory of the self-fulfilled form. He illustrates the process perhaps better than do his Romantic contemporaries—though they may be the greater artists—for he places one foot conspicuously in the idea of apocalyptic vision as prophecy, something about to be, and one in the notion of vision as autotelic; that is, the vision finds its closure not in its external fulfillment but in itself. These images of the apocalypse are the only apocalypse we shall experience, though their structural features are durable and continue to be passed down—"images that yet / Fresh images beget," as Yeats was to say in "Byzantium."[19] De Quincey plays a significant part in the refathering process.

NOTES

1. Harold Bloom, *Poetry and Repression: Revisionism from Blake to Stevens* (New Haven, Conn.: Yale University Press, 1976), p. 116.
2. My own commentary on this work in *Thomas De Quincey: The Prose of Vision* (Toronto: University of Toronto Press, 1980), pp. 96–116, touches on these biblical resonances but focuses on *The English Mail-Coach* chiefly as a kind of psychomachia. For a more traditional and extensive treatment of the religious and messianic elements in the work see Robert Hopkins, "De Quincey on War and the Pastoral Design of *The English Mail-Coach*," *Studies in Romanticism* 6 (1967): 129–51.
3. *Jerusalem*, plate 12:45–53, in *The Complete Poetry and Prose of William Blake*, rev. ed., ed. David V. Erdman (Berkeley and Los Angeles: University of California Press, 1982). Five lines below this passage (plate 12:58) Blake cites Ezekiel as his predecessor in fourfold visions. All subsequent citations from Blake are to this edition.
4. Ibid., plate 98:24–27.
5. See Walther Eichrodt, *Ezekiel: A Commentary*, trans. Cosslett Quin (London: SCM Press, 1970), p. 29. A strong historical emphasis, of course, informs the whole of Hebrew prophecy.
6. This theme is trenchantly analyzed in the fine essay of Robert M. Maniquis, "Lonely Empires: Personal and Public Visions of Thomas De Quincey," in Eric Rothstein and Joseph Anthony Wittreich, Jr., eds., *Literary Monographs*, vol. 8 (Madison: University of Wisconsin Press, 1976), pp. 47–127. Of the "Dream-Fugue" Maniquis says, "No more mind-boggling fantasy of patriotism was ever written in the nineteenth century.

The self, the nation, the world, Christendom are gathered into one historical light cast against the darkness" (p. 75).

7. J. Hillis Miller, *The Disappearance of God: Five Nineteenth-Century Writers* (1963; reprint, Cambridge, Mass.: Harvard University Press, Belknap Press, 1975), pp. 67-69.

8. Harold Bloom, *Shelley's Mythmaking* (New Haven, Conn.: Yale University Press, 1959), pp. 144, 232-36.

9. Percy Bysshe Shelley, *Prometheus Unbound*, 4.238-52, in *Shelley's Poetry and Prose*, ed. Donald H. Reiman and Sharon B. Powers (New York: Norton, 1977); all subsequent citations from Shelley are to this edition.

10. Ibid., *Prometheus Unbound*, 2.4.153-55.

11. Shelley, *The Triumph of Life* (1822), lines 86-106.

12. This is not the occasion to become embroiled in the critical controversy over whether Shelley intended to provide a pessimistic or a meliorist conclusion to his poem. Suffice it to say that, in the poem as we have it, the options for escape from Life's chariot are made so exquisitely narrow that it is difficult to imagine where Shelley would have found material to flesh out a hopeful conclusion.

13. John Keats, *The Fall of Hyperion*, 1.61-71, 81-92, in *The Poems of John Keats*, ed. Jack Stillinger (Cambridge, Mass.: Harvard University Press, Belknap Press, 1978); all subsequent citations from Keats are to this edition.

14. Ibid., 1.107-20.

15. Contrasting De Quincey and Blake, Maniquis observes that "De Quincey, despite his immersion in dialectical visions, is afraid of their seeming unendingness and seeks ... some hope of an absolute, a hypostatized, a Godly truth" ("Lonely Empires," p. 71).

16. For a particularly fine exposition of this view see D. J. Hughes, "Potentiality in *Prometheus Unbound*," *Studies in Romanticism* 2 (1963): 107-26.

17. Alfred, Lord Tennyson, *Idylls of the King*, "Gareth and Lynette," lines 272-74, in *The Poems of Tennyson*, ed. Christopher Ricks (London: Longmans, 1969).

18. W. B. Yeats, "Sailing to Byzantium," line 24, in *The Variorum Edition of the Poems of W. B. Yeats*, ed. Peter Allt and Russell K. Alspach (New York: Macmillan, 1957).

19. Ibid., lines 38-39.

3

"In a Stranger's Ear":
De Quincey's Polite Magazine Context

JOHN C. WHALE

De Quincey's most famous works derive much of their complexity from an unresolved combination of extreme experiential concerns and a politeness which is in keeping with their periodical magazine context. The Romantic extremist and the essayist frequently join together to produce a crossing over of viewpoints which can be intimidating and even morally disturbing to the reader: confession and formal reticence, decadence and sentimentality intertwine in provocative ways. The results of this combination are most interesting in those works where the act of polite delivery is not assumed to be straightforward and where, as a consequence, the context becomes a significant factor in determining the nature of the text concerned.

The polite and sentimental aspect of De Quincey's work remains as problematical for his critics as its magazine context. It can be irritating to find interruptions to the serious depiction of extreme experience, or to find his working out of Romantic archetypes and myths interspersed with capricious humor and whimsical geniality. In his fiction the Gothic mode frequently engenders a comfortable combination of sentimentality, politeness, and horror. In his purely scholarly writings the accurate presentation of knowledge is assumed to predominate; no obvious disjunction between the point of view of the scholar and his authoritative information can be detected. But in De Quincey's various autobiographical writings—particularly *Confessions of an English Opium-Eater*, *The English Mail-Coach*, and *Suspiria de Profundis*—and in his papers on murder the combination is more complex because it is less constrained: it has greater freedom to debate its own place and the values of its context.

The persona of the magazine journalist, whether in the role of autobiographer or scholar (or, as is frequently the case, a mixture of both), can then be considered an important stratagem in the writing.

The most obvious way in which De Quincey's works refer to their own context is through the numerous footnotes, prefaces, and apologies which overtly draw attention to certain formal restrictions. It is, for example, easy to see a clash of interests between the demands of an autobiographical narrative and a serialized form of publication. In *Suspiria de Profundis* the supposition of an intimate act of revelation exists uneasily alongside reminders of the public context in which it is taking place. This tension is neatly encapsulated in De Quincey's phrase "in a stranger's ear."[1] There is clearly an ambivalent conception of publicity present in De Quincey's work. The degree to which his writings register their context can be seen either as an indication of difficulty (the context at odds with his Romantic concerns) or as an exploration and exploitation of the strategies and conventions available within it. Just as De Quincey's works evidence an ambivalent response to imaginative power,[2] so too they evidence an ambivalent response to their mode of publication, both crying out against an uncongenial form of presentation and manipulating the reader through the tactics available in this type of writing.

The "Introductory Notice" to *Suspiria de Profundis* contains an extreme example of this ambivalence in De Quincey's work. By explaining what the "true object" of his earlier "'Opium Confessions'" (*SP,* p. 158) actually is, he reveals the extent to which he is engaged in a mixed mode of writing. Not only is the essentially creative aspect of his work described as occupying a subordinate role, but it also is seen in terms that are negative versions of the usual analogies of Romantic organicism:

I tell my critic that the whole course of this narrative resembles, and was meant to resemble, a *caduceus* wreathed about with meandering ornaments, or the shaft of a tree's stem hung round and surmounted with some vagrant parasitical plant. The mere medical subject of the opium answers to the dry, withered pole, which shoots all the rings of the flowering plants, and seems to do so by

some dexterity of its own; whereas, in fact, the plant and its tendrils have curled round the sullen cylinder by mere luxuriance of theirs....
   ... Not the flowers are for the pole, but the pole is for the flowers. Upon the same analogy, view me as one ... *"viridantem floribus hastas"*—making verdant, and gay with the life of flowers, murderous spears and halberts—things that express death in their origin. [*SP*, pp. 157-58]

De Quincey's ambivalent response to his own creativity—the problem about the origin and status of his work—is linked to its profoundly digressive quality.[3] That the above passage is to be found in an "Introductory Notice" is not fortuitous: at the same time that De Quincey explains to his "critic" the nature of an antecedent work and thereby reveals the characteristics of his own imaginative power, he also highlights the magazine context. The reader is asked to focus on the connections that exist between the different works, to consider the status of a text which refers backwards and which requires such preliminary explanations. Its title, *Suspiria de Profundis,* might suggest obscure experiential material, but it intimates as well the problems of being understood in such a public medium.

The special relationship with the reader which is a familiar feature of De Quincey's work may be constructed to counter this evident difficulty in the magazine context.[4] It is a means of stabilizing the text, of establishing an ideally intimate system of address. Through a series of appeals to the reader De Quincey not only promotes a mediatory device in keeping with the confessional aspect of his work but also confirms the magazine identity of his writings. The development of the persona of the scholarly journalist takes place in conjunction with this system of address. Although the form of writing may well be described as familiar, it is a familiarity set up to challenge certain notions of publicity. The reader immediately enters as an outsider into a seemingly private arena; however, from the standpoint of the magazines the reader is suddenly admitted into an exclusive coterie. This effect accords with the uneven composition of *Blackwood's Edinburgh Magazine* and its readership. In common with other successful early-nineteenth-century periodicals, *Black-*

wood's took its lead from the *London Magazine* in its attempt to cater equally to the "many" and the "few," retaining an "air of exclusiveness and authority" while at the same time encouraging a "relaxed, personal, and intimate ethos."[5] Installments of the "Noctes Ambrosianae" promoted this sense of coterie by using magazine personalities, including that of the Opium-Eater, in dialogues which served to define the journalistic identity of *Blackwood's*.

The most consistent and perhaps most evident example of this construction of a polite address to the reader is to be found in the *Confessions* of 1821-22, where it simultaneously defines the identity of the anonymous opium-eating scholar. As he locates his reader with a series of single adjectives, including "courteous," "logical," "humane," "observing," and "understanding," De Quincey also fabricates a magazine personality for himself: the terms of the address reflect indirectly the values and attributes of the autobiographer. Like the qualification of the subtitle, "An Extract from the Life of a Scholar," this aspect of the text suggests respectability and conformity sensationally at odds with the immorality of the subject of drug taking. The opening section, titled "From the Author to the Reader," plays a crucial part in initiating this double-edged system. It professes to be anticonfessional, a reluctant publication, but also plays on this publicity because of its anonymity and tantalizing suggestion that certain eminent public figures are also addicts. The preface thus can be seen as a denial, or at least a forestalling, of expectations. In aligning itself with the respectable norm of the magazine, however, the preface does not cut itself off irretrievably from the possibility of sensationalism: the figure of the scholar lends respectability to the work and also enlivens the thrill of immorality.

In De Quincey's autobiographical writings the authority created by this scholastic pose, this acting out of the role of expert, joins with the authority based on the claim of personal experience. Once again, this characteristic of De Quincey's work is typical rather than exceptional, illustrating in its own particular combination the more general mixture of *Blackwood's*, where esoteric learning existed alongside "blatant sensationalism."⁶ De Quincey's share in this trait has been labeled a "desperate pretense and an audacious hoax."⁷ While this attack may find some justification in many essays flamboyantly displaying esoteric learning, it is much less defensible in his autobiographical works, where such a "pose" can claim its rightful place within the framework of the text. It is an important part of De Quincey's position as magazine writer and public commentator, and it is not exorcized in the act of autobiography but is consistently exploited as a tactic. In the *Confessions,* De Quincey fashions a mixed magazine personality which includes as one of its components the role of scholar. Even though it is a natural product of its periodical-magazine context, this role does not exist in a simple form: it is made to answer the demands of the particular text. The reader is confronted by the potentially disturbing combination of opium-eater and philosopher-scholar. As a result the opening promise of the *Confessions* that they "will prove, not merely an interesting record, but, in a considerable degree, useful and instructive" (*C,* p. vii) may justifiably be read as a tantalizing, ultimately perplexing ploy.

This combination of esoteric learning and sensationalism is memorably parodied in Edgar Allan Poe's "Loss of Breath," subtitled "A Tale Neither in nor out of 'Blackwood'":

I forbear to depict my sensations upon the gallows; although here, undoubtedly, I could speak to the point, and it is a topic upon which nothing has been well said. In fact, to write upon such a theme it is necessary to have been hanged. Every author should confine himself to matters of experience. Thus Mark Antony composed a treatise upon getting drunk.⁸

Here Poe himself combines the two forces comically by making the claim for sensationalism in a declamatory manner and by ending with the learned jest. In "How to Write a Blackwood Article" he suggests that just such a combination in the *Confessions* has an element of charlatanry about it:

Then we had the *"Confessions of an Opium-eater"* — fine, very fine! — glorious imagination — deep philosophy — acute speculation — plenty of fire and fury, and a good spicing of the decidedly unintelligible. That was a nice bit of flummery, and went down the throats of the people delightfully. They would have it that Coleridge wrote the paper—but not so. It was composed by my pet baboon, Juniper, over a rummer of Hollands and water, "hot, without sugar."[9]

Even allowing for the exaggeration of Poe's parody, the characteristics he identifies serve to promote the authority of the autobiographer at the same time that they challenge the reader. Either as a member of the public or as a member of the supposedly elite coterie, the reader might justifiably feel alienated. There is a fairly consistent, often antagonistic, gap between the public commentator and his audience. The potentially exciting and disturbing mixture of vision and analysis in De Quincey's work is presented in a tense public context in which certain of the roles, like those of polyhistor and scholar, available and to some degree conventionalized there reinforce the isolation of the public commentator. In other words, the mode of delivery does not simply register the difficulties but plays a significant part in determining and originating their extent and nature. While such tactics offer an apparently consistent system of address, they have the effect of destabilizing the text, for they provide the foundation upon which the digressive aspect of De Quincey's work can take place. The magazine persona, with its related system of address, takes part in a process of fluctuation between the polarities of De Quincey's work. In his autobiographical writings and in his papers on murder the two sides depend upon each other in an act of counterdefinition.

The flexibility generated by the shifting movement and ambivalent authority of such a magazine persona achieves its most interesting result in the *Confessions,* where the shift from one basis of authority to another can be a successfully aggressive tactic. In the following passage from that work the approach toward the supposed subject is carefully modulated, consisting of a leisurely playfulness not without an element of mockery. The reader who allows for this pretext in anticipation of the nominal subject might easily be baffled or disappointed as the *Confessions* characteristically masks its promised goal with a succession of seemingly preparatory discourses. The experiential claim in this instance hides its assertiveness behind a genial humor and an elaborate though significantly informal development:

> I have said already that on a subject so important to us all as happiness, we should listen with pleasure to any man's experience or experiments, even though he were but a ploughboy, who cannot be supposed to have ploughed very deep in such an intractable soil as that of human pains and pleasures, or to have conducted his researches upon any very enlightened principles. But I, who have taken happiness, both in a solid and liquid shape, both boiled and unboiled, both East India and Turkey,—who have conducted my experiments upon this interesting subject with a sort of galvanic battery,—and have, for the general benefit of the world, inoculated myself, as it were, with the poison of eight hundred drops of laudanum per day (just for the same reason as a French surgeon inoculated himself lately with a cancer,—an English one, twenty years ago, with plague,—and a third, I know not of what nation, with hydrophobia),—I, it will be admitted, must surely know what happiness is, if anybody does. And therefore I will here lay down an analysis of happiness; and, as the most interesting mode of communicating it, I will give it, not didactically, but wrapt up and involved in a picture of one evening. [*C*, pp. 95–96]

Throughout this passage De Quincey maintains the effect of an expert condescending to the act of public communication. Despite the humor and a note of self-parody, sufficient gestures are made to support his image of learned philosopher-scholar. We are promised an "analysis" of happiness and saved from a didactic delivery, yet we know that precisely such a delivery is within his powers. Typically, the passage ends on what it claims to be a note of concession, having begun confidently in its act of self-justification. Though the main difference between the autobiographer and his reader in this instance is predominantly one of experience, it is supported by other tactical aspects of the text which have arisen out of its special public context.

Earlier in the *Confessions,* De Quincey's claim to be an expert on the subject of opium is made in more stark and formal terms when he justifies his own position in relation to medical opinion. It not only defines his position, of course, but allows him to promote his case by using the rhetoric and the authority of his supposed adversaries:

> And, therefore, worthy doctors, as there seems to be room for further discoveries, stand aside, and allow me to come forward and lecture on this matter. First, then, it is not so much affirmed as taken for granted, by all who ever mention opium, formally or incidentally, that it does or can produce intoxication. Now, reader, assure yourself, *meo periculo,* that no quantity of opium ever did, or could, intoxicate. [*C,* p. 68]

The rhetorical possibilities exploited in this instance reveal De Quincey's characteristic combination of experience and scholarship. The "fictional" or autobiographical element of his work is harnessed to his role as expert; his personal authority as an addict is linked to his public authority as a scholarly journalist capable of delivering facts and crucial distinctions to his audience.

The English Mail-Coach, especially in the section titled "The Vision of Sudden Death," reveals a more self-conscious and humorous version of this combination. Learning is immediately paraded before the reader as the section opens with a dispute regarding the correct distinction between the Roman and Christian ideas of "sudden death." De Quincey then defends his use of the word "diphrelatic" as follows: "Excuse, reader, a word too elegant to be pedantic. And also take this remark from me as a *gage d'amitié*—that no word ever was or *can* be pedantic which, by supporting a distinction, supports the accuracy of logic, or which fills up a chasm for the understanding" (13: 306–307). Here the reader might be excused impatience as the text leads sideways instead of straight on to deliver the "vision" which has been promised. At this point De Quincey jokes about his own reputation for procrastination.

While explanatory and scholarly commentaries often have an introductory function in De Quincey's autobiographical works, offering a justification for the main text, such authoritative statements can easily accentuate, instead of smooth over, the gap between the public world and the private world which the autobiographer is divulging. These passages can even be overtly aggressive, a register of antagonism toward the public. *Suspiria de Profundis* provides more frequent illustration of De Quincey writing against the grain of his audience than does the *Confessions*. In the latter work direct confrontation is generally avoided, the reader being subtly cajoled into an involvement which might occasionally include sensational issues impinging on public interest. Such is not the case in the *Suspiria*, however, as is typified by the different openings of the two works. The *Confessions,* in both the 1821–22 and 1856 versions, begins with a conciliatory gesture to the reader, whereas *Suspiria de Profundis,* though designated a "sequel" to the *Confessions,* opens with an attack on "the gathering agitation of our present English life" (*SP*, p. 148).

Various other sections of the *Suspiria* maintain this note of aggression. The introduction to the second installment in *Blackwood's,* for example, makes the following arrogant claim which is supported by a sequence of particularly hostile interruptions or qualifications before the main statement is unburdened:

Upon me, as upon others scattered thinly by tens and twenties over every thousand years, fell too powerfully and too early the vision of life. The horror of life mixed itself already in earliest youth with the heavenly sweetness of life; that grief, which one in a hundred has sensibility enough to gather from the sad retrospect of life in its closing stage, for me shed its dews as a prelibation upon the fountains of life whilst yet sparkling to the morning sun. . . . Is this the description of an early youth passed in the shades of gloom? No; but of a youth passed in the divinest happiness. And if the reader has (which so few have) the passion, without which there is no reading of the legend and superscription upon man's brow, if he is not (as most are) deafer than the grave to every *deep* note that sighs upwards from the Delphic caves of human life, he will know that the rapture of life (or anything which by approach can merit that name) does not arise, unless as perfect music arises, music of Mozart or Beethoven, by the confluence of the mighty and terrific discords with the subtle concords. [*SP*, pp. 257–58]

This clearly goes beyond a forestalling of the reader's presumed response: the autobiographer's claim for the peculiarity of his own experience is paralleled by a sense of antagonism growing out of the fact of his delivery.

As well as highlighting the difficulty of translating experience, *Suspiria de Profundis* provides some of the most stark examples in De Quincey's work of provocatively placed generalizations which often appear to anticipate a hostile public reception. These can be viewed not only as evidence of resistance offered to the context but also as a positive claim coming from the text itself. In the *Suspiria* as posthumously published, for example, the section titled "The Dark Interpreter" opens with the following declaration: "Suffering is a mightier agency in the hands of nature, as a Demiurgus creating the intellect, than most people are aware of" (*PW*, 1:7). This immediately asserts the importance of the work before the reader: it is an act of justification flying in the face of the public. But it is also the initial promise of relevance for what might appear to be slightly sensational or extravagant material.

Another section of the posthumous *Suspiria* clearly illustrates, from its opening sentence, the potential which lies in a provocative conjunction of the fantastic and the everyday:

There is a story told in the "Arabian Nights" of a princess who, by overlooking one seed of a pomegranate, precipitated the event which she had laboured to make impossible. . . . Yet why go to Arabian fictions? Even in our daily life is exhibited, in proportions far more gigantic, that tendency to swell and amplify itself into mountains of darkness, which exists oftentimes in germs that are imperceptible. [*PW*, 1:22]

This opening prepares for De Quincey's characteristic inclination to invest the normal with something approaching occult significance. He appeals to his public by appearing to redefine old boundaries, offering the thrill of secrecy in an area commonly accepted as mundane.

Frequently De Quincey's more sensational and disturbing commentaries are able to pierce that "delicate and honorable reserve" (*C*, p. vii), referred to in the "Introductory Notice" to the *Confessions*, owing to the construction of a genteel social discourse. Alternatively, the move toward secrecy or revelation can be made without regard to that safe and socially acceptable middle area, as it is on many occasions in the *Suspiria*. In such cases the didactic strain of De Quincey's autobiographical writing finds itself abruptly juxtaposed with intimate illustrations from his own experience. While De Quincey may adopt certain roles and tactics which bestow a learned authority on his work, thereby distinguishing the autobiographer from the reader and providing a requisite framework for his more public commentaries, the more negative aspect of his enterprise is that such commentaries are often accompanied by a curious condemnation of the public. The special relationship fabricated by an individual text often seems to be an ideal, situated in a context which is assumed to be much more hostile.

De Quincey's essay "On Murder Considered as One of the Fine Arts" (1827) takes this aggressive reaction and applies it to both coterie and the public. The essay offers a particularly complex and condensed example of the way in which the fact of magazine publication informs the very substance of his work. Here the combination of decadence and politeness depends for its success not simply on the extremity of De Quincey's interest in murder but also on the way in which this extreme is projected into a magazine context. Rather than a fluctuation between polarities based upon a scholarly persona as in the *Confessions*, "On Murder" initially subsumes the two sides under the fiction of the text of a lecture which has "fallen into [De Quincey's] hands" (13:10). The scholarly pose is again present in the form of the lecturer, but it is now overtly open to scrutiny as the belletristic norm of the magazine becomes invested with a morally suspect and occult significance. The polarities, artistic and moral, reside in the crossing over of terms. Because of this integration the work avoids De Quincey's characteristic "failing" as described by Virginia Woolf:

Here was a difficulty which De Quincey often faced and often failed to solve. . . . He must descend from these happy heights to the levels of ordinary existence. And, again and again, it is in returning to earth that De Quincey is undone. How is he to bridge the horrid transition? How is he to turn from an angel with wings of flame and eyes of fire to a gentleman in black who talks sense?[10]

In the lecture which forms the first paper on murder, we are presented with a macabre version of the "gentleman in black," and the terms which constitute his politeness actually become the agents of horror.

Despite the integration of the characteristic polarities in De Quincey's work, "On Murder" possesses a digressive nature which has led one critic to claim that "the real substance of the essay is an exercise in elusiveness."[11] An examination of this first paper reveals a play of various authorities in which the subject of the work, because it is not rigidly defined or fixed, changes as the authorities change. Although there is no specified satirical target, the terms employed in the system of address themselves become the center of attention, if not an implied target. The politeness of the work is defined by the use of terms which highlight the values of its particular magazine context.

The initial impetus of the first paper is provided by the alignment and substitution of usually separate categories. The lecture rests on the following rhetorical foundation:

Everything in this world has two handles. Murder, for instance, may be laid hold of by its moral handle (as it generally is in the pulpit and at the Old Bailey), and *that*, I confess, is its weak side; or it may also be treated *aesthetically*, as the Germans call it — that is, in relation to good taste. [13:13]

Hugh Sykes Davies recognizes this as the first English use of the term "aesthetic" and claims that it inaugurated a nineteenth-century theory that incorporated the work of Baudelaire and eventually became the "vulgarized formula of 'art for art's sake.'"[12] Although this distinction between "moral" and "aesthetic" has a more obvious historical importance, the distinction made in "On Murder" between "amateur" and "professional" would seem to be more significant in determining the nature of the work. This distinction, unlike the other, is flexible and open to the various pressures and movements of the text. The use of the term "amateur" in a system of address focuses attention on a polite coterie and creates a false division between theory and practice. The "Advertisement of a Man Morbidly Virtuous" which prefaces the society's lecture describes its members as "connoisseurs," "dilettanti," and "amateurs" (13:9, 10). The first two terms are occasionally used as support, but it is primarily the term "amateur" which plays a key role in the structure of the essay. Functioning at a basic level of sensationalism and offering the reader the thrilling possibility of criminal activity,[13] the use of the amateur-professional antithesis illustrates the shifting movement of "On Murder."

Whereas the substitution of an aesthetic for a moral attitude provides a stable foundation for what might appear to be a traditionally ironic and satirical text, the insistence on the flexible amateur-professional distinction destabilizes the text and leads to the production of a more relative structure. This arises not only because of the breakdown of the distinction but also because of an unequal balance within the distinction itself. The term "amateur" is clearly exhibited as the positive term, with "professional" providing the shock of a horrific euphemism and the possibility of a suitable antonym. We may gauge the valency of "amateur" from an article which appeared in the April 1827 installment of *Blackwood's*. Titled simply "The Fine Arts," it is signed by "An Amateur" and begins: "To the public, whom I hate, (but not you, gentle reader, whom I both love and respect,) I address this letter, or, as Blackwood calls it, Article." The ambivalence of this address to the philistine public on the one hand and the gentlemanly reader on the other centers on an interesting social split which defines the meaning of the word "amateur." The Edinburgh public is attacked because it is "so wrapt up in the miserable calculation of pounds, shillings, and pence, that, generally speaking, [it is] dead to every elegant and intellectual pursuit, especially to the Fine Arts."[14]

Within "On Murder" the dense tissue of scholarly references both literary and philosophical which constitute the lecture is, on occasion, combined aggressively with the word "amateur" to foster an elitism which scorns the wider public. Referring to Jeremy Taylor, the lecturer states that "the bishop talks like a wise man and an amateur, as I am sure he was; and another great philosopher, Marcus Aurelius, was equally above the vulgar prejudices on this subject" (13:42). As the tone becomes more paternalistic, the text of the lecture increasingly highlights the context of De Quincey's published article: "But it is now time that I should say a few words about the principles of murder, not with a view to regulate your practice, but your judgment. As to old women, and the mob of newspaper readers, they are pleased with anything, provided it is bloody enough. But the mind of sensibility requires something more" (13:46). The lecture exhibits a familiar self-congratulatory tone of the periodical magazines, especially of *Blackwood's;* it also echoes their antagonism toward newspapers and their corresponding celebration of a supposedly exclusive audience.[15] Wider publicity in terms of a broad readership is seen as anarchic and frightening. The polarities intrinsic to the lecturer's system of address are displayed most obviously in the following passage where "the world" is juxtaposed with "gentlemen": "The world in general, gentlemen, are very bloody-minded; and all they want in a murder is a copious effusion of blood; gaudy display in this point is enough for *them.* But the enlightened connoisseur is more refined in his taste" (13:48).

The lecture on murder thus may be read both as an overt attack on the public and as an implied satire on the dilettanti readership of *Blackwood's Edinburgh Magazine.* The extent to which the pseudonymous "Advertisement," in the form of a letter "To the Editor," places and initiates this double-edged attack is crucial. In its use of scholarly authority (the long quotation from Lactantius) and in its formality the letter is of course at one with the lecture. The initial address—"Sir, We have all heard" (13:9n.)—immediately promotes the idea of a coterie magazine readership. The supposedly public-spirited plea which "X.Y.Z." makes in his translated extract from the Lactantius quotation could be said to rebound upon the readers of "Maga":

Let the Society of Gentlemen Amateurs consider this; and let me call their especial attention to the last sentence, which is so weighty, that I shall attempt to convey it in English: "Now, if merely to be present at a murder fastens on a man the character of an accomplice; if barely to be a spectator involves us in one common guilt with the perpetrator: it follows, of necessity, that, in these murders of the amphitheatre, the hand which inflicts the fatal blow is not more deeply imbrued in blood than his who passively looks on; neither can *he* be clear of blood who has countenanced its shedding; nor that man seem other than a participator in murder who gives his applause to the murderer and calls for prizes on his behalf." [13:11]

The mock indignation of this public warning can be seen as an oblique attack on the sensationalist content of *Blackwood's*, an attack which implicates the readership in the guilt of murder. The aesthetic world of the amateur is turned into the criminal activity of the professional. Instead of horror issuing from De Quincey's article because an artistic viewpoint anesthetizes real events, intimidation emerges because the paper establishes an unexpected connection between the magazine article and real events. It suddenly reinvests the activity of reading the magazine with the moral responsibility accorded to actual experience. Instead of setting up a barrier between art and life, "On Murder" depends upon an alignment of the two sides. Its very starting point is the exploitation of the boundary between fact and fiction.

The text of "On Murder," therefore, is not sealed off in the manner of "art for art's sake." Like De Quincey's other texts it is structured on an ambivalent conception of publicity: it attacks the public yet is dependent on it. The magazine itself is situated in a split between art and economics: it must sell and to do so must claim aloofness from monetary concerns. Reflecting its own equivocal status, "On Murder" fluctuates between theory and practice, learning and experience, fact and fiction. The basic foundation of the work is, of course, an example of this system of relationship to publicity; treating murder as a fine art at once invokes a series of relationships spanning lurid newspapers and learned monthly periodicals, experience and scholarship, sensationalism and reason. To this extent the prefatory letter "To the Editor of *Blackwood's Magazine*" provides the appropriate framework, for it initiates a text whose status is strangely related to the workings of publication.

The contentious nature of this relationship is immediately apparent from the editor's note appended to the letter of "X.Y.Z." Although the note is rather vague and its authorship unknown, it is interesting because it takes issue not only with the main premise of the lecture, as one might expect, but also with the quotation from Lactantius:

Note of the Editor:—We thank our correspondent for his communication, and also for the quotation from Lactantius, which is very pertinent to *his* view of the case; our own, we confess, is different. We cannot suppose the lecturer to be in earnest, any more than Erasmus in his Praise of Folly, or Dean Swift in his Proposal for Eating Children. However, either on his own view or on ours, it is equally fit that the lecture should be made public. [13:11n.]

It is impossible to determine whether the editor takes issue with the quotation because it appears to blur the category of murder or because he recognizes an intimidation of the magazine reader. The purpose of the note's second sentence, however, is not in doubt: it clearly serves to alleviate the alarm of an unsuspecting reader and also to render a risqué paper respectable by citing eminent authors from the past. Even before we are given the text of the lecture, it has become involved in a series of relationships which focus on its being "made public," a phrase used by both "X.Y.Z." and the editor.

The impetus provided by a supposedly contentious publication is continued in the subsequent papers on murder. Even though the second article appeared in *Blackwood's* over twelve years later, in November 1839, it deliberately fosters the problematical reception of the earlier paper. The first paragraph of the article begins, once again, with a supposedly intimate address to the editor and a characteristically pedantic definition of a single word:

DOCTOR NORTH—You are a liberal man: liberal in the true classical sense, not in the slang sense of modern politicians and education-mongers. Being so, I am sure that you will sympathize with my case. I am an ill-used man, Dr. North—particularly ill-used; and, with your permission, I will briefly explain how. A black scene of calumny will be laid open; but you, Doctor, will make all things square again. One frown from you, directed to the proper quarter, or a warning shake of the crutch, will set me right in public opinion; which at present, I am sorry to say, is rather hostile to me and mine —all owing to the wicked acts of slanderers. [13:52n.]

The opening of the "Postscript" of 1854 is more straightforward, lacking the mannered and indirect form of address to a third party. It is an aggressive justification aimed directly at the reader, not an elaborately contrived pretense on which to construct an article. Writes De Quincey in the "Postscript":

It is impossible to conciliate readers of so saturnine and gloomy a class that they cannot enter with genial sympathy into any gaiety whatever, but, least of all, when the gaiety trespasses a little into the province of the extravagant. In such a case, not to sympathise is not to understand; and the playfulness which is not relished becomes flat and insipid, or absolutely without meaning. [13:70]

De Quincey successfully exploits the ambivalent nature of publicity by his construction of a polite essayist alongside a man of dubious experience. This dual persona plays an important part in the genesis of his series on murder, in which the sequels to the first paper emerge not only as further illustrations but also as explanations to and defenses against his readers. In this respect "On Murder" parallels the *Confessions* in its two forms and its sequels *Suspiria de Profundis* and *The English Mail-Coach*. It shares with them a gentleman-scholar figure who assumes the respectability of his readership on the subject of his own experience. The conflicts arising from this rhetorical situation are prominent features of the introductory paragraphs and notes of the subsequent works. In the *Confessions* the sequels contain defenses concerning the very subject of the work and the question of its encouraging others in drug taking. The status of De Quincey's texts—their inconclusiveness and their growth— is bound up with this twin impulse, the contradictory impulse of amateur-professional combinations, alternately revealing similarity to and difference from the respectable norm of the magazine. The success of De Quincey's works results from the disturbing effect of such combinations, intimidating the reader not only by an apparent disparity between subject and style but also by an alarming flexibility in the use of crucial terms and in the adoption of different authoritative positions. The characteristic nature of De Quincey's works, therefore, is not to be found in the static presentation of such polarities as murder and fine art or drug addiction and scholarship. Some of De Quincey's most famous works could be said to be parasitical upon their own context, highlighting their own tactic of address and place of publication. An awareness of this self-reflexive aspect of De Quincey's texts clarifies and particularizes Mario Praz's description of De Quincey, under the heading of "Romanticism Turns Bourgeois," as an "ambiguous figure," a "forerunner of the Decadents" who was attempting a "mixture of the intimate, the pathetic, the fantastic, and the humorous."[16] By considering this mixture in some of De Quincey's most provocative works, one can appreciate that his challenge to the reader resides not only in his extreme experiential concerns but also in the way such extremes feed off their polite context. This polite context does not moderate the extremes of his Romanticism but actually provides the means of making them more provocative. Those extremes are at their most provocative when successfully integrated into the bourgeois context.

Notes

1. I borrow the phrase from the installment of *Suspiria de Profundis* published in *Blackwood's Edinburgh Magazine* 57 (March 1845): 277. Presumably owing to a compositor's error, the Ticknor, Reed, and Fields reprint of 1852 of the original *Suspiria* series in *Blackwood's* renders the phrase "for a stranger's ear" (*SP*, p. 154). Although I elsewhere cite parenthetically from the reprint of 1852, which is otherwise faithful to the original *Suspiria* text, I here prefer to use "in a stranger's ear" as an index to my argument in this chapter.
2. See V. A. De Luca, *Thomas De Quincey: The Prose of Vision* (Toronto: University of Toronto Press, 1980), p. 147.
3. See J. Hillis Miller, *The Disappearance of God: Five Nineteenth-Century Writers* (1963; reprint, Cambridge, Mass.: Harvard University Press, Belknap Press, 1975), pp. 28–30.
4. Although she does not address the issue of De Quincey's magazine context, Elizabeth W. Bruss offers several insights on De Quincey's relationship with his audience in her *Autobiographical Acts: The Changing Situation of a Literary Genre* (Baltimore, Md.: Johns Hopkins University Press, 1976), pp. 93–126.
5. Michael Allen, *Poe and the British Magazine Tradition* (New York: Ox-

ford University Press, 1969), p. 23. See also Josephine Bauer, "The London Magazine: 1820–29," in *Anglistica*, vol. 1 (Copenhagen: Rosenkilde and Bagger, 1953); and Marie Hamilton Law, *The English Familiar Essay in the Early Nineteenth Century* (Philadelphia: N.p., 1934), pp. 31–56.

    6. Allen, *Poe and the British Magazine Tradition*, p. 23.

    7. Albert Goldman, *The Mine and the Mint: Sources for the Writings of Thomas De Quincey* (Carbondale: Southern Illinois University Press, 1965), p. 27.

    8. *Collected Works of Edgar Allan Poe*, ed. Thomas Ollive Mabbott (Cambridge, Mass.: Harvard University Press, Belknap Press, 1978), 2:69.

    9. Ibid., 2:339–40. Although De Quincey's *Confessions* appeared in the *London Magazine* in 1821, the work was originally intended for publication in *Blackwood's*.

    10. Virginia Woolf, *Granite and Rainbow* (New York: Harcourt, Brace, 1958), pp. 35–36.

    11. De Luca, *Thomas De Quincey*, p. 45.

    12. Hugh Sykes Davies, *Thomas De Quincey*, Writers and Their Work, no. 167 (London: Longmans, Green, 1964), p. 24.

    13. That the reader is supposed to suspect the lecturer's amateur status is evident from the audience's reaction at one point during the lecture: "'It was no obscure baker, gentlemen, or anonymous chimney-sweeper, be assured, that executed this work. I know who it was. *(Here there was a general buzz, which at length broke out into open applause; upon which the lecturer blushed, and went on with much earnestness.)* For heaven's sake, gentlemen, do not mistake me; it was not *I* that did it. I have not the vanity to think myself equal to any such achievement; be assured that you greatly overrate my poor talents'" (13:37).

    14. "The Fine Arts," *Blackwood's Edinburgh Magazine* 21 (April 1827): 401. The article is usually attributed to Francis Grant.

    15. See Allen, *Poe and the British Magazine Tradition*, pp. 20–29, 35–40.

    16. Mario Praz, *The Hero in Eclipse in Victorian Fiction*, trans. Angus Davidson (London: Oxford University Press, 1956), pp. 76, 75, 81.

4

"The True Hero of the Tale": De Quincey's *Confessions* and Affective Autobiographical Theory

MICHAEL COCHISE YOUNG

As Thomas De Quincey himself admits, "Every species of composition is to be tried by its own laws" (10:101); the code governing his *Confessions of an English Opium-Eater*, therefore, would appear self-evident. Yet in the work's subtitle and in the pretensions set forth in the author's introduction, the generic label becomes more ambiguous. As "An Extract from the Life of a Scholar," De Quincey's work suggests a preexisting, complete life from which the *Confessions* itself is drawn. He will present, the subtitle suggests, not the spontaneous and irregular development of a personality but a calculated and representative set of incidents. Substantiating this sense of the *Confessions* as having a predetermined end is De Quincey's avowed didactic purpose in breaking literary decorum by exhibiting his nightmare-ridden opium existence:

But, on the one hand, as my self-accusation does not amount to a confession of guilt, so, on the other, it is possible that, if it did, the benefit resulting to others, from the record of an experience purchased at so heavy a price, might compensate, by a vast overbalance, for any violence done to the feelings I have noticed, and justify a breach of the general rule. [*C*, p. ix]

These introductory remarks conclude with the promise of "the *moral* of [his] narrative" (*C*, p. xiii), emphatic evidence of his instructive, utilitarian (and therefore nonconfessional) designs.

Yet the reality of his narrative personality is transparently specious when compared to this standard. Such claims to a preordained method and public urbanity are a far cry from the examination of the tortured and tortuous designs of the irrational mind which De Quincey actually presents. Far from offering a study which will place his life in a broad cultural context, dignifying its vicissitudes by aligning them with the larger fluxes of history, or ordering his materials to ensure their accuracy, De Quincey admits himself unable to bring perspective or logic to the range of either public or personal affairs. He abandons his commentary on David Ricardo's *On the Principles of Political Economy and Taxation* (1817), for instance, because he cannot maintain order in his domestic, much less the political, economy.

Even this case for establishing the generic claims of the *Confessions* is not as convincing as it might at first appear, for elsewhere in his canon De Quincey questions the very premises of any autobiographical writing. He discounts as legitimate grounds of interest the convolutions of any individual life, suggesting that to inquire into those elements of character which distinguish a person is prurient or voyeuristic. And such sensationalism he deems an unsuitable basis for legitimate, protracted concern. As he admits, "An interest of personality cannot be other than fugitive" (10:119). Such a statement, it seems, would undermine the bases of both the composition and the reading of most autobiographical works, since it is the attraction provided by that personality which engages and sustains the readers' attention and which generates the energy impelling the confessional narrative. Does he then intend his works to be fugitive: transient in the initial experience of them; surreptitious in the enjoyment of them; seemingly ephemeral yet in their effects as cumulatively insidious as the opium dreams he records in them?

The extent to which De Quincey effaces his personality, subordinating it to (or making it partly a function of) the external influences, like opium, which impinged on it or focusing his readers' interest on the plights of people among whom he moves, could lead to that conclusion. In the mode of such confessional authors as Rousseau, Wordsworth, and Byron, he does permit outside forces to absorb his personality, sometimes to the extent of seeming to abdicate even the narrative control of his *Confessions* to his implied readers. De Quincey's deliberate obfuscation of the boundaries between author-narrator and reader raises a theoretical question implicit in many confessional works: the function of the confessor, or the hearer-recipient of the confession, in structuring the work and in determining its efficacy for the sinner-narrator.

In the Roman Catholic tradition the priest holds the "power of the keys"—the ability, in other words, to absolve the sinner from his guilt or to bind his sins if, in the priest's estimation, the confession is neither complete nor sincere. Yet it is also the duty of that same judgmental priest to lead the penitent through his confession, to ensure its exhaustiveness, and to prompt the sinner's memory and encourage his expression of remorse. In the dissenting tradition which rejects such episcopal guidance, the penitent's audience consists of God and his own conscience — a conscience racked by doubt and looking in the confession for affirmation of its hoped-for election, or convinced of its salvation and using the confession as an occasion of praise and instruction. But De Quincey, like Rousseau in the opening paragraphs of his *Confessions* (1781-88), conflates the natures and functions of his audiences, denying God the authority to judge while attributing to his mortal, common readers a divine expansiveness of vision. De Quincey resorts to "an audience of his own creation, a half-imaginary readership."[1] None of these situations, however, seems quite exactly to apply to De Quincey's. His continual dwelling on the past as both explanation of and justification for his present behavior is strongly Catholic, while his resistance to external authority is markedly Protestant. And he seems simultaneously to welcome and avert a dialogue with his implied readers, recognizing in them both a necessary device in the conduct of such interchange and a threat to his narrative and personal autonomy.

With logical justification students of autobiographical writing concentrate on the intentional and structural aspects of a work. Such texts, by definition, almost universally focus their attention on the author-speakers even when they are powerless to affect the situation around them. As De Quincey complains, "I, as is usual in dreams (where, of necessity, we make ourselves central to every movement), had the power, and yet had not the power, to decide [the crisis]" (*C*, p. 123). Unlike many characters of fictional memoirs, however, the narrators of confessions cannot right the imbalance of that power without outside aid. The therapeutic value of confessional writing requires the attention of analytic readers to draw out the suppressed memory; the confessing party must receive absolution. Yet from the beginning De Quincey denies both the need for and the possibility of such relief by refusing to admit any taint of guilt. Rejecting the normative Protestant view of original sin, he goes further by refusing to accept responsibility for his addiction and resulting aberrant behavior; as a victim of circumstances—familial, constitutional, social—he displaces onto others the blame for his actions which they cannot countenance. By eschewing one standard rationale of confessions—justification—De Quincey can invert the expected pattern and indict not himself but his environment.

De Quincey's preface to the version of 1821–22 insists on a rather haughty separation between the author and the audience allowed to view its martyr, a separation indicating both his assumed moral superiority and his disdain for those so tied to conventional morality that they regulate their behavior by the presumed disapprobation of nonopium-eaters: "Guilt, therefore, I do not acknowledge; and, if I did, it is possible that I might still resolve on the present act of confession, in consideration of the service which I may thereby render to the whole class of opium-eaters" (*C*, p. x). The only unqualified statement in the sentence, a clause of denial, introduces the projected audience of addicts whose role is clouded by the speaker's apparent irresolution. By attracting notice to the fictiveness of these readers through his recurrent subjunctives, the speaker affirms the reality of his own identity as a creative force. Yet having thus undermined the existence of his putative audience, De Quincey thwarts the possibility of dialogue with them, an interchange central to the confessional undertaking.

Following Jean Starobinski's model, the " 'I' is confirmed in the function of permanent subject by the presence of its correlative 'you,' giving clear motivation to the discourse."[2] For Starobinski, then, autobiographical works depend, always implicitly and often for their organization, on the distinction between self and other implied by the author-narrator's conventional obligation to establish himself as an "I"—an entity which can be understood only by being contrasted with another entity external to himself. This dialectical tension persists between the self and other—between the author as protagonist and another character in the autobiographical work, or between author as narrator and his implied audience, or even between historical author and contemporary readers.

But if De Quincey's imagined readership is a projection of his opium-laced fantasy, he similarly proposes that the readers physically perusing the volume could also be drug-induced manifestations of his fancy. Elizabeth W. Bruss, in a different context, raises this issue but avoids exploring its implications:

Close enough to overhear what is hardly a communication, to perceive the symptoms of passion without the need to be told, the reader of *Suspiria de Profundis* must become almost the narrator's other self. The reader endures the very same process of grief, shares the identical emotions and memories.... In the dream sequences, the reader is admitted as a full participant.... In the "Vision of Life," the text becomes a mutual undertaking of narrator and reader.[3]

The concept which Bruss derives from the *Suspiria* applies equally to the *Confessions*. One particularly striking illustration of this collaboration is the description of the scholar's study provided in the version of 1821-22. From this depiction of the Opium-Eater's snug winter retreat, expressly commissioned as an illustration by De Quincey's speaker, the figure of the narrator is oddly absent:

But as to myself, there I demur. I admit that, naturally, I ought to occupy the foreground of the picture; that being the hero of the piece, or (if you choose) the criminal at the bar, my body should be had into court. This seems reasonable; but why should I confess, on this point, to a painter? or, why confess at all? If the public (into whose private ear I am confidentially whispering my confessions, and not into any painter's) should chance to have framed some agreeable picture for itself of the Opium-eater's exterior,—should have ascribed to him, romantically, an elegant person, or a handsome face, why should I barbarously tear from it so pleasing a delusion,—pleasing both to the public and to me? No: paint me, if at all, according to your own fancy; and, as a painter's fancy should teem with beautiful creations, I cannot fail, in that way, to be a gainer. [*C*, p. 100]

Adopting the stance suggested by Louis A. Renza, one could read such a passage as the writer's paranoiac attempt to exalt himself through humility by making his absence the most vigorous reminder of his existence.[4] Unlike the nominal protagonist of *Childe Harold's Pilgrimage*, however, the narrator here withdraws himself from the reader's view; he is not overwhelmed by the personality of his narrative alter ego. But, this time like the Harold of cantos 1 and 2, De Quincey's persona here assumes that what sympathy or attempted identification is extended to him from the implied audience is basically well intentioned but misguided. The sympathetic, complimentary portrait they might frame is, he suggests in a faintly pitying tone, not at all representative. He refrains from correcting it, not through any vanity of his own but through consideration of his readers', whose judgment of his character (based in part on physiognomy) would be proved wrong. This concern with the reflection of internal traits in both the demeanor of the individual and the cosmographical glass in which he finds his reflection is an issue which concerned De Quincey and which will be taken up later.

More interesting, however, is the unnaturally active role assigned to the readers as the principal creators of the projected artwork. De Quincey, exploiting the nuances of his artistic metaphor, foregrounds the narrative elements usually relegated to the middle distance; the reading (or listening) public assumes momentarily a status equal to that of the speaker. Its collective ear not only receives the confessional outpouring but also projects its own fantasies to constitute an image of the shadowy speaker. This act of bestowing form engages the readers with the text in a way that temporarily draws them within the frame distinguishing the artwork. Suddenly self-conscious, they no longer merely overhear the confession but become themselves the potential performers of autobiographical acts.

Such creation by the audience of the work it contemplates leads it vertiginously to the limits of the same neurosis from which De Quincey himself suffers, one in which "the sentient organ *project*[*s*] itself as its own object" (*C,* p. 116). To try to contemplate the organ or faculty of perception is, for De Quincey, to precipitate oneself into an infinitely deepening vortex, one which draws into itself not only the perceiving mind but also the rhetoric in which the resulting vertigo attempts to find expression. As he observes in his essay on style:

> Direct objective qualities it is always by comparison easy to measure; but the difficulty commences when we have to combine with this outer measurement of the object another corresponding measurement of the subjective or inner qualities by which we apply the measure; that is, when besides the objects projected to a distance from the spectator, we have to allow for variations or disturbances in the very eye which surveys them. The eye cannot see itself; we cannot project from ourselves, and contemplate as an object, our own contemplating faculty, or appreciate our own appreciating power. Biasses, therefore, or gradual warpings, that have occurred in our critical faculty as applied to style, we cannot allow for. [10:153]

It is this inability to escape the limitations of one's individual perspective which drives De Quincey, reluctantly, to tolerate the presence of these intrusive, sometimes obtrusive, implied readers. Only in the image of himself cast back by them—only in the manipulation of his public avatar—can he establish his private identity. Yet insofar as they recreate him in their own image, he becomes reified and thus gains a measure of the "objectivity" and stability he yearns for.

The readers themselves are saved from a precipitous fall into this psychic chasm, however, because of the distance deliberately established between them and the work—and between the speaker and his own self. While the readers are metonymically described by their capacity to hear and see, only the speaker is endowed with the capacity to speak, to utter the confession which is both the performance and subject of the autobiographical act. In the *Confessions* it is the capacity for articulation which propels the narrative and distinguishes the roles of the implied interlocutors. Moreover, in the passage from the *Confessions* quoted above, De Quincey continues to manipulate his public role. By threatening to explode that public's delusions, the sole manifestation of its creative power within the text, he reasserts the conventional hierarchy of power in which the readers' vision is subordinated to that of the author. In the end, De Quincey avers, his existence is not absolutely posited on the fantasies of his readers. First differentiating the painter of the study from the creative audience, then extending to it the option of refusing to create ("paint me, if at all"), De Quincey establishes an existence independent of the persona which that public attempts to impose on him.

But he further compounds the schizophrenia of both the text and his narrative ego by becoming his own audience: "Long before that fifteenth year of mine, I had noticed, as a worm lying at the heart of life and fretting its security, the fact that innumerable acts of choice change countenance and are variously appraised at varying stages of life—shift with the shifting hours" (3:296). The process of maturation, he suggests, is not marked by a single turning point around which, like a magnetic pole, the currents of his life are organized, a pattern typical of autobiography. Rather, it is a continual task of retrospection and revaluation in which the number of vantage points is potentially infinite, corresponding to the number of infinitely divisible moments of which the life is composed. To accommodate these multiple possibilities, De Quincey would have been compelled (if he had not already been temperamentally so inclined) to multiply his autobiographical writings in proportion to record them all: the two versions of his *Confessions,* the autobiographical components of *Suspiria de Profundis,* and the *Autobiographic Sketches.*[5]

Despite this multiplication of and alienation from himself, the stylistic retention of the first person implies a stability in De Quincey's self-image; by his continued assertion of the "I" he alerts the reader to a situation that underlies the paradox fundamental to the interpretation of the work and to the establishment of an adequate autobiographical theory. As Starobinski suggests, such a device implies the permanent assumption of responsibility by the speaker for past events and asserts a unity of identity, a continuity of existence.[6] One encounters here a situation in which the putative and actual images of De Quincey are placed in a Blakean opposition, the existence of one implying that of its counterpart. In so projecting this divided self, he invites the situation described by Francis R. Hart in which the speaker's narrative existence is "*more true* somehow than the 'versions of self' historically recoverable."[7] From the perspective of a historic present the speaker's earlier selves assume for him an air of unreality, of fictiveness; from the same temporal framework, however, the reader is tempted to extrapolate from the text an image of the speaker which may bear only tangential, although more palpable, relevance to the author's life.

This fluctuating acceptance and rejection of the biographical legend surrounding an author becomes an influential convention in the De Quincey canon. Particularly in the *Confessions* he influences the readers' reception of the work by opposing the expected, publicly created personality with a persona yet more idiosyncratic. Thus the audience, while removed from the process of designing the actual text, is implicitly charged with the development of the author's character, both as a narrative device and in his social capacity. Therefore, even while his use of the first person, his refusal to hide behind a transparently fictional persona as Byron does, suggests his willingness to accept responsibility for his actions, his exploitation of his audience as coauthors of his work belies that moral courage.

Such intimacy on the boundaries of life and art imposes upon the audience moral claims which verge on the casuistic. Its anticipated intolerance or violation of his confessional confidences, De Quincey hints, absolves him as speaker from obligatory honesty in his narration. Thus the reader senses the necessity to accept De Quincey at his word for the sake of maintaining the appearances which permit the continued operation of the literary marketplace, the advancement of the narrative.[8] This preoccupation with his authorial veracity, De Quincey claims, originates in his concern for an image of rectitude with (and concomitant sympathy from) his readers: "It would vitiate the interest which any reader might otherwise take in this narrative, if for one moment it were supposed that any feature of the case were varnished or distorted. From the very first, I had been faithful to the most rigorous law of accuracy—even in absolute trifles" (3:293n). That his interest in the truth springs equally from a concern with the audience's eventual granting of pardon has already been suggested. As in a Shakespearean epilogue, the exercise of that audience's "good hands" is required to set free the artist who has labored to entertain them. If the conduct of his lived existence does not require their assent, that of his literary life does. For that reason he is himself often chary of his criticism, vilifying only those individuals or institutions no longer in a position to damage his prospects and currying the favor of those in a position to be of further assistance. "To blame might be hazardous," De Quincey observes in his essay "Rhetoric" (1828), "for blame demands reasons; but praise enjoys a ready dispensation from all reasons and from all discrimination" (10:124). Such rationalization, while it explains one reason for his self-serving circumspection, also sounds suspiciously like Rousseau's self-justification of his conversion to Catholicism. Blame, like Protestantism for Rousseau, demands active assent and evidential support; both suggest an aesthetic which continually questions its basis and its appropriateness.

The *Confessions*, therefore, is riddled with conflicting allusions to the need both for factual accuracy and for the artistic license which governs De Quincey's revision of past events, notably his treatment of Charles Lawson, headmaster of the Manchester Grammar School. In that instance, as De Quincey acknowledges in the edition of 1856, the version of 1821-22 inflated Lawson's academic pretensions in the interest of soliciting the favor of his family and colleagues. The need to "evade too close an approach to the realities of the case" (3:249) there forced De Quincey's equivocations—equally suggested, he claims, by the ostensible interests of his reading public. The interplay of author and readers thus affects both the content and the continuity of the work.

De Quincey's continued insistence on this pretense of honesty and accuracy despite his own acknowledged self-contradictions is a matter of some concern. Continually mistrustful, he anticipates his audience's betrayal of the aesthetic and moral confidence he places in them and is the first to violate their pledge of reciprocal good faith. His definition of truth refers, it seems, only to the immediate present in which he presumably utters his discourse. For if De Quincey indeed views time as infinitely divisible, then he can assume neither a continuous personality nor consistent behavior for either himself or the audience whose behavior is modeled after his own. Assuming that they are as changeable as himself, he adapts his discourse to that audience, producing statements without reference to the interpretations or assumptions offered earlier in the text. His speech writing is ahistorical, as disjunctive and displaced from a stable context as the listener-readers to whom it is addressed.

In his discussion of autobiography as poem, William L. Howarth proposes that the author "writes solely for himself, in the *lyric* genre, but the hero of his book is its reader, who alone can master its final form."[9] Howarth's emphasis on the solipsism and self-indulgence, psychological and artistic, of the author and on the separation of author and audience recognizes two of De Quincey's principal affectations. As De Quincey notes in a discussion of the pleasures of music, the listeners' fulfillment derives not from passive acquiescence to the linear progression of the score but from the continual process of arranging the discrete metrical units of which a piece is composed into new associative patterns:

The mistake of most people is, to suppose that it is by the ear they communicate with music, and therefore that they are purely passive as to its effects. But this is not so; it is by the reaction of the mind upon the notices of the ear (the *matter* coming by the senses, the *form* from the mind) that the pleasure is constructed. [3:390]

Such enjoyment, moreover, is nondiscursive; that is, the listener-composers participate in a manner which defies rational reduction to language. Their perception of the event resides in an emotional, not a logical, approach to reality. Neither ideas nor words, De Quincey insists, deserve a place in the apprehension of this intellectual activity. The vocabulary with which one deals with the phenomenon of music eludes codification: " 'But,' says a friend, 'a succession of musical sounds is to me like a collection of Arabic characters: I can attach no ideas to them.' Ideas! my dear friend! there is no occasion for them; all that class of ideas which can be available in such a case has a language of representative feelings" (3:391).

An analogy can be drawn between the hearers' response to music and the readers' role in the *Confessions*. In imposing a continuity upon the discrete experiential units which De Quincey presents as his confession, the readers are similarly compelled not only to negotiate the often refulgent outpouring of the author's prose but also to establish a new alphabet and critical vocabulary in order to engage in the dialogue which De Quincey posits. In light of the fascinated revulsion with which he relates his Oriental vision, his allusion to the Arabic derivation of its language indicates both its unfamiliarity to the readers and the accompanying difficulty—and reluctance—with which it is mastered. Recalling his frustration in learning the piano, De Quincey concludes that the exertion required in the production of music detracts from the enjoyment of the product:

Too soon I became aware that to the deep voluptuous enjoyment of music absolute *passiveness* in the hearer is indispensable. Gain what skill you please, nevertheless activity, vigilance, anxiety must always accompany an elaborate effort of musical execution: and so far is that from being reconcilable with the entrancement and lull essential to the true fruition of music, that, even if you should suppose a vast piece of mechanism capable of executing a whole oratorio, but requiring, at intervals, a cooperating impulse from the foot of the auditor, even *that,* even so much as an occasional touch of the foot, would utterly undermine all your pleasure. [3:270]

The very activity which De Quincey attempts to impose on his projected audience, therefore, is one which seems to preclude its enjoyment of the work. Such a deduction, however, assumes that the modes of apprehension employed by reader and speaker are identical, and that is not the case. Referring to his childhood prodigiousness as a Grecian, De Quincey boasts of his facility in establishing relationships among disparate concepts—a skill, he argues, superior to the simple mastery of the lexicon and grammar of a language. He boasts his possession of a talent "for feeling in a moment the secret analogies or parallelisms that connected things else apparently remote" [3:332]. These associations he understands as independent of the functions of memory, occurring as instantaneous and intuitive acts of recognition outside of time. Opium, he reminds his readers, is valuable in part for its efficacy in liberating this comprehensive vision. Yet those same readers are effectively denied access to such an omniscient perspective by the fact that their experience of the text is necessarily a progression through linear time. In the act of reading they are bound by conventional chronology, despite De Quincey's efforts to arrange his illustrations "either in their chronological order, or any other that may give them more effect as pictures to the reader" (*C*, p. 112).

Significantly, De Quincey distinguishes between visual and self-consciously literary ways of conceiving of the *Confessions*. From the point of view of the speaker the work stands as a painting, a pictorial representation whose value does not rely on sequential presentation but which may be comprehended instantaneously. Such an analogy is usually reserved, appropriately, for the visionary experiences of the opium dreams or the reveries induced by a nontextual form such as music. But in his status as mediator between the opium world and the gross mortality in which the readers move, De Quincey adopts the persona of author, invoking the self-referential vocabulary of literature to describe the process in which his *Confessions* is ostensibly engaged: the fulfillment of "the desire [he] had to spell backwards and re-compose the text" (3:250) of his life. The "backwards" here signals the uncomfortable limitation imposed by the act of composition, a restriction impinging equally on the naïve readers of the text. The situation alters significantly, however, for the reader already familiar with the text. As one's acquaintance with the text increases, one presumably draws asymptotically toward the condition of the author by merit of one's ability to range freely—mentally—through the text, anticipating patterns and reassigning values to incidents in proportion to their foreknown import. Yet each reading, presumably, assumes the revaluation of the work anew, according to De Quincey; although the teleology of a work may remain the same, the progression to that end must be traced afresh continually:

> Even the character of your own absolute experience, past and gone, which (if anything in this world) you might surely answer for as sealed and settled for ever—even this you must submit to hold in suspense, as a thing conditional and contingent upon what is yet to come—liable to have its provisional character affirmed or reversed, according to the new combinations into which it may enter with elements only yet perhaps in the earliest stages of development. [3:314-15]

In this instance De Quincey suggests the impossibility of arriving at a definitive interpretation of his life or of his work. The act of composition and the interpretative event are coterminous and mutually defining occurrences whose alliance precludes the observation of one without consideration of its complement.

Another way of approaching this dilemma is to realize the impetus of the forces of time which both speaker and listener resist. The autobiographer's translation of his life into the atemporal region of art attempts to collapse the antagonistic forces of time, over which individuals extend their existence, and timelessness, which permits the "never ending, still beginning" (3:252) cosmology of the artwork. Augmenting the force of this dialectic is the comparable tension established within the time-bound perimeter of the individual life. In it the past continually threatens to well up and overcome the present, just as in the opium visions "immemorial tracts of time" (*C*, p. 117) obliterate present historical reality. The compulsive detailing of biographical minutiae and cultural commentary which critics perceive as the principal flaw of the *Confessions* of 1856 represents De Quincey's response to this threat of dissolution in time. By exhibiting the minute particularity of his historically verifiable past, he tries to hold in check the unregulated encroachments of that past into the dream realm. Where Byron used the same technique to camouflage his protagonist's extended absence in *Childe Harold,* De Quincey multiplies details to establish himself more specifically and concretely in his own mind. The incarnation of lived experience in textual form breaks the nightmare repetition of past events not only for De Quincey, however, but also for his interlocutors, real or imagined. Apostrophizing his wife, Margaret, he remarks: "But these troubles are past, and thou wilt read these records of a period so dolorous to us both as the legend of some hideous dream that can return no more" (*C,* p. 62).

One Romantic view of time perceives history as tending toward apocalypse, toward the obviation of time and of the opportunity for further progression and change; in this scheme time's cessation poses a threat. De Quincey's view is quite the opposite. To him the threat of history for the individual lies in the possibility of its indeterminate continuance and the limitation of the individual's vision to what may be realized within the confines of time: "Over every form, and threat, and punishment, and dim sightless incarceration, brooded a sense of eternity and infinity that drove me into an oppression as of madness" (*C,* p. 119).

This preoccupation with the completion of time impels De Quincey's work in two mutually exclusive directions: toward a sense of absolute closure within time and to a transcendence of chronological limits. Thus, while confessions typically avoid the issue of the speaker's potential death as threatening the creative process which sustains the work, De Quincey invokes images of mortality in the coda to each version of the *Confessions.* By inviting posthumous dissection by the College of Surgeons in the version of 1821-22, he projects himself no longer as the performer of an autobiographical act but as the subject of future analysis, both physical and psychological, by those who are his present readers. And these imagined readers, like the De Quincey of the volume's subtitle, are themselves scholars engaged in preparing "extracts" from the Opium-Eater. The body of his work has become congruent with his own body:

No man, I suppose, employs much of his time on the phenomena of his own body without some regard for it; whereas the reader sees that, so far from looking upon mine with any complacency or regard, I hate it and make it the object of my bitter ridicule and contempt; and I should not be displeased to know that the last indignities which the law inflicts upon the bodies of the worst malefactors might hereafter fall upon it. [*C*, p. 142]

This opprobrium which he calls upon himself effectively forestalls the readers' temptation to criticize the speaker's previously demonstrated self-indulgences. Like Rousseau he feels free to criticize himself in the harshest terms but swells in self-righteous indignation if the same charges are leveled by another. Furthermore, in thus figuratively laying himself exposed to public examination, he himself becomes an equally detached spectator of the probing initiated by his erstwhile audience.

In the end narrator and audience are afforded the omniscient perspective to which the text aspired. The "Daughter of Lebanon" dream which concludes the version of 1856 performs a similar, albeit more sophisticated, function. By rounding off the work with a prophecy, De Quincey inverts the expected chronological patterns of the text: he looks forward rather than back. The allusion immediately preceding this passage establishes as historic context the Miltonic expulsion of Adam and Eve from Eden to begin the historic process, looking back upon their lost paradise (or, for De Quincey, the debased paradise offered by his dreams) as a region "'with dreadful faces thronged and fiery arms'" (3:449). But "in the final segment of the text, the autobiographical world is upended, memory becomes prophecy and the problem of death and things past becomes the problem of birth and things to come."[10] The escape from time which De Quincey here effects is, nevertheless, one which implies the preexistence of a significant pattern to his life and suffering. The prophet's responsibility, he reminds the reader, is to part "the curtain from the secret counsels of Heaven. He declared, or made public, the previously hidden truths of God" (3:452n.). Thus, while the version of 1821-22 implies the readers' ongoing duty to impose, even after death, an organizing pattern on the circumstances of his life, De Quincey here points toward the completion of life and its direction toward some ordained end independent of the readers' participation.

But such an observation cannot league De Quincey's *Confessions* absolutely with autobiographical rather than with confessional works. For his central concern, especially in the version of 1856, is to document and thereby explain the circumstances of his early life. He does this not from any obeisance to childhood as an especially privileged state but from his conviction, supported elsewhere in his canon, of the explanatory power of origins. If each moment contains within itself infinite options, the most choices were available to him during that time when the consequences of some of those choices had not barred future avenues of exploration to him. And at a period when he least understands his present situation, recourse to a past imagined as stable offers a distraction from the fluid and perplexing present. Thus emerges his obsession with tracing origins when he cannot understand a phenomenon itself:

It is a natural resource that whatsoever we find it difficult to investigate as a result we endeavour to follow as a growth. Failing analytically to probe its nature, historically we seek relief to our perplexities by tracing its origin. Not able to assign the elements of its theory, we endeavour to detect them in the stages of its development. [10:168]

This passage offers some assurance that De Quincey possesses one major confessional prerequisite: he either does not know or else resists stating the teleology of his work, a contention supported by the profusion of labyrinths as motifs in the *Confessions* and by the equally labyrinthine arabesques traced by his prose. Or does it only mean that he as architect of this literary structure knows its secret center and inflicts the tracing of it on his readers? But like Daedalus, the originator of such mazes, De Quincey is himself imprisoned by the labyrinth he created: he remains immured in his own elaborate mental structure.

Notes

1. Elizabeth W. Bruss, *Autobiographical Acts: The Changing Situation of a Literary Genre* (Baltimore, Md.: Johns Hopkins University Press, 1976), p. 93.
2. Jean Starobinski, "The Style of Autobiography," in *Literary Style: A Symposium*, ed. and [in part] trans. Seymour Chatman (London: Oxford University Press, 1971), p. 288.
3. Bruss, *Autobiographical Acts*, pp. 123-24.
4. See Louis A. Renza, "The Veto of the Imagination: A Theory of Autobiography," *New Literary History* 9 (1977): 18.
5. Similar epistemological problems have led to the production of comparable multiple versions of a life in the canons of Rousseau (whose *Confessions* are further expanded and corrected in his *Reveries of a Solitary Stroller* of 1782) and Byron (whose *Childe Harold's Pilgrimage* and *Don Juan* each invert the structural devices, tone, and ideology established in the other), to cite only two Romantic instances.
6. Starobinski, "The Style of Autobiography," p. 290.
7. Francis R. Hart, "Notes for an Anatomy of Modern Autobiography," *New Literary History* 1 (1970): 496.
8. Those inclined to underrate the importance of reciprocal honesty in the literary marketplace as defined by Barbara Herrnstein Smith ("The Ethics of Interpretation," in her *On the Margins of Discourse: The Relation of Literature to Language* [Chicago: University of Chicago Press, 1978], pp. 133-54) are well advised to heed De Quincey's warning: "No; believe all that I ask of you, ... believe it liberally, and as an act of grace, or else in mere prudence; for, if not, then, in the next edition of my Opium Confessions revised and enlarged, I will make you believe, and tremble; and, *à force d'ennuyer*, by mere dint of pandiculation, I will terrify all readers of mine from ever again questioning any postulate that I shall think fit to make" (*C*, pp. 87-88). Those critics of De Quincey unkindly disposed toward the version of 1856 might admit to the self-fulfillment of this prophecy.
9. William L. Howarth, "Some Principles of Autobiography," *New Literary History* 5 (1974): 377.
10. Bruss, *Autobiographical Acts*, p. 107.

5

De Quincey's Retrospective Optics: Analogues of Intoxication in the Opium-Eater's "Nursery Experiences"

MARTIN BOCK

The first entry in Thomas De Quincey's diary of 1803 explores "the intimate connection, which [exists between the] body and the mind" (*D*, p. 141). Although at eighteen De Quincey is simply postulating the salutary effects of exercise on the human mind, he remained interested for much of his writing career in the relation of "physical economy" to the imaginative life. This early fascination with the connection between the mind and body probably springs from his admiration of the Lake Poets, whose sensationist theories articulated new metaphors of mind and concepts of sense perception. For the young De Quincey the first-generation Romantics were "prophet[s] of the senses,"[1] whose spiritual optics penetrate beyond the material world in order "to treat of things not as they *are*, but as they *appear*; not as they exist in themselves, but as they *seem* to exist to the *senses* and to the passions."[2] While De Quincey's epistemology also emphasizes this Wordsworthian connection between the senses, human passions, and imagination, his theories of imaginative perception are based on an original conception of the dreaming mind as outlined in *Suspiria de Profundis:*

The machinery for dreaming planted in the human brain was not planted for nothing. That faculty, in alliance with the mystery of darkness, is the one great tube through which man communicates with the shadowy. And the dreaming organ, in connection with the heart, the eye and the ear, compose the magnificent apparatus which forces the infinite into the chambers of a human brain.[3]
[*SP*, p. 149]

Here and elsewhere in his autobiographical writings De Quincey portrays himself adopting various mechanisms—all clear analogues to opium intoxication—that offer a distinct alternative to the Wordsworthian perceptual mode.

The evidence suggesting that De Quinccy is a Wordsworthian disciple is ample and sound: his letters and writings that predate his estrangement from Wordsworth praise the poet to an embarrassing degree (see *D,* pp. 167–68, 185–88); he uses the solitary prospect to produce a coalescence of subject and object; and he exalts the child's innocent eye which perceives with a visionary clarity that the adult cannot approximate. "I maintain steadfastly," he writes, "that into all the *elementary* feelings of man children look with more searching gaze than adults. . . . Children have a specific power of contemplating the truth, which departs as they enter the world" (*SP,* p. 208). He also observes that "the heart in this season of life is apprehensive; and, where its sensibilities are profound, is endowed with a special power of listening for the tones of truth" (1:121–22). Both passages refer contextually to Wordsworth, but neither reflects the complexity of De Quincey's treatment of childhood experience in *Confessions of an English Opium-Eater, Autobiographic Sketches,* or *Suspiria de Profundis.*

In all these autobiographical works De Quincey modifies Wordsworth's theory of a prelapsarian childhood state by investing his own nursery experiences with images of intoxication, sensations garnered from his addiction to opium. Unlike Wordsworth, who maintained that "the human mind is capable of excitement without the application of gross and violent stimulants,"[4] De Quincey rhetorically compares the freshness of perception incident to childhood with the hyperaesthetic imagery of an opium landscape: "The nursery experience had been the ally and the natural coëfficient of the opium. For that reason it was that the nursery experience has been narrated. Logically it bears the very same relation to the convulsions of the dreaming faculty as the opium" (*SP,* p. 223). In the autobiographical literature the infant De Quincey is portrayed as using various distorting lenses, much like the "machinery for dreaming," which facilitate his youthful visions. More than Wordsworth and Coleridge's "modifying colours of imagination,"[5] De Quincey's apparatus involves dynamic, disorienting mechanisms which intensify and distort infant experience so that it more closely resembles the mature visions of the adult.

Throughout his writing career De Quincey struggles with a tension between his desire to celebrate the child as an autonomous self enjoying "rural seclusion" in the "silent garden" (1:34) of Greenhay and his psychological need to collapse the distinction between his adult and childhood selves. A poignant dramatization of the search for continuity between these various selves closes the "Introduction to the World of Strife," the third chapter of *Autobiographic Sketches,* which records his encounter with a rabid dog that pauses during its flight from a mob of shouting hunters. He reports that as a child unaware of his own danger he "looked searchingly" into the dog's eyes which were "glazed, and as if in a dreamy state," and the dog, in turn, "looked most earnestly" (1:118) at its intuitive human sympathizer. The scene illustrates a moment of understanding between kindred souls, as if the persecuted and "deranged" animal were a projection of De Quincey's deepest fears about his adult self. Symbolically, the infant child and the tortured adult contemplate each other and establish a fleeting union: the uncomprehending child looks with searching gaze at the disoriented outcast who is vengefully pursued because of his derangement.

Since the pariah figure is one of De Quincey's primary involutes that characterize the adult self,[6] this momentary union metaphorically collapses their dual selves. They are separate because of their differences yet united in a bond of sympathy identical to that which unites the child and adult selves:

An adult sympathizes with himself in childhood because he *is* the same, and because (being the same) yet he is *not* the same. He acknowledges the deep, mysterious identity between himself, as adult and as infant, for the ground of his sympathy; and yet . . . he feels the differences between his two selves as the main quickeners of his sympathy. [*SP,* pp. 154-55]

This quickening of sympathy between De Quincey's two selves invites the adult De Quincey to portray his younger self as a precocious participant in the "horror of life" which "mixed itself . . . in earliest youth with the heavenly sweetness of life" (*SP*, p. 257). As this mixture is clearly analogous to the pleasures and pains of opium, De Quincey uses the concept of spiritual disorientation to characterize part of his life experience from the very beginning of his consciousness.

De Quincey uses the imagery of disorientation, even in his early nursery experiences, to suggest the fragmentary, discontinuous nature of his divided but potentially integrated self and existence.[7] The use of this technique divorces De Quincey from the Wordsworthian tradition. Critics have long recognized the central aim of Wordsworth's poetry to be a wedding of the "majestic intellect" with the natural world, a dovetailing of the noumenal and phenomenal worlds which results in a coalescence of mental and physical landscapes. As Paul de Man argues about the resulting poetic landscapes: "It becomes difficult to distinguish between object and image, between imagination and perception. . . . The vision almost seems to become a real landscape."[8] The imagery of De Quincey's work seeks the opposite. Unlike Wordsworth, who rejected the "pictorial" in his poetry because it was a "highly artificial way of looking,"[9] De Quincey exploits the pictorial frame to stress the self-conscious nature of his visions which go beyond the limits of normal perception. To achieve this, De Quincey adopts disorienting perceptual frames. To approximate a sense of spiritual disorientation, De Quincey precedes the vision that he seeks by a moment of sensory derangement in which the normal cultural episteme is disjoined and rendered inchoate. Only after such a discontinuous moment can he attain a vision that transcends ordinary perception. Morse Peckham proposes that this experience of defamiliarization is the basis of the Romantic creative process and epistemology: "The task of the artist was to create a perceptual field to which psychological adaptation was anything but easy, a field which would permit and require and force the artistic observer to experience perceptual and cognitive disorientation and in grasping that field to engage the power of the creative imagination."[10] J. Hillis Miller notes an analogous sense of structural disorientation in De Quincey's writing style. Referring to De Quincey's digressive wanderings, Miller remarks that "to read an essay by De Quincey is to experience a strange and exasperating sense of disorientation" or "a kind of dizzy amazement."[11]

There are virtually unlimited examples of stylistic and imagistic disorientation in the literature of De Quincey's adult experiences. The descriptions of London are particularly full of "such knotty problems of alleys, alleys without soundings" (3:393). This kind of sensory derangement, induced or intensified by opium, offered De Quincey an idiom for presenting his adult experiences, an idiom which demanded a lens of disorientation that would eventually become a mechanism for introducing similar events into his sympathetic nursery experiences. In De Quincey's works on his adult life an example of this disorienting perceptual frame is the double lens of distortion in *The English Mail-Coach*. The reader's perceptual frame is most obviously distorted by the narrator's opium imagery: the driver's metamorphosis into a Cyclops, the narrator's hyperaesthetic sensitivity to sights and sounds, and his exaggeration of time and space before the coach and the lovers' gig nearly collide. The second disorienting apparatus, which doubly refracts the reader's perception, is the coach itself, a machine of disorientation that compels a synaesthetic view of reality. The "glory of motion" which the prose fantasy celebrates invades virtually all the perceptive faculties so that the kinaesthetic sense is confounded with all the others: the velocity of the coach provides "grand effects for the eye between lamp-light and the darkness upon solitary roads" (13:271) and even inspires the narrator to *hear* the sound of motion some four miles distant (13:311). This distorting mechanism is intimately associated with the intoxicating properties of opium, yet analogous "machines" of disorientation are presented as equally fascinating to the juvenile De Quincey who had never taken opium.

A close comparison to the mail-coach in this regard is the problematical antigravity "humming-top" that would allow De Quincey's brother William to walk like a fly on the ceiling: "He would make an apparatus (and he made it) for having himself launched, like a top, upon the ceiling, and regularly spun. Then the vertiginous motion of the human top would overpower the force of gravitation" (1:64). On the one hand, De Quincey's fascination with this fabulous device is merely childish fancy, but the impetus for the older De Quincey's description of the machine is his deep-seated need to experience extraordinary perception, personally or vicariously. Like the mail-coach, the "humming-top" is an instrument that deranges the senses and induces a radical view of the world. The fascination that young Thomas had for his brother's vertiginous mechanism is the same that prompts the older De Quincey's synaesthetic voyage on the mail-coach, an analogous machine of disorientation.

Not all of De Quincey's devices that induce sensory disequilibrium are physical mechanisms. Some are visual lenses that metaphorically or actually distort the perceptual field. An important early example of this technique occurs in De Quincey's diary when he imagines himself "looking through a glass" and seeing a man in "dim and shadowy perspective and (as it were) in a dream" (*D*, p. 156). Such disorienting moments are among the most important of De Quincey's adolescent and nursery experiences because they are so intimately connected with the visionary imagination. In "The Affliction of Childhood," where he describes his grief after the death of his sister, sensory disorientation plays a critical role in shaping a reality that transcends the corporeal world:

> Into the woods or the desert air I gazed, as if some comfort lay hid in *them*. I wearied the heavens with my inquest of beseeching looks. I tormented the blue depths with obstinate scrutiny, sweeping them with my eyes, and searching them forever after one angelic face that might, perhaps, have permission to reveal itself for a moment. The faculty of shaping images in the distance out of slight elements, and grouping them after the yearnings of the heart, aided by a slight defect in my eyes, grew upon me at this time. And I recall at the present moment one instance of that sort, which may show how merely shadows, or a gleam of brightness, or nothing at all, could furnish a sufficient basis for this creative faculty.
> [*SP*, p. 184]

It is unclear whether by "defect" De Quincey refers to his myopia, apparently rather severe, or to an inflammation of the eye which occasionally troubled him.[12] What can be said with confidence, however, is that in the early and unrevised "Affliction" he embraces this "defect," or "mechanic affection of the eye" (*C,* p. 109), as a means of engaging the "palimpsest" of the human brain and of exciting the imaginative, visionary faculties. His welcoming of this dysfunction, of sensory disorientation preceding altered awareness, is analogous to opium taking and, as such, radically transforms Wordsworth's dictum of seeing things "as they *seem*" into a Rimbaudian *dérèglement de tous les sens.*

The phenomenon of sensory disorientation inducing the child's visionary moment is clearly demonstrated by the vision of grief and death which De Quincey experiences in church. As he mourns the loss of his sister, the child's tears distort his perceptual frame and thereby prepare for his prophetic experience: "Raising my streaming eyes to the windows of the galleries, [I] saw, on days when the sun was shining, a spectacle as affecting as ever prophet can have beheld." His blurred vision deepens the "purples and crimsons" through which "streamed the golden light" and intensifies the "emblazonries of heavenly illumination mingling with the earthly emblazonries" (*SP*, p. 185). Because of its mechanical nature this imaginative flight is thought by some critics to be "inadequate" as a visionary experience.[13] Admittedly the mild disorientation results in a *self-conscious* vision, perceptually framed by an opaque section of glass, but the intensity of the vision, which explores the relation of life and death to the finite and the infinite, must also be recognized. Writes De Quincey:

I saw through the wide central field of the window, where the glass was uncolored, white fleecy clouds sailing over the azure depths of the sky; were it but a fragment or a hint of such a cloud, immediately under the flash of my sorrow-haunted eye, it grew and shaped itself into visions of beds with white lawny curtains; and in the beds lay sick children, dying children, that were tossing in anguish, and weeping clamourously for death. [*SP,* pp. 185–86]

De Quincey's perceptive and cognitive frame is suddenly disoriented, disrupted by the *"flash"* (italics added) of his "sorrow-haunted eye" which immediately projects, through an artificial lens, the transcendent vision of anguish and death, a vision that might well have been the product of the pains of opium but is clearly beyond the ken of a six-year-old.[14]

There are other visionary moments in De Quincey's nursery experiences which are described through opium imagery, but none is so vividly portrayed or so explicitly associated with the drug as his trancelike vision as he stands over the corpse of his sister: "Whilst I stood, a solemn wind began to blow,—the most mournful that ear ever heard. . . . It was a wind that had swept the fields of mortality for a hundred centuries" (*SP*, p. 175).

This experience becomes a De Quinceyan involute, a complex of emotional associations that coalesce in a symbolic object or situation and that represents the interplay between the visionary imagination and the sensible world. This interplay is emphasized by the auditory and visual images which prompt the vision: "Instantly, when my ear caught this vast Aeolian intonation, when my eye filled with the golden fulness of life, . . . instantly a trance fell upon me. A vault seemed to open in the zenith of the far blue sky, a shaft which ran up forever" (*SP*, p. 176). The adult interpolations of the childish vision appear in the expanded consciousness of a child who conceives of a "hundred centuries" and who witnesses the infinite expansion of space. These hyperaesthetic distortions are identical to the intoxicating effects of opium, which "may intensify or distort sense-perception, especially audition and the visual apprehension of space, structure, light, and color."[15] The young De Quincey, in effect, has an opium vision. His synaesthetic ear catches the "*vast* Aeolian intonation" (italics added), and his earthly vision is arrested by the "golden fulness" and the "far blue sky."

Immediately after describing the vision, De Quincey inversely compares the contraction of time in his recent childish vision to the elastic expansion of time experienced under the influence of opium:

But why speak of it [the vision] in connection with opium? Could a child of six years old have been under that influence? No, but simply because it so exactly reversed the operation of opium. Instead of a short interval expanding into a vast one, upon this occasion a long one had contracted into a minute. I have reason to believe that a *very* long one had elapsed during this wandering or suspension of my perfect mind. [*SP,* p. 177]

With this comparison De Quincey complicates matters, revealing his tendency to fictionalize his nursery experiences and, in all likelihood, his adult experiences as well. Despite his disclaimer De Quincey describes both time and space in his vision as expansive: intonations are "vast," the vault into heaven runs up "forever," and these hyperaesthetic exaggerations seem "to go on for ever and ever." After his vision De Quincey confesses, "I slept—for how long I cannot say" (*SP,* p. 176). Why then does De Quincey contradict himself on the next page, suggesting that the trance seemed to contract the time, of which he has no objective measure? And why does his discussion of the effect of opium upon temporal duration contradict what he writes elsewhere?[16] The answer lies in his emotional reaction of guilt regarding his visionary vigil over his sister's corpse. Not wanting to be observed, De Quincey slinks "like a guilty thing with stealthy steps from the room" (*SP,* p. 177). In the same way that he introduces opium imagery into the vocabulary of the child, De Quincey here transfers the guilt he feels as an adult onto the child or at least compels his earlier self to share his guilt fictionally through a sympathetic experience.

This vivid sense of foreboding and anticipated guilt in the absence of any true cause is equally apparent in what might well be called De Quincey's last childhood event, his evening in the Shrewsbury hotel as recounted in the *Confessions.* Like the Welsh walking tour that preceded it, the event is given symbolic significance:

All through the day, Wales and her grand mountain ranges . . . had divided my thoughts with London. But now rose London— sole, dark, infinite—brooding over the whole capacities of my heart. . . . More than ever I stood upon the brink of a precipice; and the local circumstances around me deepened and intensified these reflections, impressed upon them solemnity and terror, sometimes even horror. [3:346]

The symbolic precipice and the image of London as "sole, dark, [and] infinite"—products of the natural and architectural landscapes typical of opium visions—produce a psychological state of vertigo which further deepens and intensifies the experience into a "mighty vision":

> The unusual dimensions of the rooms, especially their towering height, brought up continually and obstinately, through natural links of associated feelings or images, the mighty vision of London waiting for me afar off.... This single feature of the rooms—their unusual altitude, and the echoing hollowness which had become the exponent of that altitude—this one terrific feature (for terrific it was in the effect), together with crowding and evanescent images, . . . all this, rising in tumultuous vision, whilst the dead hours of night were stealing along,—all around me, household and town, sleeping,—and whilst against the windows more and more the storm outside was raving, and to all appearance endlessly growing,—threw me into the deadliest condition of nervous emotion under contradictory forces, high over which predominated horror recoiling from that unfathomed abyss in London into which I was now so wilfully precipitating myself. [3:346–47]

Although De Quincey credits the visionary experience to the "local circumstances," the vocabulary is again that of an opium-eater: whether distorted, intensified, or conflated, all the senses are deranged. The height of the room is "towering," and, although the room is "echoing [with] hollowness," it is also full of "crowding and evanescent images." The room, the solitude, and the growing storm contribute to a view of reality that vibrates in a tumultuous, hyperaesthetic vision worthy of the mature opium addict:

> Often I looked out and examined the night. Wild it was beyond all description, and dark as "the inside of a wolf's throat." But at intervals, when the wind, shifting continually, swept in such a direction as to clear away the vast curtain of vapour, the stars shone out, though with a light unusually dim and distant. Still, as I turned inwards to the echoing chambers, or outwards to the wild, wild night, I saw London expanding her visionary gates to receive me, like some dreadful mouth of Acheron. [3:347]

The "echoing chambers" of the hotel and the "visionary gates" of London are imagistic anachronisms used for dramatic effect. Although the experiences are those of an uninitiated adolescent, the description is the product of an adult who has already crossed the threshold and knows the horror that lies beyond.

De Quincey's lyrical shift at this point in his narration not only reveals the manner by which he reshapes remembered experience but again demonstrates his departure from the Wordsworthian tradition. Immediately after invoking the "visionary gates" of London, De Quincey compares them to the phenomenon of the Whispering Gallery:

Thou also, Whispering Gallery! once again in those moments of conscious and wilful desolation didst to my ear utter monitorial sighs. For once again I was preparing to utter an irrevocable word, to enter upon one of those fatally tortuous paths of which the windings can never be unlinked. [3:347]

De Quincey refers similarly to the Whispering Gallery with regard to his departure from the Manchester Grammar School in July 1802, an occasion that marked not only his liberation from the confines of school and familial guardianship but also his being "launch[ed] . . . into the world" (3:294). With his eyes open the seventeen-year-old De Quincey "dream[s] ominously" (3:296) in his Manchester study of his past and future until a voice, seemingly audible, warns him:

"Once leave this house, and a Rubicon is placed between thee and all possibility of return. Thou wilt not say that what thou doest is altogether approved in thy secret heart. Even now thy conscience speaks against it in sullen whispers; but at the other end of thy long life-gallery that same conscience will speak to thee in volleying thunders." [3:297]

The metaphor of the Whispering Gallery is an adolescent memory reshaped by the adult De Quincey for aesthetic reasons. As such it is a clear example of his fictionalizing process in which he transforms a remembered event into a symbolic recreation of an emotional state: "At the earlier end of the gallery had stood my friend, breathing in the softest of whispers a solemn but not acceptable truth. At the further end, after running along the walls of the gallery, that solemn truth reached me as a deafening menace in tempestuous uproars" (3:296). Here was the perfect involute for De Quincey: the coalescence of intense emotions, of powerful sense experience, and of the "solemn truth" of a symbolic situation. The amplification of sense experience—a characteristic not of the Whispering Gallery but rather of opium intoxication—is another mechanism by which De Quincey can explore the relation of childhood experience and adult addiction.[17] The Whispering Gallery in altered form offered De Quincey a symbolic mechanism for collating, without collapsing, the adult and nursery experiences within the context of an extraordinary sense perception. As Alethea Hayter points out, this method is central to De Quincey's creative fictionalizing process:

The symbol restores the theme—that was the essence of De Quincey's discovery of this process of the imagination. Only when the original experiences have been drawn into symbolic shape, and that shape has been transmuted by a passage through the mysterious realms where man's nature comes into contact with hidden truth, can it re-emerge into consciousness and be fully communicated as a literary theme.[18]

The Whispering Gallery thus provides De Quincey not only with a theme but also with a model of the literary imagination that, dependent upon the operations of memory and the mechanism for dreaming, is analogous to the opium experience.

Since it suggests man's need but inability to unify or integrate his life experience, the Whispering Gallery involute is also a clear index to De Quincey's departure from the Wordsworthian tradition. If, as Romantic critics have maintained, Wordsworth's poetry reveals a paradigm of the cyclical Christian journey—in which a fallen Adamic figure pursues a circuitous journey through an alien land back to reintegration with paradise and God—then De Quincey offers a heretical variation.[19] The Whispering Gallery becomes an involute for what one critic suggests is an obsessive determinism, at once a model for both the continuity and discontinuity of life experience.[20] Although the circular form of the Whispering Gallery symbolizes cyclical continuity, the exaggeration and disorientation of the senses are associated with "those fatally tortuous paths of which the windings can never be unlinked."

The guilt and disorientation associated with De Quincey's involute thus provide a different model of the journey, a journey whose landscape is intimately connected with the socially, psychologically, and spiritually disorienting properties of opium. De Quincey's nursery experiences are not "recollected in tranquillity" but come to him in "tempestuous uproars." His life journey, from the very beginning, is punctuated by a series of critical visionary events which determine the course of his life and for which he will always bear a guilty conscience. Although these events in his autobiographical writings are related to the Wordsworthian "spots of time," De Quincey's moments are analogues of intoxication which prohibit "'all possibility of return'" and the kind of reintegration characteristic of Wordsworth. These moments in De Quincey's nursery experience — as he pauses over his sister's corpse, dreams in the church, leaves the Manchester Grammar School, or spends a turbulent night in the Shrewsbury hotel — all offer fictional comparisons to his later adult visions, visions that a child probably could not have interpreted but that are entirely consistent with the emotional tenor of his nursery experiences and his predisposition for dreaming.

The fact that these experiences or their symbolic geography are part of a mental landscape that De Quincey had not yet inhabited is less important than what this fact tells us about De Quincey's motivation for writing and about the fictionalizing process of his autobiographical works. Since much of De Quincey's work is an apologia that serves to explain the nature and causes of his opium addiction, very often he is less interested in the mere verisimilitude of his work than in the winning of the reader's sympathetic interest and the assuaging of his own lifelong feelings of guilt. Accordingly, his writing must be assumed to be rich in fictionalized detail that is intended to establish a bond of sympathy between himself and the reader, much like that between the adult and child selves. It is for this reason that the nursery and adolescent experiences are narrated in De Quincey's lifework. They are an account of his adult experiences of pleasure and pain grafted onto the experiences of childhood. As such they seek to explain the origins of his addiction as grief coupled with a precocious but "constitutional determination to reverie" (*SP*, p. 147); at the same time they tend to naturalize and sanctify the adult addiction to the "celestial drug" (3:381), thereby lessening the older De Quincey's poignant sense of guilt.

Notes

1. Georg Roppen and Richard Sommer, *Strangers and Pilgrims: An Essay on the Metaphor of Journey* (Oslo: Norwegian Universities Press, 1964), p. 170.

2. William Wordsworth, "Essay, Supplementary to the Preface (1815)," in *Literary Criticism of William Wordsworth*, ed. Paul M. Zall (Lincoln: University of Nebraska Press, 1966), p. 160.

3. Cf. Alethea Hayter, who singles out De Quincey from among all the Romantics as "the first writer . . . to study deliberately, from within his personal experience, the way in which dreams and visions are formed, how opium helps to form them and intensifies them, and how they are then re-composed and used in conscious art" (*Opium and the Romantic Imagination* [Berkeley and Los Angeles: University of California Press, 1968], p. 103).

4. William Wordsworth, "Preface to *Lyrical Ballads, with Other Poems* (1800)," in *Literary Criticism of William Wordsworth*, p. 21.

5. Samuel Taylor Coleridge, *Biographia Literaria*, ed. James Engell and W. Jackson Bate, vol. 7, pt. 2, of *The Collected Works of Samuel Taylor Coleridge*, Bollingen Series 75 (London: Routledge and Kegan Paul; Princeton, N.J.: Princeton University Press, 1983), p. 5.

6. In his "Introduction to the World of Strife" De Quincey discusses at length the "pathos of that great idea" of the pariah (1:100); in *Suspiria de Profundis* he celebrates the "everlasting Jew" (*SP*, p. 178), the German equivalent of the Wandering Jew; and later in the same work he introduces Mater Suspiriorum, "Our Lady of Sighs," one of the three sisters of sorrow who reign over the world of the forgotten, the pariahs, and the wandering guilt-ridden (*SP*, p. 242). See also Hayter, *Opium and the Romantic Imagination*, pp. 236–37.

7. For a full treatment of this sense of a fragmented self see J. Hillis Miller, *The Disappearance of God: Five Nineteenth-Century Writers* (1963; reprint, Cambridge, Mass.: Harvard University Press, Belknap Press, 1975), pp. 17–80.

8. Paul de Man, "Intentional Structure of the Romantic Image," in *Romanticism and Consciousness: Essays in Criticism*, ed. Harold Bloom (New York: Norton, 1970), p. 70.

9. Christopher Salvesen, *The Landscape of Memory: A Study of Wordsworth's Poetry* (Lincoln: University of Nebraska Press, 1965), p. 68. For a discussion of the pictorial qualities of De Quincey's imagination see Albert Goldman, *The Mine and the Mint: Sources for the Writings of Thomas De Quincey* (Carbondale: Southern Illinois University Press, 1965), p. 91.

10. Morse Peckham, *Victorian Revolutionaries: Speculations on Some Heroes of a Culture Crisis* (New York: George Braziller, 1970), p. 21.

11. Miller, *The Disappearance of God*, p. 28.

12. These two physiological explanations for De Quincey's "defect" in his eyes are discussed by Horace Ainsworth Eaton, *Thomas De Quincey: A Biography* (London: Oxford University Press, 1936), pp. 179–80; and in a letter of 16 August 1809 from De Quincey to Dorothy Wordsworth, included in John E. Jordan, *De Quincey to Wordsworth: A Biography of a Relationship* (Berkeley and Los Angeles: University of California Press, 1962), pp. 243–44.

13. See, for example, V. A. De Luca, *Thomas De Quincey: The Prose of Vision* (Toronto: University of Toronto Press, 1980), p. 67.

14. De Quincey's various selves and the discrepancy of understanding between them are discussed by Stephen J. Spector, "Thomas De Quincey: Self-effacing Autobiographer," *Studies in Romanticism* 18 (1979): 501–20. See also Elizabeth W. Bruss, *Autobiographical Acts: The Changing Situation of a Literary Genre* (Baltimore, Md.: Johns Hopkins University Press, 1976), p. 98.

15. M. H. Abrams, *The Milk of Paradise: The Effect of Opium Visions on the Works of De Quincey, Crabbe, Francis Thompson, and Coleridge* (1934; New York: Harper and Row, 1970), p. ix.

16. We may take as an example the compression of time in De Quincey's "Dream-Fugue" on the theme of sudden death. While time is psychologically stretched by the influence of opium in *The English Mail-Coach*, in the subsequent "Dream-Fugue" the effect of opium seems the reverse: "Thus as we ran like torrents—thus as we swept with bridal rapture over the Campo Santo of the cathedral graves—suddenly we became aware of a vast necropolis. . . . Yet, in the first minute, it lay like a purple stain upon the horizon, so mighty was the distance. In the second minute it trembled through many changes, growing into terraces and towers of wondrous altitude, so mighty was the pace. In the third minute already, with our dreadful gallop, we were entering its suburbs" (13:323-24). The purple laudanum stain clearly associates the vision with opium, yet here the velocity of the coach dramatically compresses time.

17. Grevel Lindop argues that De Quincey's account is probably unconsciously wrong: "As so often in cases of experience embodying what De Quincey liked to call 'the dark sublime,' imagination blended insensibly

into memory, transmuting a fact into a poetic symbol" (*The Opium-Eater: A Life of Thomas De Quincey* [New York: Taplinger, 1981], p. 35).

18. Hayter, *Opium and the Romantic Imagination*, p. 122.

19. According to Northrop Frye's early theories (*A Study of English Romanticism* [New York: Random House, 1968], p. 17), this archetype is apparent in the Christian prototype of a "gigantic cyclical myth, outlined in the Bible, which begins with the fall of man, is followed by a symbolic vision of human history, under the names of Adam and Israel, and ends with the redemption of Adam and Israel by Christ." M. H. Abrams (*Natural Supernaturalism: Tradition and Revolution in Romantic Literature* [New York: Norton, 1971], pp. 165, 255) suggests that the Romantic journey is a descendant of a biblical prototype such as the story of the Prodigal Son, in which the post-Adamic wanderer leaves his native land to journey through an alien land in quest of another, better land. See also Bernard Blackstone, *The Lost Travellers: A Romantic Theme with Variations* (London: Longmans, 1962), p. 10; Roppen and Sommer, *Strangers and Pilgrims*, pp. 75–109.

20. Kathleen Blake, "The Whispering Gallery and Structural Coherence in De Quincey's Revised *Confessions of an English Opium-Eater*," *Studies in English Literature, 1500-1900* 13 (1973): 632–42, esp. p. 639.

6

Thomas De Quincey and Sigmund Freud: Sons, Fathers, Dreamers—Precursors of Psychoanalytic Developmental Psychology

CHARLES L. PROUDFIT

Death we can face: but knowing, as some of us do, what is human life, which of us is it that without shuddering could (if consciously we were summoned) face the hour of birth?

—DE QUINCEY, *Suspiria de Profundis*

But she delighted not in infancy, nor infancy in her.

—*De Quincey Memorials*

. . . [with] nothing on the stage but a solitary infant, and its solitary combat with grief—a mighty darkness, and a sorrow without a voice.

—DE QUINCEY, "General Preface"

When Thomas De Quincey, aged seventy-four, died peacefully on the morning of 8 December 1859, at 42 Lothian Street, Edinburgh, Scotland, a two-and-a-half-year-old Jewish boy, Sigmund Freud, was quite likely playing in his nursery at his birthplace, 117 Schlossergasse, Freiberg, Moravia. Although the lives of De Quincey and Freud barely overlap, the two men demonstrate remarkable similarities in their life cycles, and their writings offer common insights into the worlds of dreams and childhood. Even though Freud did not know De Quincey's works firsthand, his *The Interpretation of Dreams* (1900) and *Three Essays on the Theory of Sexuality* (1905) share with De Quincey in the investigation of the nature of dreams and the importance of the first few years of life in the psychological development of the human being. De Quincey's *Confessions of an English Opium-Eater, Autobiographic Sketches, Suspiria de Profundis,* and selected "Reminiscences" place him among the important contributors to the knowledge of human psychology in the light of contemporary psychoanalytic understanding of dreams and early childhood development. His psychological insights, especially in the matter of dreaming, anticipate several of Freud's major discoveries, and his observations on children show him to be a precursor of what is now termed psychoanalytic developmental psychology —that is, the study of the psychological birth of the human infant.

As we compare De Quincey and Freud in terms of their families of origin, their roles as sons and fathers, their reputations as great dreamers, and the circumstances that surround the composition and publication of writings that contain many of their most significant psychological insights, we may entertain the notion that certain similarities in their lives may have fostered the creative process that led to their discoveries. Both De Quincey and Freud were born into middle-class families. De Quincey's father, Thomas, the son of a Leicestershire squire, had inherited a small fortune and had been successful as a linen draper. He was involved in foreign and wholesale trade when Thomas, his second son and fourth child,[1] was born on 15 August 1785 in the industrial town Manchester. De Quincey's mother, born Elizabeth Penson, was the daughter of an army officer attached to the king's household. Freud's father, Jakob, was born in Tysmenitz, Galicia, and was a fairly successful merchant who dealt primarily in wool. Freud's mother, Amalie Nathansohn, was from Brody, in northeast Galicia near the Russian border.

De Quincey and Freud were reared in large families, and their relationships with their parents offer several interesting contrasts. The De Quinceys had eight children, four sons and four daughters, during their twelve years of marriage. Two daughters died in childhood and a son in adolescence. Since De Quincey's father was often absent for long periods of time owing to business or to efforts to find a more healthful climate for his tubercular condition, and since his older brother, William, was usually away at school, Thomas spent the first seven years of his life in a female household composed of his mother, three sisters, and female nurses and servants. He was a small, sickly child who suffered a chronic ague from his second through his fourth year. His first six years of life were spent at "The Farm," a cottage in the environs of Manchester. He then moved with his family into a mansion called "Greenhay" built by his father about a mile outside Manchester. It was to Greenhay that Thomas's father returned to die in 1793, when his son was almost eight. De Quincey never really knew his father, and his recollections of him have an idealized quality (see 1:17–27). This is not the situation with his mother, whom he describes as follows:

> But she delighted not in infancy, nor infancy in her. The very greatness of some qualities in her mind made this impossible. Let me make a sketch of her; for she well merits it. Figure to yourself a woman of admirable manners, in fact as much as any person I have ever known, distinguished by lady-like tranquillity and repose, and even by self-possession, but also freezing in excess. Austere she was in a degree which fitted her for the lady president of rebellious nunneries. Rigid in her exactions of duty from those around her, but also from herself; upright, sternly conscientious, munificent in her charities, pure-minded in so absolute a degree that you would have been tempted to call her "holy,"—she yet could not win hearts by the graciousness of her manner. That quality which shone so brightly in my sister [Elizabeth], and the expansive love which distinguished both her and myself, we had from our father. [Japp, 1:8–9]

De Quincey's portrait of his mother, though respectful, is chilling.

Jakob and Amalie Freud also had eight children, three sons and five daughters. It was the third marriage for Jakob, who married Amalie when he was forty and she not yet twenty. She was twenty-one when her first child, Sigmund, was born on 6 May 1856 in the quiet little town of Freiberg. When Freud was nineteen months old, his eight-month-old brother, Julius, died. And when Sigmund was three, his father moved the family first to Leipzig and a year later to Vienna. Freud was the decided favorite of his mother; his biographer Ernest Jones records that in later years, after Freud had achieved fame and renown, Amalie still referred to her son as "*'mein goldener Sigi.'*"[2] The adult Sigmund paid a visit to his mother every Sunday morning, usually accompanied by several family members, and on Sunday evenings his mother and all his sisters would go to his home for a family meal. Freud was also very close to his gentle father, and it was not until a year or two after his father's death, in October 1896, that through his own personal analysis Freud became aware of his once deeply buried and hostile feelings toward the father of his childhood.

Both De Quincey and Freud were themselves heads of large families, and their biographers describe them as attentive and loving husbands and fathers.[3] De Quincey and his wife, Margaret Simpson, had eight children, five sons and three daughters. One son died in childhood and another in adolescence. Freud and his wife, Martha Bernays, had six children, three sons and three daughters, all of whom reached maturity. Their love of children, however, extended beyond their immediate families. De Quincey was devoted to the children of Wordsworth and Coleridge, and Freud demonstrated sincere interest in the children of relatives and the births of his friends' children.[4]

More important for the purposes of this chapter, however, is the manner in which De Quincey and Freud related to children and entered into their world to discover its secrets. One of De Quincey's daughters, Mrs. Florence Bairdsmith, offers several recollections which show how her father responded to her first as a small child and then as a young girl entering puberty:

> My father's love for children, and power of winning their confidence, was one of his loveliest characteristics. My own first awaking to the fact that I had a father grew out of the restless nights of a delicate childhood, when my small ill-regulated uproar was sure to bring the kind, careful arms which rescued the urchin from a weariful bed and the wisdom of nursery discipline, and brought it to the bright warm room, and the dignity and delight of "sitting up with papa." This papa, after a petting and soothing process of inexpressible sweetness, and coffee well loaded with sugar, had always some delightful book, exquisite to the sense of smell, as a book always was to the family nose, and to the eyes, because of pictures, about which, when they became too amazing for the restraining sense that "papa must not be disturbed," he had always

something wonderful or beautiful to tell. The leaves of this book had generally to be cut, and much breathless joy came of the careful teaching how this was to be done, so that there might be no ragged edges; reverence for the person of a book being among our early lessons. The triumph of the small operator and the applause of the audience over a well-executed work was the chorus to each opened page. . . .

As a girl between ten and twelve, I was his constant and almost only companion, and was never so happy as with him. The unfailing gentleness of his temper, and tender attention to the feeblest of girlish thoughts and interests, the unconscious way to both of us in which he turned these into high meanings, without overshooting the power of the child, was one of those wonderful and gracious gifts, like his power of conversation, which it was as impossible to catch and bottle for future use, as it would have been to have bottled the sunshine of those days. [Page, 1:359–60]

In his daughter's first recollection we observe De Quincey's sensitivity to childish distress, his unconditional love, and his support of a child's efforts to accomplish a difficult task. In the second recollection we note his ability to enter into the thoughts and interests of a young adolescent girl and to help her understand herself without overwhelming her. All are attributes that parents must possess in some measure if they are to help their children successfully pass through the developmental stages of infancy, latency, and adolescence.

Freud, like De Quincey, was also very responsive to his children, and his letters to Wilhelm Fliess, written between 1887 and 1902, are replete with references to his growing family. Since it was also during this period that Freud was involved in his own analysis, he looked to the psychological development of his children to help him understand his own past. His comments to Fliess about his children often contain psychological observations and speculations, as seen in this account of a daughter's brief illness and its aftereffects:

Do you think that children's talk in their sleep belongs to their dreams? If so, I can introduce you to the very latest wish-dream. Little Anna, aged one-and-a-half, had to fast for a day at Aussee, because she had been sick in the morning, which was attributed to eating strawberries. During the night she called out a whole menu in her sleep: "Stwawbewwies, wild stwawbewwies, omblet, pudden!"[5]

It was such direct observation of children, coupled with the analysis of his own dreams, that enabled Freud to assert in *The Interpretation of Dreams* that *"a dream is a (disguised) fulfillment of a (suppressed or repressed) wish."*[6]

Freud also observed and listened to his grandchildren. Perhaps the most famous example of this attentiveness is recorded in *Beyond the Pleasure Principle* (1920), where he recounts how his observations of a one-and-a-half-year-old child at play over a period of several weeks helped him formulate his theory of the repetition compulsion—a repetitive, purposeful human activity that attempts to master earlier traumatic experiences, such as the inevitable separation from the mother.[7] This child, who served as the principal figure in one of the first direct, observational studies of children, was Freud's grandson, Ernst.[8]

Besides De Quincey's and Freud's great skills in penetrating into the secret world of childhood, each was able to turn his observational powers inward and make discoveries about dreams and the dreaming apparatus that have continued to receive confirmation. Each had been a great dreamer since childhood, and each published his insights in works that still have value for the student of the dream as part of man's complex psychic life. The inciting reasons for the publication and subsequent public reception of De Quincey's *Confessions* as well as *Suspiria de Profundis* and Freud's *The Interpretation of Dreams* differ substantially, however.

De Quincey's *Confessions* was written out of dire economic necessity in London during the summer of 1821. Published anonymously in the September and October numbers of the *London Magazine* that year, the work received considerable attention from reviewers and reading public alike, leading to a reprinting in book form in 1822. According to one of De Quincey's editors, six editions in England and four in America had appeared before the author revised it substantially in 1856.[9] In a similar fashion De Quincey's publication of the *Suspiria* in four installments during 1845 in *Blackwood's Edinburgh Magazine* occasioned further critical attention.

Freud's *The Interpretation of Dreams*, however, was written out of a psychic, rather than economic, necessity, and, according to Jones, the work is a selection of Freud's dreams from his own analysis which began in the summer of 1897 and extended into the summer of 1899, when he completed the book.[10] Freud considered *Die Traumdeutung* his most important work, a valuation evident in his preface to the third English edition (1932), where he wrote that "insight such as this falls to one's lot but once in a lifetime."[11] Only 351 copies were sold in the first six years after publication, however, and Freud's failure to reach the medical audience he intended caused him to be depressed. When a second edition was called for nine years later, Freud shared the following with his readers in his preface:

> For this book has a further subjective significance for me personally—a significance which I only grasped after I had completed it. It was, I found, a portion of my own self-analysis, my reaction to my father's death—that is to say, to the most important event, the most poignant loss, of a man's life. Having discovered that this was so, I felt unable to obliterate the traces of the experience.[12]

This theme of loss runs throughout the contributions of both De Quincey and Freud to dream theory; as we shall see, it also anticipates one of the major tenets of contemporary psychoanalytic developmental psychology.

Before proceeding to show how certain of Freud's discoveries about the nature of dreams and the dreaming process in *The Interpretation of Dreams* are foreshadowed by De Quincey in the *Confessions* and *Suspiria de Profundis*, I would like to emphasize that Freud apparently had no firsthand knowledge of De Quincey's writings. In his text Freud refers to at least twenty-nine articles and books on dreams published either on or before 1845, and De Quincey's are not among them.[13] Freud also lists another eighteen works published on or before 1845 *not* referred to in his text, and De Quincey is not mentioned there either.[14] De Quincey's name is mentioned once by Freud, in *Jokes and*

Their Relation to the Unconscious (1905), and then only as quoted by the American psychiatrist A. A. Brill in an article written by him on "Freud's Theory of Wit."[15] Although it seems safe to assume that Freud was not directly influenced by De Quincey's writings, it does seem evident that much of what both men tested upon their pulse and found to be valid for them was alive in the intellectual and emotional climate of nineteenth-century Europe.

Perhaps one of De Quincey's most significant insights into man's mental activity that anticipates Freud's view of the unconscious mind is that *there is actually no such thing as forgetting.* De Quincey remarks in the *Confessions* that a study of the contents of one's dreams reveals that "the minutest incidents of childhood, or forgotten scenes of later years, [are] often revived" (*C,* p. 111) and that these memories are not available to us in our waking hours. He asserts that "there is no such thing as *forgetting* possible to the mind; a thousand accidents may and will interpose a veil between our present consciousness and the secret inscriptions on the mind," and he likens the mind to "the dread book of account, which the Scriptures speak of" (*C,* p. 112).

De Quincey elaborates upon his view that the mind never forgets in the *Suspiria,* where he compares the human brain to a palimpsest—"a membrane or roll cleansed of its manuscript by reiterated successions" (*SP,* p. 226). "What else than a natural and mighty palimpsest is the human brain?" he asks. "Such a palimpsest is my brain; such a palimpsest, oh reader! is yours. Everlasting layers of ideas, images, feelings, have fallen upon your brain softly as light. Each succession has seemed to bury all that went before. And yet, in reality, not one has been extinguished" (*SP,* p. 233). De Quincey believes that the hour of death, fever, and the use of opium can revive these seemingly forgotten experiences. Furthermore, even preverbal experiences can be found embedded in our minds:

In some potent convulsion of the system, all wheels back into its earliest elementary stage. The bewildering romance, light tarnished with darkness, the semi-fabulous legend, truth celestial mixed with human falsehoods, these fade even of themselves, as life advances. The romance has perished that the young man adored; the legend has gone that deluded the boy; but the deep, deep tragedies of infancy, as when the child's hands were unlinked forever from his mother's neck, or his lips forever from his sister's kisses, these remain lurking below all, and these lurk to the last. [*SP*, p. 236]

The truth of such psychological retention, De Quincey goes on to say in the same passage, is probably available "experimentally [to anyone] who passes through similar convulsions of dreaming or delirium from any similar or equal disturbance in his nature." Further, in a footnote appended to this statement he writes:

As an argument for this mysterious power lurking in our nature, I may remind the reader of one phenomenon open to the notice of everybody, namely, the tendency of very aged persons to throw back and concentrate the light of their memory upon scenes of early childhood, as to which they recall many traces that had faded even to *themselves* in middle life, whilst they often forget altogether the whole intermediate stages of their experience. This shows that naturally, and without violent agencies, the human brain is by tendency a palimpsest. [*SP*, p. 236n.]

Freud likewise argues, of course, for the mind's retention of early experiences, asserting in *The Interpretation of Dreams* that "*we find the child and the child's impulses still living on in the dream.*"[16] He also maintains that "what we describe as our 'character' is based on the memory-traces of our impressions; and, moreover, the impressions which have had the greatest effect on us—those of our earliest youth—are precisely the ones which scarcely ever become conscious."[17] Thus, when one compares De Quincey's metaphor of the mind as a palimpsest with Freud's concept of the unconscious, both are seen to be drawing attention to the generally accepted view today that the mind does not forget any experience strong enough to leave a memory trace in our brains.

Another of De Quincey's seminal psychological insights is that man does not divest himself of the child within but rather retains a subtle relationship with the experience of childhood:

An adult sympathizes with himself in childhood because he *is* the same, and because (being the same) yet he is *not* the same. He acknowledges the deep, mysterious identity between himself, as adult and as infant, for the ground of his sympathy; and yet, with this general agreement, and necessity of agreement, he feels the differences between his two selves as the main quickeners of his sympathy. He pities the infirmities, as they arise to light in his young forerunner, which now, perhaps, he does not share; he looks indulgently upon the errors of the understanding, or limitations of view which now he has long survived; and sometimes, also, he honors in the infant that rectitude of will which, under *some* temptations, he may since have felt it so difficult to maintain. [*SP*, pp. 154-55]

Although De Quincey also asserts that "man is doubtless *one* by some subtle *nexus* that we cannot perceive, extending from the newborn infant to the superannuated dotard," yet "as regards many affections and passions incident to his nature at different stages, he is *not* one; the unity of man in this respect is coextensive only with the particular stage to which the passion belongs" (*SP*, p. 178).

In exactly similar fashion Freud posits that the child lives on in the adult. Like De Quincey, he finds that man has "affections and passions incident to his nature *at different stages*" (italics added). Turning his attention to the first several years of life, Freud, in *Three Essays on the Theory of Sexuality*, postulates the oral, anal, and phallic stages of psychosexual development in infancy.[18] De Quincey's emphasis on specific "passions" for specific "stages" of man's development also anticipates the developmental stages in object relations in infancy delineated within contemporary psychoanalytic developmental psychology.[19] In a general way his outlook also reminds us of the "Eight Ages of Man" as defined by Erik Erikson in *Childhood and Society*.[20]

In addition to foreshadowing Freud's view of the human mind as a receptacle of one's individual past and his observation that the child lives on in the adult, De Quincey's insights into dreams and the dreaming process parallel those of Freud in an almost uncanny way. Both men believe, for instance, that dreams offer a very special access to the depths of the human psyche. In

Suspiria de Profundis, De Quincey makes this observation about the "magnificent apparatus" of dreams and their heuristic value:

> The machinery for dreaming planted in the human brain was not planted for nothing. That faculty, in alliance with the mystery of darkness, is the one great tube through which man communicates with the shadowy. And the dreaming organ, in connection with the heart, the eye and the ear, compose the magnificent apparatus which forces the infinite into the chambers of a human brain, and throws dark reflections from eternities below all life upon the mirrors of the sleeping mind. [*SP*, p. 149]

Similarly, in *Five Lectures on Psycho-Analysis* (1910), Freud asserts that "the interpretation of dreams is in fact the royal road to a knowledge of the unconscious; it is the securest foundation of psycho-analysis and the field in which every worker must acquire his convictions and seek his training."[21] Furthermore, both De Quincey and Freud have very similar things to say about daydreams that precede nightdreams, the "day residue" of dreams, affective states during and immediately following dreams, and dream distortion.

In the "Introductory Notice" to the *Suspiria,* De Quincey states that "habitually to dream magnificently, a man must have a constitutional determination to reverie" (*SP*, p. 147). This "constitutional determination" is observed in childhood:

> I know not whether my reader is aware that many children, perhaps most, have a power of painting, as it were, upon the darkness, all sorts of phantoms: in some that power is simply a mechanic affection of the eye; others have a voluntary or semi-voluntary power to dismiss or summon them; or, as a child once said to me, when I questioned him on this matter, "I can tell them to go, and they go; but sometimes they come when I don't tell them to come." [*C*, p. 109]

Freud conceptualizes this process in the following terms:

> Dreams think essentially in images; and with the approach of sleep it is possible to observe how, in proportion as voluntary activities become more difficult, involuntary ideas arise, all of which fall into the class of images. Incapacity for ideational work of the kind which we feel as intentionally willed and the emergence . . . of

images—these are two characteristics which persevere in dreams and which the psychological analysis of dreams forces us to recognize as essential features of dream-life."[22]

Concerning the same phenomenon De Quincey reports in the *Confessions* that, in the middle of 1817, this "constitutional determination to reverie" became "positively distressing to me: at night, when I lay awake in bed, vast processions passed along in mournful pomp; friezes of never-ending stories, that to my feelings were as sad and solemn as if they were stories drawn from times before Oedipus or Priam, before Tyre, before Memphis" (*C*, pp. 109–10). Here De Quincey appears to be describing what Freud and others have called "hypnagogic hallucinations." "These are images," writes Freud, "often very vivid and rapidly changing, which are apt to appear—quite habitually in some people—during the period of falling asleep; and they may also persist for a time after the eyes have been opened."[23]

De Quincey goes on to observe that, in 1817, "a corresponding change took place in my dreams; a theatre seemed suddenly opened and lighted up within my brain, which presented, nightly, spectacles of more than earthly splendor." After a careful analysis of these changes in his dream-life, he lists four facts about these psychic experiences. First, ". . . whatsoever I happened to call up and to trace by a voluntary act upon the darkness was very apt to transfer itself to my dreams." Second, his dreams "were accompanied by deep-seated anxiety and gloomy melancholy, such as are wholly incommunicable by words," for "I seemed every night to descend—not metaphorically, but literally to descend—into chasms and sunless abysses, depths below depths, from which it seemed hopeless that I could ever reäscend. Nor did I, by waking, feel that I *had* reäscended." Third, "The sense of space, and in the end the sense of time, were both powerfully affected. . . . Space swelled, and was amplified to an extent of unutterable infinity. This, however, did not disturb me so much as the vast expansion of time. I sometimes seemed to have lived for seventy or one hundred years in one night." And, fourth, "The minutest incidents of childhood, or forgotten scenes of later years, were often revived" (*C*, pp. 110–11). All four observations anticipate Freud's comments on the "day residue" of dreams, affective (emotional) states during and immediately upon waking from dreams, and dream distortion.[24]

Finally, De Quincey provides an early basis of support for Freud's view that dreams, in the last analysis, defy *complete* understanding. In "The Apparition of the Brocken" section of the *Suspiria*, De Quincey asserts that "no man can account for all things that occur in dreams" (*SP*, p. 251). Freud utters a similar observation in *The Interpretation of Dreams:* "There is at least one spot in every dream at which it is unplumbable—a navel, as it were, that is its point of contact with the unknown."[25] Each of these interpreters of dreams thus acknowledges that dreams resist ultimate interpretation.

Besides sharing many comparable insights into the nature of dreams, the dreaming process, and the human psyche, De Quincey and Freud recorded observations of infancy and childhood and reflections upon these observations that show them to be precursors of psychoanalytic developmental psychology. Those who subscribe to this view believe that the first three years of life are crucial for one's development of a sense of self, sound object relations, and a basic sense of trust in oneself and one's surroundings. All are necessary if the child is to pass more or less successfully through later stages of development. While not discounting the importance of maturation and cognitive development, psychoanalytic developmental psychologists place special emphasis upon the mother-child relationship during the first three years of life. They maintain that developmental failures at this time are primarily responsible for many adult psychotic disorders as well as for borderline and narcissistic disorders of the self.[26]

While Freud was aware of the importance of the mother-infant relationship for the psychological development of the adults whom he treated, most of his interest was centered on the neurotic conflicts that originate usually in the so-called Oedipal period (two and a half to seven years). He clearly realized, however, the importance of the mother (object) for the development of the infant's ego[27] and saw that the child's identification with the mother involved a close emotional tie,[28] though he left it to others to research this area more fully. Thus Freud entered the nursery occasionally and emerged with his theories of the repetition compulsion, infantile sexuality, and the Oedipus complex. René A. Spitz, Anna Freud, and Margaret S. Mahler have devoted their professional lives to observation in the nursery,[29] and the full effect of the results has yet to be felt in childrearing practices and the treating of emotionally disturbed children.

De Quincey, unlike Freud and others, was not a trained psychologist seeking scientific answers to scientific questions, yet many of his nursery observations and reflections have been validated in clinical settings. For instance, the innumerable, subtle, conscious as well as unconscious communications that pass between mother and infant, clinically verified today, are captured in De Quincey's description of this important maternal bond:

> The loveliest sight that a woman's eye opens upon in this world is her first-born child; and the holiest sight upon which the eyes of God settle in Almighty sanction and perfect blessing is the love which soon kindles between the mother and her infant: mute and speechless on the one side, with no language but tears and kisses and looks....
> ... The true paradise of a female life in all ranks, not too elevated for constant intercourse with the children, is ... that sequestered chamber of her experience, in which a mother is left alone through the day, ... where ... she is attended by one sole companion, her little first-born angel, as yet clinging to her robe, imperfectly able to walk, still more imperfect in its prattling and innocent thoughts, clinging to her, haunting her wherever she goes as her shadow, catching from her eye the total inspiration of its little palpitating heart, and sending to hers a thrill of secret pleasure so often as its little fingers fasten on her own. [*PW*, 1:29, 31]

Although idealized and written in the language of the time, De Quincey's description highlights the exclusiveness and mutuality of the mother-infant bond.

De Quincey was also aware that when this bond is threatened or momentarily severed through absence, illness, or emotional withdrawal by the mother, the infant is quick to register his discomfort. And, according to De Quincey, the preverbal child has an array of communicative responses: "In watching the infancy of my own children, I made another discovery—it is well known to mothers, to nurses, and also to philosophers—that the tears and lamentations of infants during the year or so when they have no *other* language of complaint run through a gamut that is as inexhaustible as the Cremona of Paganini" [*PW*, 1:11]. Furthermore, De Quincey observes that when this temporary severance of the mother-infant bond becomes permanent, the results can be dire. He writes that six-year-old children "torn away from mothers and sisters . . . not unfrequently die. I speak of what I know. . . . Grief of that sort, and at that age, has killed more than ever have been counted amongst its martyrs" (*SP*, p. 239). Recent clinical studies of object loss and subsequent depression and death tend to support De Quincey's assertions.[30]

Besides anticipating the mother-infant bond so important to psychoanalytic developmental psychology, De Quincey's comments in a personal letter on what lies ahead for a recently born granddaughter, Eva, suggest that he had an awareness of the complex and hidden interaction between infant and mother upon which are built stable internal representations of the objective world of reality:

Tuesday Night, December 5, 1854

MY DEAREST MARGARET,—I felicitate you upon your recovery, upon the beauty of little Eva, and upon the prospect (not by any means unimportant) that she, with her earliest capacities of enjoyment, will find herself in the grandest of all spectacles—viz., in the carnival of spring. What I mean is, that her birth has been felicitously timed; for grandeur would be thrown away upon the eye that cannot connect, and upon the ear that cannot distinguish. In April next, when dear little Eva will have completed her sixth month, when, first of all, she will be capable of enjoying, there will be something *extra* to enjoy. That is, speaking Germanically, and therefore pedantically, as the *subjective* (viz., the power of spectating) will then be in the very meridian of its development in Eva, so correspondingly will the *objective* (viz., the thing to be spectated, or in base vulgar the spectacle), be travelling for three months—April, May, June—through all the stages of its revelation. *Before* April, for want of developed faculties in Eva, any spectacle would be thrown away. *After* April, when she will be ready, yet if spring were not ready, her powers would be thrown away for want of an object. But now, . . . taking Eva as the centre of a secret and insulated world, the contemplating and the contemplated, the beholding and the thing beheld, the subject and the object, will blossom concurrently. [Page, 2:87–88]

De Quincey's observation that at six months little Eva will have undergone enough significant internal development to enable her to become more involved in the world around her is partly the boasting of a proud grandfather who prefers little girls to little boys (Page, 2:82) and partly the remark of an astute observer of infants. Six months is one of the major turning points in the psychological birth of the infant; according to Spitz, between six and eight months the infant develops the internal capacity to differentiate between mother and a stranger. When a stranger approaches a child at this age, the infant reacts with a variety of responses from lowering the eyes or covering them with its hands to weeping or screaming. Spitz terms this pattern of behavior in the presence of a stranger with the mother momentarily absent *"eight-month anxiety."*[31] When infants lose their mothers at this age and suitable surrogates are not found, severe depression and sometimes death follow. Many clinicians also believe that adult depression and severe forms of psychopathology often have their origins in either the psychological or the physical loss of the mother in the second half of the first year of life.

In addition to his observations on the importance of the mother-infant bond and the possible consequences when this bond is severed, De Quincey also has left us a record of his own consciously remembered losses in his dream visions and autobiographical writings. Before he was eight, De Quincey lost through death his maternal grandmother, two sisters, and a father. During a turbulent adolescence his brother died, and he lost contact with Ann, the young prostitute of Oxford Street later immortalized in the *Confessions* who had befriended him when he was seriously ill during his London sojourn. And in early adulthood, when his beloved Catherine Wordsworth, the three-year-old daughter of the poet, died unexpectedly, De Quincey was plunged into a four-month depression.

This theme of loss, which permeates the very fabric of De Quincey's "impassioned prose" (1:14), has received considerable attention from literary critics. Some follow De Quincey's own lead and focus on the Opium-Eater's archetypal fall from paradise, which, according to De Quincey, occurred with the death of his sister Elizabeth.

About the close of my sixth year, suddenly the first chapter of my life came to a violent termination; that chapter which, even within the gates of recovered Paradise, might merit a remembrance. *"Life is Finished!"* was the secret misgiving of my heart; for the heart of infancy is as apprehensive as that of maturest wisdom in relation to any capital wound inflicted on the happiness. *"Life is Finished! Finished it is!"* [1:28]

In the *Suspiria* he elaborates further on this pivotal event in his psychic experience:

I grieved, indeed, that my sister should lie in bed; I grieved still more sometimes to hear her moan. But all this appeared to me no more than a night of trouble, on which the dawn would soon arise. O! moment of darkness and delirium, when a nurse awakened me from that delusion, and launched God's thunderbolt at my heart in the assurance that my sister *must* die. Rightly it is said of utter, utter misery, that it "cannot be *remembered*." . . . Enough to say, that all was soon over; and the morning of that day had at last arrived which looked down upon her innocent face, sleeping the sleep from which there is no awaking, and upon me sorrowing the sorrow for which there is no consolation. [*SP,* pp. 170–71]

Citing this episode, J. Hillis Miller finds the theme of loss to be the paradigm of De Quincey's spiritual condition: "Lost in the abysses within and without, his fate, after all his attempts to escape, is to spiral ceaselessly in echoing repetitions of the definitive event in his life: the death of his sister and his exile from Paradise, the 'everlasting farewells' with which it all began."[32] And V. A. De Luca argues for a reading of the *Confessions* that incorporates "the fundamental thematic concerns of De

Quincey's imaginative work in general, concerns which centre upon the situation of the solitary individual in a post-lapsarian state of lost community."[33]

Other critics with a psychological orientation often approach this theme in De Quincey's writings in terms of loss experienced during the Oedipal period, and their studies variously examine the Oedipal nature of De Quincey's dreams, his incestuous longings, his Oedipal guilt, and his unconscious death wishes.[34] One critic, however, Elizabeth W. Bruss, attempts to understand the theme of loss from a developmental perspective. In a comparison of *Suspiria de Profundis* and *Autobiographic Sketches* she observes that, whereas the latter is an autobiographical record "composed . . . of developmental stages and divided according to the distinct epochs of the young man's life," commencing with the death of Elizabeth and concluding with "the final form of De Quincey's identity," the *Suspiria* has a confused chronology and "mimics, in the way chronologically separate scenes lie together in the text, the workings of a subconscious mind."[35]

Bruss's emphasis upon the developmental stages of a young man's life, stages that begin with the Oedipal period and include latency, adolescence, and young adulthood, leads one to speculate about those losses experienced by De Quincey in earliest childhood before his consciously remembered early losses. De Quincey himself alludes to such losses in infancy when he tells us, in two passages already noted, that his wakeful night reveries were of "friezes of never-ending stories, that to my feelings were as sad and solemn as if they were stories drawn from times *before Oedipus or Priam*" (italics added), and when he speaks of "the deep, deep tragedies of infancy, as when the child's hands were unlinked forever from his mother's neck, or his lips forever from his sister's kisses," adding that "these remain lurking below all, and these lurk to the last." Although such losses in infancy can never be known directly, they can be experienced indirectly through the power of the theme of loss as manifested in De Quincey's autobiographical and visionary writings. De Quincey himself cautions us not to confuse the child who experienced with the adult who remembers: "I, the child, had the feelings; I, the man, decipher them. In the child lay the handwriting mysterious to *him;* in me, the interpretation and the comment" (*SP,* p. 187n.).

Had De Quincey made no literary effort to "decipher" the "feelings" of the child within, and had he made no attempt to understand the "solitary infant, and its solitary combat with grief—a mighty darkness, and a sorrow without a voice" (1:9), generations of readers of nineteenth-century English prose would have been denied the challenging pleasures afforded by De Quincey's *Confessions, Suspiria de Profundis,* and other autobiographical writings. Had Freud not grappled with a crippling depression in midlife and submitted himself to a rigorous self-analysis, his monumental *Interpretation of Dreams* and *Three Essays on the Theory of Sexuality* would not have been written, and the course of human psychology would have taken a different turn. It is appropriate in the bicentenary year of De Quincey's birth that we acknowledge his contribution to human psychology as well as his contribution to English literature. His insights into the human mind, dreams, and the world of childhood herald many of the discoveries of Freud and psychoanalytic developmental psychologists, but the record of his life suggests that he paid a heavy price for this psychological knowledge. "When he sate," remarks Thomas Carlyle, "you would have taken him, by candlelight, for the beautifullest little child; blue-eyed, sparkling face, had there not been a something, too, which said '*Eccovi*—this child has been in hell.'"[36]

Notes

1. Some confusion surrounds the relative ages and correct order of birth of the De Quincey children. See Judson S. Lyon, *Thomas De Quincey* (New York: Twayne, 1969), pp. 188–89n.
2. Ernest Jones, *The Life and Work of Sigmund Freud,* 3 vols. (New York: Basic Books, 1953–57), 1:3.
3. See, for example, Horace Ainsworth Eaton, *Thomas De Quincey: A Biography* (London: Oxford University Press, 1936), pp. 224, 362–65; Edward Sackville-West, *Thomas De Quincey: His Life and Work* (New Haven, Conn.: Yale University Press, 1936), pp. 220–25; Grevel Lindop, *The Opium-*

Eater: A Life of Thomas De Quincey (New York: Taplinger, 1981), pp. 325-26; Jones, *Life and Work of Sigmund Freud*, 1:139-53.

4. See John E. Jordan, *De Quincey to Wordsworth: A Biography of a Relationship* (Berkeley and Los Angeles: University of California Press, 1962), pp. 59, 208-209; Jones, *Life and Work of Sigmund Freud*, 3:179.

5. Sigmund Freud, *The Origins of Psycho-Analysis: Letters to Wilhelm Fliess, Drafts and Notes, 1887-1902*, ed. Marie Bonaparte, Anna Freud, and Ernst Kris, trans. Eric Mosbacher and James Strachey (New York: Basic Books, 1954), p. 227.

6. Sigmund Freud, *The Standard Edition of the Complete Psychological Works of Sigmund Freud*, trans. and ed. James Strachey, 24 vols. (London: Hogarth Press, 1953-66), 4:160; hereafter cited as *Works*.

7. Freud, *Works*, 18:14-17.

8. See Jones, *Life and Work of Sigmund Freud*, 3:41.

9. Thomas De Quincey, *Confessions of an English Opium-Eater*, ed. John E. Jordan (London: J. M. Dent, 1960), p. x.

10. Jones, *Life and Work of Sigmund Freud*, 1:355-59.

11. Freud, *Works*, 4:xxxii.

12. Ibid., p. xxvi.

13. Ibid., 5:687-708.

14. Ibid., pp. 708-13.

15. Ibid., 8:21-22.

16. Ibid., 4:191.

17. Ibid., 5:539-40.

18. Ibid., 7:197-200.

19. See, for example, Margaret S. Mahler, Fred Pine, and Annie Bergman, *The Psychological Birth of the Human Infant: Symbiosis and Individuation* (New York: Basic Books, 1975), pp. 39-120.

20. Erik H. Erikson, *Childhood and Society*, 2d ed. (New York: Norton, 1963), pp. 247-74.

21. Freud, *Works*, 11:33.

22. Ibid., 4:49.

23. Ibid., p. 31.

24. See, respectively, ibid., 4:163-88, 5:460-87, 4:134-62.

25. Ibid., 4:111n.

26. See, passim, Margaret S. Mahler, *On Human Symbiosis and the Vicissitudes of Individuation*, vol. 1, *Infantile Psychosis* (New York: International Universities Press, 1968); James F. Masterson, *The Nacissistic and Borderline Disorders* (New York: Brunner/Mazel, 1981); Donald B. Rinsley, *Borderline and Other Self Disorders* (New York: Jason Aronson, 1982).

27. Freud, *Works*, 14:237-58.

28. Ibid., 18:65-143.

29. See René A. Spitz, *The First Year of Life: A Psychoanalytic Study of Normal and Deviant Development of Object Relations* (New York: International Universities Press, 1965); Anna Freud, *The Writings of Anna Freud*, rev.

ed., 8 vols. (New York: International Universities Press, 1966-81); Mahler, Pine, and Bergman, *Psychological Birth of the Human Infant.*

30. See René A. Spitz, "Hospitalism: An Inquiry into the Genesis of Psychiatric Conditions in Early Childhood," *Psychoanalytic Study of the Child* 1 (1945): 53-74; René A. Spitz, "Anaclitic Depression: An Inquiry into the Genesis of Psychiatric Conditions in Early Childhood, II," *Psychoanalytic Study of the Child* 2 (1946): 313-42; C. M. Dennehy, "Childhood Bereavement and Psychiatric Illness," *British Journal of Psychiatry* 112 (1966): 1049-69; J. Birtchnell, "Depression in Relation to Early and Recent Parent Death," *British Journal of Psychiatry* 116 (1970): 299-306; Edith Jacobson, *Depression: Comparative Studies of Normal, Neurotic, and Psychotic Conditions* (New York: International Universities Press, 1971).

31. Spitz, *First Year of Life*, p. 151.

32. J. Hillis Miller, *The Disappearance of God: Five Nineteenth-Century Writers* (1963: reprint, Cambridge, Mass.: Harvard University Press, Belknap Press, 1975), p. 72.

33. V. A. De Luca, *Thomas De Quincey: The Prose of Vision* (Toronto: University of Toronto Press, 1980), p. 21.

34. See Wilhelm Stekel, *Die Träume der Dichter: Eine vergleichende Untersuchung der unbewussten Triebkräfte bei Dichtern, Neurotikern, und Verbrechern* (Wiesbaden: J. F. Bergmann, 1912), pp. 236-44; Françoise Moreux, *Thomas De Quincey: la vie, l'homme, l'oeuvre* (Paris: Presses universitaires de France, 1964), pp. 499-533; Robert André, "Les rêves de Thomas De Quincey," *Nouvelle revue française* 12 (1964): 681-90; Brooks Wright, "The Cave of Trophonius: Myth and Reality in De Quincey," *Nineteenth-Century Fiction* 8 (1954): 290-99; David Sundelson, "Evading the Crocodile: De Quincey's 'The English Mail Coach,'" *Psychocultural Review* 1 (1977): 9-20; Michael Haltresht, "The Meaning of De Quincey's 'Dream-Fugue on . . . Sudden Death,'" *Literature and Psychology* 26 (1976): 31-36.

35. Elizabeth W. Bruss, *Autobiographical Acts: The Changing Situation of a Literary Genre* (Baltimore, Md.: Johns Hopkins University Press, 1976), pp. 96, 101, 105.

36. Thomas Carlyle, *Reminiscences,* ed. James Anthony Froude (New York: Harper, 1881), p. 127.

7

The Dark Interpreter and the Palimpsest of Violence: De Quincey and the Unconscious

ROBERT M. MANIQUIS

> *Now reader, I have told my dream to thee,*
> *See if thou canst interpret it to me,*
> *Or to thyself, or neighbour: but take heed*
> *Of misinterpreting; for that, instead*
> *Of doing good, will but thyself abuse:*
> *By misinterpreting, evil ensues.*
>
> —BUNYAN, *The Pilgrim's Progress*

John Bunyan's warning of the self-destructive evil in misinterpretation may have long frightened the pious, but not those today who thrive beyond belief in Nietzschean "as ifs," in supreme fictions, in creative misreading, in deconstructive gazes cast from textual margins, in insightful blindness. These will be no more scared off by Bunyan's warnings than will archaeologists by a pharaoh's curse. Academic interpretation is less likely to abuse than continually to extend itself with interpretative signifiers of signifiers claiming a shared authority with that which, in Bunyan's day, they only humbly pointed to—the ultimate signifieds.

This state of affairs is a familiar one on any pilgrimage we make down the highway of criticism that begins, and some would say ends, in Ferdinand de Saussure's elegant circuit of *signifiant* and *signifié*. Bunyan's warning is for those who reject structuralist closures or deconstructive deferrals of "meanings" and hold to a sign pointing from *here* to *there*, where meaning is found. Virtuoso interpreters from Bunyan to Freud have usually pointed in this way. Freud may often have discovered the unconscious there where it has always been, in the language with which it is spoken. But Freud's entwined signifier and signified, much like Hegel's, often *mirrors* a dialectical unity to which signifier and signified refer, as he veers away from mirror labyrinths down the road to meaning elsewhere, dark and imageless, beyond the signs.

To this extent John Bunyan and Sigmund Freud share common assumptions of Western civilization. Both seek meaning in silent but certain being. Though both are self-conscious artificers of signs, neither Bunyan nor Freud could ever have uttered anything like Wittgenstein's postulate that "whenever we interpret a symbol in one way or another, the interpretation is a new symbol added to the old one."[1] Such hermeneutical Chinese boxes are not to be found along the straight roads traveled by Christian to the Celestial City or by Freud to the mysterious meaning at the center of dreams. Despite their own blending of interpreter and interpreted, Freud banished erring disciples and Bunyan aggressively implied that, if we cast away his "golden" meanings, he will come back and dream up another self-defensive text: "If thou shalt cast all away as vain, / I know not but 'twill make me dream again."[2]

Bunyan and Freud may seem as distant from Thomas De Quincey as at first they may seem from each other. But De Quincey's language preserves a Bunyanesque emblematic tradition as well as Bunyan's Protestant faith in dream visions. Many readers think that his writings also look forward to Freud. It is not unusual to hear, for example, that *Confessions of an English Opium-Eater* is "a pioneering study of the operation of the subconscious mind in dreams" or that De Quincey "twenty-five years before Freud was born" delivers up Freudian discoveries.[3] But does De Quincey remind us of the Freudian topographical unconscious where causes become mythical origins that explain, as in *The Interpretation of Dreams,* individual and, as in *Civilization and Its Discontents,* collective neurotic woes? Or does De Quincey anticipate the Freudian unconscious not metaphorically *there* but always *here*, within a linguistic structure of self-substantiating signs?

Like many other Romantic writers, De Quincey constructs mental places elsewhere, in the anima, the moving Spirit, historical tendency, or salvational secrets. But he also anticipates a Freudian unconscious always to be uncovered yet always manifest in the constructed language of interpretation. De Quincey could not help but anticipate both Freuds, for Freud repeats, like other writers, modern indecision between submission to the signified and a sense of the signified as a function of its signifiers. There is often a crisis in this sensed contingency, felt as the loss of autonomy that flatters interpreters, even Freud, however well he knew that the ego was dynamically produced from shifting symbolic reflections. Elsewhere I have shown how both De Quincey's dream visions and journalism, in his own moments of such crisis, bristle with images of an imperial self.[4] There are better moments in his writing when he sees past fake autonomies to his mirrored self without aggressively mirroring it upon the world. His awareness of this need occurs in scattered passages, mostly fragments of intricate meditations destined for *Suspiria de Profundis*. Here De Quincey is disarmed of the overweening central self he transforms elsewhere into collective imperial power. Here he gazes at mechanisms of the unconscious and of violence and helps us understand his lifelong contradictions. To this we must respond with respect, as we begin our interpretation with the looming figure to whom De Quincey allusively pays his own respects—Bunyan's Interpreter in *The Pilgrim's Progress*.

I. The Dark Interpreter

Some men by feigning words as dark as mine,
Make truth to spangle, and its rays to shine.

—BUNYAN, *The Pilgrim's Progress*

Christian comes upon the House of the Interpreter early in his pilgrimage. There he sees, among other things, a picture of Christ, a man and a damsel sweeping up dust, two children named Passion and Patience, a man eternally quenching fire, and a man named Despair in an iron cage. As Christian goes from room to room and sees emblematic picture, person, or thing, he asks the Interpreter what each means. The Interpreter tells him and they pass tranquilly on to the next. This House of the Interpreter is a comfortable place where the Interpreter, even when called upon to interpret a man dreaming, speaks with calm authority. Such a guide upon Christian's perilous path is wondrous. As he says to Piety, whom he meets farther down the road, "I could have stayed at that good man's House a twelve-month, but that I knew I had further to go."[5] And who would not want to while away time with the Interpreter who kindly assures us that signs are signs and meanings are meanings?

Certainly De Quincey would not have spurned a twelve-month there, conscious as he was of living in historical uncertainty, when everything threatened to decay into fleshly torpor or spin into madness unless principles of religion or philosophy were found (see *SP,* p. 148). Speaking of his dreams, as Bunyan speaks of his, driven by his own interiorized Protestant quest, the Opium-Eater meets no kindly Bunyanesque guide, only an eerie figure he must call the Dark Interpreter.[6] He is most extensively described in a passage intended for *Suspiria de Profundis* about the Spectre of the Brocken, a natural curiosity much sought after by nineteenth-century tourists in the Hartz Mountains of northern Germany. De Quincey presents the Spectre in typically "impassioned prose" (1:14), to which he attaches a typically objective note explaining what actually it is he has just passionately portrayed:

"*Spectre of the Brocken.*"—This very striking phenomenon has been continually described by writers, both German and English, for the last fifty years. Many readers, however, will not have met with these descriptions; and on *their* account I add a few words in explanation, referring them for the best scientific comment on the case to Sir David Brewster's "Natural Magic." The spectre takes the shape of a human figure, or, if the visitors are more than one, then the spectres multiply; they arrange themselves on the blue ground of the sky, or the dark ground of any clouds that may be in the right quarter, or perhaps they are strongly relieved against a curtain of rock, at a distance of some miles, and always exhibiting gigantic proportions. At first, from the distance and the colossal size, every spectator supposes the appearance to be quite independent of himself. But very soon he is surprised to observe his own motions and gestures mimicked: and wakens to the conviction that the phantom is but a dilated version of himself. This Titan amongst the apparitions of earth is exceedingly capricious, vanishing abruptly for reasons best known to himself, and more coy in coming forward than the Lady Echo of Ovid. [*SP*, p. 247n.]

As matter-of-fact as this account may be, De Quincey moves from natural curiosity to a poetic Spectre-image he cites from Coleridge, who wonders whether all ideas are not like optical illusions:

> And art thou nothing? Such thou art as when
> The woodman winding westward up the glen
> At wintry dawn, when o'er the sheep-track's maze
> The viewless snow-mist weaves a glistening haze,
> Sees full before him, gliding without tread,
> An image with a glory round its head;
> This shade he worships for its golden hues,
> And *makes* (not knowing) that which he pursues.
>
> [*SP*, p. 248n.]

The question Coleridge asks, "And art thou nothing?" (from "Constancy to an Ideal Object"), rhetorically invites a negative answer to affirm the idealizing imagination. But the question is put sharply enough to remind De Quincey of his common fears of threatening illusions and nothingness. He was probably thinking as well of the note about self-projections that Coleridge (quoting himself from *Aids to Reflection*) attached to his poem:

Pindar's fine remark respecting the different effects of Music, on different characters, holds equally true of Genius—as many as are not delighted by it are disturbed, perplexed, irritated. The beholder either recognizes it as a projected form of his own Being, that moves before with a Glory round its head, or recoils from it as a Spectre.[7]

The projected self as an empty shadow would be an appropriate inhabitant of De Quincey's often intuited abyss of nothingness. To circumvent the abyss, he can cry to a distant God; to circumvent an endless circle of self-generated signs, he plays a mirror game with the Spectre of the Brocken. In this game the "I" of the narrator-reader—for it is the reader who will play the role for both—must survive intact in a defense against a "projected form of his own Being."

The game and the struggle begin with De Quincey's invitation. "Ascend with me on this dazzling Whitsunday the Brocken of North Germany," he says, leading the reader with priestly intonation to the mountain forest summit. There he (the reader and narrator blended into one) comes upon the shadow he knows is his but pretends is not, sharing neither the naïveté of Coleridge's woodman nor his idealizing contentment: "Who and what is he? He is a solitary apparition, in the sense of loving solitude; else he is not always solitary in his personal manifestations, but, on proper occasions, has been known to unmask a strength quite sufficient to alarm those who had been insulting him" (*SP,* pp. 247–48). Why is the shadow insulted? Why does he wish to alarm? De Quincey, in a circle of self-reflections, is also in a circle of unspecified violence. Nothing is more common to his opium nightmares than circles of ritual violence in which he is both sacrificer and sacrificed. But here he is neither pariah nor doubled priest and ritual offering, only the observer of doubling played in a historical tableau. The tableau actor strikes the attitudes and repeated gestures of suspected brutal, pagan violence that must be turned into proven signs of pure sacrifice. But the self-dissolving swirl of sacrifice is the worst of the Opium-Eater's nightmares. Here even holy sacrifice will be turned into self-affirming gesture in which all violence, including the metaphorical violence in linguistic fracture, will be removed.

Ensuing tests of authenticity applied to the shadowed self must, as we shall see, exclude all possibility that the shadow acts from vestigial violent impulses: "Make the sign of the cross, and observe whether he repeats it.... Look! he *does* repeat it; but the driving showers perplex the images, and *that,* perhaps, it is which gives him the air of one who acts reluctantly or evasively" (*SP,* pp. 248–49). Even the sign of the cross is not sufficient; it may be duplicitous. Another test is called for:

Pluck an anemone, one of these many anemones which once was

called the sorcerer's flower, and bore a part, perhaps, in this horrid ritual of fear; carry it to that stone which mimics the outline of a heathen altar, and once was called the sorcerer's altar; then bending your knee, and raising your right hand to God, say,—"Father, which art in heaven, this lovely anemone, that once glorified the worship of fear, has travelled back into thy fold; this altar, which once reeked with bloody rites to Cortho, has long been rebaptized into thy holy service. The darkness is gone; the cruelty is gone which the darkness bred; the moans have passed away which the victims uttered; the cloud has vanished which once sate continually upon their graves, cloud of protestation that ascended forever to thy throne from the tears of the defenceless, and the anger of the just. And lo! I thy servant, with this dark phantom, whom for one hour on this thy festival of Pentecost I make *my* servant, render thee united worship in this thy recovered temple." [*SP*, p. 249]

De Quincey's emphasis above is not on the Christian symbol's uniting of observer and his shadow but on the increasingly precise exclusion of all instinctive violence from Christian symbolizing. The narrator pretends to overpower the mysterious Spectre, making him his "servant," forcing him to adapt his gestures to a purified sacrificial moment. But even this is not enough. The narrator then pretends that the shadow makes the sign of the cross with intentions still stained with the memory of bloody sacrifice. Perhaps the shadow is a dissembler, as Hamlet first thought his father's ghost was, an instigator not to purifying but to perpetuating violence. "Perhaps," the test continues, "on this high festival of the Christian church he may be overruled by supernatural influence into confession of his homage, having so often been made to bow and bend his knee at murderous rites" (*SP*, p. 250). Perhaps the Spectre, in other words, has been so habituated to blood symbolism that the paradox of Christian blood symbolism is negated, transformed from the mystical healing of all fracture into just another repeated fracture. If the cruciform gesture cannot be decisive, what gesture can? What sign can identify the continuous self and its images?

The narrator finds another test in a veiling of the head and a withdrawal into voiceless grief. De Quincey of course always somehow signals Christian redemption that should end the spilling of blood, the sacrificial death that ends death. But as if in the Christian symbol itself there is still too much resonance of ancient violence, the narrator steps past all ambiguity, even in the cross, to the gesturing griever who is all victim. The "high festival of the Christian church" at which the shadow is seen is Pentecost morning, when, it will be remembered, the Holy Spirit appeared in the sound of a "rushing mighty wind" and "cloven tongues like as of fire" and graced the apostles with the gift of tongues (Acts 2:1-4, AV). De Quincey drives the paradox in this Christian legend—the simultaneous sounding of all languages in a total transparency that denies all boundaries of language—to a different extreme. And in this extreme he finally implies a different idea, one of withdrawn silence, in which the victim speaks devoid of all signifying words, enfolded into himself, and as far distant as a Christian believer like De Quincey could imagine from the sacrificial celebration and implicit guilt of those who "have taken" and "by wicked hands have crucified and slain" (Acts 2:23, AV):

If, then, once in childhood you suffered an aff[li]ction that was ineffable,—if once, when powerless to face such an enemy, you were summoned to fight with the tiger that couches within the separations of the grave,—in that case, after the example of Judaea (on the Roman coins),—sitting under her palm-tree to weep, but sitting with her head veiled,—do you also veil your head. Many years are passed away since then; and you were a little ignorant thing at that time, hardly above six years old.... Therefore now, on this dovelike morning of Pentecost, do you veil your head like Judaea in memory of that transcendent woe, and in testimony that, indeed, it surpassed all utterance of words. Immediately you see that the apparition of the Brocken veils *his* head, after the model of Judaea weeping under her palm-tree, as if he also had a human heart, and that *he* also, in childhood, having suffered an affliction which was ineffable, wished by these mute symbols to breathe a sigh towards heaven in memory of that affliction, and by way of record, though many a year after, that it was indeed unutterable by words. [*SP,* pp. 250-51]

As all Christendom celebrates redemption in plenitudinous

language, the shadow is fixed in the unutterable, the unvoiced affliction of the victim.

With this supposedly definitive test the narrator can testify that the apparition is indeed his shadow. Mute symbolism with which De Quincey speaks this self-identity had already pervaded nineteenth-century melodrama, a symptom of bourgeois discomfort with signs as indices of metaphysical order and their increasing cultivation as desperate expression of psychic purity.[8] Intentional silence here is an illusionary escape from linguistic fracture which De Quincey uses to shape narrative arrival at self-identity. Though the Spectre's previous gestures were also mute, this gesture expels all self-generating stain, all guilt, all violent impulse. Ambiguous self-reflection ends by piercing the ambiguous hidden will to violence. The Spectre is transformed from suspected sacrificer into innocent victim, from a Spectre defending against aggression into a Spectre that, though called to wrestle with the "tiger" of the grave, turns inward to identify itself. The narrator shrewdly turns all nefarious "hidden" motives of the Spectre into a "veiling" that paradoxically signifies transparency. Moral purity of will is thus linked to this silent gesture that signifies with the illusion of no gap to be crossed, no *there* of meaning to be reached, no symbolic exchange. This is no Saussurean enclosure of the self in the sign but of the sign within the self. And yet the urgency with which De Quincey would arrive at identity and presence is channeled with the awareness of dialectical mirror relations contained within all "pure" mimetic signifying. This awareness often seems about to break through De Quincey's mimetic allegorizing, not simply because he inherits Bunyan's doubt or anticipates Freud's unveiling of the hidden but rather because he participates in the common self-conscious signifying that has preoccupied Western culture since at least the late eighteenth century.

Consider, for example, Freudian dialogues with the unconscious, which often include, as in De Quincey's mirror game, a patient as self-interpreter whom the psychoanalyst must interpret. The psychoanalyst must often witness a cogito observing some version of his own ego, resisting, testing, accepting its own reflections. The self-interpreter goes to the source of a disguised desire and, by interpreting, speaks as if the central scene of violence, once spoken, is now subdued to the interpretative will of a unified self.[9] There the *I* sees itself and says, as the narrator says of the Spectre, that is *me* and *I* speak, even in wordless gesture, what it cannot: the fractured thought within, cleansed of transformations of victim into murderer, of the excluded son into the father. Freud thus portrays the unconscious with aggressive-defensive mirroring of the self and a panoply of psychic mechanism. But he also portrays it with Greek and Hebrew stories and with grand clashes of life-and-death forces. Freud separated his metapsychology—hypothetical psychic structure and its historical projection into myth and legend—from his clinical theories of repression and substitution. Metapsychology was speculation and stories; the clinical theories were supposedly scientifically verifiable. But Freud's versions of the great stories are untellable without some sense of the clinically analyzed mechanisms. And Freud often tells the stories *as if* they had interpretative power and historical truth bearing a reliable paradigm of a continuous, however neurotic, historical subject.

De Quincey's tableau of the Spectre of the Brocken can be accurately compared with Freud's tableau of the unconscious only if we see that, in the ideal transparency each interpreter aims at, the "hidden" in De Quincey and the "unconscious" in Freud disappear, its spatiality given over to the mirrored self in dialogue with itself. This imagined transparency, when conscious and unconscious or signifier and signified disappear in a feeling of self-identity, can, of course, always slide back into the narrative suspense of a secret to be discovered. This is not surprising, after all, since it is by narrative that Freud and here De Quincey *imitate* the unveiling of what is manifest in the verbal surface of symbolic substitutions. De Quincey's game with the Spectre, like much Romantic myth interpretation, cuts through layered ritual to gaze on the mythless, storyless mind in order to understand historically elaborated myths and stories. That is why he imitates the unlayering from his Spectre of aggression, concealing, even in seemingly innocent intentions, memories of old and seeds of new violence.[10]

Only one part of the mirror process in De Quincey's psychic ritual, however, has so far emerged. The Spectre, cleansed by the spectator's gestural tests of the self-identifying, pure will, must imaginatively serve the spectator. For without the purified Spectre the narrating spectator cannot speak the question of violence declined by the mute sufferer. The Spectre, cleansed of dark purposes, is now the suitable persona of what De Quincey calls the Dark Interpreter. It is the Dark Interpreter who will speak the question of whence the violence cast upon the sufferer. The question, and the answer, assigned to this self preserves the idea of another one—that persistent cogito within dialectical reflections—that will remain purified, unstained, guiltless, resistant to violence from which he has just freed himself in freeing his reflection. He can now ask the question in total purity—a dream state of interpretation—looking into the eye of violence and not becoming that which he contemplates, not turning into the aggressive sacrificer in the defense from violence. The Dark Interpreter is, to this extent, still, like Bunyan's Interpreter, beneficently alien:

> He is originally a mere reflex of my inner nature. But as the apparition of the Brocken sometimes is disturbed by storms or by driving showers, so as to dissemble his real origin, in like manner the Interpreter sometimes swerves out of my orbit, and mixes a little with alien natures. I do not always know him in these cases as my own parhelion. What he says, generally, is but that which *I* have said in daylight, and in meditation deep enough to sculpture itself on my heart. But sometimes, as his face alters, his words alter; and they do not always seem such as I have used, or *could* use. No man can account for all things that occur in dreams. Generally I believe this,—that he is a faithful representative of myself; but he also is at times subject to the action of the good *Phantasus*, who rules in dreams. [*SP*, p. 251]

Both identified with and distanced from the Dark Interpreter, that other self entwined with engulfing dream phantasmagoria becomes in the dream-interpreting self only the good Phantasus. He is more than the mystical bearer of truths; he is the other self in scenes of sacrificial violence, overwhelming to the dreamer, but who *as interpreter* speaks the violent questions of the sufferer with no danger of becoming violent.

De Quincey's narrator, in first defensively positioning himself against the Spectre of the Brocken, suspects his own shadow of defending against himself. Now the purified shadow embraces ancient, tragic forms of violent ritual, but in an idealized liberation from the aggressive-defensive projection of the self upon the other:

The Greek chorus is perhaps not quite understood by critics, any more than the Dark Interpreter by myself. But the leading function of both must be supposed this—not to tell you anything absolutely new,—*that* was done by the actors in the drama; but to recall you to your own lurking thoughts,—hidden for the moment or imperfectly developed,—and to place before you, in immediate connection with groups vanishing too quickly for any effort of meditation on your own part, such commentaries, prophetic or looking back, pointing the moral or deciphering the mystery, justifying Providence, or mitigating the fierceness of anguish, as would or might have occurred to your own meditative heart, had only time been allowed for its motions. [*SP,* p. 252]

The "fierceness of anguish" invokes that barely disguised reaction of the sufferer that so easily becomes retributive violence in response to what De Quincey earlier calls the "hailstone choruses" of a raging God. The treacherous tendency of the dreamer is to dissolve into the revengeful sufferer, uniting sacrificer and the sacrificed as in his horrible Oriental dreams:

I was the idol; I was the priest; I was worshipped; I was sacrificed. I fled from the wrath of Brama through all the forests of Asia; Vishnu hated me; Seeva lay in wait for me. I came suddenly upon Isis and Osiris: I had done a deed, they said, which the ibis and the crocodile trembled at. [3:442]

Fear, violence, and revenge in chaotic, pagan sacrificial forms often seem ready to burst through the Christian sacrifice in which De Quincey was a pious believer. The narrator does not trust the violence he senses in himself (or is it in his reflection?) as he gazes through sacrificial ritual. The Dark Interpreter, both more and less than a believer, guides him through that which can ravage Christian belief and drive it back to the violence which supposedly Christian sacrifice transcends. In this process the Dark Interpreter does not bring the "unconscious" to the surface but shares the same space as dreamer or narrator in the same scenes of primordial violence.[11]

Walking, for instance, through the submarine asylums of the dream city Savannah-la-Mar, in another fragment of *Suspiria de Profundis,* the dreamer and the Dark Interpreter gaze upon crowds of the dead. Both are shocked by this "ample cemetery" (*SP,* p. 253) and its "marble altars" (*SP,* p. 254) of dead lovers and dead babies. The Dark Interpreter, engaging the shock that the suffering self must feel, speaks first to himself as if rehearsing what he must say to the dreamer:

"They are waiting for the heavenly dawn," whispered the Interpreter to himself: "and, when *that* comes, the bells and the organs will utter a *jubilate* repeated by the echoes of Paradise." Then, turning to me, he said, — "This is sad, this is piteous; but less would not have sufficed for the purpose of God." [*SP,* p. 254]

The Interpreter intervenes in any automatic response of "fierce anguish" by the victim-dreamer. His sermonic explanation unites emblems of infinite time and the fracture sensed even in speech. Death is like the infinitesimal divisions of all moments: "Infinite declensions [of] the true and very present, in which only we live and enjoy, will vanish into a mote of a mote.... The time which *is* contracts into a mathematic point; and even that point perishes a thousand times before we can utter its birth" (*SP,* p. 225). The warped time phase by which the voice cannot speak the birth of that which has already died is one version of common Romantic continuity in process, permanence in change, death in life, eternity in grains of sand, presence in absence. But the Interpreter must also speak to that which most preoccupies the dreamer-spectator — the aggression of it all, the power in what seems no more than godly violence.

The wonder of that violence is always echoed in the potentially revengeful cry of the victim, a universal response buried in the old sacrificial violence from which the narrator, along with his shadow, must emerge. The Interpreter provides the substitution by which he can emerge, replacing the marble altar of sacrificial violence with the altar of fructifying natural process: "The future is the present of God, and to the future it is that he sacrifices the human present. Therefore it is that he works by earthquake. Therefore it is that he works by grief" (*SP,* p. 255). The word "sacrifice" itself is engaged only to extrude it from all mere violence. God's actions are progressive and productive. The Interpreter substitutes for destruction and death solemn figures of sowing and reaping: "O, deep is the ploughing of earthquake! . . . O, deep is the ploughing of grief! But oftentimes less would not suffice for the agriculture of God" (*SP,* pp. 255-56). We may think here of William Blake's "cut worm" that must forgive the plow *(The Marriage of Heaven and Hell),* a call for a different heroic response from that imagined by the sermonizing Interpreter. The Dark Interpreter, in speaking *for* a city of victims and the dreamer, allows the divided self to step outside the moment of the cut when in *Suspiria de Profundis,* these cries from the deepest depths, the innocent victim becomes the proud, crying revenger, when in the worst of De Quincey's nightmares the sacrificed becomes the bloody sacrificer. Divided voices by which to speak of violence without becoming its participant allow the speaking of that other "unconscious" in Romantic discourse, not the hidden anima but the mirrored self in voice and gesture where the artist suspects he sees his self-defensive and self-defining violence.

Blake saw the same necessities in his system of Spectres. Shelley's Prometheus listens to his own curse upon the punishing Jupiter magically repeated by Jupiter himself so that Prometheus can stand in purified demigodly presence outside circular aggression and defense. Within these mirrored selves the narrator has of course a single purpose—to draw a coherent cogito out of interdependent ego voices by extinguishing the seeds of violence that grow in self-defining and protective cries for mercy. That cogito, when nurtured with Christian orthodoxy and political purpose, can be subject, of course, to other violent aggrandizements. Once a fictionally coherent self is placed on the side of the plowing God, it is easy to invite the worms in its path to forgive the plow, as De Quincey easily justified the

English imperial plowing of the world. But here De Quincey comes closest to seeing the rhetorical substitutions of which he is often the victim. He knows that the mirror game, instead of specifying the violent cycle, can produce it. This drift of the dark but transparent interpreter back into the mere dark shadow of violence he goes on to analyze in the elementary act of murder.

II. The Avatar of Vengeance

> *Revenge, at first though sweet,*
> *Bitter ere long back on itself recoils....*
>
> —MILTON, *Paradise Lost,* 9.171-72

In another passage destined for *Suspiria de Profundis,* the Dark Interpreter makes his appearance again. He serves to bring boldly together the psychotic murderer and the innocent child. "Suffering is a mightier agency in the hands of nature, as a Demiurgus creating the intellect, than most people are aware of," a truth De Quincey says comes from the lips of the Interpreter. Though he is introduced once more as a shadowy reflection, the analogy is now to the child's shadow-projecting power:

> Perhaps you are aware of that power in the eye of many children by which in darkness they project a vast theatre of phantasmagorical figures moving forwards or backwards between their bed-curtains and the chamber walls. In some children this power is semi-voluntary—they can control or perhaps suspend the shows; but in others it is altogether automatic. [*PW,* 1:7–8]

Given the tests the narrator applies to his reflection to expel vestiges of bloody rites from the mirror, the narrator's association of this child's mental theater with pagan religion will not be surprising. "I myself, at the date of my last confessions, had seen in this way more processions—generally solemn, mournful, belonging to eternity, but also at times glad, triumphal pomps, that seemed to enter the gates of Time—than all the religions of paganism, fierce or gay, ever witnessed." It is not, however, retributive rites that interest him here but the dark places where human retribution assumes a personal shape. "Now, there is in the dark places of the human spirit—in grief, in fear, in vindictive wrath—a power of self-projection not unlike to this," writes De Quincey:

> Thirty years ago, it may be, a man called Symons committed several murders in a sudden epilepsy of planet-struck fury. According to my recollection, . . . "revenge is sweet!" was his hellish motto on that occasion, and that motto itself records the abysses which a human will can open. Revenge is *not* sweet, unless by the mighty charm of a charity that seeketh not her own it has become benignant. [*PW*, 1:8]

In the section "Savannah-la-Mar" the Dark Interpreter bears the self out of the cycle of violence to ask the questions that will avoid the victim's revenge. In a similar way Symons the murderer will bear violence away from his offended and insulted self, but in an alienated projection by which he instrumentalizes violence. Rejected by the young mistress of his employer's family and scorned by her sisters, he permits his revenge to swallow up both him and them:

> After the term of his service was over, and he, in effect, [was] forgotten by the family, one day he suddenly descended amongst the women of the family like an Avatar of vengeance. Right and left he threw out his murderous knife without distinction of person, leaving the room and the passage floating in blood. [*PW*, 1:8-9]

Symons claimed that all during his murderous fury he felt beside him a dark figure that De Quincey clearly wants to link with the child's "violent" or "automatic" shadow projections, as well as figures like the Spectre and the Dark Interpreter:

> Now, this murderer always maintained, in conversation with the prison chaplain, that, as he rushed on in his hellish career, he perceived distinctly a dark figure on his right hand, keeping pace with himself. Upon *that* the superstitious, of course, supposed that some fiend had revealed himself, and associated his superfluous presence with the dark atrocity. Symons was not a philosopher, but my opinion is, that he was too much so to tolerate that hypothesis, since, if there was one man in all Europe that needed no tempter to evil on that evening, it was precisely Mr. Symons, as nobody knew better than Mr. Symons himself. I had not the benefit of his acquaintance, or I would have explained it to him. The fact

is, in point of awe a fiend would be a poor, trivial *bagatelle* compared to the shadowy projections, *umbras* and *penumbras*, which the unsearchable depths of man's nature [are] capable, under adequate excitement, of throwing off, and even into stationary forms. [*PW*, 1:9]

Symons's projection perverts the mirror relation which De Quincey suggests in the productively shadowed self. The beneficently alien Dark Interpreter, like the Spectre of the Brocken, reflects the self back to itself miraculously unfragmented by the mirror gift of division. In the mirror the narrator also sees the violent reciprocation by which aggressor and defender define themselves against each other. Symons, on the other hand, never sees himself in the mirrored projection; he sees only the alien Other. Symons, refusing to admit at least his partial identity with the dark figure, makes himself worse by trying to make himself better. By expelling all violence upon a projection that is not him, he sets the primordial avatar of vengeance loose to do its will and thus loses his own. The narrator, however, in the specular image by which he *both is and is not* the dark figure, can use the figure truly to bear the violence away, to imaginatively transfer the violence.

Murderer and interpreter are frighteningly similar. One produces and one escapes the violent psychic moment because one does not see and the other does that his reflection is himself. But does the narrator, going down this analytic path of definition, really get far beyond Coleridge's idealizing woodman who "*makes* (not knowing) that which he pursues"? This distinction between murderer and interpreter could be analyzed to its illusionary core. Whence comes this special grace in the "voluntary" projective power, or in self-consciousness after the fact of symbolic projection? Whence comes the "dark" power of interpretation which, as Bunyan says, sometimes makes "truth to spangle, and its rays to shine"? Or is this dark power defined only by its mysterious operations, its source again to be found in the "elsewhere" within the self? Pascal thought that the "thinking human reed" achieved a liberating power greater than all the world's in knowing its own mortality; such knowledge comes in a self-dividing self that somehow in this division feels a power that comes from he knows not where, even in knowing. The self seems to have no knowledge of the source of power in its knowledge. Does De Quincey's or any Romantic or any Freudian or Lacanian positioning of oneself over against the projected self tell us more than Pascal about the magical arbitrariness of this self-consciousness?

Kant halted the infinite regression of the self observing the self with an incantatory philosophical phrase—"the transcendental unity of apperception." De Quincey finds a stopping place in a paradoxical (and impossible) mental place beyond language. But whatever the version of a locatable self, the immediate and ancient sense of its powerful source—in knowing itself—keeps threatening to spin off into mirrors of mirrors. The ideological question is then inevitably asked: are the psyche and its extension, the historicized individual subject, only a necessary fiction in an unspeakable, anonymous grid of subjectless social relations? Such a question asked even of De Quincey's limited ideological practices would carry us far into another essay. It must be enough, however inadequate, to see only how De Quincey looks for an exit door in the asserted powerful perception of the mirrored ego. He can see here a chance at sanity in self-reduplication, self-coherence in self-division. He must find an exit, for in his worst nightmares this same reduplication threatens to engulf and crush him, no less than it engulfs Symons the murderer.

De Quincey is a specialist in pain and engulfed or drowning selves. The pain and suffering which he says comprise a "Demiurgus creating the intellect" he marks in Symons as he does in himself and in the crying child. He insists that this pain must be uttered. But he also implies that in the very utterance is the beginning of both the production and the destruction by which violence done upon the self turns back toward the other. The expression of agony nothing will stop. Expressed agony may even be the necessity, we are told, by which some are "awakened" unto themselves:

Pain driven to agony, or grief driven to frenzy, is essential to the

THE DARK INTERPRETER AND THE PALIMPSEST OF VIOLENCE 127

ventilation of profound natures. A sea which is deeper than any . . . measured cannot be searched and torn up from its sleeping depths without a levanter or a monsoon. A nature which is profound in excess, but also introverted and abstracted in excess, so as to be in peril of wasting itself in interminable reverie, cannot be awakened sometimes without afflictions that go to the very foundations, heaving, stirring, yet finally harmonizing; and it is in such cases that the Dark Interpreter does his work, revealing the worlds of pain and agony and woe possible to man — possible even to the innocent spirit of a child. [*PW*, 1:12]

But in this expressed pain the Demiurgus may create from the innocent child an Opium-Eater who in nightmare interpretation learns what the reflected, dialectical ego is. Or the Demiurgus may produce the murderer-avenger. The Dark Interpreter must do his work if he is not to become the dark shadow. Analyzing the cycle of violence must continually occur, without which the mind will do nothing else than continue to construct, as he suggests, even in "stationary forms" the icons and the rites of violence.[12]

Fictional autonomous psyches are thus shown either perpetuating or halting violence. De Quincey will, of course, still invoke the shadowy underworld of the "unconscious." The language that demands that place forces him to speak of the "unsearchable depths of man's nature," though we must wonder whether he has not seen those depths in exploring the mind's mirror surface. And, in fact, De Quincey likes images of productive surfaces as much as magical incantations of secret places. One such surface is the written text itself, the stationary linguistic mirroring in which the writer can enclose his mirrored interpreter, as Bunyan does in his text and De Quincey and Freud do in theirs. It is appropriate, then, to turn to De Quincey's most famous and influential image of the mind, in which he combines sacrificial violence and the erasures by which the self writes the self into being. From Bunyan's kindly Interpreter, revealing mysteries of Crucifixion and grace, to De Quincey's Dark Interpreter we have witnessed the blending of the antitheses of death and life with signifiers and signifieds, silence and utterance, aggression and defense, conscious and unconscious.

These antitheses are overlaid in all modern translations into the text of what was once reserved for the Body of Christ. De Quincey imagines such a mental text where, from the midst of "sacrificial" erasure and substitution of its thoughts, the mind still looks back at itself. The mind is here a text to which violence is repeatedly done but whose image portrays a source from which violence cannot be allowed to emanate—like that purified self shadowed through reflections of the suspected violent self in all his texts.

III. Transubstantiated Texts

Where has the supreme miracle been achieved, this transubstantiation of irrational qualities of matter and life in human words?

—PROUST, letter to Lucien Daudet

What else than a natural and mighty palimpsest is the human brain? Such a palimpsest is my brain; such a palimpsest, oh reader! is yours. Everlasting layers of ideas, images, feelings, have fallen upon your brain softly as light. Each succession has seemed to bury all that went before. And yet, in reality, not one has been extinguished.

—DE QUINCEY, *Suspiria de Profundis*

Transubstantiation may seem at first an alien concept to link with the Protestant De Quincey. But it makes for a fair exchange, since the palimpsest image has been used by Gérard Genette not only, as we shall see, in analyzing Proust's transubstantiations but also in emblematizing an entire system of textual theory.[13] The expansion of the palimpsest into a descriptive metaphor for a modern literary preoccupation is not unreasonable. And though Genette draws no simplistic lines of influence, it is useful to remember De Quincey's image of the mind as transformable and transforming text, a place where erased words, in succeeding little murders, only seem to die. This magical text is a version of Romantic fascination with sacrificial symbology and transformational power in a universal Word made up of human words.

De Quincey's mental palimpsests invoke the vellum on which

Greek and Latin pagan texts could be discovered imperfectly erased beneath medieval Christian texts. De Quincey treats these vellum wonders of the recovered past in ways we have seen previously; he is fascinated by the spatial appearances of above and below, visible and hidden. These are illusionary spaces, however, that the eye draws onto one magical surface:

> Hence it arose in the middle ages, as a considerable object for chemistry, to discharge the writing from the roll, and thus to make it available for a new succession of thoughts.... They did the thing; but not so radically as to prevent us, their posterity, from *un*doing it.... Could magic, could Hermes Trismegistus, have done more? What would you think, fair reader, of a problem such as this, — to write a book which should be sense for your own generation, nonsense for the next, should revive into sense for the next after that, but again become nonsense for the fourth; and so on by alternate successions, sinking into night or blazing into day, like the Sicilian river Arethusa, and the English river Mole; or like the undulating motions of a flattened stone which children cause to skim the breast of a river, now diving below the water, now grazing its surface, sinking heavily into darkness, rising buoyantly into light, through a long vista of alternations? [*SP*, pp. 228–29]

The now-we-see-it, now-we-don't skipping of texts through time, like a child's skipping rock upon the water rising to and falling from the surface, counters other De Quinceyan senses of the buried, unconscious secret. It is not that one model of mental space displaces the other. Like wave and particle theories from which the physicist can choose to portray light, De Quincey's texts, like most other modern texts, alternate between the topographical unconscious and flat, mirror surfaces of self-definition.

In one of his own palimpsest images Freud, like Proust and De Quincey before him, becomes fascinated with the magical erasure and reappearance of signs upon the surface. His particular example is not of old vellum manuscripts but of the popular *Wunderblock*, the "Mystic Writing-Pad" still commonly to be found, a wax base beneath a writing paper and a celluloid protective cover. The tablet produces an image when a stylus presses the paper into the wax and erases the image when the paper is lifted. Held to a certain angle of light, as Freud points out, what has been erased can be seen again in the cuts upon the wax where the image has disappeared only to be preserved. Freud compares the parts of the amusing writing pad with his mechanisms of perception, conscious, preconscious, and unconscious.[14] He can hardly resist this pleasurable analogical play, no more than can Proust, of discovering images recovered from the past. De Quincey also moves pleasurably with the palimpsest into the place of the hidden and the dead, only to find that everything is reconstitutable in the imagined moment of complete memory.

But unlike Freud's mystic writing pad, De Quincey's palimpsest is a metaphorical mechanism and, like Proust's transubstantiating text, an image of violences conceived as disappearances and reappearances and finally complete, unbroken continuity. Convulsions of birth and death are united, as in a woman's memory of her palimpsest experience when, as a girl nearly drowning, she saw in imminent death all instants of her life before her "arraying themselves not as a succession, but as parts of a coexistence" (*SP,* p. 234). There is nothing here of modern mythical unconscious violence, for instance, of the son replacing the father. And though this anecdote may have been related to De Quincey by his mother, there is nothing special in that circumstance. His palimpsest metaphor speaks of that violence which is the subtext of all violences written in the stories that displace each other upon the vellum as they do in the human mind. Psychic mechanism and psychic ritual are aligned in the metaphors applied to the palimpsest image. The problem of understanding the beauty in this substitution of texts is, De Quincey says, no different from understanding what it is when we

> bid a generation kill, but so that a subsequent generation may call back into life; bury, but so that posterity may command to rise again. Yet *that* was what the rude chemistry of past ages effected when coming into combination with the reaction from the more refined chemistry of our own. Had *they* been better chemists, had *we* been worse, the mixed result, namely, that, dying for *them,* the flower should revive for *us,* could not have been effected. They did the thing proposed to them; they did it effectually, for they

founded upon it all that was wanted: and yet ineffectually, since we unravelled their work; effacing all above which they had superscribed; restoring all below which they had effaced. [*SP*, p. 229]

Equating killing, chemical transformation, and organic process correspondingly unites organic growth, chemical reconstitution, and resurrection. The antitheses of total disappearance and reappearance are, in Proust's sense, transubstantiated into continuous wholeness. The implication is that the metaphorical sacrifice imagined here, the commanded killing, is only illusionary. This text is filled with substitutions and erasures and chemical burning through of one text to resurrect another, and yet paradoxically none of this are we to understand as destructive violence. It is all creative process.

Few analogies draw the mind so specifically together under the metaphor of secular language to declare the always underlying Romantic obsession with psychological vestiges of the religious Word. Writes De Quincey:

In the illustration imagined by myself, from the case of some individual palimpsest, the Grecian tragedy had seemed to be displaced, but was *not* displaced, by the monkish legend; and the monkish legend had seemed to be displaced, but was *not* displaced, by the knightly romance. In some potent convulsion of the system, all wheels back into its earliest elementary stage. [*SP*, pp. 235-36]

Everything wheeling back into its origin, the Word into itself, the erased into the resurrected, magically replaces all texts and displaces none. The palimpsest contains within itself the sermonizing voice of the Dark Interpreter which we hear in "Savannah-la-Mar." But instead of speaking of the fracture unavoidable even in speech, the impossible uttering of a moment's birth before it dies, De Quincey gives, like the last tested reflection of the Spectre, an image of speaking silence in the written text. The imitated sounds of the text we need not hear to see word dissolving into word, sinking below and rising to the surface, disappearing and reappearing in unfractured presence. This magical presence of life in death and conscious in unconscious transcends the violence without which texts displacing other texts could not be born. Thus Christian salvation becomes a dying of words into the Word of the undying mental text. And that ultimate text is the Romantic mind pleasurably imagining how it has authored its own totality.

De Quincey's palimpsest can be seen beneath Genette's description of Proust's work: "As Proustian writing, Proust's work is a palimpsest where several figures and several meanings blend and get mixed up, each always present at the same time, and which are only deciphered all together, in their inextricable totality."[15] Since Proust makes only two slight uses of the actual metaphor, Genette turns to *Les paradis artificiels,* Baudelaire's translation of the *Confessions* and *Suspiria de Profundis.* De Quincey, his name unmentioned in this backward glance, would have enjoyed finding himself partly erased and yet revived — consummately "palimpsested." Relayed from De Quincey by Baudelaire and into a critical embrace of the vast domain of *À la recherche du temps perdu*, the palimpsest image helps Genette inscribe modern upon Romantic myths of psychic autonomy. But they must be artfully inscribed, for the myths are not identical. Writers like De Quincey, Baudelaire, Gide, and Proust lived in historical and social disruptions that both occasioned and fragmented those myths; the more psychic autonomy was asserted, the more accelerating disruptions kept flattening it into a shadow. Gide's Michel in *L'Immoraliste,* for example, compares himself to a palimpsest and cries out, "A new being! A new being!" in magically shedding his obsession with history: "... I compared myself to palimpsests; I tasted the joy of the scholar, who under the most recent writings discovers on the same paper a very ancient text."[16] The former historian, resurrected in the sensuous present, ironically portrays his new existence as a self-discovering historical and salvational text, now released from the dead texts of the past. And yet, even in 1902, this seems self-consciously antiquarian. Gide's tone produces a palimpsest unlike De Quincey's image of linguistic christological violence. De Quincey draws a kind of aura around these textual images of the mind in order to recuperate some version of traditional Belief. Gide's palimpsest is more like Proust's transubstantiating words. Both Gide and Proust play with the textual embodiment of sacrifice and redemption and psychic continuity. Both, even in affirmation of the self, try to recall, often ironically, what the desire to believe was like; that is to say, they can be only nostalgic. But all christological texts of bourgeois culture and all mystic writing pads have collided today with contemporary violences beyond containment even in nostalgia for the Word. The victim of this collision seems to be the individual historical subject, who has lost the last wisps of his affirming psychic shadow in postmodern culture. Jacques Derrida's texts, for instance, not only flee transcendental textual moments but also thrive in their own metaphorical violence. They have no transforming power; they in fact refuse it. Multiple collisions push the text in blinking moments out of "differential traces." No longer "content enclosed in a book or its margins," this text "overruns all the limits assigned to it so far (not submerging or drowning them in an undifferentiated homogeneity, but rather making them more complex, dividing and multiplying strokes and lines)." Such a text can reveal only its own constantly rupturing order. And the shifting voice within it must refuse all sacrificial prelude to apocalyptic illusion, all conception of the palimpsest:

Last judgment. Resurrection of the dead. Ghosts, *Doppelgänger.* (Nietzsche: I am a *Doppelgänger,* in *Ecce Homo.* The event—which *"sur-vient"* ["takes place," "occurs"; lit., "comes on"]—how will they translate this word?—consists in nothing, nothing but coming about, going on, and being gone.) Apocalypse, eschatology, the "last War," the "context" of *L'arrêt de mort.* "Come" is said to the event that comes about. An apocalyptic superimprinting of texts: there is no paradigmatic text. Only relationships of cryptic haunting from mark to mark. No palimpsest (definitive unfinishedness). No piece, no metonymy, no integral corpus. And thus no fetishism.[17]

Fighting off the palimpsest and other metonymic fetishes from a continuous footnote band parallel with his essay's text, Derrida looks out proleptically from a continually shrinking margin to his translated words about Shelley's *Triumph of Life* and Blanchot's *L'arrêt de mort.* He is here not unlike De Quincey interpreting the Dark Interpreter in his own text. But the

Romantic self is privileged, like De Quincey testing his Spectre, to test with his own authenticity that of the *Doppelgänger* he meets. The postmodern writer proclaims, with an amusingly grotesque pride, his Nietzschean lineage and the discovery that he is himself the *Doppelgänger*. He is the shadow, not the source, and without any Platonic hope that there is a source to his shadowiness. Symbolic exchange dies in such texts. Transubstantiation is dissipated into conflicting lines of force. Illusory passages between conscious and unconscious are blocked up. Bunyan's kindly Interpreter, already less comfortably metamorphosed in De Quincey's Dark Interpreter, has become a human shade only to be vaguely made out against the dark recesses and margins of violent texts.

The palimpsest has suffered its own partial erasure and become only a remembered writing surface on which no more can be written. It has fallen into historical fractures it once magically embraced and healed. Surely it will settle into some succeeding taxonomy of mental forms awaiting elaboration in our decentered culture. The narrative "chronotopes" of Mikhail Bakhtin, for example, could be arranged into a historical grid that will help us see the ascendant and diminishing force of the palimpsest and related figures.[18] Chronotopes comprise dominant spatiotemporal symbolic forms of Western narration, such as the pilgrim's road, the castle, the house, or the prison, to which I would add the body and the palimpsest. But whatever new rhetorics of narrative figuration we may need, we know that few narrative and textual figures have claimed more ideological power than the circular route between the conscious and the unconscious in images such as the palimpsest. If that particular figure has drifted into the past, it is only replaced by others in a cultural power of figuration that, of course, has not weakened—and never will. That is why Bunyan's warning in *The Pilgrim's Progress* of the evil self-abuse in misinterpretation can still usefully make us suspicious of the power both of figures and their interpretation, as long as we add that all assumed modes of correct and incorrect readings are part of the complex social and political power in communal definitions of individual imagination, the unconscious, and the political individual. If

Bunyan could carry out his gentle threat to return and dream up another text, he would not be surprised by the ideological power and many implied kinds of violence in our various circuits of *signifiant* and *signifié*. Bunyan, though often doubting the certainty of signs, knew how to wield them in disciplining a will to salvation. De Quincey, a Romantic inheritor of both Protestant self-consciousness and doubt, struggled also to preserve that ultimately unshakable will. Threatened loss of will is what erupts in his dreams of painful confusion, but it is also what drives him to gaze into those imagined mental places always to see darkly against his mirrored self the figured violences that he imagined the self *must* subdue.

And yet De Quincey never achieved a continuous self-conscious transparency that would keep him from cultivating violence especially in political, economic, and historical texts that desperately assert a psychic autonomy. He is a curiously frustrating author, always falling away from his own illuminating gazes into the power of language to fragment the will while seemingly embodying it. The emphasis we need here, however, is not on what De Quincey did not see but on what he did. That which he saw, both in the Dark Interpreter and in the palimpsest, makes it possible to read him with the same attention to complexities we invoke in Proust or Freud. Though his voice will never have the literary authority of theirs, he grasped, before they did, much of what is at stake in the metaphorical and ritual puzzles of violence. His willingness to engage those puzzles still helps us understand, if only to dissipate, that powerful spiritualized and ideological place we call the unconscious.

Notes

1. Ludwig Wittgenstein, *Preliminary Studies for the "Philosophical Investigations," Generally Known as the Blue and Brown Books* (New York: Harper, 1958), p. 33.
2. John Bunyan, *The Pilgrim's Progress*, ed. Roger Sharrock (Harmondsworth: Penguin, 1965), p. 207.
3. Thomas De Quincey, *Confessions of an English Opium-Eater*, ed. Alethea Hayter (Harmondsworth: Penguin, 1971), p. 18. The idea is to be found again and again in discussions of De Quincey, but it is only a local ver-

sion of the general idea that European Romantic writers, in one way or another, anticipated Freud. This usually means no more than that Romantic writers often spoke topographically like Freud—but of course also like the ancient Greeks—of places "below" or "beyond" consciousness. Such an outlook, to cite only a few of the senses "unconscious" can have in the nineteenth century, can include the complex doubling of the self, crypts of mental secrets, "inanimate" power, or Carlyle's enthusiastic cry that "the sign of health is Unconsciousness," by which he means the "mysterious depths" of "vital forces." Many readers would be offended if by Romantic anticipation of Freud one meant that writers actually half-imagined something like the mapped Freudian mechanisms. A general and genteel idea of anticipation serves most commentary. Recent criticism, especially that influenced by the psychological and linguistic analysis of Jacques Derrida and Jacques Lacan, for all its excesses, has raised some exacting, though complicated, questions about what the "unconscious" may mean in Western culture from the eighteenth century on. Much of this analysis has made the question of who anticipated what secondary to defining the general problem of interpretation shared by both the Romantics and Freud. Historians of psychiatry are not of much help here. Henri F. Ellenberger, in *The Discovery of the Unconscious: The History and Evolution of Dynamic Psychiatry* (New York: Basic Books, 1970), for instance, typically assumes that the Freudian unconscious (repression, libido, ego defenses, and all the rest) was only waiting to be discovered and was glimpsed here and there by writers and medical doctors in the "Romantic" tradition. Ellenberger has no doubt about what the unconscious is, only about exactly where it comes into view. One of the most superficial of these histories, Lancelot Law Whyte's *The Unconscious Before Freud* (New York: Basic Books, 1960), provides lists of quotations from dozens of writers who helped "discover" the unconscious. Whyte properly enrolls De Quincey among the discoverers (see p. 141), but Whyte thinks he was an American doing his best for the intellectual progress of the New World in its attempt to glimpse what Freud would finally unveil completely.

4. See my "Lonely Empires: Personal and Public Visions of Thomas De Quincey," in Eric Rothstein and Joseph Anthony Wittreich, Jr., eds., *Literary Monographs*, vol. 8 (Madison: University of Wisconsin Press, 1976), pp. 47–127.

5. Bunyan, *Pilgrim's Progress*, p. 81.

6. This symbolic figure has received surprisingly little commentary. His name graces the title of Tilottama Rajan's interesting book *Dark Interpreter: The Discourse of Romanticism* (Ithaca, N.Y.: Cornell University Press, 1980), but the name does little more than emblematize analyses of other writers than De Quincey.

7. Samuel Taylor Coleridge, *The Complete Poetical Works of Samuel Taylor Coleridge*, ed. Ernest Hartley Coleridge (Oxford: Oxford University Press, Clarendon Press, 1912), 1:456.

8. See Peter Brooks, *The Melodramatic Imagination: Balzac, Henry James, Melodrama, and the Mode of Excess* (New Haven, Conn.: Yale University Press, 1976), esp. pp. 56–80.

9. Freud was of course well aware of the necessity to move between various systems of explanation that inevitably embrace even the patient as interpreter. In his essay "The Unconscious" (1915) he suggests that he is virtually forced to take up the "topographical point of view" (see Sigmund Freud, *The Standard Edition of the Complete Psychological Works of Sigmund Freud*, trans. and ed. James Strachey, 24 vols. [London: Hogarth Press, 1953–66], 14:172–76; hereafter cited as *Works*). He comes close to making the same point Wittgenstein does that we cannot object to the idea of "unconscious" thoughts if we insist on the idea of "conscious" thoughts (see *Preliminary Studies for the "Philosophical Investigations,"* pp. 57–58). Still, Freud moves between the topographical and a notion of continuous "thought" in language; Wittgenstein drives the unconscious and the conscious onto one level plane of language.

10. On the difference between Freud's claims for the metapsychology and the clinical evidence of repression and other mechanisms, see Adolf Grünbaum, *The Foundations of Psychoanalysis: A Philosophical Critique* (Berkeley and Los Angeles: University of California Press, 1984), especially pp. 1–93. Grünbaum's explanation of this difference is essential to his critique of (1) blundering hermeneutic interpreters of psychoanalysis, especially Habermas and Ricoeur, who have conflated the metapsychological and clinical claims, and (2) blundering psychoanalysts who incorrectly claim verifiability for their clinical results. In brief, the psychoanalysts are profoundly mistaken, and the hermeneutic theorists are mistaken about what the mistakes are. The last word has not been said about this challenging book, and Habermas can be defended from many of Grünbaum's criticisms. Undeniably Freud needed to and did emphasize the distinction between the manifestly fabular metapsychology and clinical, "scientific" practice. And yet it is also undeniable that Freud needed the fabular to draw out implications of that clinical practice. The story of Freud's conversion to the "story" as a means of representing "scientific" understanding has been told many times. For a useful summary of the literary and epistemological implications of this conversion see Michel de Certeau, "The Freudian Novel: History and Literature," *Humanities in Society* 4 (1981): 121–41.

11. For analyses of the single space shared by mirrored selves and the violence exchanged between them see Jacques Lacan, "The Mirror Stage as Formative of the Function of the I" and "Aggressivity in Psychoanalysis," in his *Écrits: A Selection*, trans. Alan Sheridan (New York: Norton, 1977), pp. 1–7, 8–29. The other essays in this collection are also of value for this subject. Generally I have made use as well of the series *Le séminaire de Jacques Lacan*, ed. Jacques-Alain Miller (Paris: Editions du Seuil, 1975–).

12. At points De Quincey denies any primitive instinct of violence or

revenge in the child. In "The Affliction of Childhood" section of *Suspiria de Profundis* he tells the story of his first learning of "brutality and violence," from which nature forced him to "revolt." Yet even in denying "vindictive thoughts" in the "powerless infant" (*SP*, p. 164), he portrays the child instinctively turning his head away from that brutality and violence that seem to call him into consciousness of the world and of himself. Again, the violence is not part of him, but it determines all his succeeding consciousness. After experiencing this first brutality and violence, he is sure that "henceforward the character of my thoughts must have changed greatly; for so *representative* are some acts, that one single case of the class is sufficient to throw open before you the whole theatre of possibilities in that direction" (*SP*, p. 165).

13. Proust's lines on the linguistic miracle of transubstantiation with which I begin this section are from a letter to Lucien Daudet quoted by Gérard Genette in his essay "Proust palimpseste," in *Figures I* (Paris: Editions du Seuil, 1966), p. 42. More recently, in *Palimpsestes: la littérature au second degré* (Paris: Editions du Seuil, 1982), Genette has expanded the palimpsest metaphor into scaffolding for a rhetorical analysis of "transtextualité," or the "textual transcendence of the text... everything which puts it into a relationship, obvious or secret, with other texts" (ibid., p. 7). For a discussion of a self-conscious modern text in which the palimpsest metaphor thrives see Maurice Cagnon, "Palimpsest in the Writings of Hubert Aquin," *Modern Language Studies* 8, no. 2 (1978): 80–89. Cagnon points out that De Quincey is the favorite author of "Ghezzo-Quenum alias author P. X. Magnant alias the editor/narrator/scriptor" in the Quebec novelist's *Trou de Memoire* (p. 88). There is little doubt that Aquin is resurrecting De Quincey's metaphor. Cagnon also cites Genette's use of the metaphor in analysing Proust, which called forth a rather pointless note by Thomas A. Reisner, "De Quincey's Palimpsest Reconsidered," *Modern Language Studies* 12, no. 2 (1982): 93–94. Reisner says that "Cagnon suggests that Baudelaire's translation of De Quincey's essay may have been instrumental in transmitting the image to Marcel Proust, who anticipates Aquin in his use of it in modern French literature and may therefore have served as its immediate source" (ibid., p. 93). Reisner inflates one of Cagnon's footnotes into a theory that neither Cagnon nor Genette is much concerned with. Nevertheless, he gets his note off the ground with this inaccurate information in order to remind us that the palimpsest metaphor can be found in Coleridge (the prefatory note to *The Wanderings of Cain*) and in Plutarch. He then argues, with gusto, that therefore neither Coleridge nor De Quincey invented the metaphor, an assertion that, as far as I know, no one has ever made.

14. See Freud's brief essay "A Note upon the 'Mystic Writing-Pad'" (1925), in *Works*, 19:227–34. See also *Works*, 4:135 *(The Interpretation of Dreams)* for Freud's quotation from an essay by James Sully, who compares the dream and the palimpsest.

15. Genette, *Figures I,* p. 67.
16. André Gide, *Romans, récits et soties, oeuvres lyriques,* ed. Yvonne Davet and Jean-Jacques Thierry (Paris: Gallimard, 1958), pp. 398-99.
17. Jacques Derrida, "Living On," in Harold Bloom et al., *Deconstruction and Criticism* (New York: Seabury Press, 1979), pp. 136-37, 84.
18. See M. M. Bakhtin, *The Dialogic Imagination: Four Essays,* ed. Michael Holquist, trans. Caryl Emerson and Michael Holquist (Austin: University of Texas Press, 1981), pp. 84-258.

8

The Artist as Murderer: De Quincey's Essay "On Murder Considered as One of the Fine Arts"

A. S. PLUMTREE

Although De Quincey's essay "On Murder Considered as One of the Fine Arts" is acknowledged as among his finest works and is the foundation of his reputation as a humorist, it has not been accorded the critical study it deserves. In this chapter I explore the psychological grounds for his obsession with murder, place his essay in its context as an example of the genre of Romantic irony, trace the elements of sadomasochism inherent in his identification with both murderer and victim, and suggest that his intuition of the connection between art and murder marks him as an important precursor of the modern literature of crime.

I. The Growth of an Obsession

At first sight there is a remarkable discrepancy between the known facts of De Quincey's personality and his preoccupation with crime and violence. He called himself "the shyest of human beings" (1:334–35) and declared himself "incapable of cruelty."[1] To a shrewd observer like Thomas Carlyle his benignity and diminutive size suggested a child, but appearance was deceptive: "When he sate, you would have taken him, by candlelight, for the beautifullest little child; blue-eyed, sparkling face, had there not been a something, too, which said '*Eccovi*—this child has been in hell.'"[2] All his contemporaries testified to the Byzantine elaborateness of his manners, which created a distance between himself and others to protect the citadel of his secret inwardness from a hostile world. Yet De Quincey's works are littered with references to murder and display an overall preoccupation with violence. He was fascinated by confederations of murderers such as the Jewish Sicarii (7:150; 13:64), the Thugs of India (7:151; 8:428, 429n.; cf. Hogg, p. 174), and the assassins of the Old Man of the Mountains (13:21-22, 62; *PW*, 2:92). He was at home amid the murderous intrigues of the Caesars. Herod the Great, for his massacre of the innocents, he once commended for his "artistic merit as a first-rate murderer" (8:319n.). In "The Avenger" his hero, Maximilian, exacts a terrible revenge for the humiliation of his mother and sisters: his murdered victims finally include even his own wife, Margaret Liebenheim, whose name reveals her to be a thinly veiled portrait of De Quincey's own wife.

What, then, are the springs of this preoccupation? In the broadest sense it begins with his conviction of the "colossal guilt" (1:102) of the fallen human heart, which is subject to conflicting pulls: "Every man has two-edged tendencies lurking within himself, pointing in one direction to what will expand the elevating principles of his nature, pointing in another to what will tempt him to its degradation" (4:298). In his "reverie upon *Sudden Death*" (13:304) in *The English Mail-Coach* he imagined a moment "when, by any even partial failure or effeminate collapse of your energies, you will be self-denounced as a murderer" (13:303). Such a failure in moral courage presupposes the existence of "a dreadful ulcer, lurking far down in the depths of human nature," a taint of treachery through which every man participates in "the treason of the aboriginal fall" (13:304).

As ever, De Quincey's conviction of man's ineradicable guilt must be placed alongside the sources of his own guilt feelings. He felt himself to be directly or indirectly responsible for several "murders." His anxiety that he might have killed the mysterious Malay with an opium overdose precipitated some of the most horrific dreams in *Confessions of an English Opium-Eater.* He may have believed that, by leaving the child prostitute Ann and going to Eton, he had condemned her to an early grave. Perhaps he blamed himself for his wife's early death. He certainly felt that he had killed the young girl in *The English Mail-Coach* with whose frail gig he collided. He wrote copiously, out of a sense of guilt, about all these figures. And if the guilt seems disproportionate to the crimes, we must recall his own remark that "the crime that *might* have been, was in my eyes the crime that *had* been" (1:45).

For the true interpretation of his obsession with murder we must trace a critical series of relationships, starting in childhood, which fixed in De Quincey the self-image of a victim of persecution. The first of these persecutory figures was his older brother, William. The sadistic element in De Quincey's fascination with murder no doubt developed as an imaginary compensation for his actual position of subservience to his brother's cruel whims, to which his response was positively masochistic: "I had a positive craze for being despised. I doted on it; and considered contempt a sort of luxury that I was in continual fear of losing" (1:59). Viewing his little brother as weak, effeminate, and stupid, William terrorized him by provoking stone-throwing battles with the local factory boys and by pushing him to such dizzy heights on the garden swing that, had he not died young, William would "infallibly have broken [his] neck" (1:110).

These fraternal persecutions induced in De Quincey that "chronic passion of anxiety" (1:73) which remained as the root of his psychological malaise. Yet he courted, and even thrived upon, this sense of anxiety: "A certain proportion of anxiety, or even of gloomy fear, is a stimulant" (5:291), and "Even danger, kept within just limits, is a mode of pleasurable stimulation" (8:79). Persecution mania was such a dominant trait of his personality that it is often difficult to decide whether his persecutors were real or imaginary. The creditors who pursued him in 1838 were real enough, yet, as his daughter (Mrs. Bairdsmith) testified, he derived a perverse pleasure from their remorseless importunities: "It was an accepted fact among us that he was able when saturated with opium to persuade himself and delighted to persuade himself (the excitement of terror was a real delight to him) that he was dogged by dark and mysterious foes."[3] This cultivation of terror, innocent enough in itself, could occasionally border on paranoia, as is most clearly seen in his relations with Professor Wilson.

He described Wilson as "the only very intimate male friend"

(2:355) he had ever had. They had met as admirers of Wordsworth and soon developed a complementary friendship: De Quincey admired Wilson's energy and athleticism, and Wilson respected De Quincey's intellectual brilliance. In 1813, Wilson borrowed 200 pounds from De Quincey and returned the favor in 1819. In March 1820 he complained to De Quincey that he had been forced to borrow to pay off De Quincey's bills totaling £90 and found himself scarcely able to "avoid bankruptcy" (Japp, 2:41). De Quincey's financial dependence and Wilson's attempts to draw upon De Quincey's knowledge of philosophy to bolster his newly acquired position as professor of moral philosophy in the University of Edinburgh together may account for the remarkable hostility toward Wilson revealed in De Quincey's conversations with Richard Woodhouse in 1821. Wilson's character, he maintained, was "a compound of cruelty and meanness"; Wilson was furthermore jealous of men of superior talent and used his position as reviewer for *Blackwood's Edinburgh Magazine* to domineer over them. But the real reason for De Quincey's suspicion was his own insecurity: "We can never be thoroughly reconciled to a man to whom we have been too communicative and confidential and who has betrayed us." On 2 December he told John Taylor, editor of the *London Magazine*, that "he had a sort of feeling, or omen of anticipation, that possibly there was some being in the world who was fated to do him . . . a great and irreparable injury. . . . Many circumstances seemed to make it not improbable that Wilson might be that man."[4] Although his suspicions were short-lived and the balance of their friendship was soon restored, the episode shows how easy it was for De Quincey to attribute hostile intentions to others out of his own sense of vulnerability.

If he was sensitive to hostility (real or imagined) against himself, he was still more sensitive to insults directed against his wife. In 1824 he was the object of a vicious libel, probably written by the Irish scholar and wit Dr. William Maginn, in the *John Bull Magazine*. Recalling this libel in his "Reminiscences," De Quincey observed that "calamity—the degradation in the world's eye of every man who is fighting with pecuniary difficulties—exasperates, beyond all that can be imagined, a man's sensibility to insult. He is even apprehensive of insult . . . where none is intended" (3:173). It is not surprising that De Quincey was "convulsed with wrath" (3:176) when he read the accusation that Margaret

> was his servant-maid long before he married her, and had often made his bed before she ascended it. This is no blame to the woman: but who can bear to hear Quincy [sic] wondering at her stooping to servile offices, when it was to such that she was bred; and comparing a Westmoreland waiting-wench to the daughter of Agamemnon, the king of men."[5]

With enemies like this, De Quincey scarcely needed imaginary persecutors.

The years which culminated in his wife's death in 1837 were times of desperate struggle against financial ruin. Harassed by creditors, editors, and the printer's "devil," he was briefly imprisoned in 1832 and frequently sought sanctuary (sometimes with his wife) in Holyrood House.[6] Moreover, by 1838 he had come to see Margaret as a martyr to the cruelty of others, as a "lamb fallen amongst wolves" (12:163), and it is as such that she appears, in fictional disguise, as the heroine and victim of "The Household Wreck," in which he exorcised his lingering feelings of bitterness: "But my wrath still rises . . . against all the earthly instruments of this ruin; I am still at times as unresigned as ever to this tragedy, in so far as it was the work of human malice" (12:164). This "tragedy," in De Quincey's experience, centered upon his alienation from his "idol," William Wordsworth. The vicissitudes of their relationship are familiar enough, having been well documented by John E. Jordan.[7] What most pained De Quincey was the ostracism of his wife, who was of lowly social origin and had borne their first son, William, out of wedlock, by the Wordsworth ménage. Thus in a passage later omitted (in a significant act of self-censorship) from his portrait of Wordsworth, De Quincey makes the "grand confession" that, despite the "more than filial devotion" and "blind loyalty of homage" which he (and Wilson) had shown the poet, their rejection provoked "a rising emotion of hostility—nay, something, I fear, too nearly akin to vindictive hatred."[8]

In "The Household Wreck," written soon after his wife's death, these feelings of grief and resentment emerge, and the sense of vulnerability and impending catastrophe, like that in the Wilson episode of 1821, is strongly evoked. "I never ridded myself," writes De Quincey, "of an overmastering and brooding sense . . . of some great calamity travelling towards me, not perhaps immediately impending, perhaps even at a great distance, but . . . already in motion upon some remote line of approach" (12:168). It is the same feeling of unrelenting anxiety distended to the proportions of persecution mania that his friend Charles Lloyd experienced in his periodic fits of insanity. As De Quincey describes the case, "It seemed to him as if on some distant road he heard a dull trampling sound, and . . . he knew it, by a misgiving, to be the sound of some man . . . continually advancing slowly, continually threatening, or continually accusing him" (2:394). This account of Lloyd's "breathless anxiety" (2:395) conforms precisely to De Quincey's recurrent sense of a threat to his security—one at an indefinable distance yet in a state of perpetual imminence. It is what Pierre Leyris, French translator of the essay "On Murder," calls "l'imminence indéfiniment prolongée [d'une] menace multiforme, mais toujours appelant ou confirmant la même angoisse."[9]

The narrative of "The Household Wreck," like the later account of the Williams murders, reproduces exactly this sense of impotence in the face of mounting threat and accusation. As the tale unfolds with the inevitability of nightmare, we are reminded of Kafka by the fact (based on De Quincey's experience at Holyrood) that prisoners for debt and criminals are treated alike in "this huge caravanserai for the indifferent reception of crime, of misdemeanour, and of misfortune" (12:198). Above all, the dreams of the hero and heroine are pure Kafka:

> Every night I dreamed of our insecurity under a thousand forms. . . . Every night . . . I lay painfully and elaborately involved, by deep sense of wrong. . . . [A]t last all the solemnities of a great trial would shape themselves and fall into settled images. The audience was assembled, the judges were arrayed, the court was set. The prisoner was cited. Inquest was made, witnesses were called; and false witnesses came tumultuously to the bar. [12:228–29]

For De Quincey's heroine, as for Kafka's K., innocence confers no privilege when the individual is confronted by the monolithic, impersonal indifference of the Law.

Blind justice, which makes no distinction between the vicious murderer and the unfortunate debtor, brutalizes the innocent into a sense of criminal culpability. In both De Quincey and Kafka we find the imaginative expression of the inexorable Kierkegaardian formula: *"The individual in dread, not of becoming guilty, but of being regarded as guilty, becomes guilty."*[10] For most of his adult life De Quincey was rarely free of this dread of guilt stemming from "the sad anxieties, the degrading fears, the miserable dependencies of debt" (2:292). Hence his close identification with the outcast and the persecuted, developed in early childhood, was intensified by experiences which conferred on him the stigma of criminality. His sympathy with the murderer's cruelty thus grew as the logical antipole of his sympathy with the *victims* of cruelty.

This sympathetic ambivalence in which his interest is focused in turn on the pariah as victim—the "moral sublime" (1:127) —and on the pariah as criminal—the "*dark* sublime" (1:130)— lies at the heart of his obsession with murder. His first attempt to justify this obsession can be found in an editorial article in the *Westmoreland Gazette,* where he defended his policy of filling the paper with lurid reports of trials for rape and murder on the grounds that they have "a powerful and commanding interest" and teach the "uneducated classes" their "social duties" (13:95n.). He came closer to the real focus of his fascination in his essay "On the Knocking at the Gate in *Macbeth,*" which contains this germinal idea of the essay "On Murder": "At length, in 1812, Mr. Williams made his *début* on the stage of Ratcliffe Highway, and executed those unparalleled murders which have procured for him such a brilliant and undying reputation" (10: 390).

In the essay of 1823 De Quincey sought to explain the dramatic impact of the knocking at the gate in *Macbeth* by citing a comparable incident in the first Williams murders, one in which life had imitated art. The chief interest here lies in his explanation of this dramatic device as a means of manipulating our sympathy and then antipathy toward Macbeth. He observes that "murder, in ordinary cases, where the sympathy is wholly directed to the case of the murdered person, is an incident of coarse and vulgar horror." The tragedian must contrive to override this natural sympathy for the victim: "He must throw the interest on the murderer. Our sympathy must be with *him* (of course I mean a sympathy of comprehension, a sympathy by which we enter into his feelings, and are made to understand them, — not a sympathy of pity or approbation)" (10:391). This is achieved by embodying in the murderer "some great storm of passion, — jealousy, ambition, vengeance, hatred, — which will create a hell within him; and into this hell we are to look" (10:392). Human nature is eclipsed by a kind of demonic possession; the reader or audience participates in the feelings of the tragic hero by being transported "out of the region of human things." "The murderers and the murder," De Quincey elaborates, "must be insulated — cut off by an immeasurable gulf from the ordinary tide and succession of human affairs . . . ; time must be annihilated, relation to things without abolished; and all must pass self-withdrawn into a deep syncope and suspension of earthly passion." The dramatic intensity of this "awful parenthesis" is then heightened by the knocking at the gate, which serves to emphasize that "the reaction has commenced; the human has made its reflux upon the fiendish; the pulses of life are beginning to beat again" (10:393). At the same time our sympathy with the all-consuming passion of the murderer is dissipated and reverts to the victim of that passion.

It is significant that this remarkable essay in "psychological criticism"[11] should focus on this moment of cathartic release, which reverses the unbearable repression involved in our identification with the murderer, a sympathy which goes far beyond mere understanding. As we shall see, De Quincey's account of the Williams murders shows how well he had absorbed the lessons of Shakespeare's dramaturgical skill. In such a narrative, where the complex reactions of the reader can be carefully manipulated, the orchestration of sympathy and antipathy presents relatively few problems. But in the first two ironic sections of the essay "On Murder," which call for a willing participation in De Quincey's evident delight in bloodshed, the problem is more equivocal. To understand why, we must now examine the genre to which the essay belongs: Romantic irony.

II. Romantic Irony and the Ironic Double

Irony, undoubtedly, is indeed too moral to be truly artistic, as it is too cruel to be truly comic.

—VLADIMIR JANKÉLÉVITCH, *L'Ironie*

Irony may be defined as a form of indirect metacommunication in which there is a disjunction between the sign (the language of expression) and the signified (the idea which is communicated). This disjunction creates an ethical vacuum which must be filled in by the reader, and this, in turn, presupposes a reader sufficiently sensitive to nuances of style not to confuse surface statement with literal veracity. The ironist himself is aloof, detached. His method depends upon a suspension or inversion of all explicit ethical judgments. As Paul de Man expresses it, a "reflective disjunction" takes place in ironic consciousness which "transfers the self out of the empirical world into a world constituted out of, and in, language."[12]

A frequent reductio ad absurdam of the ironist's detachment is for him to disclaim authorship altogether. A common device is the "discovery" by an "editor" of a manuscript to which he has reactions of bewilderment, fascination, or horror. The end product is a fiction within a fiction, a multiple authorship which directly reflects the equivocal subject matter. In the novel the device is found in E. T. A. Hoffmann's *Die Elixiere des Teufels* (1815–16) and James Hogg's *The Private Memoirs and Confessions of a Justified Sinner* (1824). We find the same device in Carlyle's *Sartor Resartus* (1833–34) and in Kierkegaard's *Either/Or* (1843), whose pseudonymous "editor" discovers in a secret drawer the manuscripts of the aesthete A and his ethicist friend B.

All these works offer a structural parallel to De Quincey's first paper "On Murder," published in *Blackwood's* in 1827, which is prefaced by an "Advertisement of a Man Morbidly Virtuous" who has learned of the existence of a "Society of Connoisseurs in Murder."[13] Writes De Quincey:

They profess to be curious in homicide, amateurs and dilettanti in the various modes of carnage, and, in short, Murder-Fanciers. Every fresh atrocity of that class which the police annals of Europe bring up, they meet and criticise as they would a picture, statue, or other work of art. [13:9–10]

This man of morbid virtue proposes to expose their nefarious activities by publishing one of the "Monthly Lectures" read before the society, a text which of course fell "accidentally" into his hands. The fundamental principle of the lecture is soon established:

Everything in this world has two handles. Murder, for instance, may be laid hold of by its moral handle (as it generally is in the pulpit and at the Old Bailey), and *that*, I confess, is its weak side; or it may also be treated *aesthetically*, as the Germans call it—that is, in relation to good taste. [13:13][14]

This deceptively simple premise is the starting point for the development of De Quincey's irony. What follows takes the form of what Friedrich Schlegel called a "continuous self-parody"[15] which elaborates on the original theme in an ever-expanding act of reflection. The self-perpetuating momentum generated by ironic discourse is exploited by De Quincey to display all his resources of persiflage, humor, and erudition, mixing the high style of scholarly debate with a liberal scattering of slang terms from the vulgar idiom.

By his suspension of the ethical the ironist confers upon himself a freedom which brings the ethical and the aesthetic into collision. He employs, behind the mask of his incognito, an apparently objective method to assert a total subjectivity. For Kierkegaard, Romantic ironists such as Schlegel and Ludwig Tieck were guilty of abusing this freedom by claiming for themselves a freedom from all social and ethical restraints, based on a complete misapprehension of Fichtean philosophy. As he makes clear, their ethical relativism has disturbing repercussions: "But as the ironist has no continuity, so the most contrary feelings are allowed to displace each other. Now he is a god, now a grain of sand. His feelings are as accidental as the incarnations of the Brahma."[16] The accusation directly calls to mind De Quincey's dreams wherein "I was the idol; I was the priest; I was worshipped; I was sacrificed. I fled from the wrath of Brama through all the forests of Asia; Vishnu hated me; Seeva lay in wait for me" (3:442). For ironist and dreamer alike, a subjective freedom from the bonds of contingency will culminate in a disintegration of consciousness. Suspended in an ethical vacuum, he finds himself without a coherent sense of identity: he is persecutor and persecuted, idol and sacrifice.

That Schlegel had himself reached similar conclusions is shown in his ironically titled essay "Über die Unverständlichkeit" in which he displays his awareness of becoming entangled in a reflective and semantic labyrinth. After listing various kinds of irony (coarse, fine, extrafine, dramatic, and double), he expounds the "irony of irony":

> If one speaks of irony ironically without in the process being aware of having fallen into a far more noticeable irony; if one can't disentangle oneself from irony anymore, as seems to be happening in this essay on incomprehensibility; if irony turns into a mannerism and becomes, as it were, ironical about the author; . . . and if irony runs wild and can't be controlled any longer. . . .
>
> . . . what gods will rescue us from all these ironies? . . . Irony is something one simply cannot play games with.[17]

Irony, when pushed to this extreme, culminates in a dissociation of consciousness which borders on insanity. If irony becomes so all-consuming that it swallows up all other forms of reflection, it induces a fragmentation of identity. Irony is then involuted to such a degree that an impasse is reached like that which confronted Jonathan Swift when he remarked, "But my Heart is too heavy to continue this Irony longer."[18] Irony reaches this outer limit because an ironic consciousness sets in motion a displacement within the self. The exercise of irony begins as an attempt to reconcile this dividedness by treating the problem—in this case, De Quincey's obsession with murder—on the level of fiction.

Humor frequently involves an element of ironic "doubling" or *dédoublement*. In a darker sense the murderer John Williams was De Quincey's ironic double, a fictive alter ego through whom he could exact a vicarious, imaginary revenge on all those who had tormented him. "Revenge," he wrote, "is a luxury . . . so inebriating that possibly a man would be equally liable to madness from the perfect gratification of his vindictive hatred or its perfect defeat" (3:70). The phrase "vindictive hatred," it may be noted, is precisely that used about Wordsworth in the passage cited earlier. That De Quincey was, to some extent, aware of the connection between his "double" consciousness and his fascination with murder is revealed by this extraordinary remark: "If I had a *doppel-ganger* who went about personating me, . . . philosopher as I am I might . . . be so far carried away by jealousy as to attempt the crime of murder upon his carcase" (11:460–61). The remark is only half a joke. It shows, like the entire essay "On Murder," his difficulty in coming directly to terms with the cruel and vindictive impulses in his own nature, feelings which his writing both reveals and conceals, confesses and represses.

III. The Aesthetics of Murder

The development of ironic consciousness sketched above, expanding from the initial idea to a point of intoxication verging on madness, is reflected in the progressive execution of De Quincey's first two papers "On Murder" (1827 and 1839). Ironic effects which at first derive their impact from a masterly use of litotes are succeeded by a climactic scene of dizzy hyperbole. The discursive pleasantries of the first "Lecture" give way to the second paper's frenetic account of a dinner celebrating the Williams murders, where the atmosphere of mounting hilarity finally explodes in chaos and confusion.

The exposition of De Quincey's central idea depends initially on the consistency with which he maintains the parodistic parallel between murder and other branches of the fine arts. Thus "something more goes to the composition of a fine murder than two blockheads to kill and be killed, a knife, a purse, and a dark lane. Design, gentlemen, grouping, light and shade, poetry, sentiment, are now deemed indispensable to attempts of this nature" (13:12). With superb mock-seriousness he declares that "the final purpose of murder" as a fine art "is precisely the same as that of tragedy in Aristotle's account of it; viz. 'to cleanse the heart by means of pity and terror'" (13:47). Here he also implies a sly critique of the aesthetics of Edmund Burke, who argued that works of art can achieve the power of the sublime by provoking terror in their audience. A thorough mastery of the art of murder by the enlightened connoisseur, De Quincey maintains, will "humanise the heart": "A philosophic friend, well known for his philanthropy and general benignity, suggests that the subject chosen ought also to have a family of young children wholly dependent on his exertions, by way of deepening the pathos" (13:48). The ironic technique here shows the possibility of arriving at a precise reversal of empirical fact by the simple expedient of suspending the usual reaction of horror and unfolding the argument with inexorable logic. At the same time De Quincey's conception of murder as Aristotelian catharsis is, by a double irony, uncomfortably close to the truth.

His most telling effects are gained by the transplanting of familiar precepts of critical or aesthetic theory into a context where they are new and unfamiliar. One example is the remark about Williams: "Like Aeschylus or Milton in poetry, like Michael Angelo [sic] in painting, he has carried his art to a point of colossal sublimity, and, as Mr. Wordsworth observes, has in a manner 'created the taste by which he is to be enjoyed'" (13:12). (Again, there is a double irony in his quoting from Wordsworth here.) Other examples are the "cynical amateur" who dismisses the Thurtell murder as "'mere plagiarism'" (13:45), the observation that the seventeenth century's scarcity of good murders was "attributable to the want of enlightened patronage" (13:36), and then, in a fine use of litotes, the complaint about the "tendency in murder to excite and irritate the subject" (13:39).[19]

Most of the first paper is devoted to a history of murder, starting with Cain as "the father of the art" (13:17). The most entertaining section here is also the most spurious, as De Quincey attempts to establish a correlation between philosophy and murder, straining credulity to the limit:

Every philosopher of eminence for the last two centuries has either been murdered, or at the least been very near it,—insomuch that, if a man calls himself a philosopher and never had his life attempted, rest assured there is nothing in him; and against Locke's Philosophy in particular I think it an unanswerable objection (if we needed any) that, although he carried his throat about with him in this world for seventy-two years, no man ever condescended to cut it. [13:24]

De Quincey reserves his most refined malice for those philosophers most inimical to his own beliefs. Thus, by turning the philosophy of Thomas Hobbes around and using it against him, he scores another direct hit. Hobbes, he remarks,

was a fine subject for murder, . . . for I can prove that he had money, and (what was very funny) he had no right to make the least resistance; since, according to himself, irresistible power creates the very highest species of right, so that it is rebellion of the blackest dye to refuse to be murdered when a competent force appears to murder you. [13:28–29]

Some of De Quincey's *acharnement* here can be attributed to his frustrated hopes of becoming "the first founder of a true Philosophy" (Japp, 2:111). Instead of accepting that his incapacity for sustained concentration made such an ambition unlikely, he adopted an iconoclastic stance toward many past philosophers.

The second paper (1839) begins promisingly with an ironic protestation of the narrator's innocence. As proof of his unimpeachable morality he observes:

For, if once a man indulges himself in murder, very soon he comes to think little of robbing, and from robbing he comes next to drinking and Sabbath-breaking, and from that to incivility and procrastination. Once begin upon this downward path, you never know where you are to stop. Many a man dated his ruin from some murder or other that perhaps he thought little of at the time. [13:56][20]

Here the humor springs not from a complete suspension of the ethical, as before, but from a subversion of the accepted scale of values. Were it not for the inversion of cardinal and venial sins, we might be reading the language of one of the evangelical tracts of his mother's friend Hannah More. De Quincey's irony here is a trope of displacement by which the pious cant of evangelicalism is indirectly attacked. After this, however, his parodistic ingenuity fails him, and he falls back on the facetiousness typical of the *Blackwood's* idiom. But slang is no substitute for the agility of irony. The increasing strain and confusion of his account of the Williams dinner, with its series of toasts to the Old Man of the Mountains, the Sicarii, and the Thugs, are an accurate index of his difficulty in maintaining an ironic balance between the rival claims of the ethical and the aesthetic.

Something of this embarrassment is apparent in the self-defense which begins his "Postscript" of 1854. His purpose in the first two papers was, he argues,

> to graze the brink of horror, and of all that would in actual realisation be most repulsive. The very excess of the extravagance, in fact, by suggesting to the reader continually the mere aeriality of the entire speculation, furnishes the surest means of disenchanting him from the horror which might else gather from his feelings. [13:70–71]

He then cites the precedent of Swift's *A Modest Proposal* (1729), whose "own monstrosity was its excuse" (13:71). His own extravagance was simply a manifestation of "the spontaneous tendencies of the human mind when left to itself" (13:73). Yet this defense, plausible enough in its appeal to artistic license, probably masks real doubts about the validity of the ironic method, which can work effectively only where a temporal distance helps sustain the narrative on the level of fiction. Where the facts come too close to reality for comfort, as in the account which follows of the Williams and M'Kean murders, De Quincey is obliged to abandon the ironic method, exposing some of the more equivocal grounds for his obsession.

IV. Murderer and Victim

I am the wound and the knife!
I am the slap in the face and the cheek!

> *I am the limbs and the wheel,*
> *And the victim and the executioner!*
> —BAUDELAIRE, "L'Héautontimorouménos"

The narrative of the Williams murders in the "Postscript" of 1854 has proved to be one of the most influential portions of De Quincey's works. Several critics have sought to establish the link between its most dramatic episode (the "knocking at the gate" during the Marr murders) and the same device in Fyodor Dostoevsky's *Crime and Punishment* (1866), Robert Louis Stevenson's "Markheim" (1884), and D. H. Lawrence's fiction.[21] As I have pointed out, De Quincey derived his narrative method from his critical exegesis of the knocking at the gate in *Macbeth*. The murderer secures our sympathy by being isolated from the ordinary current of human affairs. He is consumed by an overwhelming passion—revenge. Being denied the heightening effects of stage drama, De Quincey exploits the devices of prose narrative: he slips from past to present tense, and he shifts in perspective from the murderer to his potential victim.

As Françoise Moreux notes, his method is diametrically opposed to that of Edgar Allan Poe, usually regarded as the father of crime literature: "Poe sees the murder from the exterior, and adopts the policeman's point of view. De Quincey, on the other hand, puts himself at the same time in the soul of the murderer and of his victims and makes the crime first and foremost a psychological drama."[22] Whereas Poe is primarily interested in the detective Dupin, De Quincey is more directly concerned with the drama of guilt and revenge in the murderer and the terror of his victims. The crime itself, not its outcome, which is known in advance, creates suspense.

A brief historical outline of the Williams murders will provide the background against which we can examine the main focus of De Quincey's obsession. At midnight on 7–8 December 1811 the Irish sailor John Williams murdered a shopkeeper named Marr, together with his wife and child, at his premises on Ratcliffe Highway in London's East End. Twelve nights later Williams struck again in the same vicinity, claiming the lives of an innkeeper, Williamson, his wife, and his housemaid. By good fortune some members of both households escaped – the Marrs' servant girl, then the Williamsons' granddaughter and an artisan lodger. Williams managed to flee the scenes of his crimes but was arrested on Christmas Eve, hanged himself in prison on Boxing Day, and on New Year's Eve was buried in bizarre circumstances, as described by Thomas Burke from contemporary newspaper reports. The murderer's body along with the tools of his trade (mallet and crowbar for knocking his victims senseless and ripping chisel for cutting their throats) were laid on an open cart and accompanied by a procession of ten thousand people to a crossroads. There, in a grave purposely dug extremely small, Williams's body was "crammed neck and heels,"[23] and a stake was driven through his heart, as if he were a vampire from Gothic romance.

Even in this bare outline of events it is remarkable how much De Quincey distorted or embroidered the facts of the case. His memory retained certain details with the minuteness of a man obsessed, yet there are innumerable distortions of verifiable facts, all of which underline the parallel between the Williams murders and the most fateful events in his own life. First, he altered the date from 1811 to 1812, the year in which Kate Wordsworth died and he became a "confirmed" opium-eater. Next he modified the name of the Marrs' servant girl from Margaret, his own wife's name, to Mary. He also changed the age of the Williamsons' granddaughter from fifteen to nine, the age at which his beloved sister Elizabeth had died. But the most remarkable distortions concern the appearance and manners of Williams himself. The newspapers described him as "of *fresh* complexion and with *sandy* hair," whereas De Quincey speaks of his "bloodless ghastly pallor" and "bright yellow" hair (13:77). Like the villain Adorni in De Quincey's Gothic tale *Klosterheim,* who "covered a temperament of terrific violence with a masque of Venetian dissimulation and the most icy reserve" (12:49), Williams is portrayed as masking his violent nature with the manners of a dandy: "It was in harmony with the general subtlety of his character, and his polished hatred of brutality, that by universal agreement his manners were distinguished for exquisite suavity; the tiger's heart was masked by the most insinuating and snaky refinement" (13:78). According to Burke, however, "landladies and other witnesses speak repeatedly of his fighting habits." By all accounts Williams was brutal and ill-tempered: his captain had observed prophetically that "next time Williams went ashore he would surely be hanged."[24]

So intent was De Quincey on presenting Williams as "the most aristocratic and fastidious of artists" (13:79) that he contradicted the facts of the case. If knocking victims senseless with a crowbar and then slitting their throats is not "brutality," then what is? The ambivalence of De Quincey's attitude is shown in his alternation between the conventional stance of moral condemnation and an avowed admiration for Williams's "artistic" qualities, with lingering traces of his former irony. Thus Williams is "one born of hell" (13:81), an "accursed hound" (13:93), a "ruffian" (13:94), and a "diabolic man" (13:100); then again he is a "solitary artist" who "walked in darkness" (13:75). This vacillation between undisguised fascination and pious horror reveals a deep-seated conflict in De Quincey. From a casual aside we learn that he was so entranced by Williams that he bought a plaster cast of the murderer's face in London. There can be no more graphic symbol of the way in which De Quincey's assumption of the "mask" of Williams gave him the *frisson* of unlimited sadistic power.

The most significant clue for deciphering his obsession lies in the name Williams itself. Although the actual cast of characters concerned in the Williams murders sounds like that of a Dickens novel (Jack Cahill, Susan Hoare, John Frederick Richter, Reuben Stroud, Sylvester Driscoll, Mrs. Vermillon), De Quincey ignored this colorful group and concentrated on the main protagonists, Marr, Williamson, and Williams. If we collect together, as in the schema below, the names of the "persecutory" figures described in the first section of this essay and the names of murderers and victims from the cases recounted by De Quincey, we find an obsessive punning on the name Williams too often repeated to be put down to mere coincidence.

Murderers: John Williams
             William Burke

Persecutors:	William Hare
	John Wilson
	William Wordsworth
	William Maginn
	William De Quincey (brother)
Victims:	Williamson
	William De Quincey (son)
	William Weare (see 13:44n.)
	William Begbie (see 13:49n.)
	William Coenen

This schema surely represents a classic case of the unconscious disclosing a repressed complex through punning variations on a single obsessive theme. The name John Williams embodies a whole network of relationships whose common denominator is the sense of persecution and the desire for revenge. The murderer is partly the self-projection of a divided psyche, partly the ruthless avenger that De Quincey wanted to be.

Turning back to the "Postscript" of 1854, we find De Quincey switching his focus from a portrait of Williams to the situation of the servant girl Mary, with whom we now identify as she returns to the Marrs' shop. Her employers and their child lie dead, and her anxiety grows into terror. De Quincey heightens the dramatic intensity by an expansion of time, a shift into the present tense, and the hallucinatory vividness of the sounds to which Mary listens:

On the stairs . . . was heard a creaking sound. Next was heard most distinctly a footfall: one, two, three, four, five stairs were slowly and distinctly descended. Then the dreadful footsteps were heard advancing along the little narrow passage to the door. . . . The very breathing can be heard of that dreadful being who has silenced all breathing except his own in the house. There is but a door between him and Mary. [13:88]

As in *Macbeth*, the tension thus created is snapped by Mary's violent knocking on the door.

Williams escapes, and we see through the eyes of a neighbor the scene he leaves behind: "The carnage of the night stretched out on the floor, and the narrow premises so floated with gore that it was hardly possible to escape the pollution of blood in picking out a path to the front-door" (13:90). Earlier De Quincey had prefaced the second series of murders by commenting on "the tremendous power which is laid open in a moment to any man who can reconcile himself to the abjuration of all conscientious restraints" (13:75). In contrast to his own dilatory temperament, there was for Williams no obstacle between his "cruel and vindictive impulses" (13:97) and their brutal fruition, no scruple dividing the will from the act: "To say was to do" (13:78). For De Quincey the mainspring of Williams's psychology was his sadistic enjoyment of crime, his "wolfish craving for bloodshed as a mode of unnatural luxury" (13:96) which, once indulged, cannot be satiated.

The motive for the second murders, then, is "murder for the sake of murder" (7:151), or, to put it another way, *l'art pour l'art*. As the fate of the Williamsons' granddaughter hangs in the balance, De Quincey pauses to observe:

To an epicure in murder such as Williams, it would be taking away the very sting of the enjoyment if the poor child should be suffered to drink of the bitter cup of death without fully apprehending the misery of the situation. . . . Murders of mere necessity Williams was obliged to hurry: but in a murder of pure voluptuousness, entirely disinterested, where no hostile witness was to be removed, no extra booty to be gained, and no revenge to be gratified, it is clear that to hurry would be altogether to ruin. If this child, therefore, is to be saved, it will be on pure aesthetical considerations. [13:110]

There is a darker form of irony here which derives from De Quincey's participation in the murderer's sadism, a relish revealed in the bizarre tone of hysterical gaiety that steals into the narrative. The murderer, for example, "is almost joyous; and, if any creature is still living in this house, . . . with that creature he would be happy, before cutting the creature's throat, to drink a glass of something" (13:107). Throughout the narrative De Quincey's attention to the minutiae of the case admittedly serves a dramatic purpose, but it also reveals the depth of his "morbid obsession."[25]

It is perhaps significant that De Quincey finally felt obliged to apologize for his narrative, saying that he could exercise "so little self-control" when composing the "Postscript" because of the "afflicting agitations . . . of my nervous malady." As a result, he wrote, "my record is far too diffuse" (13:124n.). Of all his writings, however, the "Postscript" least deserves the epithet "diffuse." The real failure in self-control was a failure of repression. Having discarded the ironic mask, he laid bare his oscillation between fascination with and repulsion at violent crime. If the conflict between the morality and aesthetics of murder reached a precarious balance in the irony of the first two papers, the "Postscript" leaves us with a sense of nausea like that induced by the Marquis de Sade's repetitive scenes of torture. And just as Sade's torturers express the rage of a prisoner in the Bastille, so De Quincey's murderers avenge a whole gallery of real and imaginary persecutors. For cruelties like theirs the essay can offer only a partial exorcism.

V. The Artist as Murderer

In November 1821, De Quincey attended a dinner at the residence of Charles Lamb. "Amongst the company, all literary men, sat a murderer, — such he proved to be upon later discoveries . . . , — and a murderer of a freezing class, cool, calculating, wholesale in his operations." The man in question was Thomas Griffiths Wainewright, aesthete and murderer, whose art criticism "Dogmas for Dilettanti," under the pseudonyms of "C. van Vinkbooms" and "Janus Weathercock," appeared in the same numbers of the *London Magazine* as De Quincey's *Confessions.* In retrospect De Quincey was fascinated, as he had been with Williams, by the contrast between "the murderer's dandy appearance and the terrific purposes with which he was always dallying" (5:246). Two years after De Quincey's first paper "On Murder," Wainewright began his career in murder by poisoning his uncle followed by his mother-in-law and sister-in-law. When reproached for this last crime, he is reported to have said: "'Yes; it was a dreadful thing to do, but she had very thick ankles.'"[26]

Had the chronology been different, De Quincey's inspiration in expounding the aesthetics of murder might have been attributed to his brief acquaintance with Wainewright. As it happens, however, a curiously symmetrical pattern warns us against dismissing the treatise "On Murder" as an insulated exercise in macabre humor. In 1823, De Quincey noted in his essay "On the Knocking at the Gate in *Macbeth*" that, in the Williams murders, life had imitated art. In 1827 his ironic paper "On Murder," inspired by the example of Williams, posited a correlation between art and murder. In 1829 the aesthete Wainewright confirmed De Quincey's prophetic insight by launching his career in homicide. Paradoxically, Wainewright's life was then reappropriated to the sphere of art as the subject of Oscar Wilde's essay "Pen, Pencil and Poison." This sequence of events reinforces Wilde's closing judgment that "there is no essential incongruity between crime and culture,"[27] a remark whose wider implications may be suggested briefly by way of conclusion.

I would propose that De Quincey's conception of the murderer as artist springs from an intuition of the artist as murderer. When Sade referred to "the moral crime which is committed by writing,"[28] what he meant was that the writer is free to commit crimes of the imagination for which, in actual life, he might feel nothing but revulsion. It is in this sense that we can interpret Jean-Paul Sartre's maxim that "a work of art is a dream of murder," a precept appropriately taken from a chapter of Sartre's study *Saint Genet* which bears the title "On the Fine Arts Considered as Murder."[29] De Quincey's own essay "On Murder" is an exercise in literary extremism, a macabre joke which nevertheless served a cathartic purpose for its author. It was John Wilson, aptly, who commented in 1829 that De Quincey's was "a nature of dreadful passions subdued by reason,"[30] and from this internal division De Quincey produced a pioneering study of the psychology of crime which retains a disturbing relevance for our times.

NOTES

1. As cited in Horace Ainsworth Eaton, *Thomas De Quincey: A Biography* (London: Oxford University Press, 1936), p. 301.

2. Thomas Carlyle, *Reminiscences*, ed. James Anthony Froude (New York: Harper, 1881), p. 127.
3. As cited in Eaton, *Thomas De Quincey*, p. 374n.
4. As cited in ibid., pp. 282-84.
5. As cited in Kenneth Forward, "'Libellous Attack' on De Quincey," *PMLA* 52 (1937): 249.
6. Regarding De Quincey's imprisonment in 1832 see Kenneth Forward, "De Quincey's 'Cessio Bonorum,'" *PMLA* 54 (1939): 511-25.
7. John E. Jordan, *De Quincey to Wordsworth: A Biography of a Relationship* (Berkeley and Los Angeles: University of California Press, 1962).
8. *Recollections of the Lakes and the Lake Poets*, ed. David Wright (Harmondsworth: Penguin, 1970), p. 145.
9. As cited in Georges Le Breton, "De Quincey et Wordsworth," *Mercure de France* 350 (1964): 649.
10. Søren Kierkegaard, *The Concept of Dread*, 2d ed., trans. Walter Lowrie (Princeton, N.J.: Princeton University Press, 1957), p. 67.
11. See John E. Jordan, *Thomas De Quincey, Literary Critic: His Method and Achievement* (Berkeley and Los Angeles: University of California Press, 1952), pp. 89-119; Sigmund K. Proctor, *Thomas De Quincey's Theory of Literature* (Ann Arbor: University of Michigan Press, 1943; New York: Octagon Books, 1966), pp. 123-47.
12. Paul de Man, "The Rhetoric of Temporality," in Charles S. Singleton, ed., *Interpretation: Theory and Practice* (Baltimore, Md.: Johns Hopkins University Press, 1969), p. 196.
13. Mario Praz has pointed out a parallel with the "Société des Amis du Crime" in Marquis de Sade, *Juliette, ou les prospérités du vice*, first published in 1796 (*The Romantic Agony*, 2d ed., trans. Angus Davidson [London: Oxford University Press, 1951], p. 179n.).
14. Cf. the following passage in an unpublished letter of 19 November 1823 from De Quincey to the publisher James A. Hessey: "The Murder is a good one, as you observe, and truly gratifying to every man of correct taste: yet it might have been better, if he would have thrown in a few improvements that I could have suggested.—I speak *aesthetically*, as the Germ. say, of course: morally, it is a damnable concern. You must allow me to look at these things in 2 lights. Perhaps it is yet too recent to be looked at by the aesthetic critic" (British Library, MS 37,215). I am grateful to Arden Reed for directing my attention to this unpublished letter.
15. Friedrich Schlegel, *Friedrich Schlegel's "Lucinde" and the Fragments*, trans. Peter Firchow (Minneapolis: University of Minnesota Press, 1971), p. 156.
16. Søren Kierkegaard, *The Concept of Irony*, trans. Lee M. Capel (New York: Harper and Row, 1966), p. 301.
17. Schlegel, *Friedrich Schlegel's "Lucinde" and the Fragments*, p. 267.
18. Jonathan Swift, "A Short View of the State of Ireland," in *Irish Tracts*,

1728-1733, vol. 12 of *The Prose Works of Jonathan Swift*, ed. Herbert Davis (Oxford: Basil Blackwell, 1955), p. 10.

19. The same tactic of applying aesthetic criteria to murder is found in George Orwell's essay of 1946 "Decline of the English Murder," in *The Collected Essays, Journalism, and Letters of George Orwell*, ed. Sonia Orwell and Ian Angus, 4 vols. (New York: Harcourt, Brace, and World, 1968), 4:100.

20. This passage should be compared to an inferior draft version, probably dated 1828, contained in an unpublished letter "To the Editor of Blackwood's Magazine." Extracts from this manuscript and another on "The Murder of William Coenen" were included by Richard H. Byrns in "Some Unpublished Works of De Quincey," *PMLA* 71 (1956): 990–1003.

21. See Albert Goldman, *The Mine and the Mint: Sources for the Writings of Thomas De Quincey* (Carbondale: Southern Illinois University Press, 1965), p. 148; Ann Gossman, "On the Knocking at the Gate in 'Markheim,'" *Nineteenth-Century Fiction* 17 (1962): 73–76; Philip Appleman, "D. H. Lawrence and the Intrusive Knock," *Modern Fiction Studies* 3 (1957): 328–32.

22. Françoise Moreux, *Thomas De Quincey: la vie, l'homme, l'oeuvre* (Paris: Presses universitaires de France, 1964), p. 289. See also Joseph J. Moldenhauer, "Murder as a Fine Art: Basic Connections between Poe's Aesthetics, Psychology, and Moral Vision," *PMLA* 83 (1968): 284–97.

23. Thomas Burke, "The Obsequies of Mr. Williams: New Light on De Quincey's Famous Tale of Murder," *Bookman* 68 (1928): 263.

24. Ibid., p. 259.

25. Praz, *The Romantic Agony*, p. 126.

26. *The Works of Oscar Wilde*, ed. G. F. Maine (London and Glasgow: Collins, 1948), p. 945. For further biographical details see Jonathan Curling, *Janus Weathercock: The Life of Thomas Griffiths Wainewright, 1794-1847* (London: Thomas Nelson, 1938).

27. Ibid., p. 947.

28. As cited in Albert Camus, *The Rebel: An Essay on Man in Revolt*, trans. Anthony Bower (New York: Alfred A. Knopf, 1956), p. 46.

29. Jean-Paul Sartre, *Saint Genet: Actor and Martyr*, trans. Bernard Frechtman (New York: George Braziller, 1963), p. 485.

30. As cited in Mary Gordon, *"Christopher North": A Memoir of John Wilson* (New York: W. J. Widdleton, 1863), p. 326.

9

De Quincey and the Dark Sublime: The Wordsworth-Coleridge Ethos

JOHN BEER

It is one mark of Romantic writers that they take up terms popular with their predecessors and give them a new significance, even a new intensity. So with "sublime" and "pathos." In the late eighteenth century these were still treated as aesthetic terms, enabling one to contemplate, detachedly, states of elevated spirit and indulged sentiment. The Romantic writers, by contrast, try to enter into such states, explore them, order their lives by them. Sublimity is now conceived in more ecstatic terms as a passing out of oneself into possession by a superior power; the sense of pathos, similarly, involves a full entering into the state of suffering rather than a sympathetic contemplation from outside.

It was for this reason perhaps that De Quincy was so attracted by Wordsworth, who seemed not simply to entertain his ideas but to live by them. Coleridge, with his interest in dreams, fantasies, and "facts of mind," was his more natural forerunner, but when De Quincey ran away from Manchester Grammar School in 1802, his first urge was to go to Grasmere; and when, having resisted it, he wrote to Wordsworth a year later, his feeling for Coleridge emerged only in the conclusion to his letter, where he said that he would not have written in such terms to any man on earth "except yourself and *one* other (a friend of your's)" (*D*, p. 188).

Coleridge was then running in his thoughts, nevertheless. When he thought of him, it was as "a compound of Ancient Marinere and Bath concert room traveller with bushy hair" (*D*, p. 192), and when he tried to figure a sublime character for himself, Coleridge's poem returned to his mind: "'What shall be my character?' ... wild—impetuous—*splendidly* sublime? dignified—melancholy—*gloomily* sublime? or shrouded in mystery—supernatural—like the 'ancient Mariner'—*awfully* sublime?" (*D*, p. 163). He had not, of course, met Coleridge at this time, and when he did, four years later, the decline had already set in: the ebullient preacher of earlier years had turned into a fixedly meditative man whose conversation—that conversation of which Carlyle was to say "no talk, in his century or in any other, could be more surprising"[1]—was now less like a spring than like a majestic river in flood.

Even if Coleridge's presence in the flesh did not live up to De Quincey's more romantic imaginings, it was still portentous; and as he came to know him better, he must have been stirred by an awareness of similarities in their early upbringing. In one of his essays he comments sympathetically on Coleridge's plight as a child who, having been the darling of his father and mother, was separated suddenly from both by the death of his father and precipitated into the wilderness of a London school (see *PW*, 2:7–59). He would presumably have seen further resemblances in the fact that Coleridge, like himself, had suffered the early death of a beloved sister. His description of Coleridge as a "flower unfolding its silken leaves only to suffer canker and blight" (*PW*, 2:57) may well reflect a sense of failed promise in his own career.

Some of De Quincey's twentieth-century critics have traced an existential weakness in him (as in Coleridge) which they have ascribed to the effects of his early circumstances. J. Hillis Miller has discussed the traumatic effects of his sister Elizabeth's death, while more recently A. S. Plumtree has argued that if we are looking for the root of De Quincey's anxieties we should look still further back to his relationship with his mother.[2] Drawing on the ideas of R. D. Laing, Plumtree claims that Mrs. De Quincey's frigidity toward her child, as described by De Quincey himself, led to an existential lack which can be traced throughout his career. But this important insight does not tell the whole story, as may be discovered from the description of the "morning parade," during which Mrs. De Quincey would inspect her children until they could be "pronounced to be in proper trim." Then, her son continues,

> we were dismissed, but with two ceremonies that to us were mysterious and allegorical—first, that our hair and faces were sprinkled with lavender-water and milk of roses; secondly, that we received a kiss on the forehead. The mystery in this last instance regarded the place; because we little silly people in the nursery never planted our kisses on foreheads, but sprang right at the lips. [Japp, 1:10]

This passage may fairly be read, as it is in Plumtree's study, with De Quincey's preceding description of her:

> Figure to yourself a woman of admirable manners, . . . distinguished by lady-like tranquillity and repose, and even by self-possession, but also freezing in excess. Austere she was in a degree which fitted her for the lady president of rebellious nunneries. Rigid in her exactions of duty from those around her, but also from herself; upright, sternly conscientious, munificent in her charities, pure-minded in so absolute a degree that you would have been tempted to call her "holy,"—she yet could not win hearts by the graciousness of her manner. That quality which shone so brightly in my sister, and the expansive love which distinguished both her and myself, we had from our father. [Japp, 1:9]

Although this lack at the center of De Quincey's childhood may well have been responsible for many of his personal problems, however, an interpretation of them in terms of an absolute frigidity misses some of the subtleties involved. For if there was a lack of direct physical cherishing and reassurance in Mrs. De Quincey's relationship to her son, there was, accompanying it, a deep and anxious concern made evident in the many letters and remonstrances which she addressed to him. Within the politics of the family the relationship of a parent toward a child may often encompass a power seeking that masks itself as love or that compensates for a personal lack by unreasonable demands for a loving self-denial. One very striking feature of Mrs. De Quincey's letters, by contrast, is the impression of a complete disinterestedness. Nor should we ignore the "lavender-water and milk of roses," which must have left an impression of sensuous love puzzlingly at variance with the detachment of the kisses themselves. De Quincey's problem seems to have been that his mother, despite her coldness, never gave him any reason to hate her, nor any indication that her motives were other than disinterested, while in subliminal ways (as through the perfume) she gave oblique indications of affection.

In trying to understand the situation, we perhaps need to read not only the writings of R. D. Laing but also the *Confessions* of Saint Augustine, seeing De Quincey among that select class of men who respond in the end to their mother's desire for their career—but not necessarily by the course that that mother had wished, since they need to reconcile the mother's (not ungratifying) sense that her child is a chosen human being with their instinctive sense that the life of self-abnegation proposed would also be suffocating. In Saint Augustine this task was realized largely by way of postponement: he did what his mother would have wished, but only after exploring other possibilities of human life. Romantic writers, caught up in a world less readily explicable in terms of orthodox Christianity, found it necessary to work the reconciliation without referring to traditional religious forms. Indeed, De Quincey's passage about the "religion" of opium, easily read as a whimsical flight of fancy, is susceptible of a more serious reading. "This is the doctrine of the true church on the subject of opium," he writes, "of which church I acknowledge myself to be the only member,— the alpha and omega" (*C*, p. 71).

In all this, it could be said, De Quincey was seizing upon one side of Coleridge's enterprise, his exploration of the dynamics of the human subconscious in the hope of discovering universal truths, and taking that to a logical conclusion, while neglecting the other side of what Coleridge had to say concerning the moral imperative in man. Against that side he had been anesthetized by his mother's very insistence; this did not mean, however, that it was dead.

If his mother's behavior and her demands upon him remained a dark enigma, there was no such problem about his feeling for his sister Elizabeth. Here he found a quickness of affection and a support for his emotions which were to be remembered as idyllic. Like others in that age he found in such a relationship of the heart qualities which seemed to him to transcend those of sexual attraction. Love of this order which might, it was hoped, provide a way forward for mankind generally seemed also to provide a permanent resource for the individual involved. A love, he wrote many years later, "which is *altogether* holy, like that between two children, is privileged to revisit by glimpses the silence and the darkness of declining years" (1:43). This love, we may suppose, also gave him the chief link with the poetry in *Lyrical Ballads,* in which, he said, he found " 'the ray of a new morning' " (2:139). For the note which runs through that volume, from the awakening of the Ancient Mariner as a spring of love gushes involuntarily from his heart to Wordsworth's Wye Valley meditations on the growth of the affections, is of a faith in the power of the human heart, as such, to illuminate one's sense of humanity at large.

This strain of thinking in early-nineteenth-century literature has been little attended to in recent criticism. It is now so generally believed that attempts to make the human heart central to a philosophy of life have had a disastrous effect on Western civilization that many critics have developed a blind spot in their sensibilities. It has become almost impossible for them to conceive that writers might once have taken such a conception seriously, studied the workings of their own hearts attentively, and tried strenuously to show what life could be like when lived under such preconceptions.

Even in the nineteenth century there were those who found such a way of life dangerously self-indulgent and even narcissistic, their opposition reproducing in a subtler form the eighteenth-century argument of the man of reason against the man of sensibility. At least, however, they could see what was at issue; others found the new development positively exciting. Shadworth H. Hodgson, writing about 1880, declared that a constellation of poets at the beginning of the century had made it what it was in literature and philosophy: "*They* are the fathers of that reaction, that reconstruction, that revival of the heart as the unifying principle against the dispersing, criticising *understanding*, as the end or *telos* of all action and of all thought."

Of the six poets he named, Hodgson singled out Wordsworth and Coleridge as paramount. He also designated two orders of individual minds: "... minds genial, flexible, and imaginative, on the one side, minds ungenial, inflexible, ratiocinative, on the other; minds that seem to be Nature's offspring and inherit her spontaneity, and minds that seem to be her handiwork and perform her tasks."[3] Hodgson's categories correspond to a division between "primary" and "secondary" consciousness which can be traced in the thinking of both Coleridge and Wordsworth.[4] It was poetically fitting, then, that he should see these two poets as exemplars of his first kind. De Quincey he also aligned with it but not in the first rank, his mind being illuminating rather than creative; like theirs, on the other hand, it could be classified as "subtle" rather than "acute." In pursuing his argument, Hodgson quoted a telling passage by De Quincey himself on the education of the sensibilities through their experience in life and literature:

When speaking of man in his intellectual capacity, the Scriptures speak not of the understanding, but of *"the understanding heart,"*— making the heart, *i.e.* the great *intuitive* (or non-discursive) organ, to be the interchangeable formula for man in his highest state of capacity for the infinite. [11:56]

This passage, posing as it does "the heart" as the organ through which man communes with infinite powers, is a central expression of this element in Romantic thought.

As in Wordsworth and Coleridge, moreover, De Quincey's cultivation of the heart's affections did not rest in detached observation of the behavior of other people; it led him naturally to emotional commitment, recalling the intensity of his affection for his sister many years before. Whether or not he knew of the deep love which Coleridge bore to Sara Hutchinson is hard to say—probably not. It is doubtful, equally, whether he fully grasped the intensity of William and Dorothy Wordsworth's love for each other. But De Quincey could hardly live in close association with these men as he did from 1808, or read their poetry, for that matter, without picking up some implications of a love of the heart which seemed to transcend sexual desire.

He had, after all, known a love of the same kind not only with Elizabeth but also with Ann, the young prostitute of Oxford Street whom he befriended. And it was fully in consonance with this cultivated feeling that he should have fallen in love, sexlessly, with Catherine, the Wordsworths' three-year-old daughter. When she died suddenly, he was overcome by a fierce "convulsion of grief" which is vividly described (2:443). Eventually, after he had indulged in his frenzy of loss for much of the summer, he was overtaken by a debilitating "nervous malady" (2:444) until finally an opposing process set in. The most remarkable feature of his recovery was that "all grief for little Kate Wordsworth, nay, all remembrance of her, had, with my malady, vanished from my mind. The traces of her innocent features were utterly washed away from my heart: she might have been dead for a thousand years, so entirely abolished was the last lingering image of her face or figure" (2:445).

De Quincey's grief over Catherine's death, and his subsequent need to work through the emotion again and again until the final cathartic illness cleared it from his mind, could hardly have been an isolated process, detachable from everything else that had been happening to him during these years. Rather we should ask whether the destruction of his love did not eliminate along with it many of the associations and emotional tensions that had been accumulating during his sojourn in Grasmere. If so, this would help explain the incompleteness of his later reminiscences, including his apparent inability to communicate what he had earlier found so overwhelming in the writing and ideas of Wordsworth and Coleridge.

The theory to be suggested, then, is that when De Quincey, sharing many of Coleridge's abilities and anxieties, was drawn to Wordsworth by a "deep deep magnet" (3:283), it was for similar reasons. After the initial excitement of speculations which pointed toward the human unconscious as an unknown territory ripe for new discoveries, a young man might easily find instead that he was afloat on an unknown sea where bearings were easily lost. In a situation of that kind strength such as Wordsworth's provided a welcome resource, exhibiting the possibility of existence in what Coleridge was to call "the dread watch-tower of man's absolute self."[5] But if that strength had been no more than a solidity, it would have been little more than another version of the dead eighteenth-century formulations against which they were rebelling. The impressive feature of Wordsworth's poetry was its ability to suggest further layers of meaning: intimations of dark fear and indications of a mysterious love, often most readily to be traced when a suffering human being experienced initiation into the infinite—"Suffering is permanent, obscure and dark, / And shares the nature of infinity."[6] Hearing Wordsworth read the drama in which those lines first appeared, Coleridge had been impressed by its "*profound* touches of the human heart,"[7] just as in hearing "Guilt and Sorrow" he had been struck by the "union of deep feeling with profound thought."[8] De Quincey evidently sensed the same qualities in Wordsworth.

Wordsworth's poetry appealed to elements in the psyche that had been excited, but not previously stirred so deeply, by the new ways of thought that were abroad; it also seemed to be calling for personal commitment. If it was true that "we have all of us one human heart" ("The Old Cumberland Beggar," line 153), the cause of humanity could surely be advanced both by behaving toward all human beings as equals and by cultivating intense personal relationships. Coleridge, falling in love with Sara Hutchinson, or De Quincey, falling in love with Kate Wordsworth, could feel that they were fulfilling the Wordsworthian program as much as Wordsworth himself in the intensity of his affection for Dorothy. With the withdrawal of Sara and the death of Kate they were left "like men betrayed"—and without guidance from Wordsworth himself, whose marriage had represented a move toward more conventional forms of human relationship. So Wordsworth remained an enigma: even if he no longer spoke or acted like a prophet, something in the man still conveyed intimations of a dark sublime which could communicate with more positive potencies in the human heart.

While Wordsworth was always wary of approaching the hiding places of his power, Coleridge and De Quincey were more ready to attempt a direct assault—even to the extent of resorting to drugs. Although opium was obviously a major point of contact between the two writers, it is not altogether clear how far De Quincey grasped the extent of Coleridge's addiction at the time when he first knew him. De Quincey's contention that opium led to a failure of the creative principle in his later work is reminiscent of Coleridge's account of a similar state of mind in "Dejection," but although the poem fascinated De Quincey as a representation of "extinguished power" (2:205), he did not, openly at least, connect it with the effects of the drug. His slow reenactment of Coleridge's career during the rest of his life may have been largely unconscious. Certainly his enslavement to opium became fearful only when the addiction was very advanced; he was then forced, like Coleridge again, into desperate straits to free himself. And just as Coleridge found new ways forward but never ceased to be haunted by what had happened to him in earlier years, so De Quincey continued to be fascinated by the implications of his opium experiences. While he could not but acknowledge the harm he had received, he continued to be drawn back to the revelatory power of the same experiences which had seemed to unlock the secrets of his own being.

The question is complicated by later bitterness, yet there seems to be a certain ambiguity and even confusion in the attitudes of both men toward their addiction. They could concentrate on either the "pains" or the "pleasures" of opium, but it was hard to hold both in the mind simultaneously. In view of this it is less surprising that De Quincey's career sometimes parallels his predecessor's so closely, features which characterized one phase in Coleridge's taking a more extended form in De Quincey's. Writing to a friend in 1810, Dorothy Wordsworth had spoken of Coleridge's irregular habits: "He lies in bed, always till after 12 o'clock, sometimes much later; and never walks out—Even the finest spring day does not tempt him to seek the fresh air; and this beautiful valley seems a blank to him." She also expressed her fear that if he were under their roof he would be "as much the slave of stimulants as ever" and asserted that "his whole time and thoughts, (except when he is reading and he reads a great deal), are employed in deceiving himself, and seeking to deceive others."⁹ De Quincey, likewise, came to spend more and more time studying far into the night and sleeping much of the day. When he speaks of himself as sitting with a decanter of laudanum and a volume of German metaphysics (3:410), the resemblance to Coleridge is particularly striking. Nor is this simply a matter of drugs. Whether or not we are to see him as under Coleridge's influence, De Quincey's intellectual dilemma was similar: he too wanted to investigate and establish the correspondence of the inner mind with the inwardness of physical nature; he too found himself torn between the intellectual stringency of Kant's logic and the subtler revelations afforded by opium.

Although the two men drifted apart after Catherine's death, certain ideas which he shared with Coleridge continued to haunt De Quincey, particularly those that helped him interpret his sometimes nightmarish experiences under opium. They also enabled him to understand madness better. He claimed, indeed, that insanity was normally based on a disorder of the liver, recalling that, as opium came to affect his own, "the whole living principle of the intellectual motions began to lose its elasticity, and, as it were, to petrify." He thus "began to comprehend the tendency of madness to eddy about one idea; and the loss of power to abstract . . . or to exercise many other intellectual acts, was in due proportion to the degree in which the biliary system seemed to suffer" (10:447). This description of the effects where the "living principle" is negated probably owes something to Coleridge, who also speaks of the tendency of madness to "eddy" round a single obsession.[10] It also links itself with the whole section concerning "The Pains of Opium" in the *Confessions,* where the title itself echoes that of Coleridge's poem "The Pains of Sleep" (the imagery of which clearly belongs to his opium-taking). On the other hand, as Alethea Hayter has pointed out,[11] the actual obsessions which fixed his mind during his opium addiction belonged to a period before he began taking the drug in any large measure: the period of his wanderings in Wales and London during the years 1802–1803, when he befriended Ann of Oxford Street and came to know something of the abyss of human misery. Just as images from his school days at Christ's Hospital haunted Coleridge's dreams, so images that visited De Quincey during his opium dreams (crowds of faces, the sacrificial girl child) dated from those years.[12]

The fact that his experiences of misery preceded his opium addiction is important, since it helps explain an element in his thought which we shall encounter again. Great as was his relief at having escaped from his Manchester predicament, De Quincey evidently felt that his time in Wales and London was one of the most "real" periods of his life. Among other things the sense of heightened realism may well account for his obsession with the "pariah" state in humanity, ranging from individuals whom he had known, such as Ann of Oxford Street and the daughters of Samuel Hall (1:101–108), to oppressed races such as the gypsies and the Jews (1:100–101), and including Oedipus and Antigone (6:149–51; 10:365). Through such references runs a supposition that pariahs, of which he counted himself one, are admitted to a knowledge which is not available to ordinary, comfortably placed human beings. It is a recurrent theme in his writings, connected with that of the Dark Interpreter in *Suspiria de Profundis*. There is also a link with the "Introductory Notice" to that work:

The machinery for dreaming planted in the human brain was not planted for nothing. That faculty, in alliance with the mystery of darkness, is the one great tube through which man communicates with the shadowy. And the dreaming organ, in connection with the heart, the eye and the ear, compose the magnificent apparatus which forces the infinite into the chambers of a human brain, and throws dark reflections from eternities below all life upon the mirrors of the sleeping mind. [*SP*, p. 149]

Coleridge, similarly, could write at the crisis of his opium-taking: "O infinite in the depth of darkness, an infinite craving, an infinite capacity of pain and weaknesses," and "O I have had a new world opened to me, in the infinity of my own Spirit!"[13]

So far as the original experiences were expressed, however, it was rather to Wordsworth that De Quincey turned as one who more deeply understood the human issues involved. I have already quoted the lines "Suffering is permanent, obscure and dark, / And shares the nature of infinity." When Wordsworth repeated them in his epigraph to *The White Doe of Rylstone*, he added others, beginning, "Yet through that darkness (infinite though it seem / And irremoveable) gracious openings lie," which link his sentiments still more closely with those of the younger writer. De Quincey could find in Wordsworth a figure whose philosophy and poetry provided a humane framework for his own thinking. Where Coleridge's speculations offered keys to the unlocking of the positive subliminal powers, Wordsworth seemed to understand more fully the connection between these powers and states of suffering and love.

The extent of De Quincey's devotion to Wordsworth throughout his career is manifested not merely by the testimony cited earlier but by the number of occasions on which he introduces—often, it seems, unconsciously—Wordsworthian phrases into his writing. Such usages often suggest not just "influence" in the simple sense but shared preoccupations behind the phrase in question. A good example may be found by putting together two passages in which a similar run of phraseology occurs. In describing his feelings after Ann of Oxford Street disappeared, De Quincey remembers his wish that

the benediction of a heart oppressed with gratitude... might have power given it from above to chase, to haunt, to waylay, to pursue thee into the central darkness of a London brothel, or (if it were possible) even into the darkness of the grave, there to awaken thee with an authentic message of peace and forgiveness, and of final reconciliation. [3:362]

The words "to chase, to haunt, to waylay" look strangely at odds with the rest of the passage, suggesting as they do a language of sexual pursuit. A similar usage occurs in a passage concerning Coleridge's self-withdrawal from nature, which De Quincey interprets as having been possibly due to the painfulness now associated with scenes that had formerly surrounded experiences of strong emotion:

Phantoms of lost power, sudden intuitions, and shadowy restorations of forgotten feelings, sometimes dim and perplexing, sometimes by bright but furtive glimpses, sometimes by a full and steady revelation, overcharged with light—throw us back in a moment upon scenes and remembrances that we have left full thirty years behind us. In solitude, and chiefly in the solitudes of nature, and, above all, amongst the great and *enduring* features of nature, such as mountains, and quiet dells, and the lawny recesses of forests, and the silent shores of lakes, features with which (as being themselves less liable to change) our feelings have a more abiding association—under these circumstances it is that such evanescent hauntings of our past and forgotten selves are most apt to startle and to waylay us. [2:204-205]

That "startle" and "waylay" at the end, taken with the "to chase, to haunt, to waylay" of the other passage, suggest that De Quincey is in fact haunted by the opening stanza of Wordsworth's "She Was a Phantom of Delight":

> She was a Phantom of delight
> When first she gleamed upon my sight;
> A lovely Apparition, sent
> To be a moment's ornament;
> Her eyes as stars of Twilight fair;
> Like Twilight's, too, her dusky hair;
> But all things else about her drawn
> From May-time and the cheerful Dawn;
> A dancing Shape, an Image gay,
> To haunt, to startle, and way-lay.

If the phrases come originally from Wordsworth, this changes their effect in the passage about Ann while also suggesting something about the underlying complex of thought involved. The very fact that De Quincey takes words which for Wordsworth characterized his wife when he first knew her and uses them to describe *himself* in pursuit of Ann suggests that he sees the imagery as transcending female beauty, being emblematic rather of relationship or a love of the heart between human beings. For the same reason he believed that he could awaken Ann, if ever he found her, with a "message of peace and forgiveness, and of final reconciliation." The second use of the words, on the other hand, moves back from this more affirmative belief (which was, after all, cheated as he failed to rediscover Ann) to psychological wonderment over the phenomenon involved in the revival of feelings over a space of many years. The implication of this reference and many others is that De Quincey found Wordsworth's poetry distinguished not only by an unusual feeling for humanity but also by its ability to describe certain unusual states of nature and of the human spirit in a way that suggested the existence of a correspondence between them. It was in Wordsworth's transmutations of Coleridge's ideas, however, that De Quincey's most acute focus of interest lay. Just as Hazlitt, meeting Coleridge when he was still something of a radical, creamed his philosophy of its enthusiasm for the heart's imagination and developed that to a higher intensity in the service of the liberal cause, so De Quincey's more conservative temperament found itself drawn to Wordsworth's balancing of the visionary against the mundane.

We have already seen his enthusiasm for "She Was a Phantom of Delight," in which Wordsworth celebrates an equivalent balance of virtues in his wife; the same qualities are expressed more fully, and in more Coleridgean terms, in De Quincey's fictional picture of an ideal wife:

This double character, one aspect of which looks towards her husband and one to her children, sits most gracefully upon many a young wife whose heart is pure and innocent; and the collision between the two separate parts, imposed by duty on the one hand, by extreme youth on the other,—the one telling her that she is a responsible head of a family and the depositary of her husband's honour in its tenderest and most vital interests; the other telling her, through the liveliest language of animal sensibility and through the very pulses of her blood, that she is herself a child,—this collision gives an inexpressible charm to the whole demeanour of many a young married woman, making her other fascinations more touching to her husband and deepening the admiration she excites; and the more so, as it is a collision which cannot exist except among the very innocent. [12:173–74]

This is not just a reconciliation of opposites. A Coleridgean combination of the organic and the vital[14] is drawn into service on *both* sides of the balance: it is there in the responsible self that looks after her husband's honor "in its tenderest and most vital interests"; it is there, equally, in the "liveliest language of animal sensibility" and the "very pulses of her blood." On both sides sensibility and vitality are set in apposition as equal participants in the twin qualities that constitute her charm.

De Quincey pursued the Coleridgean-Wordsworthian idea still deeper, seeing at the heart of that same childish sensibility and pulsing vitality a link with the subliminal source of vision described in the "Immortality" ode, where the light of the sun becomes the direct image of a sense of immortality that is " 'not to be put by' " (12:208–209). A similar identification of the immanent powers of childhood with those of the sun underlay his deep love for Kate Wordsworth, so that her death seemed all the more a violation of his deepest beliefs (2:443). A more abstract version of the same imagery is used in connection with the Wordsworths themselves. Of Dorothy he wrote, "The pulses of light are not more quick or more inevitable in their flow and undulation, than were the answering and echoing movements of her sympathizing attention" (2:239). And of Wordsworth himself De Quincey wrote that "he did not cease for years to wear something of the glory and the *aureola* which, in Popish legends, invests the head of superhuman beings" (2:304). The one other place where he uses this image of an "aureola" is in his description of his own sister, "around whose ample brow, as often as thy sweet countenance rises upon the darkness, I fancy a *tiara* of light or a gleaming *aureola* in token of thy premature intellectual grandeur" (1:35). Wordsworth had, it seems, become for him a supreme guarantor of the world into which he felt himself to have been initiated by his early relationship with Elizabeth.

This light imagery, though not common in De Quincey's writings, runs deep where it occurs. It expresses, essentially, his idea of God:

God must not proceed by steps and the fragmentary knowledge of accretion.... God must *see*; he must *intuit*, so to speak; and all truth must reach him simultaneously, first and last, without succession of time or partition of acts; just as light, before that theory had been refuted by the Satellites of Jupiter, was held not to be propagated in time, but to be here and there at one and the same indivisible instant. [10:103]

The old theory of light, he is implying, was closer to the true conception of God than the one now enforced by experimental observation. And this concept of God in terms of a supernatural light-filled vision, seeing all in one, he elsewhere holds to be a property of human consciousness in certain extreme states—notably in the moment of death. De Quincey was particularly impressed by the account of an old lady of what had happened to her when she almost drowned at the age of nine:

At a certain stage of this descent, a blow seemed to strike her; phosphoric radiance sprang forth from her eyeballs; and immediately a mighty theatre expanded within her brain. In a moment, in the twinkling of an eye, every act, every design of her past life, lived again, arraying themselves not as a succession, but as parts of a coexistence.... Her consciousness became omnipresent at one moment to every feature in the infinite review. [13:347-48]

The same story is told in a note to *Confessions of an English Opium-Eater*, where it is further asserted that "she had a faculty developed as suddenly for comprehending the whole and every part" (3:435), and it is there associated with a similar quality in certain of his experiences under opium. That powerful experiences under the influence of drugs do sometimes take such a form is supported by other testimony, but it was the evidence concerning equivalent experiences in moments of extremity given by people who did not resort to drugs that was the more welcome to De Quincey, since it suggested that they had a vitality independent of chemical accident. Wordsworth's "Immortality" ode, coming from a man who was not addicted to drugs, had a similar importance for him.

But why, in that case, did De Quincey not write more openly about Wordsworth's visionary powers, instead of leaving it to hover in echoes from the poetry? Part of the answer, we have suggested, may well have lain in the death of his love for the tragic Catherine Wordsworth, which no doubt carried in its passing some of the visionary light that had surrounded all the Wordsworths. But we have also observed a strange ambiguity in Wordsworth himself, a failure to live up to the vision of his own poetry, which De Quincey found disturbing. In a note to his essay on "Walking Stewart" he discusses Wordsworth's pride and his unwillingness to discuss certain subjects (including the beauties of nature!) outside his immediate family circle, or even to allow an acquaintance to indulge in self-justifying argument (3:198)—behavior which must have been bewildering to someone who had first been drawn to Wordsworth by the humility and general feeling for humanity displayed in the *Lyrical Ballads*. And his puzzlement was undoubtedly brought to a head by the Wordsworths' opposition to his relationship with Margaret Simpson, whom they considered beneath him.[15] That a man who had written so eloquently on the universality of the human heart should object when De Quincey put that principle into practice must have been not only socially wounding but also intellectually bewildering.

It is not difficult to see the Wordsworths' attitude in a less damaging light. De Quincey's marriage followed a period of growing depression and his first addiction to opium. That in turn followed the crisis of Kate Wordsworth's death and his response to it. We may suppose that his attachment to the Wordsworths had already been affected by that death, while his opium addiction would have roused in them memories of Coleridge's fate not long before. Their concern at what seemed to them an improvident marriage was, on that reading of the matter, not merely a result of snobbery but the culmination of a growing disquiet associated with his condition after Kate's death.

By the time that this happened, however, De Quincey had invested too much emotion in the Wordsworthian position, as he conceived it, to find an alternative easily. Just as Wordsworth himself had been stranded intellectually when the French Revolution showed its harsh side, so now De Quincey found himself isolated and forced to find a new basis for his life. There was no firm ground in the past to which he could return; emotionally his career had been a steady development along lines to which Wordsworth and Coleridge beckoned him. He might find ways of existing outside that development, but in doing so he would be forced to reconstruct himself.

We see something of the underlying problem involved in a passage about opium to which John E. Jordan has drawn attention. When the opium-eater is in "the divinest state incident to his enjoyment," De Quincey says, "crowds become an oppression to him; music, even, too sensual and gross. He naturally seeks solitude and silence, as indispensable conditions of those trances, or profoundest reveries, which are the crown and consummation of what opium can do for human nature" (3:394). As Jordan points out, the essential Wordsworthian nature is here transposed into a fitting background for the drug taker.[16] But such a proposition would have been offensive to Wordsworth, whose devotion to solitude and silence and receptiveness to profound reveries was always accompanied by an element of strenuousness, was always deliberately undrugged. Yet, while De Quincey's growing addiction would have been a matter of anxiety for Wordsworth, particularly after the melancholy example of Coleridge, De Quincey in his turn must have viewed Wordsworth's unwillingness to go beyond a certain point in his inner explorations of the psyche as a timidity—and even as a betrayal of his own insights.

De Quincey's sense of Wordsworth as a great visionary was by no means simple or straightforward, moreover. Just as it followed from the Gothic tradition that there was something terrible in the nature of any true visionary (we remember again Coleridge's Ancient Mariner or his figure of genius in "Kubla Khan"), so De Quincey sensed a darker side to Wordsworth, as can be seen in his comment on one occasion that Wordsworth had a "natural resemblance to Mrs. Ratcliffe's [sic] Schedoni and other assassins roaming through prose and verse" (8:291). The reference is made lightly enough yet suggests a serious comparison at some level, perhaps also referring to a relevant passage in *The Italian* where Schedoni is described:

There was something in his physiognomy extremely singular, and that can not easily be defined. It bore the traces of many passions, which seemed to have fixed the features they no longer animated. An habitual gloom and severity prevailed over the deep lines of his countenance; and his eyes were so piercing that they seemed to penetrate, at a single glance, into the hearts of men, and to read their secret thoughts; few persons could support their scrutiny, or even endure to meet them twice.[17]

Mrs. Radcliffe's comment on the play of passions and severity in Schedoni's face is reminiscent of descriptions of Wordsworth, whose eyes Leigh Hunt once described as "like fires, half burning, half smouldering, with a sort of acrid fixture of regard."[18] The Schedoni description also suggests the image of Cain, popular at the time, whose ravaged features bore witness to misapplied energies but who still carried with him the dark memory of a lost paradise.[19] The "mysterious character" (*D*, p. 192) who haunted De Quincey's youthful imagination no doubt owed a good deal to such Gothic characters.

If De Quincey's glancing reference to Schedoni hints at an ambiguity in his attitudes to Wordsworth, it also suggests that the fascination which he continued to find in him was associated with a sense that his upright and kindly philosophy was backed by more mysterious subliminal powers. He would have found ample food for such speculation in *The Prelude*, in which Wordsworth's belief that his growing love for humankind had been assisted both by the growth of a powerful organic sensibility and by the passionate experiences of his childhood was the major theme.

De Quincey was one of the few persons allowed to read *The Prelude* during Wordsworth's lifetime. That he could remember lines from it many years later (see, for example, 1:29, 12:228) without, apparently, having a manuscript from which to refresh his memory is evidence of the profound impression it made. De Quincey also had unusual knowledge of Wordsworth's own interpretation of the experiences which he termed "spots of time." He describes how on one occasion when they had walked up to Dunmail Raise, hoping to intercept news of the Peninsular War, Wordsworth, who had been putting his ear Indian-fashion to the ground in the hope of hearing distant wheels, rose from the effort and simultaneously caught sight of a bright star. Seen at that moment of relaxation, the star according to Wordsworth " 'penetrated my capacity of apprehension with a pathos and a sense of the infinite, that would not have arrested me under other circumstances.' " "Pathos and a sense of the infinite": these were twin factors of the typical Wordsworthian experience in which an expansion of spirit was closely associated with a response in the depths of the heart. Wordsworth went on to illustrate the phenomenon in "There Was a Boy," describing his boyhood experience of blowing "mimic hootings" to the owls by Windermere and noting (lines 19–22) how sometimes

> a gentle shock of mild surprise
> Has carried far into his heart the voice
> Of mountain-torrents; or the visible scene
> Would enter unawares into his mind.

De Quincey, who is quoting the passage from memory, foreshortens it: in his account it is the "complex scenery" which is "'carried *far* into his heart.'" Although this throws an interesting light on the processes of his own memory, it does not greatly affect his main point: "This very expression, 'far,' by which space and its infinities are attributed to the human heart, and to its capacities of re-echoing the sublimities of nature, has always struck me as with a flash of sublime revelation."[20] Whether conceived audibly or visually, the impressive point for De Quincey was that the word "far" linked the sublime of nature to the pathos of the heart.

Wordsworth's ability to make such a collocation evidently impressed Coleridge equally. Of the same lines he remarked that if he had met them running wild in the deserts of Arabia he would have instantly screamed out "Wordsworth!"[21] Yet the very unusualness of the collocation meant that there was no ready public mode for its expression. To combine an esoteric sense of the sublime with the private feelings of the heart was to create an area of possible embarrassment. Yet the compulsiveness of the idea, once engaged in, also made it difficult for the writer to extricate himself easily. Indeed, in a converse of "spot of time" revelation, he might find himself drawn into an involuted private vortex where the workings of the heart's affections were exacerbated into intensity by reinforcement from unconscious primary powers. Coleridge and Sara Hutchinson, Hazlitt and Sarah Walker, Keats and Fanny Brawne—most intensely and most impossibly, De Quincey and Kate Wordsworth: in each case we see an intense cultivation of the heart's affections enfolding the writer into a nympholepsy from which he seems powerless to escape except by way of trauma or death. For Coleridge the relationship was too private to be discussed in public; Hazlitt's account was published anonymously; Keats's was left in private letters. De Quincey's story was perhaps the most openly told, yet his impulses to reveal were still tangled with a strange reticence about his other Grasmere experiences, a reticence which may involve genuine amnesia but seems also to reflect an uncertainty about their true significance. Even the seminal account of Wordsworth and the star was removed when he reprinted his reminiscences in book form.

In the late twentieth century it remains hard to grasp the traumatic power of such experiences, since inability to regard the heart as a center of emotional life blocks apprehension of the complex as a whole. At the time, however, the effect was to leave the writer in a labyrinth from which it was difficult to find a way out. Marriage might provide a possible solution, as for Wordsworth, whose relationship with Dorothy had sometimes been unusually intense. De Quincey found a similar mediating affection in a wife whose benignity matched Mary Wordsworth's. Yet in his case the resolution was less complete. He was disappointed, even offended, at Wordsworth's failure to extend the insights of *The Prelude* into his later poetry, or, for that matter, into his dealings with other people, and remained fascinated by the balance of forces which Wordsworth's more profound poetry had earlier held in tension.

Wordsworth's final position enshrined wisdom of a different kind from De Quincey's. Unwilling to stimulate or revive his visionary power by resort to drugs of any kind, he had opted instead for a secure domestic happiness and a mediating role in his society, even if this involved the decline of his more directly passionate powers. One reason, no doubt, was his fear of the betrayals which the passions might bring about, another the perception that his visionary powers had always been best brought into play, as at Dunmail Raise, through a process of intermitted energy or attention. This made him unwilling to compromise with less strenuous methods of invocation. De Quincey eventually came to a similar position, but only many years later. It was not until his third opium crisis, in 1844, in fact, that he discovered a counterbalance to opium and a means of successful withdrawal by way of almost preternatural bouts of energy. Then he actually set himself an exercise range of forty-four yards in a circuit; treading it constantly, he was able in ninety days to cover a thousand miles (Page 1:326-27).

De Quincey could not achieve a comprehensive relationship between energy and vision, however. Like Coleridge, he believed that vision might be reached directly if only one could discover the right means or stimulus. Yet both men evidently remained fascinated by Wordsworth's recordings of visionary experiences which combined the resources of energy and pathos, supervening most characteristically in moments of transition between energy and peace. Wordsworth's most directly communicable experiences, moreover, seemed to take place at night, rather as if the nearest approach to total pathos or sublimity lay in negative experience—a dark pathos, a dark sublime. We may think of Wordsworth's nighttime meeting with the discharged soldier, when the mildness of the man's utterance helped enforce a sense of human interdependence, or the revelation on Snowdon, when his sudden awareness of the mild light of the moon was accompanied by sounds of hollow roaring, counterpointing the simple light by a suggestion of infinite energies.[22] These emblems of a dark sublime were, in one interpretation, negative images of a sunlike harmonious vision linking all human beings.

The sense of a possible hidden sublime unavailable to reason but answering to the human sense of grandeur and the numinous continued to haunt De Quincey—the more so, one suspects, because it provided a possible answer to the emotional lack to be traced in current religious thinking. J. Hillis Miller has claimed him as his first great example of a man confronting the disappearance of God in the nineteenth century.[23] For him the crucial event in De Quincey's development was the early loss of his sister and, with her, the one positive and sustaining relationship with another human being that De Quincey had known. This, his one spiritual value to put in the place of a disappearing God, could henceforth be recovered only in memory. On the reading developed here, however, his case was more complex. The Christian God had not exactly disappeared from De Quincey's world; it would seem more accurate to suggest that the divine presence was for him real but ambiguous — and mirrored with strange precision by the behavior of his own devout mother. In the name of that Christian God she had called for his spirit to refine itself in holiness while insisting that her demand was being made in the name of love, a love which in her remained inaccessible.

Like several other early Romantic writers, therefore, De Quincey's attitude was governed not by a conviction that God had disappeared but by uncertainty about the nature of a God who could so successfully hide himself. As with his mother, he had a sense of being loved, but of a love that seemed unable to declare itself directly. His experiences of the dark sublime under opium might be said in this sense to have an obliquity similar to that of the "lavender-water and milk of roses" of his childhood.

The effects of his bewilderment stand out prominently in his mind and writing. There is on the one hand an element of neurotic anxiety and on the other the sense of life as being a process in which mystery underlies everything. "What is life?" asks the narrator in "The Household Wreck," who then replies to his own question:

Darkness and formless vacancy for a beginning, or something beyond all beginning; then next a dim lotos of human consciousness, finding itself afloat upon the bosom of waters without a shore; then a few sunny smiles and many tears; a little love and infinite strife; whisperings from paradise and fierce mockeries from the anarchy of chaos; dust and ashes, and once more darkness circling round, as if from the beginning, and in this way rounding or making an island of our fantastic existence. [12:158]

The view is tailored to the pessimism of the tale that is about to unfold, but the imagery is sufficiently precise intellectually to suggest that De Quincey found such a view persuasive, at least at one extreme of his moods. On the alternative view, the "lotos of human consciousness" would prove to be a manifestation of the one life, the love and smiles by which it was from time to time blessed being direct manifestations of the true underlying order, while the "tears" and "strife" were no more than dark interpreters of that truth. De Quincey was fairly caught between these conflicting versions of the world, his neurotic pursuit of certainties being coupled with the sense of being involved in an overriding mystery which required an utmost subtlety of mind to deal with.

All in all, the surprise is not that De Quincey said so much about labyrinths but that he did not devote a separate study to the subject. The experience was perhaps so innate a feature of his own career that it was difficult for him to contemplate it in detachment. We may compare his image of taking the "wrong turning" in the Bath maze, "pathetically shadowing out the fatal irretrievability of errors in early life" (7:203), with a sentence or two in the revised *Confessions:*

Oh heavens! that it should be possible for a child not seventeen years old, by a momentary blindness, by listening to a false, false whisper from his own bewildered heart, by one erring step, by a motion this way or that, to change the currents of his destiny, to poison the fountains of his peace, and in the twinkling of an eye to lay the foundations of a life-long repentance! [3:232]

The passage refers not to his first taking of opium but to his escape from Manchester Grammar School. At the same time it was to this escapade that he dated the frame of mind in which he had allowed himself to fall into the opium addiction; his whole career during those years had, he felt, been of a piece. The excerpt is itself curiously labyrinthine, moreover. The moral implication of the surface text is clear and seems to be confirmed by certain literary echoes. The "false, false whisper" from the "bewildered heart" reminds us of the "wicked whisper" that made the Ancient Mariner's heart as dry as dust, while the "motion this way or that" suggests Wordsworth's *The Borderers,* where such action is said to leave a feeling of betrayal. Yet one need only examine these allusions a bit further to become aware of possible counterindications. For the Ancient Mariner the "wicked whisper" was later to be matched by the "spring of love" that reawakened the power of the heart. De Quincey's further references to the "currents of his destiny" and the "fountains of his peace" suggest that he may be recalling at another level the use of river and spring imagery in Wordsworth and Coleridge to describe the hidden, positive state of man.

Indeed, the subsequent period of his life was to include a chain of episodes about which his feelings would remain profoundly ambivalent. He might on the one hand deplore his decision to run away from Manchester, yet the subsequent experiences had proved crucially important. The friendship with Ann of Oxford Street had provided an introduction to his lifelong awareness of the "pariah worlds" of humanity, worlds which furnished their inhabitants with knowledge of a kind not available in ordinary life. De Quincey's feelings about opium were similar, as when he seems to switch from self-blame to self-congratulation. Indignation with Coleridge for suggesting that he took up opium as a voluptuary and insistence that his original resort to it was, like Coleridge's, for the relief of severe pain is followed, in almost the same breath, by the statement that if he had known of the drug's properties to tranquilize irritations of the nervous system, to stimulate the capacities of enjoyment, and to sustain unusually extended exertion he would have entered on his career "in the character of one seeking *extra* power and enjoyment" (3:224).

The contradictions begin to make sense, however, when we see them as a function of his own divided consciousness. Those faculties by which De Quincey related himself to the world of society, objectively and morally, could not but urge him to look back in disgust at his addiction; yet his subliminal self remained attached and fascinated, aware of the activity that had been stirred in it under those effects. And these experiences were of the same ambiguity as those in the labyrinth: nightmarish or golden by turns, bewildering yet opening out a place of security at the heart of the mazes. So for the rest of his life he would remain fascinated by them, returning again and again by way of autobiographical reminiscence.

A good example of the way in which he was pursued into later years by his inability either to comprehend or to abandon the feelings that had been aroused in him during those years is to be found in the essay "On the Supposed Scriptural Expression for Eternity."[24] Although the greater part is portentously digressive, the essay does have a point and an interesting one. De Quincey argues that when the Bible speaks of "eternal punishment" the word used is "aeonic," which means not an infinite length of time but a duration appropriate to the entity in question. Thus the aeon of an individual man would be something on the order of threescore years and ten; that of the Tellurian race, probably millions of years. The aeon of evil, it follows, is not meant to be compared with that of good, which is necessarily eternal; the duration of "eternal" punishment, therefore, will not be of the same order but corresponds simply to the proper nature of evil.

The full point of De Quincey's interest in the matter, however, emerges only when the essay is placed alongside his references to the figure of Memnon. Writing of the wind which he heard after his sister's death and had often heard on hot days, he describes it as "uttering the same hollow, solemn, Memnonian, but saintly swell: it is in this world the one great audible symbol of eternity" (1:41-42). In a note explaining the word Memnonian by the story of the Egyptian statue, he refers also to the statue of Memnon in the British Museum as "that sublime head which wears upon its lips a smile co-extensive with all time and space, an Aeonian smile of gracious love and Panlike mystery, the most diffusive and pathetically divine that the hand of man has created" (1:41n.). This description should be read in conjunction with his other account of the same statue in his "System of the Heavens." When he first saw it about 1812, he says, it struck him as the "sublimest sight" he had ever seen. It was to be regarded not as a human but a symbolic head, symbolizing

1. The peace which passeth all understanding. 2. The eternity which baffles and confounds all faculty of computation; the eternity which *had* been, the eternity which *was* to be. 3. The diffuse love, not such as rises and falls upon waves of life and mortality, not such as sinks and swells by undulations of time, but a procession—an emanation from some mystery of endless dawn. [8:17]

This passage brings out the fuller implications of De Quincey's conception of the aeonic; it was a quality which he had presumably found shadowed forth in his best experiences under the influence of opium but which he believed to have a metaphysical authenticity beyond that.

The word "aeon" which so attracted De Quincey corresponds, as it happens, with one which I have found appropriate elsewhere to describe some aspects of Wordsworth's visionary experiences.[25] I suggested that, in charting the sphere of the subliminal self and its activities, the "aionic" experience might be seen at one end of a spectrum with that of "kairos" at the other. In the state of aion (which might be called the sense of the eternal) the self is totally self-contented, entranced by the sense of a perpetual youthful resurgence that diffuses itself through consciousness as a whole, while in that of kairos (or "occasion") it is wrought into actions which bring the human psyche into a totally harmonious and integrated relationship with its environment. In Wordsworth, I argued, the aspiration toward the state of kairos was always uppermost; the "aionic" experience was simply a bonus, usually occurring in the moment of cessation from such activity and not to be cultivated for its own sake. Both, however, assisted Wordsworth's great effort, which was to trace those sources of his own creative power which might be thought of as a hidden but available resource for all human beings.

In post-Renaissance society actions which can be thought of as perfectly suited to their occasion became more difficult to achieve. Hamlet is here a prophetic figure, all the more so since one of the most undeniable of such acts might, paradoxically, be an efficient murder, a point recognized perhaps within the irony of De Quincey's own essay "On Murder Considered as One of the Fine Arts." De Quincey was also aware that the experience of aion might in certain circumstances involve a *betrayal* of kairos. The key text here is the culminating episode of *The English Mail-Coach*. The sense of disjunction which Wordsworth felt after the death of his brother John—the sense that cultivation of aionic experience might be dangerous to one's humanity, leaving one "housed in a dream, at distance from the Kind" ("Elegiac Stanzas Suggested by a Picture of Peele Castle," line 54)—was enacted equally powerfully for De Quincey when his release from the oppressions of organized time and space, assisted by a dose of laudanum, was broken in upon by an immediate demand which found him powerless to prevent the mail-coach in which he was traveling from colliding with the light gig, containing a man and a woman, which lay in its path. What kind of trust could after all be placed in a state which, for all its seductive sense of realization, had so little to do with the vicissitudes that beset simple humanity?

This sensed moral ambiguity at the core of things has many ramifications in his work. The figures of the Whispering Gallery and the echoing hall (3:295-97, 346-47) embody, respectively, his nightmares of being in a room beset by hostile whispers or in a large chamber toward which hostile footsteps are approaching, experiences which find one apotheosis in the essay "On the Knocking at the Gate in *Macbeth*."[26] Yet that is simply the obverse of his delight in being safe in the cell at the heart of a labyrinth (7:203-204). And he never lost his hope that from that cell proceeded an Ariadne thread that might connect him with the meaning of the universe at large. We are reminded again of his childhood love for the story of Aladdin in the *Arabian Nights*, where the magician who searches for a child with the power to find the enchanted lamp in its underground cell hears from six thousand miles away the steps of the child Aladdin and recognizes in them "an alphabet of new and infinite symbols" or "secret hieroglyphics uttered by the flying footsteps" (1:129). Even in the midst of his deepest miseries De Quincey believed that he could use such experiences as talismans to discover important truths. Of the power of eidetic vision in some children he wrote: "There is in the dark places of the human spirit—in grief, in fear, in vindictive wrath—a power of self-projection not unlike to this.... There are creative agencies in every part of human nature, of which the thousandth part could never be revealed in one life" (*PW*, 1:8-9).

If we want to see the forms under which such agencies might be imaged, on the other hand, we may turn to a passage such as that where he refers to Wordsworth's description of birds wheeling in the air (see "Home at Grasmere," line 213) and continues: "So also, and with such life of variation, do the *primary* convulsions of nature—such, perhaps, as only *primary* formations in the human system can experience—come round again and again by reverberating shocks" (*SP*, p. 210). The Coleridgean sense of a "primary" link between the essence of nature and the essence of man, set forward so guardedly in these words, is by its very nature almost impossible to communicate in prose or in a system of philosophy. If there is any such possibility, it is to be sought in images and energies which he tries to elicit through the subjects and powers of his own description. So in a passage about his friends the Lloyds he writes of the chanting sound of the river Brathay, which he had often listened to with Lloyd, commenting that he has sometimes heard in it the implied message "Love nothing, love nobody, for thereby comes a killing curse in the rear" (2:401–402); but he goes on to say that he has sometimes also heard, in the very early morning,

in that same chanting of the little mountain river a more solemn if a less agitated admonition—a requiem over departed happiness, and a protestation against the thought that so many excellent creatures, but a little lower than the angels, whom I have seen only to love in this life—so many of the good, the brave, the beautiful, the wise—can have appeared for no higher purpose or prospect than simply to point a moral, to cause a little joy and many tears, a few perishing moons of happiness and years of vain regret! [2:402]

Perhaps, then, at the heart of the stream's noise there was a more hopeful hint of correspondence between the destiny of man and the grandeur of his endowments.

Faced with this possibility, De Quincey found it natural to invoke Wordsworth, who had approached the question from a different point of view. In the Convention of Cintra pamphlet, which De Quincey saw through the press for him, Wordsworth lamented that the true tragedy of man lay not in the failure of the mind of man but in the fact that "the course and demands of action and of life so rarely correspond with the dignity and intensity of human desires."[27] Yet in his own celebration of a "little mountain river," the sonnets dedicated to the River Duddon, he had faced the same query that De Quincey raised concerning "the good, the brave, the beautiful, the wise" in words which De Quincey seems in fact to be echoing. Wordsworth's "Afterthought" concludes:

> While we, the brave, the mighty, and the wise,
> We Men, who in our morn of youth defied
> The elements, must vanish;—be it so!
> Enough, if something from our hands have power
> To live, and act, and serve the future hour;
> And if, as toward the silent tomb we go,
> Through love, through hope, and faith's transcendent dower,
> We feel that we are greater than we know.

His solution takes up the tentative sense of a correspondence between the potentialities of mankind and some hidden principle in nature into a more practical sense that in the service of the future, at least, there is scope for the exercise of love, hope, and faith. The conclusion to *The Prelude* makes clearer the indispensability of that tentative faith for Wordsworth's backing of any practical program. In the same way De Quincey, describing what he means by the "literature of power," characterizes it as that "exercise and expansion to your own latent capacity of sympathy with the infinite, where every pulse and each separate influx is a step upwards, a step ascending as upon a Jacob's ladder from earth to mysterious altitudes above the earth" (11:56).

About the ultimate metaphysical status of such ideas there must inevitably be dispute. It was Wordsworth's implicit contention that the final truth about them could not in this life be known: it was the role of human beings to live under the perpetual shadow of such possibilities, not to imagine that they would ever be physically enacted in time. For Wordsworth it was enough if men could feel that they were greater than they knew. De Quincey, on the other hand, believed that final revelations might sometimes take place, for example, in dreams.

There are at least two great climaxes in his works where such a transmutation is seen in action. The first is in "The Affliction of Childhood," where the dream echoes ten years later take up all the elements of his former vision of endless suffering and transpose them into a vision of hope:

> And now all was bound up into unity; the first state and the last were melted into each other as in some sunny, glorifying haze. For high in heaven hovered a gleaming host of faces, veiled with wings, around the pillows of the dying children. And such beings sympathise equally with sorrow that grovels, and with sorrow that soars. Such beings pity alike the children that are languishing in death, and the children that live only to languish in tears. [1:50]

The other is in the "Dream-Fugue" appended to *The English Mail-Coach*. As the carriage bringing the news of victory is bearing down inevitably on a fairy chariot bearing a baby, the dynamics of the scene are reversed: everything in motion is frozen, while the dying trumpeter sculptured on a stone comes to life and blows three times. At the third blast all the forms which had been in their turn frozen to a bas-relief are released again, but this time into a beneficent scene from which the baby has disappeared: "The seals were taken off all pulses; life, and the frenzy of life, tore into their channels again; again the choir burst forth in sunny grandeur, as from the muffling of storms and darkness; again the thunderings of our horses carried temptation into the graves" (13:325). Sublimity turns to pathos: the baby, now grown to a woman, is elevated high above the scene, gesturing in terror and despair, while at her side her better angel pleads for her deliverance and wins. This vision is then itself cast back into a final all-inclusive sublimity, as the deliverance which he had witnessed for the lady in the gig is wrought up, again and again, into something more like cosmic event:

> A thousand times in the worlds of sleep have [I] seen thee followed by God's angel through storms, through desert seas, through the darkness of quicksands, through dreams and the dreadful revelations that are in dreams; only that at the last, with one sling of His victorious arm, He might snatch thee back from ruin, and

might emblazon in thy deliverance the endless resurrections of His love! [13:326-27]

In such experiences the dialectic between stasis and frenzy within which the subliminal self normally works is transformed into visionary terms, a process where kairos is no longer impermanent but becomes the truly eternal.

Opium dreams, with their extremes of pleasure and terror, their ability to expand and contract the normal perceptions of time and space, seemed to De Quincey to provide one touchstone by which to question conventional orderings of time and space; others were the experiences of delirium in high fever and the extraordinary vision at the moment of apparent death which had been reported to him in such matter-of-fact fashion by the lady who had experienced it. He refers to all three in a single brief formula. Describing how griefs and joys inscribe themselves successively on the brain "like the annual leaves of aboriginal forests, or the undissolving snows on the Himalaya, or light falling upon light," he goes on: "But by the hour of death, but by fever, but by the searchings of opium, all these can revive in strength" (13:348).

Whether or not one treats the revelations experienced on such occasions as giving access to a truer reality than that apprehended by normal sense experience or simply as unusually vivid examples of fantasy is, of course, a matter for personal judgment. There is a strange appositeness in the report of De Quincey's own death, nevertheless, which for him it was apparently the scene of another such revelation, involving first his mother and then his sister:

Twice only was the heavy breathing interrupted by words. He had for hours ceased to recognise any of us, but we heard him murmur, though quite distinctly, "My dear, dear mother. Then I was greatly mistaken." Then as the waves of death rolled faster and faster over him, suddenly out of the abyss we saw him throw up his arms, which to the last retained their strength, and say distinctly, and as if in great surprise, "Sister! sister! sister!" [Page, 2:305]

That he should have felt himself reunited with his sister is appropriate enough, but the evidence suggests that this perception was preceded—and perhaps made possible—by a perception to the heart of his mother's treatment of him, so that he understood, as he had not done before, how it could be the dark manifestation of a love which had, after all, been both warm and immediate. If so, the deepest of the ambiguities that had haunted him throughout his life was resolved for him in the moment of death, as the dark sublime opened once again to reveal a visionary core.

Notes

1. Thomas Carlyle, *The Life of John Sterling* (London: Chapman and Hall, 1851), p. 71. Cf. De Quincey's comments on Coleridge's conversational eloquence (2:152).

2. See J. Hillis Miller, *The Disappearance of God: Five Nineteenth-Century Writers* (1963; reprint, Cambridge, Mass.: Harvard University Press, Belknap Press, 1975), pp. 17–23, 79–80; A. S. Plumtree, "Freedom and the Labyrinth: An Existential Study of Thomas De Quincey" (Ph.D. diss., University of Nottingham, 1977). I am indebted to Plumtree's thesis both for its general stimulus as a study of De Quincey and for a number of individual references.

3. Shadworth H. Hodgson, "The Genius of De Quincey," in *Outcast Essays and Verse Translations* (London: Longmans, Green, 1881), pp. 10–11.

4. See my discussions in *Coleridge's Poetic Intelligence* (London: Macmillan, 1977), pp. 70–94; and *Wordsworth in Time* (London: Faber and Faber, 1979), pp. 57–61.

5. "To William Wordsworth," line 40, in Samuel Taylor Coleridge, *The Complete Poetical Works of Samuel Taylor Coleridge*, ed. Ernest Hartley Coleridge, 2 vols. (Oxford: Oxford University Press, Clarendon Press, 1912), 1:405.

6. *The Borderers*, lines 1543–44, in *The Poetical Works of William Wordsworth*, ed. E[rnest] de Selincourt and Helen Darbishire, 5 vols. (Oxford: Oxford University Press, Clarendon Press, 1940–49), 1:188; all subsequent citations from Wordsworth's poetry except *The Prelude* (see n. 22 below) are to this edition.

7. Letter of 8 June 1797 to Joseph Cottle, in Samuel Taylor Coleridge, *Collected Letters of Samuel Taylor Coleridge*, ed. Earl Leslie Griggs, 6 vols. (Oxford: Oxford University Press, Clarendon Press, 1956–71), 1:325.

8. Samuel Taylor Coleridge, *Biographia Literaria*, ed. James Engell and W. Jackson Bate, vol. 7, pt. 1, of Samuel Taylor Coleridge, *The Collected Works of Samuel Taylor Coleridge*, Bollingen Series 75 (London: Routledge

and Kegan Paul; Princeton, N.J.: Princeton University Press, 1983), p. 80.

9. Letter of 12 April 1810 to Catherine Clarkson, in *The Letters of William and Dorothy Wordsworth,* ed. Ernest de Selincourt, rev. Mary Moorman, 6 vols. (Oxford: Oxford University Press, Clarendon Press, 1969–82), vol. 2, pt. 1, p. 399.

10. Samuel Taylor Coleridge, in *Shakespearean Criticism,* ed. Thomas Middleton Raysor, 2d ed., 2 vols. (London: Dent; New York: Dutton, 1960), 1:65.

11. See Alethea Hayter, *Opium and the Romantic Imagination* (Berkeley and Los Angeles: University of California Press, 1968), pp. 119–20.

12. Regarding the images that filled Coleridge's dreams see Samuel Taylor Coleridge, *The Notebooks of Samuel Taylor Coleridge,* ed. Kathleen Coburn, Bollingen Series 50 (New York: Pantheon, 1957–), vol. 1, pt. 1, entries 1176, 1250, 1649; vol. 2, pt. 1, entry 2055; vol. 3, pt. 1, entry 3404.

13. Letters of 19 December 1813 to Thomas Roberts and Mrs. J. J. Morgan, in Coleridge, *Collected Letters,* 3:463–64.

14. See my "Coleridge and Wordsworth: The Vital and the Organic," in Walter B. Crawford, ed., *Reading Coleridge: Approaches and Applications* (Ithaca, N.Y.: Cornell University Press, 1979), pp. 160–90. For further applications to De Quincey see my "The Englishness of De Quincey's Ideas," forthcoming in *English and German Romanticism: Cross-Currents and Controversies.*

15. For a full and detailed discussion of the estrangement and reconciliation see John E. Jordan, *De Quincey to Wordsworth: A Biography of a Relationship* (Berkeley and Los Angeles: University of California Press, 1962), pp. 203–36, 278–302. Jordan suggests that the Wordsworths' disapproval was aroused primarily by the initial illicitness of the relationship.

16. See ibid., p. 358. One might also note how, when the opium-eater in his best state "feels that the diviner part of his nature is paramount—that is, the moral affections are in a state of cloudless serenity, and high over all the great light of the majestic intellect" (3:384), De Quincey's imagery merges that of the "Immortality" ode and that of the Snowdon vision in *The Prelude.* That Wordsworth actually describes the moon as the "type of a majestic intellect" in the version of 1850 is particularly interesting. De Quincey might have seen a version later than that of 1805, where the moon is the "image of a perfect Mind"; it is even possible that Wordsworth picked up the phrase in the *Confessions* and conveyed it back into his own poem.

17. Ann Radcliffe, *The Italian,* ed. Frederick Garber (London: Oxford University Press, 1968), p. 35.

18. Leigh Hunt, *The Autobiography of Leigh Hunt,* ed. Roger Ingpen, 2 vols. (Westminster: Archibald Constable, 1903), 2:21.

19. See my discussion in *Coleridge the Visionary* (London: Chatto and Windus, 1959), pp. 213–18.

20. Thomas De Quincey, *Reminiscences of the English Lake Poets,* ed. John

E. Jordan (London: Dent; New York: Dutton, 1961), pp. 122-23. This edition contains the entirety of De Quincey's "Reminiscences" as they originally appeared in *Tait's Edinburgh Magazine*.

21. Letter of 10 December 1798 to William Wordsworth, in Coleridge, *Collected Letters*, 1:452-53.

22. See William Wordsworth, *The Prelude: 1799, 1805, 1850*, ed. Jonathan Wordsworth, M. H. Abrams, and Stephen Gill (New York: Norton, 1979), 4.400-504, 13.1-119 (1805). See also my discussions in *Wordsworth in Time*, pp. 121-25, 186-90.

23. See Miller, *The Disappearance of God*, pp. 17-18.

24. The essay appears in Hogg, pp. 295-313, and is acutely picked out for discussion by Miller in ibid., pp. 74-75.

25. See my discussion in *Wordsworth in Time*, pp. 30-42.

26. I am indebted here to Hayter, *Opium and the Romantic Imagination*, pp. 247-50.

27. William Wordsworth, *The Prose Works of William Wordsworth*, ed. W. J. B. Owen and Jane Worthington Smyser, 3 vols. (Oxford: Oxford University Press, Clarendon Press, 1974), 1:339.

10

Grazing the Brink: De Quincey's Ironies

JOHN E. JORDAN

Thomas De Quincey's contribution to Romantic irony has not been adequately recognized. To my knowledge there exists no substantial treatment of the subject: his name, for example, does not even appear in Anne K. Mellor's admirable *English Romantic Irony*.[1] Yet the world of the Opium-Eater was richly ironic. He lived on the edge of chaos which he was continually creating and re-creating, which horrified and intrigued him, at which he marveled, shuddered, and mocked, from which he generated considerable energy, and in which he found occasional islands of calm.

That De Quincey's mode of irony has received scant attention may stem, at least in part, from a lack of consensus on precisely what the concept entails. As Thomas G. Rosenmeyer has wittily put it, "'Irony' is up for grabs" since "there is very little in a good piece of writing that cannot, with some tugging and stretching, be called 'ironical' in one way or another."[2] Lilian R. Furst, in a very helpful survey of the problem, astutely notes that when we put together the murky term "irony" and the equally murky "Romantic" the result is an enigma.[3] Another scholar, David Simpson, proposes that "Romantic irony, broadly put, consists in the studied avoidance on the artist's part of determinate meanings," but Mellor objects that this view "inaccurately limits Friedrich Schlegel's original conception of *romantische ironie* to an epistemological nihilism."[4] She instead chooses to connect Romantic irony with Wayne C. Booth's model of "Unstable-Overt-Infinite" irony and neatly summarizes:

The artist who perceives the universe as an infinitely abundant chaos; who sees his own consciousness as simultaneously limited and involved in a process of growth or becoming; who therefore enthusiastically engages in the difficult but exhilarating balancing between self-creation and self-destruction; and who then articulates this experience in a form that simultaneously creates and de-creates itself is producing the literary mode that Schlegel called romantic irony.[5]

I cite this last definition at length to help orient us, not to suggest that it necessarily will suffice for thinking about De Quincey's irony. Although I suspect that his rich handling of eternal paradoxes can in many ways fit Mellor's reading of Schlegel, and many studies have pursued De Quincey's Germanic interests along comparable lines,[6] it is probably not profitable to try to put De Quincey's practice into the Schlegelian or perhaps any limited definition of Romantic irony. Without quite reaching epistemological nihilism, De Quincey certainly toys with the indeterminate. It might even be concluded that it may be the nature of this enigma to remain enigmatic. At any rate, although De Quincey was attracted to speculation about literary theory and had much to say about such terms as "rhetoric" and "sublime," I am not aware of his trying to come to grips with the concept of "irony." And although he appears to claim familiarity with the work of Schlegel and recognizes him as a man of "talent," in the third of his "Letters to a Young Man Whose Education Has Been Neglected" he condemns Schlegel's criticism as "utterly *worthless*" (10:43).

For purposes of this chapter, therefore, I use the term "Romantic irony" to mean broadly the kind of irony employed by the Romantics, most notably Byron, which is based on a cosmic awareness of a world of incongruity and uncertainty, an awareness that produces principally not savage indignation or even biting turns of wit but a self-conscious acceptance and exploitation, frequently a semicomic glorification. The Romantic ironist has his tongue in his cheek, knows that he has his tongue in his cheek, knows that some of his truest observations are made with his tongue in his cheek—and wants his readers to know also. He is both skeptical and idealistic; he scoffs and he dreams. He sees and delights in simultaneously both the doughnut and the hole. He values chaos and order and recognizes them as an inevitable part of what De Quincey calls the "systole and diastole" (1:270) of life. Thus Romantic irony is always reaching for what it realizes can never be attained, for what would be less desirable if it could be attained.

That second clause is the crux of the matter. There may be, for instance, *some* irony in Shelley's "desire of the moth for the star" or Wordsworth's "something evermore about to be."[7] Probably irony is inevitable to any meditation on the uncertainty of the human condition. But we are here more interested in the conscious manipulation of an enjoyment of that uncertainty. The paradigm is well sketched in De Quincey's description of Piranesi's engravings:

Many years ago, when I was looking over Piranesi's "Antiquities of Rome," Coleridge, then standing by, described to me a set of plates from that artist, called his "Dreams," and which record the scenery of his own visions during the delirium of a fever. Some of these (I describe only from memory of Coleridge's account) represented vast Gothic halls; on the floor of which stood mighty engines and machinery, wheels, cables, catapults, &c., expressive of enormous power put forth, or resistance overcome. Creeping along the sides of the walls, you perceived a staircase; and upon this, groping his way upwards, was Piranesi himself. Follow the stairs a little farther, and you perceive them reaching an abrupt termination, without any balustrade, and allowing no step onwards to him who should reach the extremity, except into the depths below. Whatever is to become of poor Piranesi, at least you suppose that his labours must now in some way terminate. But raise your eyes, and behold a second flight of stairs still higher, on which again Piranesi is perceived, by this time standing on the very brink of the abyss. Once again elevate your eye, and a still more aerial flight of stairs is descried; and there, again, is the delirious Piranesi, busy on his aspiring labours: and so on, until the unfinished stairs and the hopeless Piranesi both are lost in the upper gloom of the hall. With the same power of endless growth and self-reproduction did my architecture proceed in dreams. [3:438–39]

It is well known that this fugal motif fascinated De Quincey as, for example, in his famous "Dream-Fugue," the third section of *The English Mail-Coach,* which repeated in different keys the drama of a mysteriously threatened and miraculously saved female. We ought to recognize that there is here more than ingenious displacement and curious psychological economy which puts every detail to multiple use. There is at bottom a joyous glorification of being intermeshed with a titillating fear of not-being, a combination which is reflected structurally in the fugal process of repetition ironically modified by tantalizing incompletion like Piranesi's vision. Each pattern is constructed, deconstructed, and reconstructed in a version of what Schlegel called *"Selbstschöpfung und Selbstvernichtung"* (self-creation and self-destruction).[8] In fact, the artistic satisfaction comes chiefly in the balancing interplay of being and not-being. De Quincey regularly had it both ways. The ironic reciprocity is neatly captured in his culminating image of the animated bas-relief: "By horror the bas-relief had been unlocked unto life. By horror we, that were so full of life, . . . were frozen to a bas-relief" (13:325). A resonating ambivalence is characteristic of De Quincey's imaginative art. He trembled at "cancerous kisses, by crocodiles" and "unutterable abortions, amongst reeds and Nilotic mud" (3:443), but he also courted his crocodiles and uttered the unutterable. It was his stock-in-trade.

Something of Yeats's "fascination of what's difficult"[9] may be involved in this technique, which is partly sheer manipulation. However, De Quincey delights not only in the skillful display of architectonics but also in the complicated becomingness of truth. Denis Donoghue has recently commented that William H. Gass's criticism of Donald Barthelme's fiction balances the impulse to communicate with the impulse to treat the medium as means and thus is a "minor scandal because it offers, instead of wisdom, an exhibition of skill."[10] De Quincey's response, and probably the characteristic reaction of Romantic ironists, would have been that the impulse to communicate is appropriately controlled and directed by the medium and that the relation to wisdom is not necessarily "instead of" but often an intricate "along with." Furst argues the case persuasively: "Romantic irony is, thus, sited primarily between the author and his work; the reader, even when he is specifically addressed, is no more than an audience of the creative spectacle at best, and at worst merely an eavesdropper."[11] Such seems to be the fundamental situation of De Quincey's readers; for, although he frequently speaks directly to readers in footnote asides, he reveals his underlying attitude in a telling comment found in *Confessions of an English Opium-Eater:* "My way of writing is rather to think aloud, and follow my own humours, than much to inquire who is listening to me" (3:413-14).

To trace the unique cast of De Quincey's ironies, we may isolate some of their most representative features. When De Quincey remarks that his mind "almost demanded mysteries" (2:154), he is really talking about an ironic quality of sustained opposites by which "the highest form of the incredible" becomes "sometimes the initial form of the credible" (7:178). This mode of thought is at the root of his writing about opium. "For opium," he declares "*is* mysterious; mysterious to the extent, at times, of apparent self-contradiction" (3:414). The essential elements in his patterns of thought and feeling are contradictions that are somehow self-involved, are in some sense apparent—which is to say that they are both real and not real.

A famous tour de force of De Quincey's art appears in his series of three papers under the title "On Murder Considered as One of the Fine Arts." This exercise is typical of Romantic irony—a deliberate, joyous exploitation of incongruity left finally ambiguous. For De Quincey the operation is not simply an artful turn to make salable articles, although of course he often did that out of financial necessity. In the prefatory matter to his collected works, significantly titled *Selections Grave and Gay,* he asserts that some of his writings were intended "primarily to amuse," others to "offer some considerable novelty," others to rise to "impassioned prose," and some to have a "mixed character" (1:9, 14). Most could be considered intricately mixed. These characteristic pieces on the artistry of murder underscore the philosophical contortion that marked De Quincey's world.

It is typical in a number of ways that De Quincey should think of murder as a fine art. He knew well that life was messy, chaotic, and uncontrollable, and he also knew that life was capable of being seen as an art, that everything has its rhythms, its discipline, its techniques, its refinements. He was, he said, "an intellectual creature; and intellectual in the highest sense my pursuits and pleasures have been, even from my schoolboy days" (3:211). The intellectual in him wrought an artistic control through words. By this means he superimposed order on, or underlined order in, the world's chaos. Since De Quincey is wont to take the kind of wide, logical circuit he defended in Coleridge's conversation (2:152-53), that of the angelic intelligence to which everything is related to everything else, the result in De Quincey's style is often ritual verbosity that is attenuating. What, therefore, sometimes is perilously close to rigamarole—those incessant, droning digressions which he persisted in considering the cream of his writing—actually serves as a sort of incantation, a laying on of words, words, words. The irony comes partly in his perceiving this need, partly in the reader's recognition of the manipulation, and finally in the reader's ambivalence that arises somewhere between aesthetic satisfaction and logical or moral confusion. De Quincey's palaver builds a bridge between life and art, and at the same time as he brings them together he recognizes that they are separate.

Irony clearly suffuses the macabre humor characteristic of De Quincey. It is a heavy-handed, awkward sort of humor that makes some modern readers vaguely uneasy; nevertheless, it was highly regarded in the late nineteenth century, when De Quincey was sometimes compared with Aristophanes. We need to see such humor, I think, as a defense mechanism, as a protective device. De Quincey does not laugh to keep from crying; he laughs instead to imply that this is a world in which laughing is as appropriate as crying, a world in which any wise man will teeter on the edge like a clown on a tightrope. The precarious submergence of ironic comedy is neatly indicated in a political comment: "England owes much of her grandeur to the depth of the aristocratic element in her social composition, when pulling against her strong democracy. I am not the man to laugh at it. But sometimes, undoubtedly, it expressed itself in comic shapes" (13:274).

Whether or not in explicitly "comic shapes," the "pulling against" of ideas wryly balancing each other, and true as a set of contraries, appears pervasively in that "mind play" of rhetoric which is one of De Quincey's favorite subjects. He considered the province of rhetoric to be found

> amongst that vast field of cases where there is a *pro* and a *con*, with the chance of right and wrong, true and false, distributed in varying proportions between them. There is also an immense range of truths where there are no chances at all concerned, but the affirmative and the negative are both true: as, for example, the goodness of human nature and its wickedness; the happiness of human life and its misery; the charms of knowledge, and its hollowness; the fragility of human prosperity in the eye of religious meditation, and its security as estimated by worldly confidence and youthful hope.[10:91]

This "immense range" of inevitable and irreconcilable opposites sounds like "those contradictions, apparently fundamental and irresolvable," which D. C. Muecke says are the basis for "General Irony," in which the ironist is a victim along with the rest of mankind.[12] Such irony becomes more than just "cosmic bellyaching" when the ironist, while accepting the human condition, also uses it for artistic constructions, exploiting the very circumstances he fears. So did De Quincey. Although he could practice the rhetorician's art of "giving an impulse to one side" (10:91) and sometimes argued polemically, De Quincey was most at home when the argument was complex and multifarious and the subject as implacably two-sided as grief and death.

Death was a subject which forcibly impressed itself upon De Quincey's childhood. With some irony, perhaps, he applauds Wordsworth's "We Are Seven" for seizing the truth that children cannot comprehend death (3:461). Yet, in reality, some sense of death is behind the "spots of time" of Wordsworth's childhood, as it is behind De Quincey's well-known boyhood visions beside the bier of his sister. A major difference, however, is that Wordsworth is content to stop at a statement of "kindred spectacles and sounds / To which I oft repaired, and thence would drink, / As at a fountain." Wordsworth emphasizes the consonance of things, the idea that "feeling comes in aid / Of feeling."[13] De Quincey rather stresses the ironic disparity of things: "Nothing met my eyes but one large window, wide open, through which the sun of midsummer at mid-day was showering down torrents of splendour" (1:38). The contrasting splendor of a summer day becomes for him a symbol of the uncertainty of human tenure.

As V. A. De Luca has shown,[14] De Quincey's Christian background gave the scene a positive slant. "Many times since," writes De Quincey, "upon summer days, when the sun is about the hottest, I have remarked the same wind arising and uttering the same hollow, solemn, Memnonian, but saintly swell: it is in this world the one great audible symbol of eternity" (1:41-42). But it is a curious eternity which, as J. Hillis Miller has pointed out,[15] seems to amount to eternal uncertainty:

> Instantly, when my ear caught this vast Aeolian intonation, when my eye filled with the golden fulness of life, the pomps of the heavens above, or the glory of the flowers below, and turning when it settled upon the frost which overspread my sister's face, instantly a trance fell upon me. A vault seemed to open in the zenith of the far blue sky, a shaft which ran up for ever. I, in spirit, rose as if on billows that also ran up the shaft for ever; and the billows seemed to pursue the throne of God; but *that* also ran before us and fled away continually. The flight and the pursuit seemed to go on for ever and ever. Frost gathering frost, some Sarsar wind of death, seemed to repel me; some mighty relation between God and death struggled to evolve itself from the dreadful antagonism between them; shadowy meanings even yet continue to exercise and torment, in dreams, the deciphering oracle within me. [1:42]

Although God probably had not disappeared, his throne "fled away continually," and what is constant is the "gathering frost" on dying faces and the "pomps" of "glory" in nature. No resolution of this problem is offered; we are left with a sustained balance of "shadowy meanings." Appropriately, De Quincey declared himself often struck "with the truth, that far more of our deepest thoughts and feelings pass to us through perplexed combinations of *concrete* objects, pass to us as *involutes* (if I may coin that word) in compound experiences incapable of being disentangled, than ever reach us *directly,* and in their own abstract shapes" (1:39). These combined experiences are often ironically compounded from the "dreadful antagonism between them."

This handling of his experience is clearly an operation of De Quincey's ubiquitous "law of antagonism," a law which expresses itself in countless bifurcations and negations throughout his writings, from foil characters to the idea of "similitude in dissimilitude." At one level this is a manifestation of a principal tenet of the then-reigning psychology, associationism. But only go on to the folk wisdom of "opposites attract" and you have added a wry element of irony. De Quincey exploited this attraction of opposites coexisting with and enhancing each other.

Even so basically solemn a passage as the following carries an underlying awareness of almost ludicrous paradox: "Grief! thou art classed amongst the depressing passions. And true it is that thou humblest to the dust, but also thou exaltest to the clouds. Thou shakest as with ague, but also thou steadiest like frost" (1:44). Perhaps we will admit that grief can be both depressing and also strangely exalting. But we realize uneasily that the dust and clouds which are here rhetorical opposites are capable of merging, and often do so, and that a perverse reversal has taken place when value is found in the stiffening of frost. It is hard to say how much of this equivocation is intentional in this passage and how much is the habit of De Quincey's mind. In his vision of his sister's death he is obviously intending to be serious, to relate the association of death and summer not only through the "antagonism between the tropical redundancy of life in summer, and the frozen sterilities of the grave" (1:38) but also through Palm Sunday and blue skies connected with resurrection concepts. But the pattern of fancy footwork, of smothering the situation with rhetoric so as to hold the ironies in suspension, is clearly discernible here as frequently elsewhere in De Quincey's writings.

If, as this vision by his sister's bier indicates, the great antinomy of Death pervaded De Quincey's imagination in a compound "involute" from his childhood (and we always have to remember that we have chiefly his adult formulations to vouch for his youthful experience), understandably it continued its complex sway in the man whom the child fathered. We can see this fascination reflected in a number of ways. For one, the columns of the *Westmoreland Gazette* during De Quincey's editorship were filled with assize reports of the most grisly sort. His most famous piece of literary criticism, "On the Knocking at the Gate in *Macbeth*," again uses the tensions of death and the oppositions of worlds. The moment of suspension is a curious compound of the profound and the trivial, murder and a drunken porter, death and a piece of stage business. The knocking is an ironic pivot. And De Quincey's well-known paean of bardolatry at the end of the essay in effect praises Shakespeare as a Romantic ironist whose works "are to be studied with entire submission of our own faculties, and in the perfect faith that in them there can be no too much or too little, nothing useless or inert, but that, the farther we press in our discoveries, the more we shall see proofs of design and self-supporting arrangement where the careless eye had seen nothing but accident" (10:394). The design is not apparent to the careless eye because it is so comprehensive as to include much that is not obviously part of the design. Whether or not this is true for Shakespeare, it certainly is for De Quincey.

It ought to be noted that the already mentioned, and most Byronic, of De Quincey's approaches to death, "On Murder Considered as One of the Fine Arts," occupied him through most of his creative life, from the first essay of that title published in *Blackwood's Edinburgh Magazine* in 1827 through a second paper in the same journal in 1839 and a long "Postscript" in 1854, when he prepared his collected works, a postscript which begins with a defense of his method. Critics, he says, had suggested

> that perhaps the extravagance, though clearly intentional, and forming one element in the general gaiety of the conception, went too far. I am not myself of that opinion; and I beg to remind these friendly censors that it is amongst the direct purposes and efforts of this *bagatelle* to graze the brink of horror, and of all that would in actual realisation be most repulsive. The very excess of the extravagance, in fact, by suggesting to the reader continually the mere aeriality of the entire speculation, furnishes the surest means

of disenchanting him from the horror which might else gather from his feelings. [13:70–71]

Thus the reader sees the horror, but it becomes so horrible that it loses its credibility. It is there and it is not there, through rhetorical legerdemain. This is brinksmanship for its own sake, an ironic pattern of grazed horrors which are recognized and ridiculed, feared and disarmed simultaneously. So De Quincey presents his amateurs of murder, notably Toad-in-the-Hole (Tod in der Hölle?—we remember that De Quincey fancied himself a German scholar). And then comes his famous inversion in which he sets his face against murder: "For, if once a man indulges himself in murder, very soon he comes to think little of robbing, and from robbing he comes next to drinking and Sabbath-breaking, and from that to incivility and procrastination" (13:56). The progression is of course designedly ridiculous. Nevertheless, for all of us, whatever our personal habits of promptness, it contains a weirdly perverse wisdom. And for the Opium-Eater, whom Dorothy Wordsworth declared to be "eaten up by the spirit of procrastination,"[16] it perhaps was an inverted truth: procrastination is the murderer of time.

The irony is compounded, however, by De Quincey's insistence, in a letter written in 1857, that at birth he had been given by a good fairy the gift of never procrastinating but cursed by a bad fairy to suffer "in [the] midst of *too-soonness* . . . the killing anxieties of *too-lateness*" and the "endless reproach of procrastinating." No doubt he did not expect his daughter, to whom he was addressing this bit of fantasy, to agree with his description of himself as the "leader upon earth of all misoprocrastinators" (Page, 2:142), but he is serious enough about the "killing anxieties": he mocks himself and sympathizes with himself simultaneously. Perhaps this is something like what Schlegel meant by his statement that "irony is self-polemic overcome."[17]

Death is only one of the many foci of Romantic irony in De Quincey's writings. Another is his favorite figure of the "pariah," a term which for him carried overtones of conflicting grandeur and debasement, the quintessence of humility. Mater Suspiriorum is "the visitor of the Pariah" (13:366); Ann of Oxford Street belonged to "the outcasts and pariahs" (3:359). De Quincey also inserted the word "pariah" in his translation of Phaedrus's account of a statue of Aesop because "in that way only could I decipher to the reader by what particular avenue it was that the sublimity which I fancy in the passage reached my heart. This sublimity originated in the awful chasm, in the abyss that no eye could bridge, between the pollution of slavery . . . and the starry attitude" (1:125–26) of the pedestaled slave. His rhetoric indeed bridges the chasm, or at least keeps both the height and the depth before us. The sublimity and the interest reside in the continually felt, and even enjoyed, sense of ironic contrast.

A deliberate leitmotif of the revised *Confessions* is De Quincey's experience in the Whispering Gallery of Saint Paul's, where he had "a thought [that] turned upon the fatality that must often attend an evil choice" (3:296). Throughout his autobiography, as various consequences ensue from casual decisions, De Quincey regretfully reminds the reader of this fatal truth. The theme is the old implacable one which Jephthah found: the inability to recall a disastrous word. But in De Quincey's myth the basis is the "gentlest of whispers" which "reverberated . . . in peals of thunder" (3:296n.) — the trivial and insignificant grossly exaggerated, magnified into the overwhelming. The phenomenon is ludicrously true to human experience; one feels a disparity in the tenor and vehicle but recognizes an authenticity even in that fact. Both the ludicrous and the solemn, for De Quincey, are true and important — and inseparable.

Most of us, in conclusion, like to have our cake and eat it too. But for the operation to be successful, we more or less have to hide that contradiction from our conscious selves; we may even develop subtle rationalizations to persuade ourselves that there is really no contradiction. If we do let any awareness of untenable opposition break through in our own consciousnesses, we hope that others do not see the conflict, but we do not flaunt it. De Quincey did. That is the essence of his art. When he added a footnote to his essay on "The Antigone of Sophocles" stating that "I see a possible screw loose at this point: if *you* see it, reader, have the goodness to hold your tongue" (10:373n.),

De Quincey was compounding his ironies. Indeed, he was disposed to glory in loose screws, to declare that appropriate loose screws were essential to any effectively operating machine, that one might even see the universe as a monument to loose screws. One more example of this perverse virus of Romantic irony in De Quincey, this simultaneous holding of inconsistencies and even glorying in uncertainty: his celebrated *Confessions*— what does the work confess? If you, reader, suppose confession to imply some stance of mea culpa, you are mistaken. In his original preface De Quincey begins apologetically: "Guilt and misery shrink, by a natural instinct, from public notice" (3:210). Then he goes on to assert, "Guilt, therefore, I do not acknowledge," but "if I did, it is possible that I might still resolve on the present act of confession" (3:211). So the work seems to be a confession and not to be; it is both, and richer thereby. At the beginning of the third part ("The Pains of Opium") De Quincey continues: "You will think, perhaps, that I am too confidential and communicative of my own private history. It may be so. But . . . if once I stop to consider what is proper to be said, I shall soon come to doubt whether any part at all is proper" (3:413-14). Thus no part is proper, or it all is proper, or is it? De Quincey rejoices in "darkness visible" or, as he puts it, "dark lustrous brilliancy" (13:351). We can imagine his interjecting a learned footnote at this point and concluding puckishly that the essence of art is oxymoron. This self-conscious and gratuitously displayed manipulation is, to modify another critic's definition of Romantic irony, the art of holding the mirror up to art holding the mirror up to life.[18]

Notes

1. Anne K. Mellor, *English Romantic Irony* (Cambridge, Mass.: Harvard University Press, 1980).
2. Thomas G. Rosenmeyer, "Irony and Tragic Choruses," in John H. D'Arms and John W. Eadie, eds., *Ancient and Modern: Essays in Honor of Gerald F. Else* (Ann Arbor: Center for Coördination of Ancient and Modern Studies, University of Michigan, 1977), p. 31.
3. Lilian R. Furst, *The Contours of European Romanticism* (Lincoln: University of Nebraska Press, 1979), p. 17.

4. David Simpson, *Irony and Authority in Romantic Poetry* (Totowa, N.J.: Rowman and Littlefield, 1979), p. 190; Mellor's review of Simpson's book in *Wordsworth Circle* 12 (1981): 196.

5. Mellor, *English Romantic Irony*, p. 24. Wayne C. Booth discusses "Unstable-Overt-Infinite" irony in his *Rhetoric of Irony* (Chicago: University of Chicago Press, 1974), pp. 253–57.

6. See William A. Dunn, *Thomas De Quincey's Relation to German Literature and Philosophy* (Strassburg: Heitz and Mundel, 1900), and the following essays by Peter Michelsen: "Der Träumer und die Ratio: Zu Leben und Werk Thomas De Quinceys," *Deutsche Universitäts-Zeitung*, 20 December 1954, pp. 9–11; "Thomas De Quincey und Schiller," *German Life and Letters* 9 (1955–56): 91–99; "Thomas De Quincey und Goethe," *Euphorion* 50 (1956): 86–102; "Thomas De Quinceys Lessing-Bild," *Monatshefte* 50 (1958): 97–103; "Thomas De Quincey und die Kantische Philosophie," *Revue de Littérature Comparée* 33 (1959): 356–75; "Thomas De Quincey und Jean Paul," *Journal of English and Germanic Philology* 61 (1962): 736–55.

7. "One Word Is Too Often Profaned," line 13, in Donald H. Reiman and Sharon B. Powers, eds., *Shelley's Poetry and Prose* (New York: Norton, 1977); Jonathan Wordsworth, M. H. Abrams, and Stephen Gill, eds., *The Prelude: 1799, 1805, 1850* (New York: Norton, 1979), 6.608 (1850). Subsequent references to Wordsworth's *Prelude* will be to the above edition.

8. As cited in Furst, *The Contours of European Romanticism*, pp. 26–27.

9. "The Fascination of What's Difficult," line 1, in W. B. Yeats, *The Variorum Edition of the Poems of W. B. Yeats*, ed. Peter Allt and Russell K. Alspach (New York: Macmillan, 1957).

10. Denis Donoghue, *Ferocious Alphabets* (Boston: Little, Brown, 1981), p. 89.

11. Furst, *The Contours of European Romanticism*, pp. 27–28.

12. D. C. Muecke, *Irony* (London: Methuen, 1970), pp. 67–69.

13. *The Prelude*, 12.324–26, 269–70 (1850).

14. See V. A. De Luca, *Thomas De Quincey: The Prose of Vision* (Toronto: University of Toronto Press, 1980), pp. 63–64.

15. See J. Hillis Miller, *The Disappearance of God: Five Nineteenth-Century Writers* (1963; reprint, Cambridge, Mass.: Harvard University Press, Belknap Press, 1975), pp. 17–80.

16. *The Letters of William and Dorothy Wordsworth*, 2d ed., rev. and ed. Mary Moorman and Alan G. Hill, vol. 3, pt. 2 (Oxford: Oxford University Press, Clarendon Press, 1970), p. 230.

17. As cited in Mellor, *English Romantic Irony*, p. 15.

18. Cf. Muecke, *Irony*, p. 81.

11

Innocence and Revenge: The Problem of De Quincey's Fiction

Grevel Lindop

Critics have not found much to praise in De Quincey's fiction. Most would agree with V. A. De Luca that "De Quincey's faults as a fiction-writer are glaring—a deaf ear for the rhythms and idioms of actual dialogue and an incapacity for dramatizing sequences of plot (though his powers of suggesting visual spectacle provide substantial if sporadic rewards)."[1] Certainly De Quincey lacked the novelistic imagination, and his adherence to the conventions of Gothic fiction strengthened his tendency to rely upon stereotyped characterization and stylized settings while also curbing those energies of his prose which the discursive essay, with its lack of narrative constraints, set free. Yet his clumsily contrived, passionately felt stories contain much that is of interest in adding to our understanding of the tensions that structure his work as a whole.

Discussion of De Quincey's fiction, however, enters uncertainty at the first step. To put the question plainly, How many original novels and stories did De Quincey write? David Masson's standard edition reprints one novel, *Klosterheim* (1832), and two tales, "The Household Wreck" and "The Avenger" (1838). But a second novel, *The Stranger's Grave* (1823), and another tale, "The Peasant of Portugal" (1827), have been tentatively attributed to him,[2] and part of my task here will be to argue that these works should now be accepted as De Quincey's. Our problems, however, do not end there, for it has been suggested that De Quincey's acknowledged fiction may not be "original" and that unidentified German sources may exist for *Klosterheim* and "The Avenger."[3] In fact, this doubt need not trouble us too much, for all De Quincey's known works of fictional translation or *rifacimento* were first published explicitly as such, a feature which distinguishes them clearly from the "original" stories. One might add that *Klosterheim* and "The Avenger" bear the marks of De Quincey's preoccupations and attitudes so prominently as almost to proclaim their own authenticity.

We turn now to the first problem of attribution. *The Stranger's Grave,* a novel in one volume duodecimo, was published anonymously in October 1823 by Longman of London. It was first identified as De Quincey's in 1870 by Mortimer Collins, who, in an essay on Praed, mentions the village of Wetheral in Cumberland and remarks in passing that "De Quincey was there for a while, and wrote a weird wild story, *The Stranger's Grave,* which is not to be found in his collected works."[4] In 1914, William E. A. Axon added the information that "local tradition" at Wetheral related that "De Quincey visited a brother resident" in the village and "whilst there he wrote the novel."[5] At that time there was no reason to believe that De Quincey had ever been to Wetheral, but in 1920, J. Scott Duckers offered documentary evidence that De Quincey's brother Richard had owned a house there between 1814 and 1816.[6] Because De Quincey lived at Grasmere, about fifty miles away, and was very fond of his brother, it is altogether likely that he visited him. There is thus good reason to take the Wetheral tradition seriously.

Longman's archives have yielded nothing to identify the novel's author, but we may note that De Quincey had worked closely with Longman during the printing of Wordsworth's pamphlet on the Convention of Cintra in 1809. Moreover, during 1822 and 1823 he was under pressure to produce a novel. At the end of 1821 he had undertaken to write a novel for Taylor and Hessey, publishers of the *London Magazine,* who paid him in advance £157 10s. He failed to supply the novel, but in a letter dated 17 March 1824 he writes to Hessey angrily answering a demand for repayment of a substantial sum of money and strenuously denying having had dealings with other publishers.[7] If we accept that in his then severe financial straits De Quincey's response to his publisher may have been disingenuous, these circumstances are at least consistent with the possibility that he wrote a novel but, having spent his advance, sold it to Longman for anonymous publication. It also is possible that Hessey learned of the transaction and wrote to accuse him of double-dealing.

It may as well be admitted at the outset that *The Stranger's Grave* is poorly constructed and often crudely written, bearing all the marks of a hastily produced potboiler. If De Quincey wrote it, he had good reason for concealing his authorship. Indeed, the immaturity of the style and the fact that De Quincey's family connection with Wetheral ended in 1816 suggest that parts of the novel were written in or before 1816 and then hurriedly patched up into a salable commodity when De Quincey came under financial pressure in 1823.

The novel belongs, insofar as it can be classified, to the Gothic tradition and may owe much to the youthful De Quincey's avid reading of violent and sentimental fiction. The narrative is framed by an "Advertisement," supposedly by an elderly editor, who explains that the main text is compiled partly from an account left by the late Vicar of Wetheral, the Reverend William Townsend, and partly from a manuscript left by the ill-fated hero. The opening chapters describe the arrival at Wetheral of a mysterious, melancholy young stranger who shuns company and whose health seems to be "rapidly decaying under the influence of sorrow."[8] He heroically saves the vicar's son from drowning after a skating accident, and the vicar's daughter Elizabeth falls in love with him, but he continues to decline and before dying confesses to the astonished vicar that he is "an incestuous person, a murderer and a parricide."[9] He entrusts to the vicar a bundle of papers containing the story of his life.

The stranger, it appears, is Edward Stanley, a well-intentioned but feckless youth whose great crime has been his incestuous love for his niece, Emily Gordon, who is only three years his junior. Meeting for the first time when he is twenty and she seventeen, they fall in love but conceal their feelings from each other until they are brought together by a sense of shared guilt when they are involved in a boating accident and Edward, in his anxiety to save Emily, allows his former sweetheart, Sarah Franklin, to drown. They consummate their guilty love, and Emily becomes pregnant. Edward, who has a commission in the army, flees with Emily to Spain, where he hopes to obtain military employment, but remittances promised by a friend fail to arrive (the friend, unknown to them, has died suddenly). They fall into poverty, and Edward, seeking menial work at the harbor, quarrels with local laborers. After a fight breaks out, he is sentenced to a public flogging for disturbing the peace. Shocked at seeing him dragged through the streets, Emily dies while giving birth to a stillborn child. After the whipping and a period in the stocks Edward is released. Finding his wife and child dead, he becomes delirious but recovers his wits a year later in a cottage in the Pyrenees, where he has been cared for by a sympathetic Spaniard, Captain Alvarez. When Edward then returns to England only to learn that his father has died of grief and that his mother is mad, he leaves his native district and takes refuge at Wetheral.

Baldly summarized, this wild farrago sounds altogether uncharacteristic of De Quincey. But anyone familiar with his work and patient enough to read the novel through will recognize traces of his hand, and careful scrutiny reveals a substantial weight of evidence for his authorship. This internal evidence is of three kinds, which necessarily overlap at many points. First, the novel contains close parallels with people and events in De Quincey's life; second, it employs themes and motifs conspicuous in his collected writings; and third, it exhibits many similarities to his acknowledged work in style, allusion, and quotation.

To begin with biographical parallels, it is noteworthy that the novel is set in places De Quincey knew or in which he had an interest. The main episodes take place in Wetheral, Preston, and "Fontarabia" (Fuenterrabia, in northern Spain). We have seen that De Quincey had a close connection with Wetheral, which the novel describes in some detail. Preston, Edward Stanley's native town, is placed in southern England on the banks of the Thames but clearly represents Preston, Lancashire; and, although several places in England are called Preston, only Preston in Lancashire, thirty miles from De Quincey's childhood home in Manchester, could be called a "little town,"[10] as it is in the novel. The identification is strengthened by references to the driving of Scottish cattle through Preston[11] — the Lancashire town was on the main road south from Scotland — and to a house there being bought by a manufacturer from Leeds.[12] If "Preston" is on the Thames, these details are absurd; but De Quincey knew Preston in Lancashire well and frequently passed through it on journeys between London and the Lake District. Finally, although Fontarabia was not known directly to De Quincey, it could have been suggested by his deep interest in the Peninsular War aroused by his editorial work on Wordsworth's pamphlet. The town was of strategic importance in the war, and the author of *The Stranger's Grave* shows some knowledge of its military history.[13]

The most striking parallels between the novel and De Quincey's biography involve the hero, Edward Stanley. In his fifteenth year Stanley contracts a "pulmonary" complaint, which "wore at first an aspect so unfavourable, that for several months his life was despaired of," but he eventually recovers "under the influence of the mild climate of Clifton."[14] In his twentieth year De Quincey consulted physicians at Clifton and was diagnosed as consumptive; in 1812, after a period of illness, he recovered at Clifton (2:444, 3:424-25). Stanley is also briefly diagnosed as suffering from "water on the brain"[15] — a complaint of which De Quincey, who refers to it as "hydrocephalus" (*SP*, p. 167), had an obsessive fear. Stanley is unwilling "to open Sophocles or waste one thought upon university honours"[16] but goes grudgingly to Oxford to please his parents. He leaves prematurely, in debt and without a degree. De Quincey likewise went to Oxford reluctantly to please his mother and guardians, complaining of the labor he had undertaken in committing himself to the study of Greek tragedy and feeling that the incentives to take honors were "inadequate."[17] He too left in debt and without a degree.

In *The Stranger's Grave*, moreover, three episodes strikingly recall *Confessions of an English Opium-Eater*. Returning from leave after learning of Emily's pregnancy, Edward falls ill on the coach and, upon arrival, "must have fallen headlong upon the pavement, but for the timely intervention of a fellow-passenger's arm."[18] De Quincey too is memorably saved by a fellow passenger's arm from falling from a coach (*C,* p. 51; 3:369). Emily, escaping from her relatives' home to join Edward, drops "a small trunk"[19] containing her clothes; there follows a moment of suspense, but she is not detected. One recalls the dropping of De Quincey's trunk on the morning of his escape from Manchester Grammar School (*C,* pp. 24-25; 3:298). And like De Quincey before his reckless flight to London, described in the revised *Confessions* of 1856, Edward Stanley before his flight from England spends a restless evening alone in an inn room, while a storm rages outside, pondering the probable folly of the journey he is about to undertake. His mind full of "the most dreadful apprehensions," Stanley feels "quite assured, that happen what would, peace and contentment could visit his withered heart no more."[20] De Quincey remembers the Whispering Gallery and reflects that "once again I was preparing to utter an irrevocable word, to enter upon one of those fatally tortuous paths of which the windings can never be unlinked" (3:347).

In addition, Stanley's niece and later his mistress, Emily Gordon, has attributes that strongly suggest De Quincey's wife, Margaret, and the heroines of his fiction who were consistently based upon her. On her first appearance in the novel Emily has "just completed her fifteenth year"; she is "artless to an extent hardly ever seen in a young woman of these years" but "more than ordinarily womanly, both in form and notions."[21] Later, at age seventeen, she is "tall, graceful, even commanding in her deportment."[22] De Quincey also calls Margaret "artless" (13:239). In *Klosterheim* we find a "prematurity of womanly person" (12:137) in the seventeen-year-old Adeline, and in her physical double, Paulina, De Quincey stresses the "stature, the fine swell of the bust, . . . [and] the magnificent proportions" (12:151). In "The Household Wreck," Agnes is portrayed as "not much (if anything) above sixteen" but "even then . . . put[ting] forward the blossoms and the dignity of a woman." She has "childlike innocence" but, "in the first order of tall women," is "a woman of *commanding* presence" (12:165).

Other aspects of Emily Gordon recall De Quincey's portrait of "The Female Infidel," Mrs. Dashwood Lee, who shocked his mother at a Manchester dinner party. Emily has been brought up "wofully [sic] ignorant" of religious principles because her father is an "infidel," and though not herself "a professed infidel" she is only nominally a Christian.²³ Mrs. Lee, De Quincey recounts, "openly professed infidelity" (1:135). Emily's surname, Gordon, further recalls the rakish Gordon brothers with whom Mrs. Lee eloped (1:144). And we may note that the name Emily clearly appealed to De Quincey, for he gave it to his youngest daughter in 1833.

At another level Mr. Townsend's son William resembles De Quincey's older brother of the same name. William Townsend is featured chiefly in a skating scene; he is a keen skater and a rash one, for once upon the ice he "rushed forward, as usual, to the very spot where, if the ice was to give way at all, it could not fail to separate."²⁴ William De Quincey was "an excellent skater" (1:64) and had a penchant for dangerous pranks. To conclude this survey of minor characters, we may note that, while Edward Stanley has an older sister named Margaret and is loved by a girl named Elizabeth, De Quincey's older sister was named Elizabeth and his wife, Margaret.

The two cottages described in *The Stranger's Grave* also bear a close resemblance to De Quincey's accounts of his cottage at Grasmere. That rented by the hero is

> a neat cottage . . . furnished in a plain, but not inelegant style, surrounded by a pretty garden, and commanding a glorious prospect of the mountains on the one hand, and of the sea on the other. Its walls were covered with vine branches; its grass-plot adorned with myrtle and other odoriferous shrubs.²⁵

The cottage of Captain Alvarez is

> a lonely cottage, erected in the very bosom of those romantic valleys with which the eastern Pyrenees abound. Immediately behind the house stood a tall perpendicular rock, of the height of perhaps three hundred feet, . . . sloping . . . till it united itself on the right and left to two lofty mountains. In the rear of that, again, rose the stupendous precipices of the Quatrocone; whilst on each side of the vale, well-wooded and green hills sloped gently upwards, and in front the view was bounded wholly by the sea.²⁶

If for the Pyrenees we substitute the Cumbrian Mountains and for the sea the lake at Grasmere, the surroundings are those of De Quincey's cottage: a "lovely valley," a "lake lying immediately below," and behind the cottage a "vast and seemingly never-ending series of ascents rising . . . to the height of more than three thousand feet" (2:231). The cottage itself is "embowered at almost every season of the year with roses, and in the summer and autumn with a profusion of jasmine and other fragrant shrubs" (2:236).

The second category of evidence is that *The Stranger's Grave* is rich in motifs prominent in De Quincey's acknowledged writings. Perhaps the clearest example is the pivotal episode of the novel, the hero's public flogging at the orders of an arrogant Spanish mayor. The same outrage is suffered by the hero's mother in "The Avenger," and both characters are dragged through the streets followed by a howling mob. De Quincey's horror of flogging is expressed on many occasions in his essays (1:288, 293–97; 5:197; 8:400–401). The novel also parallels De Quincey's interest in divination and oracles, exhibiting two forms of oracle that occur in "The Household Wreck." One is the "Bath-col" or "echo augury" (1:123), in which words of peculiar relevance are heard by chance. Stanley is disturbed by hearing Mr. Townsend read the word "damnation" during the communion service;[27] the narrator of "The Household Wreck" is struck by the preacher's reading of the text "'Vengeance is mine; I will repay, saith the Lord'" (12:232). Book oracles are also common to both tales: the narrator of "The Household Wreck" opens a book at random and finds an ominous text from *Paradise Lost;* Stanley does the same and comes upon some threatening ballad verses. De Quincey discusses both types of oracle at length on several occasions (1:123–24, 7:44–100, 8:420–26). *The Stranger's Grave* reveals as well an interest, similar to De Quincey's, in the figure of the pariah or outcast. There are, in fact, three pariahs in the novel: the hero, who makes his appearance as the guilt-ridden stranger at Wetheral; the editor, who "has been for the last forty years a sort of wanderer upon the face of the earth";[28] and Colonel Franklin, who after his daughter's drowning "became a wanderer upon the face of the earth, and found no resting-place till he found it in the grave."[29]

INNOCENCE AND REVENGE

The other major De Quinceyan theme in the novel is that of bereavement. As in "The Affliction of Childhood" the subject is presented twice, first from the viewpoint of an innocent child and then through a consciousness that understands the full meaning of the experience. When William Townsend's mother and brothers died of typhus,

> little William, who had barely completed his sixth year, was too young to be affected, other than as the melancholy pomp of a funeral always affects a child. Occasionally, indeed, during the first few succeeding weeks, he would ask when mamma and his brothers would return; but the visits which his father and sisters paid to the three green mounds in the churchyard were to him mysterious and unmeaning.[30]

The second passage anticipates, in its clumsy way, the heights of De Quincey's "impassioned prose" (1:14) and describes Colonel Franklin's grief at the loss of his daughter:

> Oh, reader! if thou hast known what it is to be deprived by death of some single being on whom thy fondest affections were fixed; if thou hast lost a wife, a parent, or, even more than these, an only child; thou wilt then know how dreadfully the feeling of utter desolateness is increased, when even the lifeless body comes to be removed from the presence of the survivor. While the form is before our eyes, pale, cold, and inanimate though it be, we fancy that we are not totally deserted; but when the coffin has enshrouded it, when we listen to the hollow sounding of earth upon its lid, and the voice of the clergyman who consigns "earth to earth, dust to dust, ashes to ashes," then comes upon us, in all its force and bitterness, the assurance that we are alone; and fain, fain could we close our eyes upon the light of day, and lay us down beside the corpse of our beloved one, to share with it the dark bed in which it must slumber.[31]

The passage traces the process of bereavement and burial in the same manner as does the account of Elizabeth's funeral in *Suspiria de Profundis*, focusing on the same details of the burial service. Moreover, both texts lead on associatively to the idea of the pariah: Colonel Franklin immediately leaves his home and becomes a wanderer, while "The Affliction of Childhood" proceeds to a rhapsody on the Wandering Jew (*SP*, p. 178).

There remain several minor thematic parallels. Both *The Stranger's Grave* and "The Avenger" purport to be constructed partly from written memoirs consigned by the dying hero to an elderly gentleman. The "editor" of *The Stranger's Grave* offers his story as one of "many curious and interesting scraps of private history"[32] in his possession; the narrator of "The Avenger" calls his tale "a separate chapter in the private history of German manners" (12:234). Despite their interest in "private history," both De Quincey and the novelist express a disapproval of Lake District gossip: the latter mentions "the disposition to make much out of little for which the inhabitants of a Cumbrian village were and are still distinguished";[33] De Quincey told Richard Woodhouse that "he considered the minds of the people in his own neighborhood as being particularly gross and uncharitable. . . . They were fond of retailing anecdotes, however horrible, as true, without ever taking the trouble to ascertain their foundation" (Hogg, p. 89).

Anticipating the third category of internal evidence, several verbal correspondences between *The Stranger's Grave* and De Quincey's known works have already emerged. The style of the novel is in general undistinguished, but often a passage strikingly resembles De Quincey's acknowledged work. An example is the description of Emily Gordon at the moment of her first parting from Edward: "She wept not, she spoke not, her limbs moved, as it appeared, involuntarily; till her labouring bosom at length relieved itself by the utterance of a long deep-drawn sigh, which sounded as if it came from the very bottom of a heart, in which happiness might never again hope to find a habitation."[34] This "sigh from the depths" is itself a familiar motif in De Quincey's work,[35] and the opening of the passage echoes the account of "Our Lady of Sighs" in *Suspiria de Profundis:* "She weeps not. She groans not. But she sighs inaudibly at intervals" (*SP*, p. 243). The hero and heroine, moreover, after the first indulgence of their guilty love, are described as "humbled, even to the dust,"[36] a favorite De Quinceyan metaphor. In the *Suspiria* we find the phrase "thou humblest to the dust" (*SP*, p. 182) and in "The Avenger" the slight variation "I humbled myself to the dust" (12:278). Edward Stanley also confesses himself, as noted earlier, "an incestuous person, a murderer and a parricide," an indictment which matches De Quincey's judgment that Oedipus "was a murderer, he was a parricide, he was persistently incestuous" (6:142).

The range of literary allusion and quotation in the novel gives additional evidence of De Quincey's hand. Frequent allusion to *Hamlet* is perhaps to be expected in a sentimental novel of the 1820s, but our novelist also knows his Sophocles and his Wordsworth. A reference to "icicles, dropping moisture like the hair on the head of the famous Achelous, when in his bull's form he presented himself as a suitor before Dejanira"[37] alludes to lines 13 to 15 of Sophocles' *Trachiniae*, which describe Achelous "in bulk a man / With front of ox, while from his shaggy beard / Runnels of fountain-water spouted forth."[38] Allusion to Greek tragedy is, of course, quite frequent in De Quincey's work. And after describing his hero's death, the novelist breaks abruptly into verse:

> No motion has he now, no force,
> He neither hears nor sees,
> Rolled round in earth's diurnal course
> With stocks and stones and trees.

The crude misquotation ("stocks" for "rocks"), regrettable as it is, does not make De Quincey's authorship less likely. His frequent quotations from Wordsworth are scarcely ever accurate; for example, in his biographical essays on Wordsworth, among countless other inaccuracies, he seriously misquotes both "Strange Fits of Passion Have I Known" and "'Tis Said that Some Have Died for Love" (2:285).

Enough evidence, perhaps too much, has now been presented. To sum up, there is plausible external evidence pointing to De Quincey's authorship of *The Stranger's Grave;* the novel's subject matter and themes match his preoccupations; its episodes frequently duplicate his autobiographical writings; in important passages both the sequence of ideas and the phrasing are highly characteristic of his work; and close correspondences of detail exist with *Confessions, Suspiria de Profundis,* and "The Avenger." To suppose that another author could have produced this combination of De Quinceyan features by chance is to stretch credulity beyond the breaking point. There seems every reason to accept the novel into De Quincey's canon, and in the latter part of this chapter I treat it as his work.

The second attribution, a five-thousand-word story titled "The Peasant of Portugal," may be dealt with briefly, for in style and plot it is so characteristic of De Quincey that there can be little doubt of his authorship. The external evidence is good, though not conclusive. In a letter dated 18 June 1826, Wordsworth promised Alaric Watts, editor of *The Literary Souvenir; or, Cabinet of Poetry and Romance,* that "I will with pleasure speak to Mr. De Quincey of your wish to have him among the contributors to your *Souvenir.*"[39] Upon examination Watts's duodecimo annual, the *Literary Souvenir* for 1827 (published, we may note, like *The Stranger's Grave,* by Longman), turns out to contain, amid much prose and verse that could by no effort of the imagination be taken for De Quincey's, one story that is clearly his.

"The Peasant of Portugal" is set during the Peninsular War and concerns a young peasant, Juan Taxillo, whose beautiful wife, Marguerita, is raped and killed by cuirassiers of the invading French army. Vowing to exterminate every man of the regiment concerned, Juan takes to the mountains and wages a solitary campaign of terror, stealthily assassinating soldiers until the survivors are convinced that "some fiend possessed of supernatural powers" is at work.[40] On the rare occasions that he is glimpsed, "bullets whizzed harmless by his head,"[41] and he seems invulnerable. When at last he is betrayed, the survivors of the regiment set out to capture him. His hiding place, a cave in a cliff face, seems to be empty, but when all have entered, Juan reveals himself and flings away the ladder which is the only means of escape. After a rousing speech he fires a train of gunpowder, destroying both his enemies and himself. The story is consonant with De Quincey's interest in the Peninsular War and centers on a motif common to *Klosterheim* and "The Avenger," that of the invulnerable and secret avenger. Moreover, the hero's interview with the dying Marguerita, an episode full of Miltonic echoes, takes place in a "luxuriant grove attached to her dwelling," a "delicious bower" which with its "perfume of orange flowers and lemon trees"[42] recalls the "fragrant shrubs" whose luxuriance "embowered" De Quincey's cottage. And three important passages display De Quincey's style and patterns of thought so transparently as to render further comment unnecessary.

The first of these passages is an analysis of the hero's psychology in terms of "power": before his marriage to Marguerita, Juan possesses "an inward sense of power not yet modified into distinct form and nature"; upon the arrival of the invaders, "one great passion in its mighty flow had aroused every dormant faculty of his being, and that with such rapidity as to seem to give birth to the powers it merely called into action."[43] The second passage is a description of Juan at the side of his dying bride: "He spoke not—he moved not; but seemed rooted by horror to the spot on which he stood—spell-bound, yet retaining a terrible consciousness of his fate."[44] The third passage conjures up a highly characteristic De Quinceyan *frisson* and occurs at the moment when Juan hurls the ladder from his cave "down the dread abyss": "When it had reached the lowest depths the faint and dull sound it occasioned tolled the death of hope in every manly breast, for it was the single fragile barrier between them and the grave."[45] This is the sound which so often in De Quincey's work signals the intersection of the ordinary world with the realm of the sublime and the terrible: the rattle of earth upon Elizabeth's coffin, the step on the stairs outside her death chamber, or the knocking at the gate in *Macbeth*. There can be no real doubt that "The Peasant of Portugal" is De Quincey's work and that, whether or not we now know the full extent of De Quincey's fiction, we are at least in a better position than before to perceive its overall pattern and development.

As soon as we consider De Quincey's fiction as a whole, we notice a consistent interest in the linked opposites of suffering innocence and triumphant revenge. It is clear that De Quincey is grappling with an intricate psychological and moral problem, for though in most of his fiction it is the spectacle of undeserved suffering that produces the rage for vengeance, revenge itself is completely inimical to innocence. The avenger, paradoxically, commits brutal acts in affirmation of virtue and justice; he thereby is likely to become as guilty as those whose crimes he deprecates. De Quincey's ambivalence toward the figure of the avenger and his uncertainty about where to place moral responsibility for revenge lead to frequent hints of "doubling" in his fiction: characters and settings are split or duplicated as the tensions and ambiguities of the theme force themselves into the texture of the narrative.

The Stranger's Grave is unique among De Quincey's tales in that the hero is both suffering innocent and victim of righteous vengeance. We follow him sympathetically through his ordeal in Fontarabia and admire his romantic melancholy at Wetheral; he even is granted a Wordsworthian epitaph. Yet he is a murderer and parricide guilty of incest. His sufferings which from one point of view are inconsequent products of sheer ill luck — the death of a friend, the bigotry of Spaniards — are from another, perhaps, signs of divine displeasure. Edward on the night of his flight from England looks at the stormy sky and reads in it the marks of God's anger. Yet how could he have avoided his guilt? He and Emily are "both children of nature, unaccustomed to question the impulses which arose within their bosoms, and absolutely ignorant that they ought ever to be restrained."[46] They begin, then, from a state of quintessential innocence, yet even before they meet, their virtuous family has done its part in preparing for their fall: "It was a standing joke in the family, — a joke with which Emily never professed herself displeased, — that Emily was over head and ears in love with her uncle, and that a dispensation ought to be applied for to the pope, in order to enable them to marry."[47]

Edward is scarcely more blameworthy than Oedipus, who was "loaded with an insupportable burthen of pariah participation in pollution and misery, to which his will had never consented" (6:142). And his sufferings constitute a kind of crucifixion, for after his procession before the enraged mob he is tied to a stone cross in the town square for the flogging. Like "The Household Wreck," *The Stranger's Grave* explores an extreme of powerless misery. No solace is left to the hero: even his last redeeming action, his rescue of William Townsend from the icy river, results in the drowning of his dog, his sole companion. It seems that for his sins Edward Stanley is being punished by an implacable Providence. Furthermore, he is preoccupied with the fear of damnation: hearing the vicar read the liturgy verbatim, warning unworthy communicants of their "damnation" (rather than softening the word, as was customary, to "condemnation"), he reacts "as if this were the very test for which [he] had waited"[48] and leaves the church. Reassured on his deathbed that "God's mercies are boundless,"[49] he admittedly dies in peace. Yet one senses the presence of a cruel and predestinarian God behind the story, a God probably owing much to the somber evangelicalism of De Quincey's mother.

The hero, it seems, cannot be defined unequivocally as either guilty or innocent, and his ambiguity is expressed by a duplication of settings and viewpoints in the novel. We have seen that the cottage at Fontarabia rented by Edward and Emily duplicates the cottage of Captain Alvarez, where Edward recovers from his ordeal, and that both are fictional idealizations of De Quincey's Grasmere home. In the first cottage the lovers hope to evade the evil consequences of their guilt; the second is a sanctuary where Edward, now enduring those consequences, is given leisure for repentance. Moreover, the places where Edward's career begins and ends—Preston and Wetheral—are differentiated only in name. Both are near scenic rivers where offsetting accidents take place, Edward's rescue of William Townsend at Wetheral symmetrically balancing his failure to save Sarah Franklin at Preston. The Townsend family at Wetheral also mirrors the Stanley family at Preston in that each contains an elderly clergyman, a single son, and two young girls. As Emily falls in love with Edward at Preston, so at Wetheral does Elizabeth Townsend. It seems clear that the two places and the two households are essentially the same, differentiated chiefly by their view of the hero, the family at Wetheral which takes pity on Edward being a revision of the family against whom he has sinned at Preston. One sees a romantic and lovable stranger where the other sees a scapegrace son. The reader is offered these two views and has no choice but to remain suspended between them.

In "The Peasant of Portugal" attention focuses on an active hero whose task is to avenge the wrongs suffered by another, but the ambivalence is as strong here as in the previous tale. Juan has to harden himself against the perception that his vengeance renders him akin to his enemies. "Shall the thought of their bereaved wives and children stay my hand?" he asks. No, he decides, for "they have torn from me my young and blooming bride."[50] Irresistibly, however, parallels between Juan and the French commanding officer emerge. They are crudely differentiated in physique—Juan is "of gigantic height, and extraordinary muscular power," while Colonel Vermont (like De Quincey) is "slight and elegant, but somewhat diminutive," but both are "young intrepid spirit[s]."[51] Both have curly hair; both are devoted to beautiful young women. Colonel Vermont, impressed by a premonition of misfortune before his fatal expedition to Juan's cave, entrusts "the miniature of a beautiful young female"[52] to a friend's keeping. He even expresses, in an almost schizophrenic speech, De Quincey's ambivalence toward the hero: "This mistaken man," he says of Juan, "has endured irreparable injury at our hands, red and hot as they were with the blood of their victims. . . . By heavens, I care not if I leave my bones to whiten in Portugal, so that I arrest the progress of this infatuated assassin." As if further to diminish the guilt of Juan's vengeance, the soldiers of the regiment beg that they, and they alone, make the expedition to Juan's lair. "'We have no right,' said they, 'to claim exemption from this service, for we are the offending party; and you cannot ask others to assist you in this enterprize.'"[53] Conscious of their collective guilt, they accept their doom without resentment.

De Quincey's most ambitious novel, *Klosterheim*, again concentrates our attention upon the avenger, but this time the murders and abductions seemingly perpetrated by the hero are illusory. Appropriately, the novel is permeated by three symbols of deception: the labyrinth, the masque, and the theater. The first of these is pervasive in De Quincey's work, and it is no surprise to find it applied to the novel's three main settings. De Quincey speaks of the "labyrinths of the forest" (12:54), the "labyrinths of . . . tortuous passages" (12:72) in the palace, and the "labyrinth of passages . . . [in] the interior of the convent" (12:122). In the convent too we hear "sublime fugues" from the organ filling the chapel with "floating labyrinths of sound" (12:110), and at the first masqued ball the dancers are easily counted because of the precise numbers in which they must combine as they "glided through the fine mazes of the Hungarian dances" (12:97) — a detail which reminds us that the maze or labyrinth indicates not disorder but a hidden order known only to the initiate. The plot of *Klosterheim*, with its twists and deceptions, is itself labyrinthine, intelligible at first only to the author and the hero, Maximilian, who construct the maze and lead us through it.[54]

Against Maximilian is pitted, ineffectually enough, the Landgrave's minister Adorni, who "delighted in . . . the most tortuous labyrinths of political manoeuvring" and "covered a temperament of terrific violence with a masque of Venetian dissimulation" (12:49). This combination of labyrinth and masque also characterizes the architecture of the city's central edifice. The palace's interior is a Piranesian nightmare of dungeons, "gloomy halls of audience," and "vast corridors" surmounting "innumerable flights of stairs" (12:72). But this visible structure is a masque: within it are secret passages unknown even to the Landgrave, and the palace, apparently distinct from and emblematically opposed to the convent, is eventually revealed as structurally one with it. When the partitions are removed, "the two vast establishments, which on one side were contiguous to each other, were thus laid into one" (12:141) — a unification which heralds the reunion of Maximilian and Paulina and the reestablishment of political harmony.

This easy transformation calls our attention to the theatrical nature of *Klosterheim*. The town itself is a series of theaters within theaters: the city walls form a grandstand from which the people look down upon spectacles of flight and battle; the convent has "antique galleries of wood" (12:11) like those in a playhouse; the Landgrave equips the antechapel with a "stage" (12:142) on which the rebels are to be executed; the great chapel has galleries "capable of containing with ease from seven to eight thousand spectators" (12:148); and in the novel's climactic scene a curtain rises to reveal these galleries full of imperial troops, witnesses and enforcers of the hero's claim, at once actors and audience. The people of the city are repeatedly referred to as "spectators," and their role is most often simply to act as audience for the dramatic tableaux contrived by the author.

In the midst of this intricately stylized world the righteous hero is somewhat lacking in interest. He embodies an obvious duality, inspiring terror in his role as "The Masque" but being in reality harmless. Those he has "trepanned," we learn, have gone willingly; signs of bloodshed have been theatrically faked; and the only real murder has been perpetrated by the Landgrave, upon whom vengeance falls as an incidental result of his own actions and not through any plan of Maximilian's. De Quincey has solved the problem of the hero's guilt by rendering his crimes illusory.

Nevertheless, signs of another and deeper duality appear which De Quincey does not succeed in realizing, for early in the novel are hints that Maximilian is somehow paired with the ruffian who steals the trunk from Paulina's coach as she and other travelers to Klosterheim pass the night in a forest encampment. Paulina's uneasy dreams involve the "malicious gaze" (12:21) of an insolent farmer whom she has noticed earlier in the evening, and upon awakening she sees him approaching her carriage through the darkness. She determines to watch his movements, but, strangely, her mind drifts off to thoughts of Maximilian, her absent lover. The theft of the trunk follows, along with the abduction of a sentry in a manner which anticipates the acts of "The Masque." The villain, apparently invulnerable to bullets, escapes amid mocking laughter, and immediately afterward Maximilian appears. When Paulina next sleeps, her dreams are disturbed only by her joy and excitement, and at each waking she sees her lover on guard beside her. Clearly the thief's brief appearance prefigures Maximilian's part in the novel. The latent possibilities of the episode, however, are not developed.

The heroine also briefly acquires a double. At one point Paulina, having fallen into the hands of the Landgrave's agents, is threatened with torture and confronted with "an iron machine, with a complex arrangement of wheels and screws" (12: 136), the ominous vagueness of the description recalling the "mighty engines and machinery, wheels, cables, catapults, &c." (3:439) which De Quincey in the *Confessions* attributes to Piranesi. As the machine is about to be applied, Paulina evades her captors and, fleeing down a corridor, encounters Adeline, the Landgrave's daughter. Adeline uses her authority to protect Paulina but is subsequently mistaken for Paulina and executed. In Adeline's death lies the Landgrave's punishment, and it is one that saves the novel's ending from banality. Although Maximilian's hands are clean, evil is punished by the death of innocence—a disquieting conclusion that calls into question the simplistic moral perspective that governs the rest of the novel.

In "The Household Wreck," first published in January 1838, the pointless destruction of innocence becomes the ostensible subject. The story portrays a peculiarly frightening world in which comfortable trivialities, such as a visit to the haberdasher's, open upon gulfs of horror as the blameless heroine, falsely accused of theft by a shopkeeper whose sexual advances she has rejected, is sentenced to ten years' hard labor in a quasi-medieval prison. This bizarre juxtaposition of realistic and Gothic conventions is enough to take the story into a Kafkaesque realm of the absurd, but in addition the narrative is full of internal contradictions which make us painfully aware of the narrator's disturbed state of mind. The chief actors in the tale, he says, have been dead for "upwards of fifty years" (12:161), but again the events took place only twenty-eight years before (12:200). He tells us at first that "from the very constitution of society and the tone of manners in the city which we inhabited, there seemed to be a moral impossibility that any dangers of consequence" (12:175) should befall his wife on her solitary shopping expedition. Yet as the story proceeds, we learn successively that one of the paths to the heroine's home leads through a "dangerous and disreputable suburb" (12:178), that the city is "overflowing with profligacy" (12:181), that the narrator "could not trust" one of his own household servants (12:183), and that "a very malignant typhus" is raging in the city (12:200). It is as if, retrospectively, the Eden in which the protagonists have lived is revealed as having always been a hell, or as if the environment has no qualities independent of the narrator's extreme emotional states.

Not surprisingly, the story is full of Miltonic echoes. In a crucial episode the narrator, alarmed by his wife's prolonged absence, picks up a book at random; the book is *Paradise Lost*, which falls open, ominously, at the passage describing Eve's rash separation from Adam, the separation which exposes her to Satan's temptation. Clearly an identification between Agnes and Eve is implied. As the narrator perceives, however, the parallel is a false one. "'*My* Eve!' I exclaimed. . . . 'Much *failing* thou wilt not be found, nor *much deceived;* innocent in any case thou art; but, alas! too surely by this time *hapless'*" (12:185). If Agnes is an Eve, then James Barratt, her destroyer, is a Satan armed with force as well as fraud, with power to harm the innocent as well as those who freely fall. Indeed, it is essential to the horror of the tale that Agnes should be pure and even saintly. She is "dovelike," a "lamb," an "angel" (12:163); she is Christlike in that "the bitter cup" of her suffering "might not be put aside" (12:164); she has "childlike innocence" and "more than cherub loveliness" (12:165); and she is repeatedly compared to a Christian martyr.

The narrator's rage at Agnes's public degradation is proportionate to her virtues and is enhanced by his powerlessness to act. Mentally dooming Barratt to a "bloody atonement," he yet dares not act while Agnes lives for fear of jeopardizing her. His resolution to kill Barratt seems to participate in divine authority even as he recognizes its futility: thus it "was settled in my thoughts with the stern serenity of a decree issuing from a judgment seat. But that gave no relief, no shadow of relief, to the misery which was now consuming me" (12:190). One reason for his caution is fear that Barratt might himself become an avenger; when Agnes's brother horsewhips Barratt before her trial, the narrator is anxious lest "[Barratt's] malice might now assume the nobler aspect of revenge" (12:203). Revenge, in short, confers a measure of nobility on acts that would otherwise be altogether evil. As such it is a privilege to be jealously guarded. But what form of vengeance could be commensurate with Barratt's crime? "The momentary shock of a pistol bullet, —what is it? Perhaps it may save the wretch, after all, from the pangs of some lingering disease" (12:231). The narrator is already persuading himself of the futility of revenge when a chance overhearing of the text, "'Vengeance is mine; I will repay, saith the Lord,'" confirms his inclination to refrain from action. He is rewarded, for Barratt is caught "attempting to play off the same hellish scheme" (12:232) upon another young woman. Before dying from his assault by a furious mob, he confesses his misdeeds and clears Agnes's name; "my revenge," concludes the narrator, "was perfect" (12:233).

Nevertheless, it is an odd sort of revenge, for though it vindicates Agnes, her husband has had no hand in it. Instead, the energies of vengeance have been diffused into the populace. In any case the revenge is not "perfect," for at the beginning of his story the narrator has confessed that "still it happens that at times I do, I must, I shall perhaps to the hour of death, rise in maniac fury, and seek, in the very impotence of vindictive madness, . . . for that tiger from hell-gates that tore away my darling from my heart" (12:164). That thirst for vengeance remains unsatisfied, and we realize that the narrative itself has been a substitute for revenge—its verbal elaboration a compensation for the inability to act, its hyperbolic eulogy of the suffering heroine's virtues a plea to some imaginary tribunal that might exact a revenge impossible in the real world.

The reflection that vengeance is God's alone can, as we have seen, lead to two very different conclusions. One is that revenge must be eschewed as a kind of blasphemy; the other is that the avenger participates in the divine, becoming God's instrument or even an aspect of God himself. It is upon the latter view that De Quincey's last story, "The Avenger," published in August 1838, is constructed. At first sight a fairly conventional Gothic tale, "The Avenger" upon examination reveals itself as a rich tissue of religious allusion and irony. Like "The Peasant of Portugal" and *Klosterheim,* it centers on the exploits of a hidden avenger who terrorizes an entire community. There is, however, a new emphasis on the bloody nature of his vengeance, and the injuries he comes to avenge form a catalogue of atrocities still more appalling than those of the other tales. Once again the hero is called Maximilian, and this time he seeks vengeance upon the aging dignitaries of the city in which during his boyhood his father was tortured to death, his mother publicly flogged, and his sister raped—horrors tolerated and even encouraged by the city authorities because his mother was Jewish.

Part of the story's interest, as V. A. De Luca has pointed out, lies in its dual narrative: Maximilian's arrival, his falling in love with Margaret Liebenheim, and the series of shocking murders are recounted by Maximilian's tutor, a passive onlooker who describes with naïve astonishment the splendor of Maximilian's accomplishments and the horror of the murders. The professor's narrative is followed by Maximilian's testament, which explains the murders and the grievance that lay behind them. Whereas the professor sees the town as "a perfectly average city, intent on its humble pursuit of daily affairs," to Maximilian it is "a place of dungeons, tortures, and tribunals of tyrants."[55] The duality, it might be observed, corresponds to that found in the single narrator's account of his city in "The Household Wreck."

Into this ambiguous environment Maximilian descends like a god. A veteran of Waterloo, he arrives "fresh from the most awful battle of this planet since the day of Pharsalia,—radiant with the favour of courts and of Imperial ladies,— . . . an Antinous of faultless beauty." For the professor the "grandeur" of Maximilian's appearance "existed in such excess, so far transcending anything I had ever met with in my experience, that no expectation which it is in words to raise could have been disappointed" (12:239). He is overwhelmed by "the supremacy of beauty and power which seemed to have alighted from the clouds before me," and, though the professor does not yet know that this young prodigy is of Jewish blood, his narrative contains a clue for the reader that strengthens the sacred aura surrounding Maximilian. The hero is reported to have "an eye such as might be looked for in a face of such noble lineaments," specifically one "'Blending the nature of the star / With that of summer skies.'" The lines (slightly misquoted) are from Wordsworth's poem "A Jewish Family," published in 1835, and De Quincey is citing a passage which compares a young Jewish boy to the infant Saint John portrayed by Raphael. Moreover, Maximilian's eyes have also "a light of sadness . . . more profound than seemed . . . commensurate to a human sorrow; a sadness that might have become a Jewish prophet, when laden with inspirations of woe" (12:240).

In retrospect these sacred attributes, applied to a merciless avenger, acquire a curious irony which is deepened by the association of the story's most violent moments with crucifixion. Maximilian's account of his mother's sufferings—she was scourged through the streets at noonday in front of a "shouting populace" (12:278)—irresistibly recalls Christ's progress to Calvary. In the first household visited by Maximilian and his accomplices, an elderly woman is killed clasping the golden pillars of the altar in her private oratory, where she "had turned, perhaps, her dying looks upon the crucifix" (12:248). Later the city's chief jailer is found crucified on a tree in the forest. It appears that those who participated in the crucifixion of Maximilian's family are themselves crucified in retribution. Finally, in his testament Maximilian implicitly associates himself with Christ, calling Margaret "the one temptation to put aside the bitter cup which awaited me" (12:272), since out of compassion for her he was tempted to spare her grandfather, who was "amongst the guiltiest" (12:283) toward his mother. Having resisted this temptation to mercy, he now sees Margaret's subsequent death not as proof of the futility of his vengeance but as a final sacrifice demonstrating the purity of his will.

This is a bleak conclusion. De Quincey may have intended Maximilian's devastating "second coming" to have apocalyptic implications, but this Christlike avenger seems as far removed from real humanity as the tyrants who tortured his mother. As a consequence of his actions, innocence in the person of Margaret is destroyed. Maximilian's hopes that his crimes will "carry . . . into the councils of princes" (12:285) a warning against the bigotry that martyred his family seem an evasion of the truth that his vengeance is merely a final acknowledgment of impotence: the past cannot be changed, and innocence must exist in its own vulnerability or not at all.

One senses that fantasies of vengeance held an attraction for De Quincey, perhaps as a compensation for the powerlessness he felt in struggling with the practical difficulties of his own life. He seems, however, to have realized that "The Avenger," with its attempt to deify revenge, had exhausted the theme. It is noteworthy that, while a preoccupation with suffering innocence remains central to much of his best work after 1838, De Quincey does not return to the theme of vengeance. Perhaps he recognized his own interest in revenge as an essentially private concern and accordingly expressed it in his fiction, which he regarded as inherently minor work and deliberately excluded from the collected edition of his writings. If so, it may not be too fanciful to view his fiction as a "repressed" portion of his oeuvre: in part fugitive and anonymous, and banished from his canon because it rendered too explicitly pressures of guilt, frustration, and resentment which shaped his creativity but which he finally preferred not to acknowledge.

Notes

1. V. A. De Luca, *Thomas De Quincey: The Prose of Vision* (Toronto: University of Toronto Press, 1980) p. 47.

2. See Mortimer Collins, "Praed's Country," *Belgravia: A London Magazine* 12 (1870): 445-52; William E. A. Axon, "The Canon of De Quincey's Writings, with References to Some of his Unidentified Articles," *Transactions of the Royal Society of Literature of the United Kingdom*, 2d ser., 32 (1914): 1-46; Grevel Lindop, *The Opium-Eater: A Life of Thomas De Quincey* (London: J. M. Dent, 1981), pp. 264-67, 281-82.

3. Albert Goldman, *The Mine and the Mint: Sources for the Writings of Thomas De Quincey* (Carbondale: Southern Illinois University Press, 1965), pp. 156-57.

4. Collins, "Praed's Country," p. 450.

5. Axon, "The Canon of De Quincey's Writings," p. 23.

6. J. Scott Duckers, "The De Quincey Family," *Times* (London) *Literary Supplement*, 21 October 1920, p. 684.

7. See Horace Ainsworth Eaton, *Thomas De Quincey: A Biography* (London: Oxford University Press, 1936), pp. 286, 296.
8. *The Stranger's Grave: A Tale* (London: Longman, Hurst, Rees, Orme, Brown and Green, 1823), p. 45.
9. Ibid., p. 68.
10. Ibid., p. 209.
11. Ibid., p. 188.
12. Ibid., p. 131.
13. Ibid., p. 217.
14. Ibid., pp. 74, 75.
15. Ibid., p. 56.
16. Ibid., p. 76.
17. See John E. Jordan, *De Quincey to Wordsworth: A Biography of a Relationship* (Berkeley and Los Angeles: University of California Press, 1962), pp. 87-88.
18. *The Stranger's Grave*, p. 168.
19. Ibid., p. 211.
20. Ibid., pp. 203, 201.
21. Ibid., pp. 85, 87.
22. Ibid., p. 94.
23. Ibid., pp. 86-88.
24. Ibid., p. 48.
25. Ibid., p. 221.
26. Ibid., p. 277.
27. Ibid., p. 43.
28. Ibid., p. vi.
29. Ibid., p. 131.
30. Ibid., p. 6.
31. Ibid., p. 130.
32. Ibid., p. vi.
33. Ibid., p. 13.
34. Ibid., p. 151.
35. See J. Hillis Miller, *The Disappearance of God: Five Nineteenth-Century Writers* (1963; reprint, Cambridge, Mass.: Harvard University Press, Belknap Press, 1975), p. 23.
36. *The Stranger's Grave*, p. 140.
37. Ibid., p. 47.
38. *Sophocles*, trans. F. Storr, Loeb Classical Library, vol. 2 (1913; reprint, London: William Heinemann; New York: G. P. Putnam's Sons, 1919), p. 259.
39. *The Letters of William and Dorothy Wordsworth*, 2d ed., rev. and ed. Alan G. Hill, vol. 3, pt. 1 (Oxford: Oxford University Press, Clarendon Press, 1978), p. 455.
40. "The Peasant of Portugal," in Alaric Watts, ed., *The Literary Souvenir; or, Cabinet of Poetry and Romance* (London: Longman, Rees, Orme, Brown

and Green, 1827), p. 214.
41. Ibid., p. 215.
42. Ibid., pp. 209, 210.
43. Ibid., pp. 207-208.
44. Ibid., p. 210.
45. Ibid., p. 221.
46. *The Stranger's Grave*, p. 97.
47. Ibid., p. 91.
48. Ibid., p. 43.
49. Ibid., p. 69.
50. "The Peasant of Portugal," p. 212.
51. Ibid., pp. 206, 222, 216.
52. Ibid., p. 218.
53. Ibid., p. 217.
54. Cf. Robert Lance Snyder, "*Klosterheim:* De Quincey's Gothic Masque," *Research Studies* 49 (1981): 129-42.
55. De Luca, *Thomas De Quincey*, p. 51.

12

De Quincey as Gothic Parasite: The Dynamic of Supplementarity

JAN B. GORDON

For what purpose have I repeated this story?

—DE QUINCEY, *Autobiographic Sketches*

The whole course of this narrative resembles, and was meant to resemble, a caduceus *wreathed about with meandering ornaments, or the shaft of a tree's stem hung round and surmounted with some vagrant* parasitical [emphasis added] *plant.*

—DE QUINCEY, *Suspiria de Profundis*

A short essay published in *Tait's Edinburgh Magazine* in September 1838 as, originally, an article in the series of De Quincey's autobiographical "Reminiscences" is surely one of the most curious fragments in a career filled with interruptions. The circumstances surrounding its composition and, as reported by David Masson (14:132n.), its subsequent disappearance from the collected works until it was reprinted in 1871 are intriguing for their revelations about De Quincey.

In the 1820s the fashionable Gothic romances of Sir Walter Scott had swept to ever-higher heights of popularity. To capitalize on the vogue, a number of writers began imitating Scott's style, and a veritable industry in "instant" and occasionally counterfeit Gothic romance sprang up. In September 1824, the customary yearly *Waverley*-type novel not having appeared, an enterprising German bookseller resolved to have one forged in three volumes entitled *Walladmor*, "freely in accordance with the English of Walter Scott. From W.... Berlin: at F. A. Herbig. 1824. 3 volumes." De Quincey was sent a copy of the forgery for review in the *London Magazine*. Having only two days to read the book, he quoted three rather long and typical Sturm und Drang passages and spliced them into what amounts to a rough summary. He did indeed see through the imposture of *Walladmor*, which he termed the "boldest hoax of our times" (14:136n.). But upon reading the passages which he had cited, the editors of the *London Magazine,* recognizing an opportunity when they saw one, asked De Quincey to do a complete translation of the fake, which would then be reimported, as it were, into England. The result was a supplementary hoax, as De Quincey described it. And in fact he worked day and night to keep up with the demands of the printer:

> And hence arose this singular result,—that, without any original intention to do so, I had been gradually led by circumstances to build upon this German hoax a second and equally complete English hoax. The German *Walladmor* professed to be a translation from the English of Sir Walter Scott; my *Walladmor* professed to be a translation from the German; but, for the reasons I have given, it was no more a translation from the German than the German from the English. It must be supposed that writing into the framework of another man's story fearfully cramped the freedom of my movements. There were absurdities in the very conduct of the story and the development of the plot which could not always be removed. [14:138]

Having made himself a party to the gross fraud perpetrated upon the reading public, De Quincey excuses himself by saying that his "translation" of the forged German translation is not really a translation at all but a work which fills the frame of another work. He attempts to achieve originality by denying in effect that his work is a translation, and in the process he endows it with the status of a supplementary forgery: "Therefore [I] took the only *honourable* [italics added] course open to me in so strange a dilemma—viz. that of substituting a readable, and at all events not dull, novel for the abortion I had been betrayed into sanctioning" (14:141). Of course the dynamic by which that supposed betrayal was effected is never really broached. But believing himself "betrayed" into translating a forgery, De Quincey transforms his translation into a kind of cure through which he remedies the illness of the original imitation. As he first took opium to palliate a stomach ailment and, then, upon finding himself betrayed by addiction, made claims for the drug as a contraceptive to consumption, so De Quincey in a reversal of that process, finding himself initially betrayed, resorts to a cure that will deny the antecedent status of the object of imitation. The consequence is the same: the construction of a therapeutic "case," an "experiment," out of a betrayal.

One of the ways in which the sow's ear of the German forgery is redeemed to become a presumed silk purse is by careful excision. De Quincey's *Walladmor* appears in two volumes rather than Scott's imitator's three volumes in the hopes that he will thereby betray the previous betrayal. "Metaphysical doubts fell upon me," protests De Quincey, "and I came to fear that, if to a new beginning and a new catastrophe I were to add a new middle, possibly there might come some evil-minded person who might say that I also was a hoaxer, an English hoaxer building upon a German hoaxer" (14:143-44). Being unfaithful to that which was unfaithful perversely restores a kind of faith.

This is the De Quincey who, long before the more careful recent authentication of the extent of Coleridge's plagiarism by Norman Fruman and Thomas McFarland,[1] made the scandalous charge, again in *Tait's Edinburgh Magazine* in 1834, that Coleridge had plagiarized "Hymn Before Sun-rise, in the Vale of Chamouni" from the work of a Danish-German poet, Frederica Brun (2:143-44). This is the De Quincey who wrote a long letter to the editor of the *Edinburgh Saturday Post* on 3 November 1827 claiming that there was no defense for "real plagiarisms of a subtler kind, which shroud themselves in disguises that deceive the injudicious, or which ... disfigure, like gypsies, the children which they have stolen."[2] Albert Goldman has argued persuasively what anyone who has read De Quincey already feels: "In any matter requiring merely intellectual ability De Quincey is not likely to have plagiarized; but when it is a question of special knowledge, facts and ideas that can only be obtained by thorough research, then in almost every instance he is dependent on a single source."[3] Surely we are in the domain of yet one more of De Quincey's demons, that Dark Interpreter of a different but related sort, who inhabits the realm of the "perpetual supplement" which provides a narrative enclosure for the fraud and the forgery, thereby enabling it to be passed on, to become part of a literary canon—in short, to have a genealogy of its own.

De Quincey's "translation" is paradoxically unique in direct proportion to its status as a derivative, supplementary document which amends an antecedent forgery. In the process of "correcting" and hence interrupting an original through a process of supplementarity, he reduces all of *Walladmor* to the provisionality of yet another "version," which of necessity must remain incomplete. Although it pretends to correct, the supplement actually verifies both the incompleteness and the inadequacy of the source simply by virtue of its existence. Although his "version" of the Gothic forgery appears as a kind of plagiarism, in fact its relationship with its source is far more complicated than that. For the "supplement" extends the life of the forgery, not merely through its inclusion in De Quincey's corpus but by modifying the status of its "source," of literary paternity. The writer whose modus vivendi gave him a reputation as a sort of literary parasite is actually participating in a virtual metaphysics of parasitism.

De Quincey's version "feeds off" an original which paradoxically "needs" his supplement to gain existence as a source, to transcend the status of the forgery. The parasitical originally appears as an interrupter, as a sort of structural amendment, dwelling in the incompleteness of the host. It is at times both a carrier and a transformer of information, depending upon the way in which the host's survival is manifested. The parasitical amendment appears in the guise of a cure, but its derivative status ensures that the illness is made endemic by guaranteeing that criminality has historical legacy. The original German forgery needs De Quincey's "supplement" as much as De Quincey's *Walladmor* needs its source. Neither host nor guest has a life of its own; each depends upon "otherness" for its survival. The ways in which the interrupter strives for acceptance and systematic inclusion furnish a pattern through which we can understand De Quincey's fascination with the Gothic, his interest in radical Protestantism, his attempt to create a sort of self-supplementing prose style, and even his effort to make the autobiographical mode itself a supplement.

In many ways the Gothic is the inevitable formal extension of a provisionality inherent in Romantic discourse. As Edward E. Bostetter reminds us, each of the major Romantic poets left behind an incomplete fragment of a larger epic, the traces of one last abortive quest.[4] And the field of Gothic narrative is invariably inhabited by the underdeveloped—atavistic monsters, unfinished or forged manuscripts, unacknowledged claims. The Gothic is the genre appropriate to the discontinuous "clue" striving to be appropriated by a pattern or connection that might lend it meaning, that might enable it, like the missing volume in De Quincey's translation manqué of a "forged translation," to become evidence even in its absence. Gothic discourse represents the traces of a profound discontinuity, usually epitomized as some crisis in communication—an ellipsis that concludes a manuscript, Heathcliff's catatonia, the Monk's inability to communicate with an innocent Immalee, perhaps even De Quincey's "sighs from the depths."

The history of critical response to the Gothic mode, however, from Mario Praz to Judith Wilt, persists in imagining it in Dionysian terms.[5] The Gothic, whatever its disguises, appears as an interruption to another system, a revolutionary mode submerged beneath a more or less "mainstream" Romantic impulse. Our critical response tends to collude with its appearance, confining Gothic discourse to the fragmentary. Yet surely the opposite is more nearly the appropriate pattern. Gothic discourse represents a dynamic process by which an alien intruder, desacralized as a "trace," strives for acceptance, for narrative enclosure within a genealogy or a genre that will give it continuity within a larger "family" or discourse. Only if it is enclosed narratively—within someone else's story—can the Gothic be passed on, inherited not as the discontinuous, the metaphysics of the instant forgery, but as an authentic utterance.

The truth of the matter is that most Gothic monsters encountered in literature do not at all enjoy their loneliness. Like most of us, they strive for acceptance, for inclusion within civilization's traditional forms of exchange, either as in *Frankenstein* by asking for a mate or as in Heathcliff by appropriating the world in an attempt to recover the lost Cathy who for him had been the world. Above all, the Dark Interpreters of literature strive for completion, even as the desire which torments them replicates itself as the vehicle of the endless wanderer, the "pariah" who recurs over and over again in De Quincey's work. The Gothic itself thus exists as a paradox, a peculiar instrument for transforming information. Although the monstrous seeks acceptance so that its secrets may be passed on, the intense striving for enclosure can be shown only by its absence; hence the status of the Gothic, its ontic condition, is invariably unfinished, fragmentary, or unenclosed—whether it be in art (Ruskin), music (Schubert), or narrative (Walpole).

The Gothic mode is part of a mythology of the *recovery* of narrative origins; as it discovers, it also covers over and stops. The interrupter in Gothic discourse is therefore a veritable Maxwell's Demon when not appearing in the guise of De Quincey's Dark Interpreter. It is important to note the systemic quality of the connections which the parasitical enforces, for the obstructor appears initially as a carrier of either new or clarifying information. Gossip and the imaginary opinions of others which recur in De Quincey's reviews always appear as an amendment to a preexisting order. Gossip repeats received discourse with a difference which in turn is supplemented each time the story is retold. Every attempt by the subject to effect the flow of discourse merely extends its life, as the denials become one more "version" in the perpetual supplement. Traces of the "original" remain, much as they do on the vellum-as-palimpsest, but originary value can never be recovered except as another trace, a vestige of some abandoned preexistent system. The systematic perpetuation of the derivative through a process of self-renewal yokes De Quincey's dreams, his addiction, his view of history, his quasi-plagiarism, and his more or less continuous experimentation with Gothic romance as a genre, including most notably *Klosterheim*.

The persistence of the Gothic, its very durability, owes much to the way in which its very incompleteness grounds a necessary supplementation. The self-replicating sequel that makes its antecedent model or structure provisional is not unknown to Hollywood, of course, where *Exorcist II* invariably follows hard on the heels of *Exorcist I*. The use of supplementary narrative "frames" which enclose often competing versions of the same events is a structural feature of the mode, most visible perhaps in a novel like *Wuthering Heights*. Just as the narrative has several structural incarnations, so the monstrous itself often gains a kind of uncanny longevity through an ability to disguise its presence as an interrupter. The Gothic sequel, like the narrative frames and the monstrous, serializes a discontinuity by sublating the "original" even as it extends it. The lack of an ending, the crisis of the deferred transitive, is at the heart of the Gothic mystery. The Gothic intruder, whether Heathcliff or Count Dracula, initially appears as an alien force which threatens order, but his real strength lies in his ability to assume the values of the world he appears to subvert and hence to go undetected, save as a trace or an absence.

De Quincey uses the metaphor of the palimpsest, as J. Hillis Miller has suggested,[6] to describe the operations of consciousness, but the model of the palimpsest also epitomizes the operation of a parasitical network. Before the invention of movable type, writing had been "carried" on parchment that was reusable, a perfectly self-supplementary system. The parchment was the ideal marriage between vehicle and thought, but the process of incremental supplementation, the overlay of writing, eventually compromised the relationship by distorting an exchange system. As a historical artifact the material parchment came to be more valuable than the writing. The vehicle came to be the usurper of what it carried:

> Once it had been the impress of a human mind which stamped its value upon the vellum; the vellum, though costly, had contributed but a secondary element of value to the total result. At length, however, this relation between the vehicle and its freight has gradually been undermined. The vellum, from having been the setting of the jewel, has risen at length to be the jewel itself; and the burden of thought, from having given the chief value to the vellum, has now become the chief obstacle to its value; nay, has totally extin-

guished its value, unless it can be dissociated from the connection. [*SP,* pp. 227–28]

Because it is a historical repository of supplementarity, the vellum is a usurping parasite with respect to its message. History-as-vellum does what writing can never do: it has a value independent of itself. A symbiotic pattern is altered when one of the partners assumes a demonic life of its own, when "identity" becomes "relationship."

De Quincey was intrigued by those instances in history during which some guest had gradually usurped power through a recognition that value lies in exchange rather than in use. Invariably some interrupter (or carrier) usurps value in direct proportion to its ability to enclose a succession of "traces" within an order of supplementarity. Whether it be an originary document, a source, or a religion, the *hôte* suddenly lives up to the full meaning of its French etymology: the host becomes a kind of guest, almost unwittingly.

De Quincey's more than amateur interest in the history of economic thought reveals his fascination with symbiotic relationships whose partners alternately supplement and supplant one another. His championing of David Ricardo's contribution over that of Adam Smith is a case in point. For De Quincey, the author of *The Wealth of Nations* had created an invariable distinction between value in use and value in exchange to demonstrate the incompatibility of utility and demand. Ricardo, by contrast, realized that it was entirely possible for a man to pay a greater price for a commodity than what that same man conceives its intrinsic value to dictate. For De Quincey the word *use* occasionally breaks free from its etymological condition as part of the verb *to use*: "The two eternally co-present forces essential to the idea of exchange nevertheless govern alternately one by one: each alternately becoming inert, and neither modifying the other by the smallest fraction, when that 'other' is raised by circumstances into the true controlling principle" (9:144–45). Ricardo's system sees price as determined, often alternately, by value in use *and* difficulty of attainment; it further recognizes that both of those determinants tend to vary in their relationship to each other. Water has little value in exchange, but its value in use—particularly if one is in the desert for long—tends to effect its exchange value and may even usurp it altogether.

Similarly, in his essay "Malthus on Population," De Quincey correctly saw the fallacy in Thomas Malthus's pessimistic notion of the consequences of the inversely proportional ratios of population growth and food supply. If human population growth were to continue in geometric progression for long, it would have to effect a revolution in the arithmetic progression of the food supply in order to sustain itself. Neither ratio was permanently fixed, and mankind was by no means doomed to eventual starvation. Rather, first food and then man usurped the prerogative in an attempt to restore equilibrium. Value and meaning always constitute a derivative project for De Quincey: a symbiotic dependency within a closed system is altered by a sudden mutation which changes the balance of power in such a way as alternately to shift the dominant parties. And that mutation is brought about by an interrupter's assumption of a disguise through which it identifies with the host. In the later stages the disguise, the means by which the usurpation was achieved, becomes the operator in a newly modified systemic order.

De Quincey's "Historico-Critical Inquiry into the Origin of the Rosicrucians and the Free-Masons" reveals a similar interest in the Dark Interpreter that effects a newly mutated symbiosis. Discounting any pre-Renaissance notions of the Oriental or Arabic antecedents of these two secret societies, De Quincey locates the supposed origin of the Rosicrucians in three books written by one John Valentine Andreä, a Lutheran cleric of "Wirtemberg" during the Thirty Years' War. To promote the reformist ideas of Martin Luther during an age of theosophy, cabbalism, and alchemy, Andreä "baited" his reform movement by portraying it as the repository of ancient Oriental wisdom and mystery. De Quincey remarks:

Many would seek to connect themselves with such a society, [and] from these candidates he might gradually select the members of that real society which he projected. The pretensions of the ostensible society were indeed illusions; but, before they could be detected as such by the new proselytes, those proselytes would become *connected* with himself and (as he hoped) moulded to nobler aspirations. [13:408; italics added]

Candidates for the mysterious order began to submit specimens of their skill in alchemy or cabbalism, each applicant attempting to gain admittance by demonstrating some unique knowledge which might qualify him. Quarrels and partisanship became an inevitable by-product of the presumed initiation. "It was remarked," furthermore, "that of the many printed letters to the society, though courteously and often learnedly written, none had been answered; and all attempts to penetrate the darkness in which the order was shrouded by its unknown memorialist were successively baffled" (13:411). The "bait" assumes finally a life of its own and proliferates as an independent system of discourse: "The public had accredited the *charlatanerie* of his books, but gave no welcome to that for the sake of which this *charlatanerie* was adopted as a vehicle. The Alchemy had been approved, the moral and religious scheme slighted" (13:416).

Andreä's attempt to counteract the spread of Rosicrucianism should have been familiar to the "translator" of the counterfeit translation of *Walladmor*. According to De Quincey, Andreä wrote a supplement, a fourth volume titled *Chemical Nuptials of Christian Rosycross,* in which he attempted to poke fun at theosophists, pedants, and alchemists. But the supplement, the presumed antidote to that which has taken on a life of its own, becomes part of that life, incorporated within the new system of discourse: "Unfortunately for the purpose of Andreä, however, even this romance was swallowed by the public as true and serious history" (13:417). The supplement, necessitated by some unforeseen usurpation as a contraceptive to its mysterious proliferation, becomes part of the illness rather than a cure. No matter what its telos, the supplement cannot help but be derivative in some way which, paradoxically, virtually ensures its systemic inclusion.

The dynamic by which one truth supplants and then extends another in the guise of amending or correcting it is for De Quincey the secret of all revelation. No matter what the attempt to amend through interpretative discourse, renewal by supplement—by secret connection—ensures survival:

> In the same way, with the same effect of alternate resurrections, all scriptural truths reverberate and diffuse themselves along the pages of the Bible; none is confined to one text, or to one mode of enunciation; all parts of the scheme are eternally chasing each other, like the parts of a fugue; they hide themselves in one chapter, only to restore themselves in another; they diverge, only to recombine, and under such a vast variety of expressions that even in that way, supposing language to have powers over religious truth—which it never had, or can have—any abuse of such a power would be thoroughly neutralised. The case resembles the diffusion of vegetable seeds through the air and through the waters: draw a *cordon sanitaire* against dandelion or thistledown, and see if the armies of earth would suffice to interrupt this process of radiation. [8:281]

Throughout De Quincey's essays there looms an almost impulsive fear of entropy, and the dynamic of supplementary renewal—the "self-restorative virtue" (8:281)—is always found in whatever subject he happens to be talking about. Thus in "System of the Heavens as Revealed by Lord Rosse's Telescopes" he responds as follows to the growing geological debate over the age of the earth:

> Perhaps, in reality, the Earth is both young and old. Young? If she is not young at present, perhaps she *will* be so in future. Old? If she is not old at this moment, perhaps she *has* been old, and has a fair chance of becoming so again. In fact, she is a Phoenix that is known to have secret processes for rebuilding herself out of her own ashes. [8:10]

Clearly the palimpsest appears everywhere for De Quincey. Although it keeps everything in a kind of eternal present, it also provides the basis of an underlying connection.[7] Yet the breaking of this secret connection is absolutely essential to the maintenance of the interrupter. Again the trace-laden vellum and its necessary dissociation from that which lends it value is necessary to the creation of new value. De Quincey observes:

> Hence it arose in the middle ages, as a considerable object for chemistry, to discharge the writing from the roll, and thus to make it available for a new succession of thoughts.... They expelled the writing sufficiently to leave a field for the new manuscript, and yet not sufficiently to make the traces of the elder manuscript irrecoverable for us. Could magic, could Hermes Trismegistus, have done more? [*SP*, pp. 228–29]

That other champion of Hermes, Michel Serres, would term the vellum-as-palimpsest a perfect parasitical system.[8] Written thought, once having been the chief value of the vellum, becomes the obstacle to that value. Parasitism, for Serres, involves a triangulated sequence of relationships. Given two stations and a channel between them, an exchange of messages is possible. If the relation succeeds and if it is perfect, optimum, and immediate, then it disappears as a relation and appears only as some hidden power. If the relation is there, if it exists at all, that would suggest a failure, for the relationship would be deflected into mere mediation. The "carrier" would disappear into immediacy, obviating the need for any spaces of transformation. The best relation would be no relation at all, something which, by definition, never exists. It also would in effect mark the end of the supplement. For Serres, the importance of parasitism—its ability both to interrupt and to consolidate a system of exchange—makes it the nexus of all transformation. Although *The Parasite* is confined to a discussion of fables and folktales, it is clear that evolutionary theory, for example, would conform to his model: the mutant begins its career as an interruption, but through a process of supplementation it consolidates. Literary criticism, as most of us have long suspected, would similarly qualify as a form of parasitical transformation. Beginning with an attempt to clarify the unfinished or "open" quality of textuality, criticism establishes itself as an interruption which simultaneously deforms the work that it describes. It clarifies an antecedent text even as it supplants it, becoming finally part of received opinion about the work. The mysterious connection with the text is both relation and nonrelation at the same time. A "perfect" reading would become enclosed within the meaning of the host, as does De Quincey's "On the Knocking at the Gate in *Macbeth*."

The mysterious system of self-renewal whose supplements have no defined limits, whose hidden lineaments can never be discovered because they are part of a secret network comprised of stored information awaiting transfer or transformation, is for De Quincey *power*. Such a dynamic provides the paradigm, in fact, for one of his better-known analogies in *The English Mail-Coach*. He declares:

> No dignity is perfect which does not at some point ally itself with the mysterious. The connexion of the mail with the state and the executive government—a connexion obvious, but yet not strictly defined—gave to the whole mail establishment an official grandeur which did us service on the roads, and invested us with seasonable terrors. Not the less impressive were those terrors because *their legal limits were imperfectly ascertained*. [13:279–80; italics added]

The permutation of secret societies through a process of supplementary tracing combined with an interest in systems of information storage and exchange which defy entropy give one strand of De Quincey's achievement an uncanny resemblance to the interests of Thomas Pynchon. But whereas Pynchon as a "living" writer has virtually ceased to exist as the result of voluntary isolation, a radical act of self-effacement, De Quincey's notion of an authorial self is entirely derivative or secondary, as in fact is so much of his writing. Inhabiting a proliferation of dwellings which he abandoned in turn when their studies held so many books and papers that he could no longer find what he was looking for, De Quincey lived a life littered with the traces of self-perpetuating, abandoned enclosures to which access was denied—a veritable architecture of the Gothic fortress. But the landscape of the incomplete fragment and the derivativeness of all attempts to enclose it are surely part of the meaning.

De Quincey's *Autobiographic Sketches* participates in the same problematic of the derivative as does the "translation" of *Wal-*

ladmor. Written late in his career, it was made up almost entirely of material excerpted from his earlier writings to satisfy an audience for whom the "Opium-Eater" had become a curiosity. De Quincey assembled these fragments into a single text only under the pressures of publishing his collected works. In the General Preface of 1853 he described the belated autobiography as a mere amusement; yet, as Elizabeth W. Bruss astutely reminds us, the *Autobiographic Sketches* may well represent some crisis in the genre of autobiography itself.[9] More specifically, the later version impoverishes its originary by suggesting that there were impediments to the kinds of pure subjectivity that it sought to establish.

The *Autobiographic Sketches* incessantly reminds us that it is but a copy of an original to which it owes both allegiance and dependency. Whereas *Confessions of an English Opium-Eater* and *Suspiria de Profundis* are referred to in the General Preface as "modes of impassioned prose ranging under no precedents" (1:14), the material of the sequel is clearly ordered by a recognition that it belongs to the domain of literature rather than dreams. The author's life, instead of being presented in a kind of eternal present, is arbitrarily demarcated into "periods" or "episodes" and later even "chapters." Although the *Suspiria* embodies the fuguelike structure of a dream, *Autobiographic Sketches* is but a re-presentation of the content of dreams. The narrator of the sequel is clearly in a different role—that of interpreting antecedent experience. The intensely subjective but spontaneous quality of the antecedents now yields instead to a narrator who is always clarifying, reminding us that "he always maintained such and such." The supplement is totally dependent upon an extrinsic power which is never internalized, as were drugs and dreams, but which must remain forever part of the intransitive. Moreover, its effects depend upon various rhetorical strategies: the use of the indicative to depersonalize and to universalize the earlier experiences, a deployment of sentimentality to defer the immediacy of the terrors felt in the earlier *Confessions* and *Suspiria,* and the blunting of direct and unmediated experiences by the use of mediating constructions like indirect speech. The *Autobiographic Sketches* also makes abundant use of modals to add a sense of necessity and hence direction to what, in the earlier versions, had been a random accumulation of experience in an eternal present. This heightened impersonality of the sequel is best illustrated by the appearance of anonymity whenever there is an occasion for self-referentiality: De Quincey as perceiver is repeatedly muted into "the man who reports" or the speaker of "open-hearted sincerity."

In almost every sense the *Autobiographic Sketches* conforms to Paul de Man's model of "de-facement."[10] The self therein presented is entirely derivative. De Quincey amends and changes crucial experiences but almost invariably in the same way: to make what had been a condition into a source for sequential reflection. The consequence is a literary dependency; neither the earlier versions nor the sequel can stand alone. The fragmentary quality of experience in the *Confessions* and *Suspiria* becomes a genetic fragmentation in the *Autobiographic Sketches*, as the latter work breaks off almost in midparagraph upon relating De Quincey's matriculation at Oxford.

In creating an autobiography which lies within another autobiography, De Quincey was doing to his own life what he had done to the lives of the great men of history and to history itself. Plato was of interest as a result of a duality inherent in his achievement. Just as Andreä had laced his religious reform movement with the "bait" of the occult only to found unwittingly the Rosicrucian order, so Plato's works contain the "affectation of a double doctrine: esoteric, the private and confidential form authorized by his final ratification; and exoteric, which was but another name for impostures with which he duped those who might else have been calumniators" (8:45-46). De Quincey is intrigued by the second book of Plato's *Republic* with its imposing dialogue between Glauco and Adeimantus over the disguises by which injustice pays homage to justice while attempting to undercut it: "If, to win upon men's practice, it must previously connect itself with artificial bounties of honour and preferment—all this is but another way of pronouncing an eulogy on justice" (8:51). The operative concept in so many of De Quincey's writings is in fact "connection," which recurs with almost incredible frequency. In his essay "On Christianity as an Organ of Political Movement," De Quincey thus sees the perpetuation of Christianity in the modern world as a function of its secret growth: "It is because Christianity burrows and hides itself that it towers above the clouds; and hence partly it is that its working comes to be misapprehended" (8:207). Good and evil exist never as coordinates but always as a set of parasitical dependencies, much as for Ricardo economic use in exchange and use in demand were in a relationship of mutual containment until one or the other, like De Quincey's famous Dark Interpreter in the *Suspiria,* was no longer recognized as a necessary parhelion.

The parasitical Dark Interpreter usually cloaks himself in the role of therapeutic agent; he supplies a remedy, a palliative, to the indisposition or fragmentation of the host. He either corrects by modifying or restores a fresh originality to a potentially entropic situation, but he always appears initially as an interruption. De Quincey's reading of the history of Christianity itself furnishes the most notable example. Christ's very name in Greek denoted "healer," yet his role as "hakim" inevitably came into conflict with the proselytizing aims of the early Church. His therapeutic dimension, in De Quincey's eyes, took on a life of its own in the transitional period during which the new religion was gradually insinuating itself. And that independent life is in effect a Kingdom of Miracles which has ineluctably become part of the revelatory dimension of Christianity—a vestige, as it were, vulnerable to assault by empiricists such as Hume, even though it is no longer an organic part of the faith. "It is clear," writes De Quincey, "that a Christianised earth never can want polemic miracles again; polemic miracles were wanted for a transitional state, but such a state cannot return" (8:166). The relationship is that of an unbreakable connection through which the parasite makes its own contribution to the furtherance of the faith, which is simultaneously furtherance of itself: "Christianity could not unroot itself now, though every trace of evidential miracle should have vanished. Being a true religion, once rooted in man's knowledge and man's heart, it is self-sustained; it never could be eradicated" (8:167). The miraculous which had attached itself to Christianity as a vehicle is now working against its acceptance by those who demand empirical verification. The vehicle for the therapeutic becomes a betrayer.

That progressive relation always follows the same structural pattern in De Quincey's thought: the early need for a therapeutic interrupter or supplement to serve as a vehicle, a succeeding stage in which the parasite metastasizes so as to become inextricable from the "message" of the host, and the final betrayal of the vehicle when the interrupter is mistaken for the host. Hence the history of Christianity is replete with need and dependency followed by betrayal and separation. In De Quincey's view the relation of the Protestant Reformation to Catholicism is exactly the same: the derivative parasite lodges itself within the same systemic order (Christianity) as Catholicism, but with an original purpose of purifying and amending its antecedent host. "Protestantism, we must recollect, is not an absolute and self-dependent idea; it stands in relation to something antecedent, against which it protests—viz. Papal Rome" (8:251). That which is dependent then establishes for itself the same antecedent status as that claimed by the host: "It would be no great triumph to Protestantism that she should prove her birthright to revolve as a *primary* planet in the Christian system; that she had the same original right as Rome to wheel about the great central orb, undegraded to the rank of satellite or *secondary* projection" (8:252; italics added).

Structurally, De Quincey's view of the historical mandate of Protestantism is akin to the role of addiction and plagiarism in his own life. Those critics who see De Quincey's opium dependency as furnishing merely another metaphor for the Romantic imagination are assuredly overlooking its central importance.[11] If my very self—as revealed for example in the *Autobiographic Sketches*—is necessarily derivative, along with everything else that I admire, then maybe that which is "not me" as found in drugs or in the work of others is, perversely, the real "me." Creation is merely an adjunct to an already extant system of relationships by which agents renew and are renewed. Hence the man who declaimed against Kant at one point as being often unoriginal can say, upon borrowing from Themistocles, in another essay: "Yet, gentlemen, hear me—

strike, but hear me. That's a sort of plagiarism from Themistocles. But never mind. I have as good a right to the words, until translated back into Greek, as that most classical of yellow admirals" (8:374). We are forever in the domain of *agency* in De Quincey's thought; as a consequence, "originality" is always a myth for him.

The supplementary figure of the Dark Interpreter who, with the same presumed rights as the "Opium-Eater," spends much of its creative life exploring a process by which the sources of inspiration might be made coterminous with the productions of that inspiration is surely related to Harold Bloom's concept of *tessera*.[12] In *The Anxiety of Influence* the revisionary movements of *clinamen* and *tessera* are deployed to prevent the periodic collapse into an identity with sources in the history of poetic influence. Yet that "temporary" identity—the process by which the autotelic nature of the parasite is restored so that it might work a transformation to guarantee its own dependent genealogy—is crucial to the operation of De Quincey's mind. If nothing is ever entirely original, then creativity is a network of binding valences, a necessary incarnation of power as opposed to knowledge. History is the history of unintended effects.

In 1832, long after the major phase of the Gothic vogue had run its course, De Quincey wrote *Klosterheim*, a belated sequel to an episode in literary history. The work can be regarded as an attempt to "re-cover" an original and curious involvement with the strange transformation of *Walladmor*. But *Klosterheim*, like its forerunner, is derivative of a German antecedent, now reimported into England. Supplementarity is a part of the strange life of literary texts. *Klosterheim*, published as a separate volume by De Quincy only later to be deleted from his collected works, is the generic Gothic supplement that participates in the historical and authorial problematic of supplementarity.

The temporal setting of De Quincey's novel is a winter lull in the protracted struggle of the Thirty Years' War—that historical occasion when Protestantism, having detached itself from its host for which it had been an agent of purification, was establishing a separate existence within the fringes of the Hapsburg principalities. At the commencement of the story war has been reduced to the entropic condition of a winter stalemate, partly as the consequence of a triangulated political situation. The principality of Klosterheim has fallen into the hands of a tyrannical Landgrave who has threatened to compromise the city's traditional alliance with the Emperor in favor of a secret pact with the Protestant armies of Sweden. The Landgrave plays off both sides against a center formed by his secondary alliance with a robber-brigand named Holkerstein, "one of the many monstrous growths which had arisen upon the ruins of social order in this long and unhappy war" (12:16). The rightful heir, Maximilian, is made aware of the compromised politics of the city by evidence of a displacement in that repository of knowledge, the library:

In the library, some of the officers had detected sufficient evidences of the Swedish alliances clandestinely maintained by the Landgrave; numbers of rare books, bearing the arms of different Imperial cities, which, in the several campaigns of Gustavus, had been appropriated as they fell into his hands, by way of fair reprisals for the robbery of the whole Palatine library at Heidelberg, had been since transferred . . . to the Landgrave. [12:36]

Displaced books, interrupted letters, and indeterminate communications, along with rumors and gossip, float about the city. Neither sources nor entitlement can be ascertained.

Klosterheim itself has a curious role by virtue of its geographical and political provisionality as an "appanage" (12:46) in the family of the previous Landgrave. It is curiously neutral, capable of being a proxy of either Protestant or Catholic interests, and is filled with spies of the antagonists. Like the labyrinthine underground tunnels which afford clandestine ingress to and egress from the palace (and the spaces of deflected desire in so much Gothic fiction), the city is porous with secret connections at a time "when the religious and political attachments of Europe were brought into collisions so strange" (12:46).

Entropy and ontic neutrality are perfect conditions for the operation of the parasitical, for it affords the possibility of double agency, of the simultaneous coexistence of relationship and nonrelationship. De Quincey observes:

But, whilst on the outside of her walls Klosterheim beheld even this unpopulous region all alive with military licence and outrage, she suffered no violence from either party herself. This immunity she owed to her peculiar political situation. The Emperor had motives for conciliating the city; the Swedes for conciliating the Landgrave: indeed they were supposed to have made a secret alliance with him, for purposes known only to the contracting parties. [12:60]

Klosterheim is both hidden, a repository of the repressed, and open at the same time. This condition which grounds its role as an agent also grounds Maximilian's attempt to recover the throne. He announces his campaign initially by textuality, by notices affixed randomly to public places: "'Landgrave, beware! henceforth not you, but I, govern in Klosterheim.' (Signed) The Masque" (12:77). The parasite does what it always does in De Quincey's thought: it establishes a virtually secondary kingdom, a nighttime order, by dispensing judgment and ad hoc justice, hearing petitions in absentia, and effecting political reform. This alternative realm, however, mirrors the Landgrave's diurnal despotism in that it appears disembodied. No one can ever find the Masque except as a "trace": "It was true that no man knew where to seek him: personally he was hidden from their reach; but everybody knew how to find him: he was amongst them; in their very centre" (12:80). The derivative nature of the Masque's conduct feeds doubts about the authenticity of the "traces"; even his estranged Paulina, concerned about his disappearance, is uncertain whether the letters she receives are really his or forgeries. The anonymous edicts of the Landgrave, whose author disappears within a tyrannical cloak of silence, feed in the parasite a different kind of sourcelessness: the counterfeit missive.

Gothic discourse parallels the archaeology which provides its setting.[13] It is unfinished, partly and incompletely enclosed, like the convent of Klosterheim: "One or other of them would attend at a particular station, easily recognised by the description added, in a ruinous part of the boundary wall" (12:121) The weathered ruin in one sense is all "middle" in that its historical antecedents appear not as presence, a cause, but as a source infinitely detached, much as the hidden sources of all the disembodied correspondence and pronunciamentos which appear suddenly and imperatively in *Klosterheim*. Only when this free-floating language is contained and enclosed within a system of exchange (answered by the woman imprisoned within the palace-convent-dungeon) can it have a legacy, can it be "passed on," as it were. The parasitical, having become internalized, then would cease to exist as a fragment, as a threat. The Gothic, particularly as it is adopted by De Quincey, plays with this process by which the fragmentary interrupter is internalized and preserved. The crucial condition for the activity of the host, in De Quincey's thought, is the palimpsest where nothing is ever extinguished but is only transformed into something else. The plagiarism, the drug addiction, and the predisposition to Gothic "adaptations" are all agents for that transformation.

In one of her imprisonments Maximilian's beloved Paulina discovers the "traces" of disembodied communication—a trunk of letters stolen during their retreat: "The fragments which she left remained strewed upon the ground; and Paulina, taking them up with a careless air, was suddenly transfixed with astonishment on observing that they were undoubtedly in a handwriting familiar to her eye" (12:128). Later she discovers them to be "mere copies of originals in the chancery at Vienna" (12:129). In an attempt to compromise her betrothed, one of Maximilian's enemies has stolen the diplomatic correspondence with which he has been entrusted. The potential betrayer of the Masque, hoping to reap a reward from the sale of politically compromising letters, discovers like De Quincey himself that supplementarity is the essential feature of communicative exchange and its rewards. De Quincey remarks:

Bringing them [the letters] forward separately and by piecemeal, he had probably hoped to receive so many separate rewards. But, as it would often happen that one paper was necessary in the way of explanation to another, and the whole, perhaps, were almost essential to the proper understanding of any one, the result would inevitably be—grievously to mislead the Landgrave. [12:133]

Meaning is inherent in the sequential, sublating order of discourse on one or another "parchments." Since writing never really disappears, never entirely vanishes, it is forever a partner in a dialectic involving attachment to and severance from antecedents.

Even in De Quincey's fictional work the body of literature, not unlike his own style, is comprised of a succession of footnotes, occasionally to other footnotes, always in quest of some elusive whole. Literature is a system which feeds upon itself, extending its boundaries through a delicate and fragile displacement of internalized antecedents appropriated within a succession of parenthetical, parasitical supplements. Its continuity is a function of its necessarily derivative status. The boundaries of personal possession are as thin as the partitions within the convent of Klosterheim; literary (and other) echoes are everywhere as the consequence of a network of whispers and dependent secrets. The structure of such a Gothic system is analogous, of course, to the structure of gossip, that concept of narrative supplementarity which derives a perverse authority from the way in which it obscures its (author)itative source, often internalizing it as "overheard."

The concept of a "literary career" as in some sense parasitical should not of itself be assumed to be entirely pejorative; in fact, it may in some larger sense be salvational. The literary critic as parasite would be an antidote to both the traditional obsession of Western criticism with discovering connections of continuous, centered rationality and the competing deconstructionists who find ellipses and discontinuous epistemes. Within this framework De Quincey seems to be involved in some act of repetitioning antecedent texts in order to find space for an "inscription" of their latent potentiality. Literature is never unfinished but never finished either, a condition which could serve as a kind of epigraph for De Quincey's career. The war between the merely dependent and the derivative, between destruction and creation, is assuredly a battle fought as much between Blake's Urizen and Los and Coleridge's primary and secondary imaginations as between De Quincey's hosts and his various Dark Interpreters.[14] The parasitical, that alternatively free and dependent interrupting trace from an alien systemic order which always blurs the distinction between past and present, is one agent of Romantic replenishment.

NOTES

1. See Norman Fruman, *Coleridge, the Damaged Archangel* (New York: George Braziller, 1971); Thomas McFarland, *Coleridge and the Pantheist Tradition* (Oxford: Oxford University Press, Clarendon Press, 1969), pp. 1-52.
2. *New Essays by De Quincey: His Contributions to the "Edinburgh Saturday Post" and the "Edinburgh Evening Post" 1827-1828*, ed. Stuart M. Tave (Princeton, N.J.: Princeton University Press, 1966), p. 182.
3. Albert Goldman, *The Mine and the Mint: Sources for the Writings of Thomas De Quincey* (Carbondale: Southern Illinois University Press, 1965), p. 81.
4. Edward E. Bostetter, *The Romantic Ventriloquists: Wordsworth, Coleridge, Keats, Shelley, Byron* (Seattle: University of Washington Press, 1963).
5. The "liberal" bias toward reading the Gothic in subversive terms is revealed in any of the following treatments of the mode: Mario Praz, *The Romantic Agony*, 2d ed., trans. Angus Davidson (London: Oxford University Press, 1951); Coral Ann Howells, *Love, Mystery, and Misery: Feeling in Gothic Fiction* (London: Athlone Press, 1978); and, most recently, Judith Wilt, *Ghosts of the Gothic: Austen, Eliot, and Lawrence* (Princeton, N.J.: Princeton University Press, 1980).
6. See J. Hillis Miller, *The Disappearance of God: Five Nineteenth-Century Writers* (1963; reprint, Cambridge, Mass.: Harvard University Press, Belknap Press, 1975) pp. 34-37. It is intriguing to consider Miller's role as an adapter of French deconstruction to a specifically American context in terms of his earlier interest in the relationship between decentering and repetition as a primary theme in De Quincey's works.
7. On this point see ibid., pp. 40-44.
8. See Michel Serres, *The Parasite*, trans. Lawrence R. Schehr (Baltimore, Md.: Johns Hopkins University Press, 1982). Serres's work contains several "flow charts" detailing the operation of the parasite in a number of different cultural contexts. But the dynamic of that operation is always similar. In the flow chart below an interrupter (from the position B') disguises itself in such a way as to gain admission to the systemic order AB which ensures its survival. The parasitical interrupter (P') is assimilated at the cost of its own separate existence. Its "success" is directly proportional to the diminishment of its relationship as an intruder. Total assimilation or total dependency is absence. Its renewed existence is possible only when it has effected a supplement which renders it no longer necessary to the symbiotic relationship.

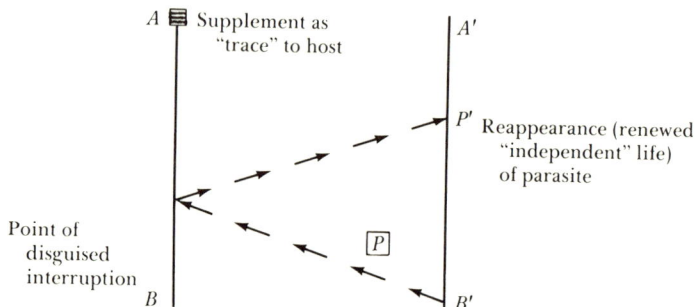

9. See Elizabeth W. Bruss, *Autobiographical Acts: The Changing Situation of a Literary Genre* (Baltimore, Md.: Johns Hopkins University Press, 1976), pp. 93–126.

10. See Paul de Man, "Autobiography as De-facement," *Modern Language Notes* 94 (1979): 919–30.

11. Two critics who see addiction in metaphoric rather than structural terms and are hence betrayed into talking about Romantic "sincerity" are Alethea Hayter, *Opium and the Romantic Imagination* (Berkeley and Los Angeles: University of California Press, 1968), pp. 226–42; and Roger J. Porter, "The Demon Past: De Quincey and the Autobiographer's Dilemma," *Studies in English Literature, 1500-1900* 20 (1980): 591–609.

12. See Harold Bloom, *The Anxiety of Influence: A Theory of Poetry* (New York: Oxford University Press, 1973), pp. 49–73. Although Bloom never really discusses the problem of unacknowledged borrowing (and one must in fact wonder what acknowledgement constitutes in Bloom's scheme of things), the relationship between the Romantic "crisis of the unfinished" and the problematic of *necessary* repetition needs further discussion. If antecedents exist not as history or as education (the eighteenth-century inculcation of the classics, for example) but rather as denied origin, then in effect the meaning of history has changed drastically—from that of "source" to that of some commonly accessible reservoir. The democratization of "influence" into the shared denial of paternity as "origin" would mean that repression is always a companion of plagiarism. One would then conceivably work through (in some psychoanalytic sense) plagiarism so as to be free in the same way that one works through parasitism so as to enjoy the freedom of the trace. In this connection see Peter Shaw, "Plagiary," *American Scholar* 51 (1981–82): 325–37.

13. See my "Narrative Enclosure as Textual Ruin: An Archaeology of Gothic Consciousness," *Dickens Studies Annual* 11 (1983): 209–38.

14. My own interest in the dynamic of parasitism in the Romantics was abetted and encouraged in conversations with Bernard Blackstone about Coleridge's *Notebooks*.

13

Nexus in De Quincey's Theory of Language

FREDERICK BURWICK

Although he scorns William Paley's *Natural Theology* (1802) for its casuistry and its "confusion between the *ratio essendi* and the *ratio cognoscendi*" (8:140n.), Thomas De Quincey develops his account of the "twofold meaning" of style as *mechanic* and *organic* (10:163) in terms that seem caught within the same hermeneutic circle that confines Paley's systematic quest for nexus. De Quincey addresses basic questions to the mystery of words: By what arrangement does an arbitrary, presumably grammatical, assemblage of lexical signs become a "literature of power"? Whence comes the living spirit that transforms the dead letter? That plants and animals function according to laws which can be comprehended, at least in part, by mechanical physics Paley took to be suitable proof of divine design and agency. De Quincey, of course, was alert to the petitio principii in Paley's teleological reasoning, but De Quincey too may seem to beg the question of an organic style unless one grasps the essential difference between De Quincey's concept of a priori organization as an active process and Paley's teleology as a hypostatic replication within an already created universe. De Quincey does not argue that all language is organically vital; he concedes, rather, the mechanical basis of all syntax. Therefore, in claiming an organic style, he may seem guilty of "the dogma of the Ghost in the Machine," that philosophical crime to which Gilbert Ryle pledged his "deliberate abusiveness."[1] When De Quincey deliberates on the processes of language, whether they be historical, cultural, or individual, his organicism is made to exist inside of mechanism; and the informing vitality of organic language is said to reside outside, or rather in between, its mechanical parts, in nexus.

The apparent paradox, in relating part to whole, has a venerable tradition. Plato has Socrates employ a similar argument in regard to the letters which make up a syllable: the whole, as he leads Theatetus to conclude, is different from the sum of its parts; to Phaedrus he recommends the analogy that the language of discourse "ought to be constructed like a living creature."[2] Aristotle adds temporal dimensions to the spatiality of the part and whole when he defines the body politic: "The state is by nature clearly prior to the family and to the individual, since the whole is of necessity prior to the part." In the *Poetics*, as in the *Politics*, he argues an essential unity in which the parts are "so closely connected that the transposal or withdrawal of any one of them will disjoin and dislocate the whole."[3] With Plato and Aristotle, De Quincey appeals to the organic whole in explaining the structure of man's language and literature as well as his social and economic community. Aristotle's insistence upon *priority* was used in the context of genetic process, the growth and maturation of form. Coleridge repeats the presumption in his *Essays on the Principles of Method* (1818) in placing man's "mechanic science" within his capacities of organic perception, as a "forcible illustration of the Aristotelian axiom, with respect to all just reasoning, that the whole is of necessity prior to its parts."[4]

In presenting his discrimination between the *organology* and *mechanology* of style, De Quincey posits the concept of nexus, or *junctura*, to explain how the parts adhere in a generative whole. Instead of providing a useful direction into the mastery of style, perhaps the concept of nexus merely introduces a cursed threshold where passage is baffled by a riddling sphinx. He appears to be referring to the interstices of language—passageways, or jumping-off places, between one word or sentence and the next. But he insists that it is a crucial endeavor to move from an atomistic to a dynamic doctrine of invention and arrangement. How is it possible for language as a mechanical thing to attain vitality as organic function? Indeed, is organic function merely a convenient analogy, or is it somehow inherent in the nature of language? And if language is inherently organic, does it derive its form from mind or from community? Noam Chomsky has traced the opposition between the "mechanical principle" and the "creative principle" in language theory from Descartes through Herder and Humboldt. All fall before the sphinx of the threshold because these theoreticians fail to "reveal the organic form of language." That Humboldt could not "face the substantive question: what is the precise character of 'organic form' in language" Chomsky considers an inevitable consequence of his perpetuating the Cartesian assumption "that the sequence of words in a sentence corresponds directly to the flow of thought."[5]

Coleridge, in his *Logic,* endeavors to avoid this Cartesian dilemma of immediacy, the *logos* as both word and thought, through a Kantian scheme of a priori categories: the intuition of time and space is distinguished from "the mechanism or construction of the representations." "To object to its being called an intuition," Coleridge asserts, "would be little else than to quarrel with language itself and all the principles on which language is possible."[6] Coleridge's dodge here is patent: the intuitive reason *(nous)* is prior to the forms of thought *(logos)* and the forms of perception *(theoria),* but the latter, roused only through external stimuli, provide the only means of communicating the former. Coleridge's triad does not answer Chomsky's challenge to Cartesian linguistics; it merely regresses further into the epistemological arena and places other thresholds before the threshold of verbal discourse.

From the very outset of his account, even before he reaches the epistemological or psychological apprehension of visual images, Paley becomes ensnared in a paradox of regression as he attempts to explain the biological mechanics of perception. The eye as "perceiving organ" functions according to the mechanical laws of optics through its mechanical operation as *camera obscura,* replete with aperture and crystalline lens, a complex system of pulleys to operate the shutters of the iris, another to focus the lens, dioptric humours to limit prismatic refraction, and a sensitive retina to receive the *pictura.* After tracing "the complexity, subtilty, and curiosity of the mechanism," Paley says, "we come to something which is not mechanical, or which is inscrutable." When he reaches this juncture, he finds himself faced with an awful question:

Why should not the Deity have given the animal the faculty of vision *at once?* Why this circuitous perception, the ministry of so many means, ... to produce an image upon a membrane communicating with the brain? ... Why resort to contrivance, where power is omnipotent? Contrivance, by its very definition and nature, is the refuge of imperfection.

Paley's explanation for the mechanical regression of threshold within threshold is a stunning example of *post hoc ergo propter hoc:* "It is only by display of contrivance, that the existence, the agency, the wisdom of the Deity, *could* be testified to his rational creatures."[7]

De Quincey tells of reading the *Aleitheia* of Parmenides during his first year at Oxford. In the midst of considering the emphatic doctrine of the identity of thought and being, "to gar auto noein estin te kai einai" ("for the same thing can be thought [is for thinking] and can be [is for being]"),[8] he is met by his tutor. Their brief exchange De Quincey recalls as "the first (which happened also to be the last) conversation that I ever held with my tutor" (2:61). Not wanting to embarrass the man, whom he confidently assumed had never heard of Parmenides, he replied to the tutor's inquiry that he had been reading Paley. "'Ah! an excellent author; excellent for his matter; only you must be on your guard as to his style; he is very vicious *there.*' Such was the colloquy; we bowed, parted, and never more (I apprehend) exchanged one word" (2:62). Left to his own thoughts, De Quincey savored the ironic contrast between Parmenides and Paley, not only that Parmenides could declare that there can be no thought corresponding to a name that is not the name of something real but also that he could affirm the principle "to be" *(to eon)* without invoking divine sanction. Of course, he himself endorsed no deistic or agnostic philosophy, as Dr. Cotton discovered to his regret when he deeply hurt De Quincey with a rash charge of deism (Page, 1:113). But Paley's rationalizing spiritual faith into a "natural religion" was to De

Quincey an abomination worse than the cold intellectual piety of deism. Thus De Quincey claimed that his tutor's appraisal was a "direct inversion of the truth": "Paley, as a philosopher, is a jest, the disgrace of the age," but "for style, Paley is a master." De Quincey damns with ironic praise: "Homely, racy, vernacular English, the rustic vigour of a style which intentionally forgoes the graces of polish on the one hand, and of scholastic precision on the other—that quality of merit has never been attained in a degree so eminent" (2:62).

But De Quincey was no more a follower of Parmenides than of Paley. Parmenides' "to be" *(to eon)* disallows the universal flux *(panta hrei)* of Heraclitus and presumes a construction of the cosmos as hypostatically determined as Paley's "mechanical organisation." Furthermore, Parmenides' separation of the objects of knowing *(nous)* from those of believing *(doxa)* was too restrictive, was at odds with the reconciliation of the intuitive and discursive processes that De Quincey later identified in the organic style. His experiments in "imaging," as well as his ascertaining his *"Facility of impression,"* recorded in his 1803 diary during those frustrating months before he entered Oxford, reveal his fascination with imaginative projection and subject-object reciprocity (*D*, pp. 153, 156). There are no clues whether by this early date he had applied such ideas directly to the modulation of syntax, but he had already become facile in identifying attributes of style and had come to terms with John Horne Tooke's polemic against Lord Monboddo (*D*, pp. 165, 198). Although De Quincey would continue to play upon the historical and cultural relativity derived from Monboddo's argument that language is a product of man's political organization, he absolutely opposed Monboddo's thesis that language is not natural to man, not inherent in mind but a mere accident of environment.[9] From Tooke he may well have learned the value of scrutinizing etymology, but he could only have been entertained by the brick-and-mortar sense of a bald noun-verb style: "A consideration of *Ideas,* or of the *Mind,* or of *Things* . . . will lead us no farther than to *Nouns,"* and verbs are necessary only to communicate nouns in motion. Tooke therefore raised his caveat that every departure from the noun-verb structure, which he called the art of "abbreviation," opened a Pandora's box of evasion, deception, and propaganda.[10]

Although they may rest upon a mode of reasoning evolved from the same dualism that Chomsky objected to as "Cartesian," De Quincey's claims for the crucial vitality in the syntactic nexus of language engage a model of perception that made his theory unique. Through the elaborate scheme of *junctura,* De Quincey asserts, "the moving intellect reveals itself and prospers" (10:259). He could not, any better than Humboldt or Coleridge, satisfy Chomsky's demand for the "precise character of 'organic form,'" but he was not caught by the riddles of the threshold. Rather, he exhibited the conflict of nexus and hiatus in language as essentially the same as in perception.

Even the physiologist who cannot explain how the brain constructs the sensory data excited in the nerves of the retina nevertheless assumes in his everyday actions the intimacy between the eye and the object it beholds. The hiatus baffles the understanding, while nexus continues to inform the organic function. With the analogy of perception De Quincey constructs his argument against Hume's insistence on "a vast *hiatus* or inconsistency in the divine economy" (8:164), and he concludes with his analysis of the a priori organization which informs and transforms mechanical forces and substances:

> The planet, indeed, might form itself by mechanical laws of motion, repulsion, attraction, and central forces. But man could not. Life could not. Organisation, even animal organisation, might perhaps be explained out of mechanical causes. But life could not. Life is itself a great miracle. . . . This kind of miracle, as deduced by our reason, and not witnessed experimentally, or drawn from any past records, I call an *a priori* miracle. [8:171]

The organic principle may rest upon an "*a priori* miracle," but De Quincey considered this not a leap of faith but a valid hypothesis, applicable as he goes on to say to every exercise of man's "intellectual and moral capacities."

In his essay "Language" he states that "it is in the *relation* of sentences, in what Horace terms their '*junctura,*' that the true life of composition resides" (10:258). In explaining nexus as "the way in which one sentence is made to arise out of another, and to prepare the opening for a third," he offers three metaphors: the interstices of language are the warp and woof for the weaver's shuttle, the "great loom" for the "textile process of the moving intellect"; separate clauses are "architectural parts, aiding, relieving, supporting each other"; and the modifying reciprocity of juxtaposition in internal and external relations is as color and outline in visual perception. As in Kant's explanation that the a priori of mind is discovered only a posteriori, the whole may be prior to the parts, De Quincey affirms, but it is revealed only through the parts. The *to zotikon* of the whole depends upon the individuation of the parts:

> Periods, and clauses of periods, modify each other, and build up a whole then only when the parts are shown *as* parts, cohering and conspiring to a common result. But, if each part is separately so vast as to eclipse the disc of the adjacent parts, then substantially they are separate wholes, and do not coalesce to any joint or complex impression. [10:259]

De Quincey confronts here the riddles of the threshold: how tenuous is the organic link? when does the part break off and become a separate whole? Metaphorically, he has described the syntactic relationships as a solar system in which the revolving spheres may eclipse one another or mutually participate in the central radiation; this visual model, however, is mentally apprehended, as a "joint or complex impression."

His visual model of linguistic or stylistic coalescence differs from Aristotle's analogy of the body politic as organic community. Aristotle reasoned that "man is more of a political animal than bees or any other gregarious animal." The metropolis, no less than the coral reef or the bee hive, lives as an organic structure, as do also human history and language. The extension of this analogy informs the organic *energeia* in the language theory of Wilhelm von Humboldt.[11] Other language theories of the period derived their organicism from the traditional *logos,* the union of language and mind.

Immanuel Kant, for example, defined the various activities of the language-making process (sign, symbol, scheme, analogy) as participating in, and contributing to, "die Möglichkeit des organischen Lebens."[12] De Quincey equates the Kantian categories with "the forms of the *logos* or formal understanding" (2:100) and interprets Kant's account of causation to reside in the process of connecting *(verknüpfen)* perceptions into the categories of quality, quantity, relation, and modality, a process which in turn renders possible the formation of judgments or the predication of sentences. De Quincey states the difficulty of this doctrine: "We have no right to view anything *in rerum natura* as objectively, or in itself, a cause"; rather, we can only subsume a perception "under the notion of a cause—we invest it with that function under that relation; that the whole proceeding is merely with respect to a *human* understanding, and by way of indispensable *nexus* to the several parts of our experience" (2:101). Many a commentator on Kant's *Kritik der reinen Vernunft* has confronted the difficulty of Kant's separation of the *phaenomenon* from the *noumenon,* but only De Quincey saw the problem as rendering causation a fiction of nexus between the mobile intellect and the *Ding-an-sich,* thus leaving the perceiver with the "Blank misgivings" of Wordsworth's "Creature / Moving about in worlds not realised."[13] De Quincey had little patience with the cumbersome structure of philosophical systems; he read widely in philosophy not to comprehend a system but to glean insights into the nature of perception and the liminal predicament of man caught between spirit and flesh, mind and nature.[14]

In affirming the revelation of the "moving intellect" in the interstices of language, De Quincey is not concerned with perpetuating the Johannine moment of the divine *logos* but with explaining the task confronting the human mind in its authorial, or interpretative, labor to bridge the gap between the letter and the spirit (2 Cor. 3:6). The squeal of a pig may be considered, organically, a part of the pig, but man, with his discriminating mind, prescinds what he speaks, divorces as he espouses, and even renders his words into the written *things* of books. For De Quincey, organic vitality must be sustained in "spontaneous connexion."

In his essay "Style" he inveighs against the evils of haste and pretentious bookishness which destroy the "natural impulse of every man . . . spontaneously to use the language of life." The latter evil of "bookish idiom" he describes as "some scaly leprosy of elephantiasis, barking and hide-binding the fine natural pulses of the elastic flesh" (10:149). The former evil resides in man's natural fluency. The "flying velocities" of words urged forth by the "necessities of hurry and of instant compliance with an instant emergency, granting no possibility for revision or opening for amended thought," spill into the "plethoric form of period, this monster model of sentence, bloated with decomplex intercalations." The aesthetic harmony of part and whole, assimilating the "crude undigested masses of suggestion" (10: 150), is accomplished in the slow, ruminating process of connection and relation:

Every man who has had any experience in writing knows how natural it is for the hurry and fulness of matter to discharge itself by vast sentences, involving clause within clause, *ad infinitum;* how difficult it is, and how much a work of art, to break up this huge fasciculus of cycle and epicycle into a graceful succession of sentences, long intermingled with short, each modifying the other, and arising musically by links of spontaneous connexion. [10:149–50]

The art of nexus, like the heautonomy of "freedom in appearance" in Schiller's aesthetics, is wrought in the deliberate labor to reproduce the spontaneity of perception.[15]

To exhibit the nexus of feeling, De Quincey relies on the doctrine of sympathy; the nexus of ideas he exercises through the associationist links of similitude and contrariety, contiguity and causality. Admittedly, such patterns of connection were advocated by many other writers of the period. But De Quincey, more than any of his contemporaries, paused within the threshold to explore the workings of perception, of association and sympathy. These were the factors of liminality which distinguished *organology* from the mere *mechanology* or arrangement. I suspect that all of the memorable passages of De Quincey's prose would reveal something of the "moving intellect" in the art of nexus. The four passages which I have selected for examination, however, may well have more to do with the problem than with the art, for I want to show how he attenuates and articulates the exploration of threshold experiences. As investigations in *nexu vincti* I have taken the account of the Roman clepsydra in the "Savannah-la-Mar" section of *Suspiria de Profundis,* the Orion nebula in "System of the Heavens," the wandering Piranesi of "Il Carceri" in *Confessions of an English Opium-Eater,* and the galloping horse in *The English Mail-Coach.*

Among the prevailing "diseases" of polite discourse, De Quincey declares in his essay on "Conversation," are the "want of *timing*" to curb the excessiveness of an egoistic appropriation and the "want of some discretional power" to control the excursiveness by "subtle links of association" and keep it from lapsing into the "vagrancy" of "verbal accident" (10:285–87). For timing he proposes the cure of the Roman law court: the clepsydra which "regulated the duration" (10:286) of the advocate's pleading. The Dark Interpreter who attends the dreamer of *Suspiria de Profundis* also conjures the clepsydra as the two stare down through the "watery veil" at Savannah-la-Mar drowned in "the loveliness of cerulean depths." The clepsydra here "regulated the duration" of death for the children, "asleep through five generations" awaiting the "heavenly dawn." The mechanical clock, its coiled spring driving a series of gears whose forward motion is released by a pivoting balance called an "escape," marks time by redundancy: its mechanical movement is repeated over and over. The clepsydra, however, gives visual testimony to the continuous flow of time in "the drops as they race along" (*SP,* p. 254). In introducing his argument that contrivance must have a contriver, Paley found the mechanical clock happily suited as his model for the biological mechanism. But De Quincey's Dark Interpreter makes the clepsydra an instrument of paradox, repeating Zeno's illusion of time as continuous and infinitely divisible. Like the space between words, the space between the falling drops invites the imagination to enter and speculate. The threshold of the present moment "contracts into a mathematic point" (*SP,* p. 255) of atomistic finitude, then expands into the dynamism of God's infinity.

From the temporal nexus of the clepsydra, in which De Quincey seeks the invisible and indivisible present in the continuum of time, to his account of the spatial nexus in the Orion nebula, in which he sees "a head thrown back, and raising its face (or eyes, if eyes it had) in the very anguish of hatred to some unknown heavens," is a mere shift in liminal perspective. Zeno's paradoxes and Parmenides' repudiation of the *genesis* and *thanatos* De Quincey had deftly exploited in tolling the passage of the fiftieth drop of the clepsydra. He also knew of Plato's preoccupation with Zeno and Parmenides. In the cosmological dialogue of *Timaeus* space is considered, similar to Zeno's time, an evanescent frame for the visible order of things.[16] Space may be organized through the imposition of hypostatic types and geometric shapes, but what seem fixed "sensations" result only from the collision of the "ever-flowing stream" of external elements with the moving impulses of body and soul. The Laokoön-like head of the Orion nebula, uttering to the universe its curse of brutal malignancy in frozen silence, is such an imposed type and shape; it owes, therefore, part of its apocalyptic horror to the very chance and happenstance of its configuration, "which Sir John Herschel was able to arrest in his eighteen-inch mirror" (8:19).

De Quincey delineates in nightmarish detail the "horror of the regal phantasma" which the telescope has "perfected to eyes of flesh" (8:18). No matter that with another focus "this nebular apparition" may vanish: "It is enough that once, in a single stage of the examination, this apparition put on the figure here represented, and for a momentary purpose here dimly deciphered" (8:19n.). Where the telescope has "tortured" the cosmos "into closer compression, again let the screw be put upon it, and once again it shall shake off the oppression of distance as the dewdrops are shaken from a lion's mane" (8:22). Space, De Quincey agrees with Timaeus, can be known only in terms of the dilemma of "the collision between magnitude and distance," the "motion in ourselves doubtfully confounded with a motion in some external body," and the illusion of "real proximity" wrought by "apparent proximity . . . , though in far other depths of space" (8:24). The telescope penetrates the venerable presence of Orion only to reveal the awful apparition of the nebula, whose beauty serves "to point and envenom his ghostly ugliness" (8:19). The horrific sublime is not simply that the beholder is thus challenged by the chance illusion in this hypostatic nexus of space, but that such terror lurks infinitely in every possible visible nexus of the cosmos. In his epilogue, abbreviated from "Traum über das All," which De Quincey had earlier translated in his "Analects from Richter," the dreamer is led through the "persecutions of the Infinite" until he cries out his agony of the endless, to which the angel replies: "Lo! also there is no beginning" (8:34).[17]

In *The Prelude*, concluding his epic simile on the formative power of the imagination to give shape to the shadows that the inspired perception provides, Wordsworth proclaims "a spectacle to which there is no end."[18] In defense of his vision of the face in the nebula as the hypostatic collision of "sensation," things mediated by the organs of perception—"both what they half create, / And what perceive," De Quincey refers to the example of Wordsworth and cites his "sonnet upon cloud mimicries, drawn from 'all the fuming vanities of earth,' . . .or that labyrinth of terraces and towers which revealed itself in the very centre of a storm" (8:19n.; *The Excursion*, 2.834–51). De Quincey quotes this passage verbatim in his account of Piranesi's "Il Carceri." The Piranesi passage, because it was composed within a peculiar complexity of imaginary encounters with unseen engravings, reveals a compelling and compulsive language of delusion in describing nexus.[19] First, he candidly admits that he has never looked into the "Il Carceri"; instead, he has had before him the "Antiquities of Rome." The transformation from those architectural "realities" to the imagined prison is accomplished through De Quincey's recollection of Coleridge's recollection. Second, the "Dreams" of Piranesi's "delirium" are made to open into De Quincey's opium visions, which in turn are substantiated by Wordsworth's "cerulean" architecture. Third, and here is the essential problem of nexus, the reduplicated figure of "delirious Piranesi," everywhere discovered creeping along staircases leading nowhere, is appropriated by De Quincey as exemplifying "the same power of endless growth and self-reproduction" (3:439) in the architecture of his own dreams.

No more than logic can supply a link between the drowned

time of "five generations" preserving Savannah-la-Mar in still waters and the relentless time racing with the fiftieth drop of the clepsydra, so no more can logic provide a nexus to the wandering Piranesi, one permitting him to cross beyond each "abrupt termination" above the abyss. Here again is the illusion of Zeno's time and Parmenides' space. The "sensation" of the moment is hypostatic, yet the "collision" of self and the external world is ever repeated. Whenever De Quincey peers through the telescope, he can anticipate another frightful image of the self in the vast void. Just so the self-projection of De Quincey or Coleridge or Piranesi (who, incidentally, has *not* inserted these self-portraits into his "Invenzioni") is doomed forever to wander the trapped and isolated interstices of the immense dungeons.

The description of the galloping horse in *The English Mail-Coach* may seem to provide a contrast with the previous examples. Here De Quincey does affirm a positive bond, a sympathetic immediacy between self and nature. The horse versus the locomotive, in this description of the thrill of speed,[20] gives occasion for an excursus on the organic versus the mechanic and what he calls the *magna vivimus* over the *magna loquimur*. All that energy "incarnated in the fiery eyeballs . . . , in his dilated nostril, spasmodic muscles, and thunder-beating hoofs" is communicated galvanically:

> The intervening links that connected them, that spread the earthquake of battle into the eyeball of the horse, were the heart of man and its electric thrillings—kindling in the rapture of the fiery strife, and then propagating its own tumults by contagious shouts and gestures to the heart of his servant the horse. [13:284]

Although he tempts us to accept the excitement and dynamic confluency in this sympathetic nexus, he has set this passage in an antagonistic context. This is the nostalgic past. The organic integrity of a nation linked together by vital concerns, visually represented in the highways pulsating with the systole and diastole of the racing mail-coaches guided by "the conscious presence of a central intellect," has given way to a modern nation —mechanized, industrialized, and dehumanized. But with that "impassioned heart" (13:272) of the past, and even because of the sympathetic links that once bound the parts into an organic whole, De Quincey posits a high moral responsibility at the threshold of action. The tremendous energy, in this dramatic moment of Aristotelian *praxis*, forever threatens to break forth into that climactic moment of tragedy narrowly averted which paralyzes the beholder in "The Vision of Sudden Death." The electric immediacy becomes impotently static.

The *mechanology* of style in De Quincey's theory is easy to summarize: it is the sum of the particulars of grammar, the machinery of predication and modification, as addressed by the "discursive reason" to the tasks of a "literature of knowledge." The corresponding "literature of power" is engendered in the *play* of "intuitive reason" with "passion," of rhetoric with eloquence, through the art of connection and relation peculiar to the *organology* of style (10:47-48; 11:54-56). De Quincey as theorist of language could do little more than declare that "the use of words" should be organically "connected with thoughts, and modified by thoughts" (10:164). But he explored the thresholds of perception and the mysteries of nexus as a persistent motif in his prose, from such tight little riddles as deciphering the *heu taceo* of Aelius Lamia in the suicidal repartee "Quam vellum et Orpheutaceam" to the wide reaches of the lambent magic of words described in his essays on sortilege. The "moving intellect" is revealed in the interstices of language, and it is in the interstices that De Quincey pauses to explore.

Notes

1. Gilbert Ryle, *The Concept of Mind* (New York: Barnes and Noble, 1949), pp. 15-16; see also A. D. Nuttall, *A Common Sky: Philosophy and the Literary Imagination* (Berkeley and Los Angeles: University of California Press, 1974).

2. Plato, *The Collected Dialogues of Plato*, ed. Edith Hamilton and Huntington Cairns, Bollingen Series 71 (Princeton, N.J.: Princeton University Press, 1961), p. 911 (*Theatetus*, 204b), p. 510 (*Phaedrus*, 264c).

3. Aristotle, *The Basic Works of Aristotle*, ed. Richard McKeon (New York: Random House, 1941), p. 1129 (*Politics*, 1253a), p. 1463 (*Poetics*, 1451a).

4. Samuel Taylor Coleridge, *The Friend*, vol. 4, pt. 1, of *The Collected Works of Samuel Taylor Coleridge*, ed. Barbara E. Rooke, Bollingen Series 75 (London: Routledge and Kegan Paul; Princeton, N.J.: Princeton University Press, 1969), p. 497.

5. Noam Chomsky, *Cartesian Linguistics: A Chapter in the History of Rationalist Thought* (New York: Harper and Row, 1966), pp. 26-28.

6. Samuel Taylor Coleridge, *Logic*, vol. 13 of *The Collected Works of Samuel Taylor Coleridge*, ed. J. R. de J. Jackson, Bollingen Series 75 (London: Routledge and Kegan Paul; Princeton, N.J.: Princeton University Press, 1981), p. 171.

7. See William Paley, *Natural Theology; or, Evidences of the Existence and Attributes of the Deity*, 16th ed. (London: S. Hamilton, 1819), pp. 16-35.

8. Hermann Diels, *Parmenides Lehrgedicht: Griechisch und Deutsch* (Berlin: G. Reimer, 1897); my translation. See also John Burnet, *Early Greek Philosophy*, 4th ed. (London: A. and C. Black, 1930), pp. 169-96.

9. See James Burnett, Lord Monboddo, *Of the Origin and Progress of Language*, 2d ed., 6 vols. (1774-1809; reprint, New York: AMS Press, 1973), 1:201-206, 415-21.

10. See John Horne Tooke, *Epea Pteroenta; or, The Diversions of Purley*, 2d ed., 2 vols. (London: J. Johnson, 1798-1805), 1:17-51.

11. See Wilhelm von Humboldt, *Über die Verschiedenheit des menschlichen Sprachbaues und ihren Einfluss auf die geistige Entwicklung des Menschengeschlechts* (1830-35), in his *Werke*, ed. Andreas Flitner and Klaus Giel (Stuttgart: Cotta, 1964), 3:418.

12. Immanuel Kant, *Anthropologie in pragmatischer Hinsicht* (1798) and *Kritik der Urteilskraft* (1790), in his *Werke*, ed. Wilhelm Weischedel (Darmstadt: Wissenschaftliche Buchgesselschaft, 1966), 6:497-502, 5:483-90.

13. William Wordsworth, "Ode: Intimations of Immortality from Recollections of Early Childhood," lines 145-46, in *The Poetical Works of William Wordsworth*, ed. E[rnest] de Selincourt and Helen Darbishire, 5 vols. (Oxford: Oxford University Press, Clarendon Press, 1940-49), 4:283.

14. For discussion of De Quincey's understanding of Kant see Sigmund K. Proctor, *Thomas De Quincey's Theory of Literature* (Ann Arbor: University of Michigan Press, 1943; reprint, New York: Octagon, 1966), pp. 34-38, 293-97; and the following works by René Wellek: *Immanuel Kant in England, 1793-1838* (Princeton, N.J.: Princeton University Press, 1931), pp. 171-80; "De Quincey's Status in the History of Ideas," *Philological Quarterly* 23 (1944): 248-72 (reprinted in *Confrontations: Studies in the Intellectual and Literary Relations Between Germany, England, and the United States During the Nineteenth Century* [Princeton, N.J.: Princeton University Press, 1965], pp. 114-52). In the latter article, countering Proctor's arguments, Wellek discusses De Quincey's sporadic and shallow analysis of Kant's critical philosophy and marvels at "how little system there was in his agile and nimble mind" (p. 255).

15. See my Introduction to *Selected Essays on Rhetoric by Thomas De Quin-

cey (Carbondale: Southern Illinois University Press, 1967), pp. xxi–xxv.

16. See Plato, *Collected Dialogues,* pp. 1171–72 (*Timaeus,* 43c).

17. See my article "The Dream-Visions of Jean Paul and De Quincey," *Comparative Literature* 20 (1968): 1–26; Joel D. Black, "Levana: Levitation in Jean Paul and Thomas De Quincey," *Comparative Literature* 32 (1980): 42–62.

18. William Wordsworth, *The Prelude: 1799, 1805, 1850,* ed. Jonathan Wordsworth, M. H. Abrams, and Stephen Gill (New York: Norton, 1979), 8.741 (1805).

19. Cf. Frances Ferguson, "Coleridge on Language and Delusion," *Genre* 11 (1978): 191–207.

20. See E. Michael Thron, "Speed, Steam, Self, and Thomas De Quincey," in Norman A. Anderson and Margene E. Weiss, eds., *Interspace and the Inward Sphere: Essays on Romantic and Victorian Self* (Macomb, Ill.: Western Illinois University, 1978), pp. 51–58.

14

"Booked for Utter Perplexity" on De Quincey's *English Mail-Coach*

ARDEN REED

What is a De Quincey essay about? You might at first regard this as a schoolmarmish question, but few critical undertakings produce more perplexity than trying to settle on the theme or subject in any given piece of De Quincey's prose. He may title an article "Sir William Hamilton," for instance, yet the reader of *Hogg's Instructor* for 1852 will find less information there about Hamilton than about the history of Greek literature, certain topics in logic, or even De Quincey's own epistolary habits. The trouble is that Sir William, like almost every other subject for De Quincey, "stand[s] in a possible relation to all things" (5:326). Or consider the original *Confessions of an English Opium-Eater:* is it an autobiographical sketch, a medical treatise on opium, a record of dream visions? How can we distinguish the variations on the theme from the theme itself? The revised *Confessions,* written after he had had thirty-five years to reconsider it, seems if anything more shapeless and discursive than the first version.

What a De Quincey essay is about will likely remain an unsettled question because he writes *circumstantial* prose. Under the weight of circumstance the adverb "about" takes on the character of an adjective, so that we can say De Quincey's writing simply is *about* — as in some or all of these definitions:

... in no particular direction; with no particular destination; to a reversed position or direction; all around; on every side; in the area or vicinity; in succession; one after another; on all sides of; surrounding; in and around; here and there in; through; almost the same as; close to, near; in the possession of; ready or prepared to do something; involved with or engaged in.[1]

It is no accident that *The English Mail-Coach* repeatedly traces revolutions about a center that may or may not be hollow (since we get deflected before reaching it, we can never know for sure), in figures like the "raving of hurricanes" (13:317) or a "local vortex [that] gave a wheeling bias to her course" (13:320) so that "round a promontory of rocks she wheeled out of sight" (13:321).

Academic criticism tends to respond to De Quincey's meanderings in one of two ways. As representative of the first, René Wellek dismisses De Quincey as hopelessly digressive: "There is no more exasperating writer than De Quincey; he never seems to be able to keep to a point, digresses constantly."[2] Alternatively the critic may attempt to demonstrate the presence of a unifying structure or principle, always concealed beneath the linguistic surface but giving shape and coherence to the text at hand. Thus David Sundelson, for example, hopes to "show that the apparent digressiveness of 'The English Mail Coach' conceals a unified skeleton."[3] The second response seems the more promising, if only because it is willing to engage the texts and has produced illuminating readings. Still, such criticism runs the risk of turning defensively into the upside-down version of its apparent antagonist ("Yes, he *is* digressive." "No, he *isn't*."), and the desire to establish unity may betray pressures that are institutional as well as aesthetic. The job of professional readers is traditionally understood to entail some form of exhuming "unified skeletons," even when as in *The English Mail-Coach* nobody actually dies. This desire for unity, furthermore, ignores De Quincey's explicit remarks to the critic in his "Introductory Notice" to *Suspiria de Profundis:* "I tell my critic that the whole course of this narrative resembles, and was meant to resemble, a *caduceus* wreathed about with meandering ornaments, or the shaft of a tree's stem hung round and surmounted with some vagrant parasitical plant" (*SP,* p. 157). That is, of course, a self-serving claim and not to be taken at face value, but at least it gives warning that any criticism which insists on homogenizing digressions and fails to read them as such (assuming, provisionally, that this is possible) will have tunnel vision, will be blind to much of what De Quincey's essays are about.

These are larger issues than I can take up here except by implication. For the present I want to suspend aesthetic judgments and try simply to describe the textual movement of De Quincey's mail-coach. We may begin with the phrase "English mail-coach." However straightforward it might appear, this phrase is ambiguous. We are likely to assume that it refers to that kind of carriage invented by John Palmer, as the first sentence obligingly informs us, and used by De Quincey to shuttle back and forth to Oxford before he aborted his career there. So understood, the essay is a vivid and lyrical picture of English travel before the advent of the railroad and also a representation of De Quincey's inner world. But the phrase "English mail-coach" also refers to the essay itself and as such signifies a linguistic construct. Thus "English mail-coach" names both an object within the text and the whole of that text.

More important, this double reference is repeated within the essay, because the mail-coach functions both as the vehicle that transports the post and also as a "vehicle" in the rhetorical sense of a figure signifying the tenor "language." The beginning of the essay intimates this second meaning for it underscores the coach's role of disseminating to an anxious public the "heart-shaking news" (13:272) of the Napoleonic Wars. (In the revised *Confessions,* written shortly after *The English Mail-Coach,* De Quincey notes that "all the mails from the N, the E, the W, the S—whence, according to some curious etymologists, comes the magical word *news*—drove up successively to the post-office" [3:348].) In fact, the mail-coach moves all through the essay as a kind of writing instrument: it articulates the body politic of England corporeally and linguistically, jointing its parts into an organic whole and acting as a kind of central nervous system along which passes all written communication. Just as a pen distributes the letters of the alphabet across the page, so the mail-coach distributes its "letters" across the land in repeated "passages" (13:316). In his preface of 1854 to the essay De Quincey records as the "grandest" distinction of the mail its function "to publish over all the land" battles such as Waterloo (13:329), and besides the secondary sense of bringing something to the public's attention the word "publish" carries its primary sense of issuing texts.[4]

De Quincey's characterization of the mail-coach, its motion, and its associations points repeatedly to the vehicle's linguistic nature. On the coach takes place "communication between the horse and his master" (13:284; see also 13:276), at the same time that the coach makes "communications with . . . rural post-offices" (13:305). For De Quincey, traveling on the mail-coach means reading a scene that "wrote all its records on my heart" (13:317). He can refer, therefore, to an "incident" on the mail-coach as "furnish[ing] the text for this reverie" (13:304), to "the grandest chapter of our experience within the . . . mail-coach service" (13:290), and to the difficulties he had in "decipher[ing] the character of the motion" (13:313) of another vehicle. *The English Mail-Coach* tells the story of how to do things with words, for the only action De Quincey as passenger can perform is the linguistic act of shouting (and even this is a speech mediated by writing, since De Quincey is self-consciously imitating the shout of Achilles in *The Iliad*). Try as he might, he cannot seize the reins or influence the speed or direction of the horses. But in a linguistic world such action as a shout may suffice.[5]

The essay stages a moral dilemma for De Quincey as a passenger but also a linguistic problem for him as a narrator, and there is an ongoing relation between the path of his adventure and that of his narrative. Between Manchester and Preston there are three "stages" to the mail, and "within these . . . stages lay the foundation, the progress, and termination" (13:308)—the three stages of the tale. Now a "good" narrative ought to move through these stages like a well-oiled mail-coach, advancing directly and punctually along a straight line so as to deliver its message efficiently. At the outset De Quincey makes much of the accuracy and constancy of the system, noting how two mails traveling in opposite directions and "starting at the same minute from points six hundred miles apart, met almost constantly at a particular bridge which bisected the total distance" (13:272n.). But on the particular ride De Quincey then recounts, the driver falls asleep and his coach wanders from the center over to the margin of the road. His failure to follow the straight path before him and his inability to resist drifting into dreams is a mirror image or *mise en abîme* of De Quincey's own habits. Like the driver of the English mail-coach, the narrator of *The English Mail-Coach* begins in the waking world only to end in a "Dream-Fugue," where the straight line turns into "the caprices, the gay arabesques, and the lively floral luxuriations of dreams" (13: 291n.). The real drifter is De Quincey, who can no more steer a straight course through his subject than could Laurence Sterne's historiographer in *Tristram Shandy:*

> Could a historiographer drive on his history, as a muleteer drives on his mule, — straight forward; — for instance, from *Rome* all the way to *Loretto,* without ever once turning his head aside either to the right hand or to the left, — he might venture to foretell you to an hour when he should get to his journey's end; — but the thing is, morally speaking, impossible: For, if he is a man of the least spirit, he will have fifty deviations from a straight line to make with this or that party as he goes along, which he can no ways avoid.[6]

Sterne introduces a twist that profoundly complicates the moral and aesthetic issues which De Quincey must negotiate. In spite of its obvious ethical and material advantages, in spite of its normative function, the straight line lacks spirit. It may even be deadly — deadly dull, Sterne would argue, contrasting the straight line to Hogarth's sinuous line of beauty and to his own digressions, which he calls "the life, the soul of reading."[7] De Quincey reiterates Sterne's ratio in the figure of the caduceus, where "those parasitical thoughts, feelings, digressions, which climb up with bells and blossoms," wind around "murderous spears and halberts — things that express death in their origin (being made from dead substances that once had lived in forests)" (*SP,* pp. 159, 158). The meandering line may be a parasite, but as such it diverts life from the "murderous" straight line.

De Quincey suggests that the railroad — straightest and swiftest of lines — is fatal to the consciousness of our own experience, because its increased velocity is not "a consciousness, but . . .

a fact of our *lifeless* [italics added] knowledge, resting upon *alien* evidence: as, for instance, because somebody *says* that we have gone fifty miles in the hour, though we are far from feeling it as a personal experience" (13:283). Alienating and deadly dull, the straight line turns deadly in a literal sense in "The Vision of Sudden Death." All that saves the amorous couple (and the essay itself) is a certain swerve from "the line of absolute ruin" (13:316). Nonetheless, swerving perplexes De Quincey's negotiations with the reader. To sustain reader interest, De Quincey must vary his theme by rambling away from it into "perhaps too rank a luxuriance" (*SP,* p. 159)—"too rank" because the curling tendrils of his prose may leave the reader unable "to unravel [De Quincey's] logic" and "follow the links of the connexion" (13:328) in the essay. The mail-coach does not solve but enacts this dilemma by moving its letters inexorably forward even while it is "drawn" to "the wrong side" of the road, which is yet "the right-hand side of the road" (13:312).

Because it is both a historical and a linguistic vehicle, the English mail-coach inscribes a double path, at once straight and splayed. It proceeds directly from one point to another: "A fiery arrow seems to be let loose, which from that moment is destined to travel, without intermission, westwards for three hundred miles" (13:294–95). But at the same time its function "as the national organ for publishing" war news makes it "*diffusively* [italics added] influential" (13:272; cf. 13:294: the mail-coach's carrying the news "has an obscure effect of multiplying the victory itself, by multiplying to the imagination into infinity the stages of its progressive diffusion"), as any linguistic activity will be diffusive for De Quincey. The essay provides two analogues for the mail-coach's double motion, one psychological and the other rhetorical. As De Quincey mounts the coach for the arrowlike trip to Preston, he takes "a small quantity of laudanum" (13:306) which produces a train of lateral associations that wind in counterpoint about the unwavering geographic progression, turning from the coachman to a monster to Virgil to the *Arabian Nights* to a bottomless gulf, and so on. The rhetorical analogue is De Quincey's proceeding along a line of argument that he calls straightforward ("I am myself as little able . . . to detect any lurking obscurity, as these critics found themselves to unravel my logic" [13:328]) while at the same time winding (or unwinding) the line into vagrant thoughts, feelings, and digressions. We may best trace that wobble in the essay's governing rhetorical strategy, which is to contrast past and present and the associations that cluster about them—the mail-coach complex and the railroad complex. This contrast, as we shall see, De Quincey at once advances and confounds.

According to the conventional but seductive argument he follows, to move from past to present is to experience a kind of fall. We may schematize the contrast as follows:

Past	Present
mail-coach	railroad
the organic	the mechanic
wholeness	fragmentation and alienation
center	absence of center
harmony	dissonance
nature	culture
life	death

De Quincey imagines the old post-office service in terms of a living organism, whose parts are "all obedient as slaves to the supreme *baton* of some great leader, [and] terminate in a perfection of harmony like that of heart, brain, and lungs in a healthy animal organisation." The "conscious presence of a central intellect" guides the organism, enabling it to "overrule" (13:272) all obstacles that might deflect the coach from its destination. The heart of the system is naturally a real animal, and De Quincey expresses a Wordsworthian appreciation for the horse's "glad animal sensibilities." Communicating with the horse in turn gives De Quincey access to his own lived experience, in this case the experience of motion; but when an iron horse replaces the natural one, communication breaks down: "Iron tubes and boilers have disconnected man's heart from the ministers of his locomotion" (13:284), leaving man alienated even from his own movements.[8]

Against this backdrop of modern fragmentation De Quincey

invokes in the second section a vision of pure Romantic unity. Like Rousseau's, De Quincey's "reverie" depends on solitude, which quickly expands into a "universal lull" that integrates the calm sea, the atmosphere, and especially the light: "Moonlight and the first timid tremblings of the dawn were by this time *blending;* and the *blendings* were brought into a still more exquisite state of *unity* by a slight silvery mist, motionless and dreamy, that covered the woods and fields, but with a *veil of equable transparency*" (italics added). Behind this text stands the Coleridgean aesthetic of imagination reconciling opposites (night and day, moon and sun) and diffusing a mist that does not obscure the landscape but, paradoxically, illuminates as it harmonizes the disparate elements.[9] To complete the vision, De Quincey adds that the "atmosphere" on such nights leads man to "ascend with easy steps from the sorrow-stricken fields of earth upwards to the sandals of God." He thus evokes an Edenic scene, and the couple meandering through it carry a muted resemblance to Adam and Eve. At the heart of the vision is a dream of fluid and immediate communication—downward between man and the natural world, inward between awareness and experience, and upward: "We still believe, and must for ever believe, in fields of air traversing the total gulf between earth and the central heavens" (13:311). This might be called the logocentric dream, since its model of communication is either inward and intuitive or, if externalized, then spoken through a veil of "equable transparency" that masks nothing between speaker and listener.

Such is the direct argument of the essay which, as it happens, is also the argument of direction or straightforwardness in itself. In characteristic fashion, however, De Quincey has already deflected it long before it ever reaches its destination, for his is a perplexing vision of paradise. The typical Romantic version of the myth, in Rousseau or Wordsworth, for instance, locates Eden in childhood and identifies the Fall with growing up. But De Quincey associates childhood with a dream, from which no one escapes, of "the original temptation in Eden." Like Adam, De Quincey's child succumbs to temptation, and his dream "publishes the secret frailty of human nature—reveals its deep-seated falsehood to itself—records its abysmal treachery." Hence it is "by infinite iteration" that the Fall already occurs *within* the paradisical space of childhood, as "each several child of our mysterious race completes for himself the treason of the aboriginal fall" (13:304). In a passage De Quincey deleted from the final version of *The English Mail-Coach*, he extends the dream to its adult form. Just as Freud would, De Quincey discovers in the most *heimlich* of places the uncanny presence of the *unheimlich*: "The dreamer finds housed within himself—occupying, as it were, some separate chamber in his brain—holding, perhaps, from that station a secret and detestable commerce with his own heart—some horrid alien nature" that "contradicts his own, fights with it, perplexes and confounds it" (13:292n.). When De Quincey looks back to an earlier Edenic time, he finds traces of a later fallen time already blemishing the "equable transparency," and when he looks inward, he finds a foreigner lodged there. It grows hard to distinguish the "*alien* evidence" produced in the present by external forces like the railroad from the "alien nature" produced in the past by the self. *The English Mail-Coach* is composed of an almost "infinite iteration" of confoundings like this, of parasitical plants twisted round and choking off the "central intellect."

For my purpose the most noteworthy dislocation of past and present involves language. If De Quincey were consistent in the contrasts he draws, it would seem that he should associate speech with the past and writing with the present—the one natural and immediate, the other artificial, deferred, and alienating. It thus creates a major conceptual disturbance that the mail-coach should "diffuse" letters and that it should owe its existence to the gaps in space and time that render speech impossible. More than that, the mail-coach literally inscribes its own marking, for "the feet of our own horses . . . [were] running on a sandy margin of the road" (13:311), where they leave hoofprints and wheel tracks.[10] Now the idealized setting of "The Vision of Sudden Death" demands an unmediated vision, which is why De Quincey mentions the transparent atmospheric veil that reveals everything, even God. The detail about horses' feet and sandy margins thus makes a decisive difference, even though De Quincey presents it offhandedly in a subordinate clause, because it introduces signs that mediate the scene, making traces on the transparent setting. Even the displacement of the coach to the "margin," where this form of writing becomes possible, is a little surprising, since De Quincey has consistently associated the mail-coach with the center: it is the "central intellect" of the nation and the center of attention, for "the gatherings of gazers about a laurelled mail had one centre, and acknowledged one sole interest" (13:284-85), by contrast to the railway station crowds, who "own as many centres as there are separate carriages in the train" (13:285). But the coach is lured away from the proper, straight, and narrow path by "the luxury of the soft beaten sand as contrasted with the paved centre" (13:312), and that luxury proves, as De Quincey strikingly phrases it, a "luxury of ruin" (13:304). It is appropriate, then, that the intrusion of writing in the form of the careening English mail-coach should terminate the couple's Edenic interlude.

There is a more obvious way that the intrusion of the mail spells the Fall from paradise, of course. De Quincey repeatedly describes the relation of the driver to his horse as that of master to slave, a relationship sustained by the "galvanic cycle ... of communication" between them. Although he asserts that this cycle is "broken up for ever" (13:284) by the coming of the railroad, he shows explicitly and at length in "The Vision of Sudden Death" how the break might occur even in the days of the mail-coach. (In fact, it is only because the break does occur that there is a story to tell.) To block communication between driver and team it is unnecessary to substitute an iron horse; the same thing happens if the driver simply falls asleep. When he does, the relation between master and slave revolves, leaving everyone on the road at the mercy of the team. And its threat extends far beyond the couple, for the rebellion of the horses is an emblem for the rebellion of natural forces against the control of civilization or, following Plato's image of the soul in the *Phaedrus*, of passion against reason. In the present narrative De Quincey manages to save the couple by warning them in the nick of time—that is, by imparting a certain knowledge. But, as in Genesis, the acquisition of knowledge is coupled to the expulsion from paradise. Thus, while De Quincey clearly marks out a fall from the past to the present, he also already locates the Fall in the past, for all the contradictions he draws between the two eras, and all the reversals, may already be found in the days of the mail-coach.

Like the moving wheels of the mail-coach, *The English Mail-Coach* performs repeated revolutions on the laws and conventions of exposition and narrative. But rather than executing perfect circles, the revolutions of De Quincey's mail-coach are skewed and unstable, the kind that might be made by those "eccentric people in comets" (13:270) who appear in the essay's first sentence."[11] From then on the runaway journey of the mail-coach maps the same wayward course that a De Quincey essay takes, and the driverless coach distributing letters in "oblique and lateral communications" (13:305) is his perfect conveyance.

The disruption of narrative laws is mirrored by the mail-coach's disruption of civil laws. By underscoring the mail's royal charter (13:281-83), De Quincey heightens the irony that the agent of the law should trespass, tearing down the wrong side of the road. But like other violations in the essay, this one is perplexing because by definition the mail-coach is always on the right side of the road: legal precedent holds that "all carriages were required to give way before royal equipages, and therefore before the mail as one of them. But this only increased the danger, as being a regulation very imperfectly made known, very unequally enforced, and therefore often embarrassing the movements on both sides" (13:312n.). Such a law leaves everyone in a double bind: you are as likely to risk mortal danger if you observe it as if you transgress it. Furthermore, although the mail-coach is an integral part of English government, it nonetheless provides the perfect haven for whoever is running from the law. If you want to evade bill collectors, counseled De Quincey, who knew about such things, the best place to hide is "on the box of his Majesty's mail" since "nobody can touch you there.... No matter though the sheriff and under-sheriff in every county should be running after you with his *posse*.... It is felony to stop the mail; even the sheriff cannot do that" (13:278).

In its revolutions the essay similarly dislocates the dimensions of space and time. The inside and outside of the mail-coach, for example, prove as reversible as the inside and outside of the self in De Quincey's dreams. According to the essay, the wealthy and the aristocrats always ride smugly inside the coach and hold in disdain those who, like the Oxford men, sit on the roof. The students respond by reversing the figurative and the literal, turning their physically superior position into a moral ascendancy so that "we, the most aristocratic of people, ... *look down* [italics added] superciliously even upon the insides themselves as often very questionable characters" (13:274). This line draws a false parallel between the students, whom it recognizes as "people," and the aristocrats, whom it subverts in naming them by the metonymy "insides themselves" (rather than "those inside"). Then the text turns these "insides" out by turning what was the outside, the roof De Quincey sat on, into an interior:

> The roof of the coach, which by some weak men had been called the attics, ... was in reality the drawing-room; in which drawing-room the box was the chief ottoman or sofa; whilst it appeared that the *inside,* which had been traditionally regarded as the only room tenantable by gentlemen, was, in fact, the coal-cellar in disguise. [13:275]

We have already remarked the temporal dislocation that occurs when a later, fallen time appears in a prelapsarian setting. An equivalent reversal takes place in "The Vision of Sudden Death," when De Quincey explains how he can visualize every detail of the collision several moments before the vehicles meet:

> I pretend to no presence of mind.... The palsy of doubt and distraction hangs like some guilty weight of dark unfathomed remembrances upon my energies when the signal is flying for *action.* But, on the other hand, this accursed gift I have, as regards *thought,* that in the first step towards the possibility of a misfortune I see its total evolution; in the radix of the series I see too certainly and too instantly its entire expansion; in the first syllable of the dreadful sentence I read already the last. [13:311–12]

Up to this point De Quincey has narrated "The Vision of Sudden Death" in the past tense, so that the turn to the present tense occurs, oddly enough, at the moment when presence vanishes: "I pretend to no presence of mind." Of course, we could interpret this sentence to mean simply "Fear made me panic so that I couldn't think what to do next," and we might add that De Quincey may still be feeling the disorientation of his opium reverie. However, the text suggests a more radical explanation: there is at this instant effectively no present moment in which mental presence could situate itself, because the past has occupied the present with a "guilty weight of dark unfathomed remembrances" which so burdens De Quincey's consciousness that he has no thought remaining with which to act. But simultaneously with this intrusion of the past into the present, a proleptic vision enters his mind, as though one seat on the mail had been sold to three different riders—past, future, and present. And between the pressure of memory on the one hand and that of foresight on the other, the present is squeezed out.

But he *does* have prescience. His imagination races ahead of the coach, doubling or squaring its furious forward motion, to light up a sudden vision of death.[12] Indeed, moments of proleptic vision seem to have punctuated De Quincey's whole life. On his first visit to the Lake District, seated on a mail-coach, he had a "prophetic glimpse" (2:354) that "on this very road, I should often pass, and in company that ... would hereafter plant memories in my heart, the last that will fade from it in the hour of death" (2:355). He had a repeated dream of a grieving woman in a doorway, and she turned out to be his wife. And his prediction that love for his departed sister would "rise again for me, to illuminate the hour of death" (*SP*, p. 179) seems to have been borne out, for "Sister! sister! sister!" (Page, 2:305) were among his last words.[13] It is noteworthy that each of these presentiments should, like that in *The English Mail-Coach*, include a vision of death. De Quincey himself remarked on this connection in a passage that reads like a summary of "The Vision of Sudden Death":

That grief, which one in a hundred has sensibility enough to gather from the sad retrospect of life in its closing stage, for me shed its dews as a prelibation upon the fountains of life whilst yet sparkling to the morning sun. I saw from afar and from before what I was to see from behind. [*SP*, p. 257]

How are we to account for this association of vision and death? It follows, I think, from the Miltonic distinction that De Quincey draws between two ways of knowing, or seeing: "I saw, not discursively... or by succession, but by one flash of horrid simultaneous intuition" (13:312). A proleptic vision is thus intuitive rather than discursive. In the terms I have been using here, it moves in a direct line without divagation. It is unerring. As such, prescience is the immaterial, mental version of the straight pole in De Quincey's caduceus, while ordinary sight corresponds to the plants that meander around it. To be armed with foresight, then, is to turn the eye into a "murderous spear" that must kill whatever it gazes on. That is why, when the narrator of "The Household Wreck" has his "presentiment," it should be "of some great calamity travelling towards me, not perhaps immediately impending, perhaps even at a great distance, but... already in motion upon some remote line of approach" (12:168; cf. 2:394–95). That is why, in reading Schiller's *Wallenstein,* De Quincey appreciates Henry IV's "prophetic instinct that caught from a far distance the sound of his murderer's motions" (8:446). And that is why, in *The English Mail-Coach,* De Quincey refers to foresight with the oxymoron "accursed gift"—both gift and curse at once.

This strange gift disarticulates the syntax of time and repeats in miniature the temporal inversions that operate throughout "The Vision of Sudden Death." The future—that is, the collision—is already present before it ever comes into being, and so when the "present" finally does arrive, it appears as a repetition of an event already experienced. Our impression that the accident itself is already a past event is strengthened by De Quincey's reverting to the past tense to narrate it. In fact, he returns to the past tense directly after recounting his presentiment, so that he uses the present tense only to name a moment in which his awareness was everywhere but in the present.

Since what De Quincey foresees is the imminent demise of

the young couple, we may interpret "dreadful sentence" at the end of the passage as a kind of death sentence handed down by some mysterious court of law. This reading is reinforced by the immediate context, the assize then in session at Lancaster, and by his remark two paragraphs later that "the court was sitting; the case was heard; the judge had finished; and only the verdict was yet in arrear" (13:313)—a verdict he already knows. But like the words "letter," "publish," and "passage," "sentence" carries a second meaning here. The three instances De Quincey cites—misfortunes, series, sentence—become progressively more linguistic in character, pivoting on the double sense of "radix," which means both a mathematical and an etymological root, and finally representing the mail-coach as a purely linguistic figure, since its movement through space and time becomes the movement from one syllable to another. His "sentence" thus circles round to point back to itself. Furthermore, as repetition provides the theme of this sentence (the present appears as a reenactment of past forebodings), so repetition organizes the words into three clauses, each of which says roughly the same thing. That is, the sentence *itself* expands like a series from a radix. And it is no accident that the reference to the "last" syllable of the sentence which the *speaker* reads is so positioned as to be simultaneously the last syllable which *we* read, thereby incorporating the reader into this (dis)articulation.

However, the role of reading in this scene is more complex than I have yet indicated. De Quincey has consistently pictured himself as the writer, but in a reversal parallel to that between driver and team this sentence transforms him into a reader. The mail-coach writes in the margin, and De Quincey here reads its text. It is as though he were a character in someone else's book and could flip ahead to read about himself. (In fact, De Quincey habitually represents foresight as a kind of reading: "It appeared, then, that I had been reading a legend concerning myself in the *Arabian Nights*. I had been contemplated in types a thousand years before on the banks of the Tigris" [*SP,* p. 220; cf. 1:129].) His reading disrupts the reverie of Romantic union just as the mail's writing had, for what he reads is the death sentence of that vision. Yet De Quincey is not a reader in the same sense that we are; if anything, he is a Borgesian *lector fantástico* who can spatialize time and gaze simultaneously on past, present, and future, or first, middle, and last word. But to *narrate* this vision he must restore the temporal dimension by turning his fantastic sentence back into an ordinary one, a sentence that unfolds the vision of synchrony only in a sequential manner. When we read "the first step," we do not yet know the last, as De Quincey does. His mode of perception and ours work at cross purposes, and for us the suddenness of vision is necessarily retarded. Since he cannot make our vision equally immediate, De Quincey opts for the reverse solution—to retard our vision yet more by stating the same theme three times over. The effect of this repetition, however, is to bring our vision into line with his: if when we read the phrase "the first step" in the opening clause, we are ignorant of the last, by the time we arrive at "the first step" in the final clause, we can confidently predict what that "last" syllable will be. Furthermore, De Quincey himself never entirely escapes from time. His intuitive, angelic vision occurs, after all, on a mail-coach plunging ahead, so that while he is able to spatialize time, that space itself is carried along in time.[14]

In the same way that past and future are compressed into the present moment, so too language (which articulates itself in time) is compacted in the mail sacks, those bundles of "letters," piled on the roof of the coach. De Quincey specifies that the mail is foreign—a vast expanse of space is representatively crowded onto this spot, just as time is. But the letters are also foreign in that language on the English mail-coach is estranged and estranging, for these letters impede communication rather than facilitate it. De Quincey is seated at the front, and to seize the guard's horn and sound a warning he must move to the rear. But the path to communication is blocked by that superabundance of writing on the mail-coach, so that he can never reach the horn. Here is the linguistic equivalent of the Romantic dilemma De Quincey has been pondering—namely, that excess of knowledge hampers action.

If the mail-coach is a kind of writing instrument, it thus produces no ordinary language. Instead, the mail keeps language in a suspended but mobile condition in which it has been detached from the writer and is not directly accessible to the reader. What sort of story does it inscribe, and how is one to make sense of its marginal markings? De Quincey suggests a way around the blockage in his essay on "Style," published in *Blackwood's Edinburgh Magazine* about five years earlier. This essay distinguishes two kinds of style, the organic and the mechanic. Given the contrast De Quincey draws between the mail-coach and the railroad, we would expect him to associate the coach-and-horse system with the organic style, but in keeping with the reversals we have been tracing, the "style" of De Quincey's mail turns out to be mechanical:

> Now, the use of words is an organic thing, in so far as language is connected with thoughts, and modified by thoughts. It is a mechanic thing, in so far as words in combination determine or modify each other.... The science of style considered as a machine, in which words act upon words, and through a particular grammar, might be called the *mechanology* of style.... It is of great importance not to confuse the functions: that function by which style maintains a commerce with thought, and that by which it chiefly communicates with grammar and with words. [10:164]

The distinction rests on the force that governs the production of language, whether thoughts or words, and the "dreadful sentence" written out by the mail-coach is the death warrant of thought. When the driver falls asleep and no one else can take the reins, the connection between thought and language breaks, so that the mail-coach becomes a machine in which language is left to its own device, words or "letters" modifying each other in uncontrollable velocity with no outside intervention.[15]

This is not to say that organic style has no part in *The English Mail-Coach*. De Quincey consistently associates the organic with the "mother tongue" and with women who have not had much commerce with the language of books and newspapers: "The idiom of our language, the mother tongue, survives only amongst our women and children; not, Heaven knows, amongst our women who write books ... but amongst well-educated women not professionally given to literature" (10:142). In *The*

English Mail-Coach the young woman in the gig plays this role. Even though we never hear her speak, we know how "effective" her language must be: "From the greater excitability of females, and the superior vivacity of their feelings, they will be liable to far more irritations from *wounded* sensibilities. It is for such occasions chiefly that they seek to be effective in their language" (10:144–45; italics added). We may therefore say that *The English Mail-Coach* narrates the wounding of organic by mechanic language, and wounding of a particular kind.

Despite De Quincey's repeated references to accidents in "The Vision of Sudden Death," "Style" implies that there is a strange necessity at work in this section of *The English Mail-Coach*. According to "Style," organic language is not a given but requires some "commerce with thought" to bring it into being. In this case it is the mail-coach's encounter with the young woman's carriage that releases her from muteness, that gives her natural tongue something to say. The essay on "Style" suggests that her experience, singular and arbitrary as it appears, may be the prototype for many another natural utterance. In a remarkable sentence De Quincey intimates that the production of organic language entails doing some sort of violence to women: "Would you desire at this day to read our noble language in its native beauty, picturesque from idiomatic propriety, racy in its phraseology, delicate yet sinewy in its composition?" he asks his male reader. If so, that reader must "steal the mail-bags, and break open all the letters in female handwriting" (10:145). As if to prefigure *The English Mail-Coach* (or perhaps to recall the event it narrates), this invocation of the mails already carries with it— "by links of natural association" (13:285)—sexuality and violation. The scene of a man opening the mail-bags and breaking the seal on a woman's letter is analogous to the mail bearing down on the frail gig, for both are metaphorical displacements of rape: the male(-coach) violates the hymen.[16]

Nothing of this is stated directly in *The English Mail-Coach*, of course, but a number of oblique indications point to rape as its unspoken theme. From its first sentence the essay connects the topics of mail-coaches and marriages. Then the digression on Fanny introduces the story of De Quincey's romantic pursuit on the mail of a young woman. In "The Vision of Sudden Death" language and communication acquire an unmistakably erotic quality as the enamored youth "whisper[s his] communications" to his companion, provoking De Quincey to ask whether it is "requisite that [the youth] should carry [his] lips forward to hers" (13:314). De Quincey himself wants to communicate with the gig, and in a way that must disrupt the couple's intercourse—to insert himself between them. Ostensibly he aims to save them both, but in fact he simultaneously identifies with the young man and desires to evict him. (Hence De Quincey starts referring to the young man as "the stranger.") This ambivalence is registered in the shout of Achilles which he revealingly chooses to imitate. Although De Quincey says he shouts a well-intended warning to friends, the cry of Achilles is a threat to an enemy after a murder has already occurred. De Quincey's aggression comes to the surface when he goes on to threaten the young man with death if the latter should shrink from his "duty," even though De Quincey has just acknowledged his own constitutional tendency so to shrink: "He will die no less: and why not? Wherefore should we grieve that there is one craven less in the world? No; *let* him perish" (13:315). And throughout the passage De Quincey maintains a close identification with the mail, connecting himself to it by use of first-person plural pronouns, for like the mail his only function is to spread the word.[17]

In "The Vision of Sudden Death" the idea of an uncontaminated and virginal language turns out to be inseparable from its opposite. The only way for natural language, in De Quincey's privileged form of the female letter, to "publish" itself is by means of the mail, but the mail-coach is precisely what violates natural language. But why should the dissemination of natural language have to involve violation? Is it not possible to ascribe the reference to cutting open letters to simple coincidence? De Quincey drops a clue when he says that "the many beautiful female letters which we have heard upon chance occasions" have convinced him that "above all, the interesting class of women unmarried upon scruples of sexual honour . . . are the true and best depositaries of the old mother idiom" (10:146). This creates an evident difficulty, for the only way such women can act as depositaries of the mother tongue is by speaking and writing it—that is, by producing it—and so becoming mothers in their own rights. And the only way for an unmarried woman to become a metaphoric mother is through a metaphoric form of rape, since her "scruples of sexual honour" would never permit any dalliance. Therefore, some man must be introduced to collide with her carriage, to soil her garments, to wound her sensibilities, and to break open her seal, the seal that bears within it a letter. But it must be understood that, rather than destroying the purity of her language, this rape underwrites and perpetuates it. In this way De Quincey's essay "Style" enacts with some precision the paradox that Jacques Derrida has formulated concerning the "hymen"—at once the membrane that testifies to virginity and the god of marriage.[18]

With this earlier scene of violation in mind we may now return to *The English Mail-Coach* to follow the actual encounter between the two vehicles. De Quincey considers this incident to be "the scene ... from which the whole of this paper radiates as a natural expansion" (13:329); it is also the textual center, occupying the middle section of the essay, just as the mail-coach is the "central intellect" of the nation. Hence it is noteworthy that the origin and center of *The English Mail-Coach* should be the dramatic enactment of a digression. Etymologically, "to digress" means "to turn aside," which is exactly what the gig does here. The avenue, we recall, is "straight as an arrow," and the mail is galloping straight for a head-on collision with the gig unless the latter can swerve out of "the line of absolute ruin" (13:316). This the young man hastens to accomplish: "Raising his horse's fore-feet from the ground, he *slewed* him *round on the pivot* of his hind legs" (13:315; italics added), producing what De Quincey later refers to as a "violent *torsion* of the wheels" (13:317; italics added)—a "twisting" or "wringing" (from Latin *torquere*). Everything turns on the gig's swerving out of the line of ruin. We may call its swerve a digression, since the space in which it occurs is a linguistic one: "between the question and the answer" (13:316). It is a vehicular digression within a geographic one, for the stretch of road on which the incident occurs is deviant as well as straight. De

Quincey enters it when "our frantic horses swept round an angle of the road which opened upon us that final stage" (13:313) and resumes his original, straight course thereafter when at "right angles we wheeled into our former direction" (13:318).

To locate a digression at the center of the text means that the center displaces itself. One could make the same point by noting that in a curious manner the center never appears or materializes. Before the crucial moment De Quincey has a clear and distinct vision of what lies ahead: "I see ... I see ... I read" (13:311-12); and for years after the event, up to and including the composition of *The English Mail-Coach*, he has correspondingly vivid memories: "Epilepsy so brief of horror, wherefore is it that thou canst not die?" (13:319). But the incident itself is obscured by the "ravings of hurricanes ... at the moment of our transit" (13:317)—more revolutions about a mobile center.[19] De Quincey calls the encounter of the gig and the mail an "appalling scene" (13:328), and, besides the sense of dreadful or horrifying, the adjective here retains its etymological meaning of growing pale or fading. Even as it is a scene, or something seen, the action is in the process of disappearing; it lurks somewhere in that nether region between the visible and the invisible.

This is a hard condition to describe, except by punning oxymorons like "appalling seen," but De Quincey's language is precise. At the same time as he emphasizes the visibility of the moment ("Light does not tread upon the steps of light more indivisibly than did our all-conquering arrival upon the escaping efforts of the gig"), he casts over it "our over-towering shadow" (13:316), for all the participants turn their eyes aside as the crisis approaches.[20] A "brave man" may die "with his face to the danger" (13:314), but when the crisis arrives, the young man turns his back, and "not by sight could he any longer communicate with the peril" (13:316). De Quincey's own position is uncertain, but he must likewise have turned away because we later read: "I rose in horror, to gaze upon the ruins we *might* have caused.... I ... looked *back* upon the scene" (13:317; italics added). Had he watched the encounter he would already have known its outcome. Of the remaining actor, the woman, nothing can be said, for she is hors de combat: "It must be remembered that I read all this from the rear, never once catching the lady's full face, and even her profile imperfectly" (13:318n.).[21]

Why should De Quincey occlude this scene? One reason is that there is simply nothing to see. The couple, the narrator, and the reader all have been anticipating a murderous collision, but as it happens, the vehicles only "glance," and everyone survives. The central event of the essay turns out to be a non-event, which makes De Quincey's title, "The *Vision* of Sudden *Death*" (italics added), radically figurative. There is no death, whether sudden or otherwise, and even if there had been, it would have remained invisible. But if the encounter between the two vehicles results in no deaths, neither does it allow any of the principals to continue participating in the "one Life within us and abroad."[22] In fact, the young man is left barely sentient, for the meeting of the gig and the mail effects a chiasmus, or "revolution," that deadens him as it animates his conveyance. While the gig, "as if it sympathised with human horror, was all alive with tremblings and shiverings," the youth "trembled not, nor shivered. He sat like a rock" (13:317). Instead of either life or death, the climax issues in a certain violent vibration, or, as De Quincey puts it in another passage, a "shuddering between the gates of life and death" (13:303). This shuddering graphs a hairline path between collision and escape, so that we cannot say definitely that the vehicles either properly hit or simply miss each other. Instead, the text places the episode *sous rature*, and De Quincey's description is scrupulously careful in tracing the glancing, offsides, or marginal nature of this incident: the young man parks his carriage "*nearly* at right angles" to the mail-coach, and later De Quincey looks back to see that "we had struck the *off-wheel* of the little gig; which stood *rather obliquely*, and *not quite so far advanced as to be accurately parallel* with the nearwheel" (13:315, 317; italics added). This is a case of what we call a "near miss," an expression we ordinarily use to mean that no collision occurred, but which literally says that, although narrowly averted, a collision did in fact take place. De Quincey puts it best two paragraphs later: the encounter between the gig and the mail is an "unparalleled situation" (13:

317). Whatever "happens" between these two vehicles perplexes the opposition between catastrophe and its aversion, event and nonevent, connection and the failure to connect.

One might object that the oscillations I am referring to are only temporary. Were one to remain on the road, after a while one would probably see the young man unfreeze and the young woman settle down. No doubt they would embrace, offer thanks for salvation, and continue on their way, and life would return to normal. However, such an objection fails to take into account De Quincey's point of "view." It assumes a stable position in space and time from which to observe the scene; but the mail-coach is in constant motion: "Fast are the flying moments, faster are the hoofs of our horses" (13:316), and "in the twinkling of an eye" (13:318) they carry the mail around a bend in the road and so shut off the vista. Nor are we even free to speculate that De Quincey might at least imagine the couple's recovery. With that turn the scene loses whatever visibility it possessed: "The turn of the road carried the scene out of my eyes in an instant, and swept it into my dreams for ever" (13:318). The scene thus writes itself on the palimpsest of De Quincey's mind as it then was; indeed, this already happened when he first "looked back upon the scene" which "in a moment told its own tale, and wrote all its records on my heart for ever" (13:317). Whatever different conclusions De Quincey might come to later would be part of another text.

What are the interpretative consequences of this last swerve in the story? The twist in the road is accidental or contingent, with the result that the story stops but does not end. It denies us the sense of an ending, which would enable us to organize the narrative and give it a certain interpretative shape. Only from the end could we look back to see whether and where our path had been direct or meandering. De Quincey is very clear about the error of reading stoppings as though they were endings, for "sudden death" is a kind of stopping: "Many people are likely to exaggerate the horror of a sudden death from the disposition to lay a false stress upon words or acts simply because by an accident they have become *final* words or acts" (13:301). In *The English Mail-Coach* the narrative itself undergoes sudden death. There is only a turn in the road, one that turns the events (if that is the word) into a text, but one without closure and one that renders all our interpretative efforts inconclusive. We are left instead with a "resounding blow," a "violent torsion," "tremblings and shiverings," the "raving of hurricanes," "agitated sight."

If "the whole of this paper radiates as a natural expansion" (13:329) from that moment, its shuddering must spread and re-sound throughout the text. The encounter between the mail and the gig should therefore return in a number of other pairings, whose relationships will likewise be glancing, wheeling, and vibratory. Or, to put it differently, if the mail-coach is a writing instrument, then the blow it inflicts may be felt in all of its communications. Vibrations or slippages occur even in rudimentary pairings like nouns and adjectives, as when De Quincey piles adjectives before a noun such that each jostles for primacy (for example, "this flattering, whispering, murmuring love" [13:317-18]) or makes connections that violate logic (for example, "the larger half" [13:316]). The relation between gig and mail is also emblematic of the *junctura* in De Quincey's theory of composition:

> It is in the *relation* of sentences, in what Horace terms their *"junctura,"* that the true life of composition resides. The mode of their *nexus*, the way in which one sentence is made to arise out of another, and to prepare the opening for a third: this is the great loom in which the textile process of the moving intellect reveals itself and prospers. [10:258-59]

As De Quincey indicates, the key issue is one of relations between entities rather than aggregates of them. But while the ideal model of composition is organic, it is not the only model.

The *junctura* between sentences in *The English Mail-Coach* may be oblique and lateral, corresponding to neither alternative De Quincey mentions, no more a "synthesis of the two objects in one co-existing field of vision" than "separate wholes" that "do not coalesce to any joint... impression" (10:259). And the same is true of *junctura* involving allusions to other works, parenthetical expressions, and footnotes, or *junctura* between units of composition longer than the sentence, such as paragraphs, digressions, intercalated stories, various sections of *The English Mail-Coach*, or even the "larger whole" of *Suspiria de Profundis* from which the essay has been momentarily "dislocated" (13:328). A sign of this dislocation is the need De Quincey repeatedly feels to assert the coherence of his essay: the "paper" of December 1849 containing "The Vision of Sudden Death" and the "Dream-Fugue" is "connected with a previous paper on *The English Mail-Coach*, published in the Magazine for October"[23] (even though no reader in October would likely have predicted a second installment); the mail-coach has a "connexion" with "the government" and a "connexion" with recent "national victories," and only a dim critic would fail "to follow the links of the connexion between [the essay's] several parts" (13:328).

To characterize the unstable conjunction of reader and text, finally, we may consider De Quincey himself, since he is the prototype, the first to have "read and interpreted" the "passion of sudden death." What he reads is a text of "averted signs" (13:318) such as the mail has been tracing all along the margin of the road, signs legible in presentiment or in memory but not when looked at directly or in the present moment. As the instrument that turns out these signs, the mail-coach could hardly be less steady. It is the scene of repeated reversals between inside and outside, law and violation, organic and mechanic, master and slave, literal and figural, reader and writer; it is on a runaway course and has no proper *topos*, since it stands at once outside the text as the title and, in "The Vision of Sudden Death," at the center and origin. Its averted signs will not submit to any direct or transparent reading, composing instead a wavering text not unlike that of a certain German work which De Quincey mentions in his essay "Style." "Of a German book, otherwise entitled to respect, it was said—*er lässt sich nicht lesen*—it does not permit itself to be read" (10:167).[24] The encounter between the two vehicles may have "furnished the text" (13:304), but such is the strange nature of this text that De Quincey can read it only after the page is turned: "I read all this from the rear" (13:318n.). The perplexity and contortions this style of reading must entail may give pause to later readers.

That De Quincey cannot align himself with his own "unparalleled" text ought to be warning enough to send a shudder through any would-be easy rider on *The English Mail-Coach*.[25]

Notes

1. William Morris, ed., *The American Heritage Dictionary of the English Language* (Boston: Houghton Mifflin, 1969), p. 4.
2. René Wellek, *A History of Modern Criticism: 1750-1950* (New Haven, Conn.: Yale University Press, 1965), 3:116.
3. David Sundelson, "Evading the Crocodile: De Quincey's 'The English Mail Coach,'" *Psychocultural Review* 1 (1977): 10.
4. The backdrop of the Napoleonic Wars also raises the issue of politics, a topic that pervades De Quincey's essay. On the political dimension of *The English Mail-Coach* see Robert M. Maniquis, "Lonely Empires: Personal and Public Visions of Thomas De Quincey," in Eric Rothstein and Joseph Anthony Wittreich, Jr. eds., *Literary Monographs*, vol. 8 (Madison: University of Wisconsin Press, 1976), pp. 65-77; Robert Hopkins, "De Quincey on War and the Pastoral Design of *The English Mail-Coach*," *Studies in Romanticism* 6 (1967): 129-51.
5. De Quincey's own experience reaffirms the link between writing and the mail-coach system. In a letter of 5 March 1840 he tells Thomas Talfourd that the series of *Autobiographic Sketches* published in *Tait's Edinburgh Magazine* was "not written, as will be thought, in monthly successions and with intervals sufficient: but all at once 2 years ago; in a coffee room of a mail-coach inn, with a sheriff's officer lurking near, in hurry too extreme to allow of reading them over even once; and with no after revision" (Pforzheimer Library, MS Misc. 104).
6. Laurence Sterne, *Tristram Shandy*, ed. Howard Anderson (New York: Norton, 1980), p. 26.
7. Ibid.
8. De Quincey's nostalgia, like his application of the organic-mechanic distinction, was shared by a retired coachman: "'Them as 'ave seen coaches afore rails came into fashion 'ave seen something worth rememberin'! Them was 'appy days for old England, afore reform and rails turned everything upside down, and men rode, as nature intended they should, on 'pikes [turnpikes], with coaches and smart active cattle, and not by machinery like bags of cotton and hardware'" (as cited in Howard Robinson, *The British Post Office: A History* [Princeton, N.J.: Princeton University Press, 1948], pp. 242-43).
9. Cf. Coleridge's description of Wordsworth's "original gift of spreading the tone, the *atmosphere* and with it the depth and height of the ideal world, around forms, incidents and situations of which, for the common

view, custom had bedimmed all the lustre, had dried up the sparkle and the dew-drops" (George Watson, ed., *Biographia Literaria* [London: Dent; New York: Dutton, 1965], pp. 48–49).

10. Aural signs mediate this scene as well as visual ones, and their appearance is similarly unexpected. De Quincey had made silence a prerequisite to his paradisical reverie ("Not a hoof nor a wheel was to be heard" [13:310]), and what suddenly awakens him from that reverie is the "sullen sound" of the approaching gig. But as with the so-called transparency, the silence of the vision is radically thrown into question because the sound of De Quincey's *own* horses and wheels, like their marks on the road, must have been present but repressed over the whole course of that vision: "*Except* [italics added] the feet of our own horses,... there was no sound abroad." To tone down its mediating effect, De Quincey attempts just prior to this message to spiritualize sound into the silent music of the spheres ("The sea, the atmosphere, the light, bore each an orchestral part in this universal lull" [13:311]). In an earlier passage he similarly uses the figure of harmony to mystify the mail-coach system as an organ of speech: "For my own feeling, this post-office service spoke as by some mighty orchestra, where a thousand instruments [were] all disregarding each other... yet all... terminat[ing] in a perfection of harmony" (13:272).

11. Cf. the "wheel in the middle of a wheel" (Ezekiel 1:16, AV) from Ezekiel's chariot, an antecedent of De Quincey's mail-coach. The creatures in the chariot "turned not when they went; they went every one straight forward" (Ezekiel 1:9, AV).

12. In his "Reminiscences," De Quincey in fact images the mind as a kind of mail-coach when he speaks of "the privilege by which the mind, like the lamps of a mail-coach, moving rapidly through the midnight woods, illuminate, for one instant, the foliage or sleeping umbrage of the thickets, and, in the next instant, have quitted them, to carry their radiance forward upon endless successions of objects" (3:162).

13. Cf. Horace Ainsworth Eaton, *Thomas De Quincey: A Biography* (London: Oxford University Press, 1936), pp. 506–507.

14. The "Dream-Fugue" poses a similar problem for De Quincey because the fugal form depends in large measure on counterpoint, the simultaneous presence of two different elements, which cannot be achieved in writing. De Quincey's solution there as well is a use of repetition (see Calvin S. Brown, Jr., "The Musical Structure of De Quincey's *Dream-Fugue*," *Musical Quarterly* 24 [1938]: 341–50). In fact, one could read the whole of the "Dream-Fugue" as De Quincey's expansion of this sentence on expansion in "The Vision of Sudden Death."

15. Newspapers forge another link between the mail-coach and the mechanic. "It is in newspapers," writes De Quincey, "that we must look for the main reading of this generation; and in newspapers, therefore, we must seek for the causes operating upon the [mechanic] style of the age" (10:148). And newspapers had a long and intimate connection with the mail-coach.

Not only did the coaches carry newspapers along with letters, but also the postmasters themselves sold the papers. As Robinson puts it, "The Post Office thus became a sort of news agent on a grand scale" (*The British Post Office*, pp. 147-48).

16. Sundelson's article "Evading the Crocodile," which I discovered after writing an earlier draft of this chapter, confirms and elaborates on the erotic dimension of *The English Mail-Coach*, although, as I have noted, to ends quite different from my own. V. A. De Luca, whose book I read at the same time, concurs: "The whole episode, graphically considered, is almost embarrassingly phallic: powerful and uncontrollable animal forces plunging down a straight and tunnel-like path towards a fragile and feminine beauty" (*Thomas De Quincey: The Prose of Vision* [Toronto: University of Toronto Press, 1980], p. 158n.).

17. Elsewhere De Quincey actually imagines himself as a mail-coach: "As the mail-coaches go down daily in London to the inspector of mails, so we rolled out of the nursery at a signal given, and were minutely reviewed in succession. Were the lamps of our equipage clean and bright? Were the springs properly braced? Were the linch-pins secured? When this inspection, which was no mere formality, had travelled from the front rank to the rear, when we were pronounced to be in proper trim, or, in the language of guards, 'All right behind!' we were dismissed" (Japp, 1:10).

18. See Jacques Derrida, "The Double Session," in *Dissemination*, trans. Barbara Johnson (Chicago: University of Chicago Press, 1981), pp. 173-285, esp. pp. 182-83, 209-16. Cf. De Luca's reading of the "Dream-Fugue": "By a strange sort of logic it seems that, if the victory of Waterloo is to occur, if a dynamic Christendom is to emerge, pure innocence and pure nature must be sacrificed" (*Thomas De Quincey*, p. 112). To call this a "sacrifice," however, is to diminish the "strangeness" of De Quincey's logic that I am trying to elicit. All strangeness disappears in the synthesis that follows in De Luca's study: "Innocence cannot rise to apocalyptic consummation," he writes, "unless it is visited by the principle of destruction and assimilates the principle into itself" (*Thomas De Quincey*, p. 114). I owe the reference to "Style," as well as certain lines of interpreting it, to Mary Jacobus's "The Art of Managing Books: Romantic Prose and the Writing of the Past," in Arden Reed, ed., *Romanticism and Language* (Ithaca, N.Y.: Cornell University Press, 1984), pp. 215-46.

19. See also the earlier image of a man "running before a hurricane" (13:315) and the later one of the mail-coach running "like hurricanes that ride into the secrets of forests" (13:324). These images recall Milton's "Chariot of Paternal Deity" that "forth rush'd with whirl-wind sound" (*Paradise Lost*, 6.749-50, in John Milton, *John Milton: Complete Poems and Major Prose*, ed. Merritt Y. Hughes [Indianapolis: Odyssey, 1957]) and Ezekiel's vision of "a whirlwind [that] came out of the north" (Ezekiel 1:4, AV) enfolding his chariot. They all are related to the reversals or "revolutions" in *The English Mail-Coach*, as is the "mill-race" to which De

Quincey also compares the motion of the mail-coach. In the draft of *The English Mail-Coach*, De Quincey explains that the reference is to Dante: "Never did water run so fast through a sluice to turn the wheel of a landmill when it approaches nearest to the paddles" (*Inferno*, 23.46–48, in Dante Alighieri, *The Divine Comedy*, trans. Charles S. Singleton, Bollingen Series 80 [Princeton, N.J.: Princeton University Press, 1970]).

20. The canvas of *The English Mail-Coach* is crowded with shadows: the "gloomy shadow darkened above him" when first the young man realizes a collision is imminent, recalling the "shadow of failure" (13:315) and anticipating the "shadow of death" (13:319). And the light of the mail signifies a kind of blindness, for "our lamps, still lighted, would give [the young man in the gig] the impression of vigilance on our part" (13:312).

21. Even in its dreamlike repetition in the third section the event is obscured. The speakers are able to see the baby (a displaced version of the young woman) as long as she remains somewhat ahead in their path, and this time the trumpeter is even able to sound a warning. But "immediately deep shadows fell between us, and aboriginal silence." Further, they are rendered unconscious: "By horror we, that were so full of life, ...were frozen to a bas-relief." It is only after the fact that the trumpet blows once more, restoring consciousness, sight, and sound. The center thus remains dark, so the speaker has to ask: " 'Whither has the infant fled?—is the young child caught up to God?' " (13:325).

22. "The Eolian Harp," line 26, in Samuel Taylor Coleridge, *The Complete Poetical Works of Samuel Taylor Coleridge*, ed. Ernest Hartley Coleridge, 2 vols. (Oxford: Oxford University Press, Clarendon Press, 1912), 1:101.

23. *Blackwood's Edinburgh Magazine* 66 (December 1849): 741. The anxiety that prompts such assertions is expressed in a letter of 1844 written during the composition of *Suspiria de Profundis:* "The nexus is wanting, and life and the central principle which should bind together all the parts at the centre, with all its radiations to the circumference, are wanting" (Page, 1:325).

24. This part of the essay "Style" appeared in the July 1840 issue of *Blackwood's*. It would seem that an avid *Blackwood's* reader, Edgar Allan Poe, picked up the line and used it at the beginning and end of "The Man of the Crowd," published in December of the same year. The likelihood is increased by the fact that Poe reproduced De Quincey's error in referring to the neuter *Buch* by the masculine article *der*.

25. The phrase cited in my title comes from a letter dated 6 June 1838 written by De Quincey to his publisher Robert Blackwood (National Library of Scotland, MS 4,046). I am grateful for financial support from the Graves Award and the National Endowment for the Humanities and for hospitality from the Institute for Advanced Studies in the Humanities in the University of Edinburgh while I was writing this essay.

15

Confession, Digression, Gravitation: Thomas De Quincey's German Connection

JOEL D. BLACK

For many years I thought that the almost infinite world of literature was in one man. That man was Carlyle, he was Johannes Becher, he was Whitman, he was Rafael Cansinos-Assens, he was De Quincey.

—BORGES, "The Flower of Coleridge"

In the section of Friedrich Schlegel's *Gespräch über die Poesie* (1799–1800) called "Brief über den Roman," the fictional speaker Antonio begins his talk with a defense of the popular contemporary German novelist Jean Paul Richter. Antonio takes it upon himself to respond to a remark made by another participant in the *Gespräch* that "Richter's novels are not novels but a colorful hodgepodge of sickly wit," that "the meager story is too badly presented to be considered a story" and is at best only a "confession" *(Bekenntnis)* in which "the individuality of the [author] is much too visible."[1] Against this charge Antonio claims that "such grotesques and confessions are the only romantic productions of an unromantic age."[2] Moreover, Antonio proceeds to group the German author Jean Paul with the English writer Laurence Sterne and the French man of letters Denis Diderot, thereby creating an international triumvirate of Romantic prose stylists. In the work of these three writers we are to discover an entirely new literary aesthetic which combines the personal confession with the erratic form of the digression or, in Antonio's words, which presents "a sentimental theme in a fantastic form."[3] Through the magical combination of sentimental confession and humorous digression the novel comes into its own as a "romantic book":[4] "Ein Roman ist ein romantisches Buch."[5]

Although Jean Paul was greatly influenced by Sterne, he developed the English novelist's blend of sentimental humor into a specifically "romantic" aesthetic; that is, he integrated Sterne's art of the digression with the fantasy of dream description. Antonio claims without hesitation that Jean Paul improves on the work of his predecessor in this regard: "I . . . place Richter over Sterne because his imagination is far more sickly, therefore far more eccentric and fantastic."[6] Lest we suspect Antonio (and Schlegel) of chauvinism in their preference for the German over the English author, we should consult the opinion of Thomas De Quincey in an admittedly whimsical essay on Jean Paul: "Judge as you will . . . on the comparative pretensions of Sterne and Richter to the *spolia opima* in the fields of pathos and of humour, — yet in one pretension he not only leaves Sterne at an infinite distance in the rear, but really, for my part, I cease to ask who it is that he leaves behind him, for I begin to think with myself who it is that he approaches" (11:265). The "one pretension" to which De Quincey refers is his belief that of all modern authors Jean Paul comes closest to Shakespeare in the astonishing mercurial movement of his prose. In a passage which itself mimics the German novelist's stylistic fireworks De Quincey writes:

> The rapid but uniform motions of the heavenly bodies serve well enough to typify the grand and continuous motions of the Miltonic mind. But the wild, giddy, fantastic, capricious, incalculable, springing, vaulting, tumbling, dancing, waltzing, caprioling, *pirouetting*, sky-rocketing of the chamois, the harlequin, the Vestris, the storm-loving raven—the raven? no, the lark (for often he ascends "singing up to heaven's gates," but like the lark he dwells upon the earth),—in short, of the Proteus, the Ariel, the Mercury, the monster, John Paul,—can be compared to nothing in heaven or earth, or the waters under the earth, except to the motions of the same faculty as existing in Shakespere. [11:266]

Elsewhere I have discussed De Quincey's relation to Jean Paul in some detail; specifically I have suggested that both writers present a view of the individual and the collective genesis of man—his *Bildungsprozess*—in terms of a pedagogical metaphor of man's "up-bringing" that is in turn structured on motifs taken from religion (the Fall of Man–the resurrection of Christ), science (gravitation-levitation), and literary stylistics (gravity-levity).[7] I now wish to supplement my observations on De Quincey's thematic relation to Jean Paul by introducing the formal feature of digression into the discussion. For as Friedrich Schlegel—the foremost critic of German Romanticism—implies in the *Gespräch*, the most significant development in the emergence of Romantic aesthetics may be the appearance of a poetics of digression. What is more, Schlegel identifies the Romantic movement in the arts with what amounts to a *digressive tradition* that is visible in the direct Anglo-German line of succession that runs from Swift and Sterne to Jean Paul—a line which finds its culmination, I shall argue, in the major writings of De Quincey.

I. Friedrich Schlegel and Permanent *Parekbasis*

The association drawn by Schlegel between Romantic *Poesie*—specifically the Romantic novel *(der romantische Roman)*—and digressive technique need not be inferred from his admittedly indirect comments in the quasi-fictional *Gespräch* and his passing references to such elusive, impressionistic-sounding terms as *das Groteske* and *die Arabeske*.[8] Rather, we may turn to Schlegel's aphoristic writings, where he is more explicit on this score. "*Parekbasis* must be permanent in the fantastic novel," he writes in his notebook of the same period as the *Gespräch*.[9] Here, as in his equation that "irony is a permanent *parekbasis*,"[10] Schlegel invokes the Greek rhetorical term for digression, which literally means "a step to the side."

Digression, we too often tend to forget, is a *rhetorical* term with a long and complicated history. In its rhetorical function digression is not merely a formal feature of a text but a practical strategy of the speaker with respect to his listener. *Parekbasis* or *digressio* indeed referred in classical manuals to an integral part of a speech or an oration in which material only indirectly related to the subject at hand could be introduced, but this extraneous material was always introduced by the speaker with a specific purpose in mind—either to work a certain effect on or to establish a particular bond with the listener. Thus, if a speech was a eulogy of a deceased individual or a legal accusation or defense of a living person's involvement in a crime, the speaker might resort to a digression or an excursus to "step to the side" of his main argument for the purpose of recapitulating the events of his subject's life—his lineage, his education, his achievements, and so forth. While such factors would not necessarily be directly related to the issue under immediate consideration, they could very well affect the listener's final judgment; hence the crucial courtroom disputes between lawyers for the prosecution and the defense over the "relevance" of certain questions, testimony, or evidence to be presented before the judge or jury.[11]

In the literary genre of the novel, particularly in eighteenth-century works like *Joseph Andrews, Tristram Shandy, Jacques le fataliste,* and *Wilhelm Meisters Lehrjahre,* this rhetorical sense of digression was adapted in a manner that allowed the narrator to intrude into the story of his protagonist's adventures for the purpose of presenting his own personal views on a variety of topics having little or nothing to do with the principal narrative. Whereas the classical speech had focused on a single issue in an individual's life, opening out to a wider perspective of that life as a *whole* in the specially designated *part* of the speech called the *digressio,* in the eighteenth-century novel this part itself swelled into the whole. The hero's life from childhood on, which formerly had been restricted to the digression, now emerged as the principal subject matter of the work in its own right. Digression evolved into narration. At the same time the extended narrative of the hero's life history was punctuated by an ongoing series of secondary digressions and asides which the narrator imposed or grafted upon the original, primary digression-narration of the individual's education and growth. In the extreme case of a work like Byron's *Don Juan,* the narrator himself emerged as the principal persona in place of the rather bland "hero"; the narrator's digressions have virtually nothing to do with the young protagonist but exist entirely as a means for the narrator to present his *own* life and opinions.

Don Juan, in effect, bridges the gap between, on the one hand, the traditional novel as *Bildungsroman*, where a narrator presents the story of his young protagonist's development, and, on the other hand, the confessional mode of autobiography which we find in *Tristram Shandy* (the fictional Tristram writing about himself), Wordsworth's *The Prelude* (subtitled *Growth of a Poet's Mind*), and the *Confessions* of both Rousseau and De Quincey.

In short, as we approach the Romantic era, the emphasis in novelistic forms of writing shifts steadily from the narration of the hero's errant adventures to the narrator's aberrant digressions away from the story of his protagonist in order to confide his own life and opinions. The narrative of the youthful hero's life history increasingly becomes an excuse, a pre-text, a vehicle for the narrator's digressive reflections about his own life. Following Swift's "Digression in Praise of Digressions" in *A Tale of a Tub*, Sterne has Tristram Shandy claim that "digressions, incontestably, are the sunshine; — they are the life, the soul of reading; take them out of this book for instance, — you might as well take the book along with them."[12] Hearkening to Sterne, Jean Paul advises the would-be author: "Make digressions, but do not plant them in the footnotes but rather above — fundamentally all major material must be only the vehicle and the silver and the lectern for an author, so that within these confines all else may be addressed."[13] And perhaps hearkening back to Jean Paul, De Quincey compares his own narrative technique to "a *caduceus* wreathed about with meandering ornaments, or the shaft of a tree's stem hung round and surmounted with some vagrant parasitical plant" (*SP*, p. 157). "The true object in my 'Opium Confessions,'" he goes on to say,

> is not the naked physiological theme, — on the contrary, *that* is the ugly pole, the murderous spear, the halbert, — but those wandering musical variations upon the theme, — those parasitical thoughts, feelings, digressions, which climb up with bells and blossoms round about the arid stock; ramble away from it at times with perhaps too rank a luxuriance; but at the same time, by the eternal interest attached to the *subjects* of these digressions, no matter what were the execution, spread a glory over incidents that for themselves would be — less than nothing. [*SP*, pp. 158–59]

This digressive summary of the growing prominence in the eighteenth and early nineteenth century of digression as a structural element of literary discourse tells only half the story, however. For when Schlegel writes at the close of the eighteenth century that *parekbasis* is a permanent feature of the fantastic novel, he does not mean—or he does not mean *only*—that the episodic narrative of the protagonist's life must be subordinated to the perpetual interruptions of the narrator's whimsy. Schlegel's accomplishment has to do with the fact that he liberated the term *parekbasis* both from its classical rhetorical context, where it designated a discrete part of the orator's speech, one that was often concerned with the subject's past life and education, and from its eighteenth-century literary usage, where, as digression, it referred to the storyteller's departure from the narrative of his protagonist's life and education in order to present his own personal views or "confessions." As Michael von Poser has suggested, rather than conceive of *parekbasis* as a "rhetorical situation" between a speaker and a listener, or a narrator and a reader, Schlegel uses the term in an *antirhetorical* sense in which the speaker-listener, narrator-reader relationship is completely annulled and overcome.[14]

What Schlegel seems to have in mind in his use of the term is something akin to the Brechtian *Verfremdungseffekt* of Aristophanic comedy (parabasis) where the chorus addresses the audience-community directly, thereby destroying the dramatic illusion of the comedy. But when the illusion of the speaker-audience relation, upon which all rhetorical communication is ultimately based, is destroyed, the speaker-as-speaker can no longer address the audience-as-audience through indirect or direct, illusionistic or disillusionistic, means. What remains after the narrating persona, subject, or consciousness has been displaced is a more or less open conversation between any number of interlocutors who are alternately both speakers and auditors. In the new space opened up by this radical *parekbasis*, this side-stepping of accepted conceptual and discursive conventions, an unfamiliar or "fantastic" play of perspectives is allowed to arise which, according to the outmoded but still-ruling conventions of the day, may appear transgressive and scandalous.

Schlegel's reference to *parekbasis* as a permanent feature of the Romantic novel, then, does not merely signify digression's function in classical rhetoric as an integral part of a speech, or its function in the eighteenth-century novel as the speaker's interruption of his narrative for the purpose of directly addressing his reader. Apart from these *structural* rhetorical meanings of digression, Schlegel views *parekbasis* as a *destructuring* principle where the narrator sidesteps not only his main story line but also his own narrative function vis-à-vis the reader, thereby bypassing normative rhetorical conventions and established moral and social codes. *Parekbasis*, the act of stepping to the side, is revealed by Schlegel in its original ethical-legal-religious sense of overstepping the law. *Digression*, in short, is *transgression* — an act of excess beyond the ethical mean.

This original meaning of digression as transgression actually carries over into the rhetorical tradition. Besides referring to a legitimate structural part of a speech, *parekbasis* was also used to designate a wide range of stylistic faults — any excessive use of meter, diction, or figures of speech for the purpose of amplifying or elevating the subject. During the Romantic era there were notable instances of fusion between the two rhetorical senses of digression as stylistic excess and as structural excursus; in Byron's *Don Juan* and in the novels of Jean Paul, for example, the two types of digression are often indistinguishable. And in De Quincey the structural excursuses of his two great confessional works are complemented by the stylistic (and ethical) excesses of his series of essays "On Murder Considered as One of the Fine Arts." Despite these tendencies, however, Schlegel refused to treat *parekbasis* as a rhetorical term — either as a stylistic fault or as a structural virtue. *Parekbasis* for him was essentially antirhetorical, a means of permanently dissolving the speaker-listener, writer-reader relation, and of perpetually canceling those "framing techniques" — such as the medieval devices of the dream vision and palinode, and the modern device of the self-conscious narrator — which fiction has repeatedly adopted to differentiate itself from the "real" world.

In the Romantic novel, or "romantisches Buch," as envisioned by Schlegel, then, the specific rhetorical relation of supposed confidence and communication between the narrator and the reader is plunged into a self-consuming abyss. Poser notes that in Jean Paul's novels the narrator sometimes negates himself as well as his relation to his reader through digressions which are directed to no ostensible purpose or object—only the void of the "leersten Ausgange."[15] It is through such aimless excursions without any hope of a return, through such "permanente *Parekbase,*" as Schlegel called it, that the realm of the *Fantastisch* might prove to be accessible. Such a literature of permanent *parekbasis,* of uninterrupted interruption, provided the only available approach to a realm of pure vision, to the world of the dream.

II. The Discourse of Confession and the Discourse of Dream

Although De Quincey declared in the "Introductory Notice" to the original *Suspiria de Profundis* that "the true object in my 'Opium Confessions' is . . . those parasitical thoughts, feelings, *digressions,* which climb up with bells and blossoms round about the arid stock" (italics added), in the enlarged edition of his *Confessions of an English Opium-Eater* of 1856 he affirmed that "the final object of the whole record lay in the dreams. For the sake of those the entire narrative arose" (3:413). Digressions and dreams alternate as the stated "object" of De Quincey's writing; narrative is subordinated to one or the other. There is not necessarily any contradiction in now calling digressions, now calling dreams, the key to his confessional work, for clearly the two are related and even interdependent. Digressions were a means of displaying the dream faculty, while the "naked physiological theme" of the effect of opium itself was "the ugly pole, the murderous spear, the halbert"—in short, the stuff of linear narrative.

Like Jean Paul, De Quincey subordinated narration to digression in the *Confessions.* Specifically, he subordinated his opium excesses to the dreams which were to be the crowning climax of the work. The extended "narration of my early adventures" with which the *Confessions* begins, "in the natural order of succession, led to the opium as a resource for healing their consequences; and the opium as naturally led to the dreams. But in the synthetic order of presenting the facts, what stood last in the succession of development stood first in the order of my purposes" (*SP,* p. 150). And in the version of the *Confessions* of 1856, De Quincey writes that "in these incidents of my early life is found the entire substratum, together with the secret and underlying motive, of those pompous dreams and dream-sceneries which were in reality the true objects—first and last—contemplated in these Confessions" (3:233). If in medieval literature the dream vision was framed by the surrounding narrative, De Quincey's "dream-phantasies" were themselves to be the frame—"first and last"—which would enclose the circumstantial events of the narrative.

Unfortunately, as De Quincey admits in the preface to the *Confessions* of 1856, the "crowning grace, which [he] had reserved for the final pages of this volume, in a succession of some twenty or twenty-five dreams and noon-day visions, which had arisen under the latter stages of opium influence," had simply "disappeared" (3:221). De Quincey expresses the hope that he may yet be able to retrieve some of these visions, but several of the dreams are forever beyond recovery, having been burned in an accidental fire. It was again just such an accident which Coleridge blamed for preventing him from completing "Kubla Khan": his attempt to record the images of an opium-induced dream was irrevocably interrupted by a chance visit from a business acquaintance. As Coleridge endeavored "to finish for himself" from "the still surviving recollections in his mind" what had been "originally, as it were, given to him,"[16] so De Quincey writes that he was able to salvage the dream vision of "The Daughter of Lebanon" from "amongst the papers burned partially, but not so burned as to be absolutely irretrievable" (3:222).

Critics' suspicions cannot fail to be aroused by these references to fantastic dream visions which the authors intended to record and publish but of which only the merest remnant survives as the result of an unexpected "accident." De Quincey's explanation seems particularly contrived. The dream fantasy called "The Daughter of Lebanon" was not part of the original version of the *Confessions* of 1821–22, and it appears that at one time De

Quincey actually considered including it in the *Suspiria de Profundis* (see Masson's note, 13:332). Nevertheless, he arranged for this one surviving dream fantasy to be added to the revised *Confessions* of 1856

as appropriately closing a record in which the case of poor Ann the Outcast formed not only the most memorable and the most suggestively pathetic incident, but also *that* which, more than any other, coloured or (more truly I should say) shaped, moulded and remoulded, composed and decomposed—the great body of opium dreams. [3:222]

Whether "The Daughter of Lebanon," however, for all its intrinsic merit, is able to function as a visionary transfiguration of the climactic episode in the narrative introduction to the *Confessions* is a matter of some doubt.

One can sympathize with the uneasiness of David Masson, De Quincey's editor, about the privileged position of "The Daughter of Lebanon" at the end of the *Confessions* of 1856. To be sure, the correspondence between the dream fantasy of "The Daughter of Lebanon" and the autobiographical episode of "Ann the Outcast" seems clear enough—the central figure in both pieces is a lovely young prostitute who is the victim of a lover's treachery. When Ann mysteriously disappears, De Quincey assumes she has died; accordingly, the Lady of Lebanon, who has been disinherited by her father, is reunited at the end of the dream, through a wandering evangelist's agency, with her heavenly father. But the dream apotheosis of "The Daughter of Lebanon" does not really transform or elevate the raw autobiographical material of the Ann episode; if anything, the narrative about Ann gives the dream whatever poignancy it has. "The Daughter of Lebanon," tacked on to the *Confessions* at a later date, is an insufficient mythification of the culminating episode of the author's narrative of his "youthful distresses in London" (3:231); moreover, it is an inadequate remainder of the twenty or more dream pieces which De Quincey claims that he intended to add.

If we take De Quincey at his word and consider narrative to be only a preliminary form, or the autobiographical raw material, of dream fantasy, then the *Suspiria de Profundis*—despite its incomplete, fragmentary condition—must be judged a more successful work than the *Confessions,* if only because of the superior merits of the "Levana" legend as compared with "The Daughter of Lebanon" vision. The chief interest of the *Confessions* is in its more or less straightforward narrative; the greatness of the *Suspiria* consists not in linear narrative but in its disconnected dreams and digressions. One may value the narrative of "Ann the Outcast" over its dream transfiguration in "The Daughter of Lebanon," but it is unlikely that one would esteem the nursery reminiscences in "The Affliction of Childhood" section of the *Suspiria,* which describe the traumatic experiences of De Quincey's earliest life, over the "Levana" dream legend, which is a fully visionary transformation of those experiences. In fact, De Quincey's "pillaging," as Masson calls it (13:332), of the *Suspiria* for the Edinburgh edition of his writings is actually in keeping with his avowed disregard for narrative, and also with his conception of the "Levana" legend as a mythic condensation of the projected *Suspiria* which as such could stand, more or less, on its own. It is difficult to imagine De Quincey similarly pillaging the *Confessions:* it is a more unified, less digressive work than the *Suspiria*; but also the deficiency of actual dream material in the *Confessions*—the "twenty or twenty-five dreams and noon-day visions" which simply "disappeared"—required as complete and extended a narrative as possible to compensate for the lack. No wonder, then, that over the years De Quincey expanded the narrative section of the *Confessions* to four times its original length, while from the original *Suspiria* he dropped entire narrative sequences, such as "The Apparition of the Brocken" and even "The Affliction of Childhood," which present the raw materials of De Quincey's life.

Clearly, two opposed dynamics inform the compositional histories of the *Confessions* and its "sequel," *Suspiria de Profundis.* The former work was the result of an additive process of composition in which the narrative section was increasingly extended over the years while the projected dream component had to be virtually scrapped. The *Suspiria,* on the other hand, underwent a paring-down process of *decomposition.* The autobiographical narrative sections were slowly stripped away, ostensibly as part of De Quincey's effort to reorganize his writings for the collected edition. More significantly, however, De Quincey's subtractive method in the *Suspiria* seems to have been motivated by a desire to refine and crystallize both his confessional narrative and his digressive prose fantasies into the pure, irreducible form of dream fantasy. As Schlegel theorized, the function of *parekbasis* here is not rhetorical; digression does not create a personal bond between writer and reader so that an intersubjective discourse of confession can proceed. Quite the contrary, *parekbasis* in the *Suspiria* has the antirhetorical function of dissolving the writer-reader bond, of clearing away all the eighteenth-century confessional apparatus and confidence games between subjects through an alienating *Verfremdungseffekt*, and of opening up a space for a radically different discourse without subject matter and without subjects (speakers, thinkers, even dreamers)—in short, a pure discourse of dream.

III. Episode, Dream, Digression

Let us now look more closely at three different modes of De Quincey's literary discourse: an episode from the narrative introduction to the *Confessions* of 1821-22 which describes the author's encounter with the prostitute Ann in London, a dream fantasy from "The Pains of Opium" section of the *Confessions* in which the author imagines he is reunited with Ann after seventeen years, and finally a digression from "The Affliction of Childhood" section of the *Suspiria* of 1845 which is a distant echo of the dream of reunion with Ann in the *Confessions* and which occurs in a scene where the author remembers visiting his sister's corpse as a child. By juxtaposing these passages, we will be able to observe the thematic transformations in De Quincey's writings through the discursive forms of narrative episode, dream fantasy, and—shuttling between the two—the freely associative digression.

In the narrative section of the *Confessions* which describes his youthful encounter with Ann in London, De Quincey writes: "Being myself, at that time, of necessity, a peripatetic, or a walker of the streets, I naturally fell in, more frequently, with those female peripatetics, who are technically called streetwalkers" (C, p. 39). This comic analogy between De Quincey's peripatetic activity as an impoverished "philosopher" and Ann's streetwalking as an equally impoverished prostitute belies a much deeper bond which links them together. For as streetwalkers both Ann and the author are transgressors. Ann is, in popular parlance, a "fallen woman," while De Quincey portrays himself at age seventeen as a young man of integrity who a year later will begin taking opium. As late as 1856, De Quincey is strangely ambivalent about the moral implications of his opium habit; referring to his and Coleridge's "baptismal initiation into the use of that mighty drug," he writes:

Trespass against trespass (if any trespass there were)—shadow against shadow (if any shadow were really thrown by this trespass over the snowy disk of pure ascetic morality)—in any case, that act in either of us would read into the same meaning, would count up as a debt into the same value, would measure as a delinquency into the same burden of responsibility. [3:227]

But the "trespass" of De Quincey's opium addiction is traceable to prior transgressions, his running away as "a child not seventeen years old" from his school in Manchester to the streets of London. De Quincey explicitly characterizes this event as an "erring step," a "motion this way or that, to change the currents of [my] destiny" (3:232). In other words, De Quincey's initial fall from grace, the transgression lying behind all his subsequent transgressions, is an act of youthful errancy, a digressive or parekbastic performance of stepping to the side.

Before becoming an urban streetwalker, however, De Quincey was for a brief time a pastoral vagrant in Wales. "Here was the eternal motion of winds and rivers, or of the Wandering Jew liberated from the persecution which compelled him to move and turned his breezy freedom into a killing captivity. Happier life I cannot imagine than this vagrancy" (3:329). This life of idyllic truancy has a long literary history, especially in works of confessional literature, where it has undergone a radical revaluation over the centuries. Such aimless wandering through a seductive country landscape, as De Quincey describes it, was soundly condemned by Saint Augustine in his *Confessions*. The living soul was urged to proceed in a straight direction and not to be deflected from its goal of salvation. Digression, or virtually any kind of measurable movement whatever, was conceived as a "wandering from God" which could only lead the pilgrim away from the central goal of his "native country."[17] Thirteen centuries later, in the *Confessions* of Rousseau, such errant movement is approved as a vital expression of man's natural freedom. In the emerging Romantic view idleness, or even the act of yielding to the beguiling charms of nature, could produce only a salutary effect upon the individual. A cursory comparison of Augustine's and Rousseau's texts, moreover, will demonstrate that the former author's hostility toward random motion is reflected in his own linear, nondigressive narrative; in contrast, Rousseau's *Confessions*, in which the author flaunts his transgressions and idealizes his life of vagrancy, is far more digressive in its mode of presentation.

Clearly there is a close connection between transgression, digression, and confession in these works. De Quincey's confessional writings only reinforce this relation. Thus, in the *Suspiria*, subtitled a "Sequel" to the *Confessions*, he imagines himself stopped on a country road by an agitated tourist eager to know the shortest route to Keswick. De Quincey's response prefaces his analogy between the caduceus and narrative discourse already mentioned:

"Most excellent stranger, as you come to the lakes simply to see their loveliness, might it not be as well to ask after the most beautiful road, rather than the shortest? Because, if abstract shortness, if ... brevity, is your object, then the shortest of all possible tours would seem, with submission, never to have left London." On the same principle, I tell my critic that the whole course of this narrative resembles, and was meant to resemble, a *caduceus* wreathed about with meandering ornaments, or the shaft of a tree's stem hung round and surmounted with some vagrant parasitical plant. [*SP*, p. 157]

In the tradition of Sterne and Rousseau, De Quincey opts for the leisurely, picturesque journey rather than the rushed flight toward a fixed destination. He favors the digressive arabesques of the "vagrant parasitical plant" to the rigid pole of narrative. Yet De Quincey's digressive confessions represent a departure from, or a further twist of, the tradition of Romantic truancy in that his vagrancy is not carefree. The garland around the unbending staff is a *parasitic* plant, and the allusion to the Wandering Jew in the Wales passage suggests that there is no *physical* difference between the random movement of nature ("winds and rivers") and of man (represented by the Wandering Jew), so that man's dread compulsion to wander must be the consequence of a *moral* transgression. Idyllic as De Quincey's description of his Wales sojourn may sound, it is only a digressive interlude between Manchester, where he first "stepped to the side" by running away from school, and London, where he suffered the actual "fall" which directly preceded his opium experiment.

That fall, when it comes, is signaled by a literal collapse. It is the climactic event in the introductory narrative of the *Confessions* of 1821-22, in which the prostitute Ann is revealed as the author's spiritual mediator:

One night, when we were pacing slowly along Oxford Street, and after a day when I had felt unusually ill and faint, I requested her to turn off with me into Soho Square. Thither we went; and we sate down on the steps of a house, which, to this hour, I never pass without a pang of grief, and an inner act of homage to the spirit of that unhappy girl, in memory of the noble act which she there performed. Suddenly, as we sate, I grew much worse. I had been leaning my head against her bosom, and all at once I sank from her arms and fell backwards on the steps. From the sensations I then had, I felt an inner conviction of the liveliest kind, that without some powerful and reviving stimulus I should either have died on the spot, or should, at least, have sunk to a point of exhaustion from which all reäscent, under my friendless circumstances, would soon have become hopeless. [*C,* pp. 40-41]

The necessary "reviving stimulus" was provided by Ann, who hurried to fetch some wine at her own expense, which had "an instantaneous power of restoration" upon De Quincey. Thus the "fallen woman" became the agent of his "reäscent," became his "youthful benefactress." And after her inexplicable disappearance shortly thereafter Ann became the recurrent figure who, as De Quincey acknowledges in 1856, "more than any other, coloured—or (more truly I should say) shaped, moulded and remoulded, composed and decomposed—the great body of opium dreams." She was the "lost Pariah woman" (3:222) who, De Quincey claims, directly inspired "The Daughter of Lebanon."

In her beneficent gesture of raising De Quincey up after his fall, however, Ann bears an even stronger resemblance to the mythical figure of Levana in the *Suspiria*, whose ritual function as a pagan deity was to raise the newborn infant from the ground "lest so grand a creature should grovel there for more than one instant" (*SP*, p. 237). But, as I have argued elsewhere, Levana is by no means an exclusively beneficent agent of levitation.[18] She is associated with "that mighty system of central forces hidden in the deep bosom of human life, which by passion, by strife, by temptation, by the energies of resistance, works forever upon children" (*SP*, p. 238)—in other words, with the physical force of gravity, the demonic principle of the fall, the flywheel of the Newtonian universe. The duplicitous nature of the Levana figure is evident in the description of Ann's act of kindness. She may indeed be the agent of De Quincey's recovery after his collapse, but she remains a fallen woman, a "lost Pariah woman," who was the victim of "some shadowy malice which withdrew her, or attempted to withdraw her, from restoration and from hope" (3:222). When De Quincey imagines her whereabouts after her disappearance, he envisions her not up in heaven but in "the central darkness of a London brothel, or ... the darkness of the grave" (*C*, p. 42). For years, De Quincey claims, he searched for Ann in vain, but "I now wish to see her no longer, but think of her, more gladly, as one long since laid in the grave;—in the grave, I would hope, of a Magdalen;— taken away, before injuries and cruelty had blotted out and transfigured her ingenuous nature, or the brutalities of ruffians had completed the ruin they had begun" (*C*, p. 59).

We may now shift our attention to the transformations of this pivotal episode through the modes of dream and digression.

Toward the close of "The Pains of Opium" section of the *Confessions*, under the entry of June 1819, De Quincey records one of his early dream fantasies based on his memory of Ann. He introduces his dream with the reflection that "the deaths of those whom we love, and, indeed, the contemplation of death generally, is *(caeteris paribus)* more affecting in summer than in any other season of the year" (*C*, p. 120). He then proceeds to narrate his dream, which takes place on the morning of Easter Sunday. Outside his cottage he contemplates a peaceful country scene and a churchyard in which cattle rest "about the grave of a child whom I had tenderly loved" (*C*, p. 121). In the dream De Quincey observes to himself that " 'it yet wants much of sunrise,' " and he determines to take a walk to "celebrate the first fruits of resurrection." The dream then shifts abruptly to Easter Sunday morning in the Orient, where appears

a great city—an image or faint abstraction, caught, perhaps, in childhood, from some picture of Jerusalem. And not a bow-shot from me, upon a stone, and shaded by Judean palms, there sat a woman; and I looked, and it was—Ann! She fixed her eyes upon me earnestly; and I said to her, at length, "So, then, I have found you, at last." I waited; but she answered me not a word. [*C*, p. 122]

The dream finishes with another separation followed by a sudden reunion on Oxford Street, where De Quincey is "walking again with Ann—just as we walked seventeen years before, when we were both children" (*C*, p. 123).

Twenty-four years after the *Confessions* first appeared, De Quincey incorporated a scene in *Suspiria de Profundis* which echoes certain elements of the episode and the dream about Ann in the earlier work. In the section called "The Affliction of Childhood," De Quincey describes the obsessive trauma of his sister Elizabeth's death and his final visit to her bedside the day after her death. It is noon when the six-year-old De Quincey "steal[s] up into her chamber" (*SP*, p. 171) in what is plainly a forbidden, transgressive act. When he turns to look at his sister's face and to confront for the first time the mystery of death, he finds that the bed has been moved in such a way that the corpse is concealed; instead of his sister, his gaze is met by a large open window "through which the sun of midsummer at noonday was showering down torrents of splendor" (*SP*, p. 172).[19] At this precise instant, when the child's determined effort to see his sister alone for the last time is interrupted, De Quincey interrupts his narrative with a long digression. After quoting almost verbatim his observation of a quarter century before that "death, *caeteris paribus*, is more profoundly affecting in summer than in other parts of the year" (*SP*, p. 172), he embarks upon an extended digression ostensibly on the associations between summer and death. De Quincey observes that it is not merely the antagonism of opposites which links these motifs in his mind but a complex association of religious imagery dating back to Bible readings in the nursery with his sisters. The illustrated Bible from which his nurse read was the means by which the summery Eastern scenery of Palestine was juxtaposed with images of Palm Sunday and the story of Christ's entry into Jerusalem and his death. After a train of further childhood associations involving Palm Sunday and Jerusalem, the digression finishes by repeating its theme of the summer-death relation and returning to the main narrative of the deathbed visit.

Several points might be made here. First, in this digression De Quincey hearkens back explicitly to the opium dream of June 1819 described earlier. In both passages the author encounters a dead (or lost) female—Ann in the *Confessions*, Elizabeth in the *Suspiria* (actually, the dream in the *Confessions* refers, as we have seen, to the "grave of a child whom I had tenderly loved," perhaps already a reference to Elizabeth). Both the *Confessions* dream and the *Suspiria* digression, moreover, are triggered by the identical words expressing why death, *"caeteris paribus,"* is more "affecting" in summer than in other seasons. The correspondence between death and summer is traced back similarly to childhood impressions of an Oriental city—in the *Confessions*, "a great city—an image or faint abstraction, caught, perhaps, in childhood, from some picture of Jerusalem"; in the *Suspiria*, more explicitly, an image of Jerusalem as "the *omphalos* of mortality" derived from a "Bible illustrated with many pictures" (*SP*, pp. 174, 173). Both the dream and the digression, fittingly, present a moment of approaching summer: the *Confes-*

sions dream of June 1819 is about the morning of Easter Sunday; the *Suspiria* digression occurs during "midsummer at noonday" and refers repeatedly to Palm Sunday. Certainly implied in a comparison between the two passages is that between Palm and Easter Sunday falls the Friday when "a just man . . . suffered the passion of death in Palestine" (*SP,* p. 173). Death is not presented directly in either the dream or the digression, but it emerges in the spatial interval between the two texts and in the temporal interval between the two days specified by those texts—on the Friday between the digression on Palm Sunday and the dream of Easter Sunday. And as the digressor De Quincey does not present death directly, so the child De Quincey does not confront his sister's corpse directly. The child's distraction from the scene of death by the radiance of summer provides the occasion for the narrator's digression on death-and-summer. The child does not *feel* death directly, nor does he *see* Elizabeth immediately; accordingly, the mature narrator does not directly proceed to *tell* the episode of himself as a six-year-old setting eyes on his sister's corpse. He manages, rather, to ward off this climactic event by means of an extended digression on the interrelation of death and summer.

When De Quincey finally concludes his digression and returns to his narrative, "return[s] to the bed-chamber of my sister" and from "the gorgeous sunlight . . . turn[s] round to the corpse," he describes his overwhelming reaction:

I stood checked for a moment; awe, not fear, fell upon me; and, whilst I stood, a solemn wind began to blow,—the most mournful that ear ever heard. Mournful! that is saying nothing. It was a wind that had swept the fields of mortality for a hundred centuries. Many times since, upon a summer day, when the sun is about the hottest, I have remarked the same wind arising and uttering the same hollow, solemn, Memnonian, but saintly swell: it is in this world the one sole *audible* symbol of eternity. And three times in my life I have happened to hear the same sound in the same circumstances, namely, when standing between an open window and a dead body on a summer day. [*SP,* pp. 175-76]

De Quincey describes himself as a child poised on the brink

of some apocalyptic vision, some total transformation. Immediately there follows a trance during which a mighty revelation unfolds before the youthful De Quincey, who dreams of himself levitating skyward to God:

> A vault seemd to open in the zenith of the far blue sky, a shaft which ran up forever. I, in spirit, rose as if on billows that also ran up the shaft forever; and the billows seemed to pursue the throne of God; but *that* also ran before us and fled away continually. The flight and the pursuit seemed to go on for ever and ever. Frost, gathering frost, some Sarsar wind of death, seemed to repel me; I slept—for how long I cannot say: slowly I recovered my self-possession, and found myself standing, as before, close to my sister's bed. [*SP,* p. 176]

This ecstatic experience at age six of the "flight of the solitary child to the solitary God" will provide De Quincey with much of the material he will draw upon for his future dream fantasies. The immediate effect of the dream vision, however, is to numb the child's anguish at the sight of his dead sister: "Rupture of grief that, being too mighty for a child to sustain, foundest a happy oblivion in a heaven-born dream, and within that sleep didst conceal a dream, whose meaning, in after years, when slowly I deciphered, suddenly there flashed upon me new light; and even by the grief of a child, as I will show you, reader, hereafter, were confounded the falsehoods of philosophers" (*SP,* p. 176). In a note to this passage De Quincey explains that "the thoughts referred to will be given in final notes; as at this point they seemed too much to interrupt the course of the narrative." De Quincey hints that the content of his vision is too rich to be presented all at once; furthermore, such an exposition would be too digressive. Consequently, the vision's description must be reserved for subsequent digressions and dreams.

We know, however, that an explicit presentation of the dream, supposing it to be possible, would constitute a supreme act of blasphemy, would be a transgressive act as well as a digressive performance. We should not forget that the child's original decision to "steal" into the forbidden bedchamber, in order to "steal" a look at his dead sister, was essentially akin in its monstrousness to looking upon the heavenly host; in fact, they *were* one and the same gesture for which De Quincey nearly paid with his life. He is absolutely clear about the transgressive nature of his action, for upon coming back to himself after his trance he "slunk like a guilty thing with stealthy steps from the room" (*SP*, p. 177). But the transgression which De Quincey committed by visiting his sister would not stop him from trying to see her again, from using opium to recall or to enhance the dream he beheld in her presence by the open window, and from digressing upon the dream's infinite content in his future writing. Just as his digression on death and summer defers the climactic event of gazing upon his dead sister, so the dream which came to him in a trance at his sister's bedside provided the "happy oblivion" that prevented him from succumbing to grief and possibly even death. Digression and dream serve De Quincey well as apotropaic mechanisms of deferral, allowing him to draw close to the transcendental reality of death without being engulfed in the process. The price of such insight, however, is incomprehension and indirection; as Moses stammers from singeing his tongue, so De Quincey continues to digress from his repeated acts of sidestepping the abyss.

IV. Digression and Gravitation

I return now to the digression in the *Suspiria* which occurs just before De Quincey sees his dead sister. Standing between the corpse and the open window on a summer day, he launches into a digression on the subject of death and summer. A chain of associations leads him from Bible readings in the nursery with his sisters to the perpetual summer scenery of Jerusalem, where Christ died. "Yet what then was Jerusalem?" De Quincey wonders, continuing the digression:

Did I fancy it to be the *omphalos* (navel) of the earth? That pretension had once been made for Jerusalem, and once for Delphi; and both pretensions had become ridiculous, as the figure of the planet became known. Yes; but if not of the earth, for earth's tenant, Jerusalem was the *omphalos* of mortality. Yet how? there, on the contrary, it was, as we infants understood, that mortality had been trampled under foot. True; but, for that very reason, there it was that mortality had opened its very gloomiest crater. There it was, indeed, that the human had risen on wings from the grave; but, for that reason, there also it was that the divine had been swallowed up by the abyss; the lesser star could not rise, before the greater would submit to eclipse. Summer, therefore, had connected itself with death, not merely as a mode of antagonism, but also through intricate relations to scriptural scenery and events. [*SP*, pp. 174-75]

As much as the *Suspiria* digression appears to be a spin-off of the *Confessions* dream of June 1819 and to be—as De Quincey himself explicitly says it is—a meditation on the relation between death and summer, I suggest that this is only the ostensible theme of the digression. Its actual subject is, rather, gravitation. Jerusalem, the former omphalos of the earth, had lost its prestige "as the figure of the planet became known"—that is, as the earth's center was recognized to be its center of gravity. It is interesting that the chief difference between the text of the *Suspiria* digression of 1845 and its later version, after "The Affliction of Childhood" was transferred to the *Autobiographic Sketches*, is the addition of the word "center." The question "Did I fancy it to be the *omphalos* (navel) of the earth?" became "Did I fancy it to be the *omphalos* (navel) or physical centre of the earth?"; and the phrase "*omphalos* of mortality" became "*omphalos* and absolute centre" (1:40).

This seemingly trivial change actually opens up a whole range of cross references in De Quincey's corpus, as in his descriptions of "this storm of life so perilously centripetal towards the vortex of the merely human" (*SP*, p. 148) and of that state of ruin where "the voice perishes; the gestures are frozen; and the spirit of man flies back upon its own centre" (*SP*, p. 153). Just as Ann had been the agent of the author's "reäscent" in the streets of London before her own descent into "the central darkness of a London brothel," and just as Levana had supervised the pagan ritual in which the infant is first "laid on the ground" and then "raised ... upright" (*SP*, p. 237), so with Christ's crucifixion in Jerusalem "mortality had been trampled under foot" before "the human had risen on wings from the grave." According to De Quincey's theological mechanics, the divine fell (and continues to fall) so that mortality may rise: "The lesser star could not rise, before the greater would submit to eclipse." Similarly, Elizabeth's life is literally finished in De Quincey's description, and her descent as a child divinity back into the earth is counterbalanced by another increment of her brother's "rise" into adulthood. When the narrative describing De Quincey's childhood development falters at the crisis of his sister's death, the author's mature reflective consciousness takes over, postponing the confrontation of the corpse through the means of a digression on death's inseparable connection with summer and on mortality's reciprocal relation to divinity—in short, on the equilibrium between the descent of burial and the ascent of resurrection.

Gravitation and levitation are complementary, compensatory movements in De Quincey's writing. Like death and summer, they are inseparable. They are always intermingled with one another, and each is the condition of the other's possibility. Ann and Levana's loving gestures of levitation disguise the "mighty system of central forces" in whose power both the harlot and the goddess are themselves trapped and whose demonic, if unconscious, agents they are. In a related effect, when De Quincey expresses his love for Elizabeth in the metaphor of gravitation ("But what was it that drew my heart, by gravitation so strong, to my sister?" [*SP,* p. 169]),[20] he echoes the Christian Augustinian formula of the *pondus amoris* of God's celestial love which draws the faithful up to heaven; but he infuses this metaphor with the demonic post-Newtonian meaning of a down-drawing death force, as in his description of Ann's final destination as "the central darkness of a London brothel, or ... the darkness of the grave," or as in his image in "Levana and Our Ladies of Sorrow" of the "central forces hidden in the deep bosom of human life, which by passion, by strife, by temptation, by the energies of resistance, works forever upon children."

De Quincey's digression on gravitation in the *Suspiria* is by no means an isolated example, a fortuitous alliance of a digressive form with a theme of great "gravity." In the first volume of *Tristram Shandy* Sterne has Tristram produce a digression on precisely the same subject:

> Tho' my digressions are all fair, as you observe,—and... I fly off from what I am about, as far and as often too as any writer in *Great Britain;* yet I constantly take care to order affairs so, that my main business does not stand still in my absence.
>
> I was just going, for example, to have given you the great outlines of my uncle *Toby*'s most whimsical character;—when my aunt *Dinah* and the coachman came a-cross us, and led us a vagary some millions of miles into the very heart of the planetary system: Notwithstanding all this, you perceive that the drawing of my uncle *Toby*'s character went on gently all the time;—not the great contours of it,—that was impossible,—but some familiar strokes and faint designations of it, were here and there touch'd in, as we went along, so that you are much better acquainted with my uncle *Toby* now than you was before.
>
> By this contrivance the machinery of my work is of a species by itself; two contrary motions are introduced into it, and reconciled, which were thought to be at variance with each other. In a word, my work is digressive, and it is progressive too,—and at the same time.
>
> This, Sir, is a very different story from that of the earth's moving round her axis, in her diurnal rotation, with her progress in her elliptick orbit which brings about the year, and constitutes that variety and vicissitude of seasons we enjoy;—though I own it suggested the thought,—as I believe the greatest of our boasted improvements and discoveries have come from some such trifling hints.
>
> Digressions, incontestably, are the sunshine;—they are the life, the soul of reading;—take them out of this book for instance,—you might as well take the book along with them.[21]

In this passage it is interesting to note that the subject of digression alternates with the subject of gravitation in each succeeding paragraph. If Tristram observes that his work is informed by "two contrary motions," if he claims that it "is digressive, and it is progressive too,—and at the same time" (a formulation repeated by Schlegel in a statement that what he called "critical philology" must be "simultaneously progressive and classical"),[22] it may be permissible to add that the work is also involved in an exchange of digressive and gravitational forces. At the end of the sixth volume Tristram writes an open-ended digression on digressions that anticipates De Quincey's passage on the caduceus in the *Suspiria*. In essence Tristram asserts that the line of narrative, like the trajectory of gravitational motion, is not straight but digressive: "Pray can you tell me,—that is, without anger, before I write my chapter upon straight lines—by what mistake—who told them so—or how it has come to pass, that your men of wit and genius have all along confounded this [straight] line, with the line of *gravitation?*"[23]

Sterne's yoking of digression and gravitation in *Tristram Shandy* may help us see that De Quincey's digression on gravitation in "The Affliction of Childhood" is not an accidental linkage between a gravitational motif and a digressive form. Rather, digression and gravitation are *necessarily* interrelated in De Quincey's writing as complementary, compensatory, structural-stylistic movements, each of which makes the other possible. As the digression on gravitation in "The Affliction of Childhood" postpones, and in a sense prepares the six-year-old De Quincey for, his encounter with his sister's corpse, so the same digression enables the mature author to avoid both the sentimentality and the gravity of his potentially morbid subject. The "gravity" of a narrative preoccupied with death is counterbalanced by the levity of a digression concerned with the connection between death and summer. Indeed, I would further maintain that De Quincey's digression in "The Affliction of Childhood" and Sterne's digression in the first volume of *Tristram Shandy* are not anomalous exceptions but fully explicit instances of a general principle that *every digression is involved with, if not directly about, gravitation*. Every digression represents a transgressive impulse to escape the dull straight line of narrative, the deadly gravity of plot, and ultimately the fatal curse of the Fall.

This relation between digression and gravitation is an essentially post-Newtonian, Romantic recognition which functions as a working principle in the narratives of English authors like Sterne, Byron, and De Quincey, but which is most explicitly developed in German literary practice and critical theory. The genre of German *Bildungsliteratur*, or narratives of individual self-formation which in turn recapitulate the history of the human race, abounds in allusions to the erratic movements of planets and comets and to the hero's "rising" or "falling" star. Hence Friedrich Hölderlin's Ptolemaic reference in his novel *Hyperion* to the "exzentrische Bahn"[24] that man traverses through life, and Jean Paul's title *Der Komet* for his last and incomplete *Bildungsroman*. The further one delves into German writings of the Romantic era, the more evident the relation between digression and gravitation appears. Thus, in a fragment which echoes Tristram's statement about the curvature of gravitational motion, Schlegel writes somewhat cryptically that "the line in itself is always curved [*krumm*]; the straight line is already a plane."[25] And in Novalis's marginal notes to a study of Pierre La Place, which Novalis himself referred to as his *Gravitationslehre,* we find this query: "Should we not expect two bodies falling next to each other to describe imperceptible *curves* against each other which would be modified through their respective masses? *Serpentine lines?*"[26] In Novalis's query the digressive motion brought about by the gravitational interaction of the two falling objects is clear, but what is one to make of the emphasized question "*Serpentine lines?*" The matter cannot be settled here, but a plausible case can be made, based on a review of literary, philosophical, and scientific references to gravitation during the Romantic era, that the serpentine movement of the falling bodies around each other, like the spiraling plant in De Quincey's image of the caduceus, is intended to evoke an association between gravity and the Fall of man.

Consider, finally, this fragment of Schlegel:

> The evil principle in nature is *Gravity* [die *Schwere*]—as opposed to the Light [dem Licht entgegen]. Everything noble in nature seeks the light, and finally sinks back into gravity again. Everything that has its existential being [Dasein] in and through gravity is only *relative*, like unreason. *The origin of gravity* must be thought to be precisely as accidental [zufällig] and as necessary as the *Fall of Man* [*Sündenfall*].[27]

Indeed, Newton's formulation of a gravitational principle, and the central role of that principle in the emerging natural sciences, was registered by several Romantic writers as constituting, after the Fall in Eden caused by Adam and Eve's partaking of the fruit of the Tree of Knowledge, man's *second* fall.[28] Man's recognition of gravitation as a universal physical law had the effect of displacing him in the natural order of things, of robbing him irrevocably of the omphalos, or center. From the moment that gravity, not Jerusalem, was discovered to be the center of the planet, man was everlastingly decentered. What is more, he was henceforth compelled to permanent digression as a means of avoiding a return to the center which was now seen for what it was—a center of mortality, a center of death.

Schlegel was the first critic to recognize the digressive principle in Romantic *Poesie* as a result of his study of the novels of Sterne, Diderot, and Jean Paul. This same recognition, moreover, was intuitively understood and developed by De Quincey, who created a dialectic of digression and dream vision in his own confessional writings, and who thematized the hidden counterforce of gravitation as both the agency and the consequence of man's spiritual and moral fall. Like the writings of other Romantics in England and Germany, De Quincey's confessional works demonstrate that gravity is a potentially harrowing death principle in the universe which must be deferred, postponed, or sidestepped by a permanent performance of digressive levity. Perhaps the most convincing proof of the digressive character of Romantic discourse is to be found not in the literary writings of the time but in the literary history of the age itself, where the zigzag pattern of international influence—from Sterne in England, over to Jean Paul on the Continent, and back to De Quincey in England—is there for all to see.

NOTES

1. Friedrich Schlegel, *Dialogue on Poetry and Literary Aphorisms,* trans. Ernst Behler and Roman Struc (University Park: Pennsylvania State University Press, 1968), p. 95. Unless otherwise noted, all subsequent citations of this particular work in English translation refer to this translation. The original is cited from Friedrich Schlegel, *Kritische Friedrich-Schlegel-*

Ausgabe, ed. Ernst Behler, Jean-Jacques Anstett, and Hans Eichner, 35 vols. (Paderborn: Schöningh, 1958–), 2:330; hereafter cited as *Kritische.* Unless otherwise indicated, citations from Schlegel's original texts are to this edition.
 2. Schlegel, *Dialogue,* p. 95.
 3. Ibid., p. 98.
 4. Ibid., p. 101.
 5. Schlegel, *Kritische,* 2:335.
 6. Schlegel, *Dialogue,* p. 97.
 7. See Joel D. Black, "Levana: Levitation in Jean Paul and Thomas De Quincey," *Comparative Literature* 32 (1980): 42–62.
 8. For book-length studies of these two Schlegelian terms, both of which are relevant to De Quincey's writings and to Romantic aesthetics in general, see Wolfgang Kayser, *The Grotesque in Art and Literature,* trans. Ulrich Weisstein (Bloomington: Indiana University Press, 1963); Karl Konrad Polheim, *Die Arabeske: Ansichten und Ideen aus Friedrich Schlegels Poetik* (Paderborn: Schöningh, 1966).
 9. Friedrich Schlegel, *Literary Notebooks: 1797-1801,* ed. Hans Eichner (London: Athlone Press, 1957), p. 61; unless otherwise noted, all translations are mine.
 10. Schlegel, *Kritische,* 18:85.
 11. I discuss the rhetorical background of the structure of digression and its function as a literary structure in "The Second Fall: The Laws of Digression and Gravitation in Romantic Narrative and Their Impact on Contemporary Encyclopaedic Literature" (Ph.D. diss., Stanford University, 1979), pp. 36–48.
 12. Laurence Sterne, *Tristram Shandy,* ed. Howard Anderson (New York: Norton, 1980), p. 52.
 13. Letter of 26 March 1793 to Christian Otto, in *Jean Pauls Sämtliche Werke,* ed. E. Berend, sec. 3, vol. 1 (Berlin: Akademie Verlag, 1956), p. 375.
 14. Michael von Poser, *Der abschweifende Erzähler: Rhetorische Tradition und deutscher Roman im achtzehnten Jahrhundert* (Bad Homburg v. d. H.: Verlag Gehlen, 1969). Poser provides a detailed discussion of Schlegel's concept of *Parekbase* (see pp. 114–32). He argues that the rhetorical model upon which the eighteenth-century comic novel was based, where the author is a specifically identifiable personality who addresses the reader for a particular purpose, is incompatible with the Romantic ideal of the *"selbsttätig"* ("self-sustaining") work that is wholly independent from the author. As he explains, "The content of *parekbasis* is 'local' and 'individual.' This content did not interest Schlegel, but only the form of the *parekbatic* procedures, that is to say, their consequences for the work of art" (p. 127). For a comprehensive assessment of Schlegel's achievement in liberating literary discourse from classical rhetorical and philosophical theory, thereby preparing the way for a revolution in aesthetic culture, see Robert

S. Leventhal, "From Semiotic Interpretation to Critical Hermeneutics: The Emergence of Hermeneutic Critique in the Early Writings of Friedrich Schlegel" (Ph.D. diss., Stanford University, 1982).
  15. Poser, *Der abschweifende Erzähler*, p. 110.
  16. *The Complete Poetical Works of Samuel Taylor Coleridge*, ed. Ernest Hartley Coleridge, 2 vols. (Oxford: Oxford University Press, Clarendon Press, 1912), 1:296-97.
  17. Saint Augustine, *On Christian Doctrine*, trans. D. W. Robertson, Jr. (New York: Liberal Arts Press, 1958), pp. 9-10: "Suppose we were wanderers who could not live in blessedness except at home, miserable in our wandering and desiring to end it and to return to our native country. We would need vehicles for land and sea which could be used to help us reach our homeland, which is to be enjoyed. But if the amenities of the journey and the motion of the vehicles itself delighted us, and if we were led to enjoy those things which we should use, we should not wish to end our journey quickly, and, entangled in a perverse sweetness, we should be alienated from our country, whose sweetness would make us blessed."
  18. Black, "Levana: Levitation in Jean Paul and Thomas De Quincey," pp. 52-55.
  19. Friedrich Christoph has traced De Quincey's description of his sister's deathbed scene to a passage describing Liana's death in Jean Paul's novel *Titan (Über den Einfluss Jean Paul Richters auf Thomas De Quincey* [Hof: N.p., 1898], p. 28). Christoph, moreover, notes that both Jean Paul and De Quincey refer to the heightened effect of death in spring or early summer as compared with the rest of the year. See also De Quincey's translation of a passage from Jean Paul called "On the Death of Young Children" (11:284), in which the happiness of the "little human ephemera" who "played only in the ascending beams, and in the early dawn, and in the eastern light" is declared. See too the *Confessions* of 1856 (3:294-95).
  20. Cf. Wordsworth's reference to gravitation in the version of *The Prelude* of 1850 (*The Prelude: 1799, 1805, 1850*, ed. Jonathan Wordsworth, M. H. Abrams, and Stephen Gill [New York: Norton, 1979], 2.241-44) to characterize the "filial bond" between the child and the world: "No outcast he, bewildered and depressed: / Along his infant veins are interfused / The gravitation and the filial bond / Of nature that connect him with the world."
  21. Sterne, *Tristram Shandy*, pp. 51-52.
  22. Schlegel, *Kritische*, 16:51.
  23. Sterne, *Tristram Shandy*, p. 334.
  24. Friedrich Hölderlin, *Sämtliche Werke*, ed. Friedrich Beissner, 6 vols. (Stuttgart: Cotta, 1943-65), 3:236. See Marshall Brown, *The Shape of German Romanticism* (Ithaca, N.Y.: Cornell University Press, 1979), pp. 161-70. Brown concludes that the expression "eccentric path," used by Schlegel as well as by Hölderlin, can be regarded "not only [as] a popular phrase *in* the period, but an appropriate description *of* the period" (p. 170).
  25. Schlegel, *Kritische*, 18:156; my translation.

26. Novalis, *Schriften*, ed. Paul Kluckhohn and Richard Samuel, 2d ed., 4 vols. (Stuttgart: W. Kohlhammer, 1968), 3:71; my translation.
27. Schlegel, *Kritische*, 18:162; my translation.
28. See "The Second Fall," pp. 132–96, where I discuss the relation between Newton's discovery of gravitation as perceived by the Romantics and the scriptural account of the Fall. Among the writers whose responses to gravitational theory I consider are Blake, Byron, Kleist, Keats, and Wordsworth, as well as Jean Paul, Schlegel, and De Quincey.

16

"The Loom of *Palingenesis*": De Quincey's Cosmology in "System of the Heavens"

ROBERT LANCE SNYDER

In *Nil*, his intriguing study of nineteenth-century writers' preoccupation with the idea of vacancy, or *néant*, Robert Martin Adams describes the period as "an age of ricochet and revulsion" in which "the conviction of irrelevance, of being beside the whole point of some immense indifferent process taking place around one[,] produces a sense of inner cancellation which is one kind of void."[1] Such an analysis of the era at large can be substantiated rather easily from De Quincey's writings, especially those which trace his spiritual autobiography. No reader of "The Affliction of Childhood," for example, can fail to recognize that in the account of his sister Elizabeth's death, climaxing with his vision of the endlessly receding throne of God (*SP*, p. 176), De Quincey is retrospectively construing an etiology for his lifelong susceptibility to metaphysical angst and his confirmed horror of the "fractured and discontinuous" (5:232). Ever the uneasy pariah, De Quincey was haunted throughout his career by specters of exclusion and estrangement, by an enduring fear of his own marginal "irrelevance" in the scheme of things. This obsession comes to the fore in a variety of contexts, but generally it is accompanied by an unmistakable agoraphobia that inspires some revealing countermeasures.

The recurrent form which the experience of *Entfremdung* assumes in De Quincey's works is the sudden or unexpected expansion of spatial dimensions. At times, of course, this distension is the result of opium, as he indicates when enumerating the drug's influences upon his dreams: "Buildings, landscapes, &c., were exhibited in proportions so vast as the bodily eye is not fitted to receive. Space swelled, and was amplified to an extent of unutterable and self-repeating infinity" (3:435). But the "Piranesi effect," as J. Hillis Miller aptly calls it,[2] is not simply a function of De Quincey's narcosis; it also asserts itself within his waking and everyday life, quite apart from the pharmacology of opium. In all cases, however, the situation remains essentially the same in that, confronting some scene of more or less stable configuration, he watches it metamorphose, almost exponentially, until he becomes lost and diminished among proliferating "circumstances of never-ending diversity" (5:358). Typically, such incidents threaten De Quincey's fragile concept of the self's autonomy by immersing him in a world of contingency and disturbing relativism. One example may suffice to establish the pattern I have in mind, a pattern clearly replicated by "'the persecutions of the Infinite'" (8:34) in "System of the Heavens as Revealed by Lord Rosse's Telescopes."

In the eighth chapter of *Autobiographic Sketches*, De Quincey portrays himself, at age fifteen, making his first journey to London, in his mind less a city than a mighty nation. To convey an impression of its prodigious "power," he depicts the hordes of traffic and commerce moving steadily toward the metropolis, all drawn forward as though by some ineluctable magnetism or gravitational force. During the final stage of approach he says, shifting to the second-person indefinite pronoun, "you soon begin to feel yourself entering the stream as it were of a Norwegian *maelstrom*" until, "for the latter ten or twelve miles, you become aware that you are no longer noticed: nobody sees you; nobody hears you; nobody regards you; you do not even regard yourself" (1:181). For the young De Quincey the episode initially involves both the thrill of assimilation into a larger whole and the mounting agitation of anonymity; however, the mood grows more sinister as he finds himself amid faces that collectively seem "like a mask of maniacs, or, oftentimes, like a pageant of phantoms."[3] Compounding his disorientation is the vertiginous complexity of this terra incognita:

The great length of the streets in many quarters of London; the continual opening of transient glimpses into other vistas equally far-stretching, going off at right angles to the one which you are traversing; and the murky atmosphere which, settling upon the remoter end of every long avenue, wraps its termination in gloom and uncertainty; all these are circumstances aiding that sense of vastness and illimitable proportions which for ever brood over the aspect of London in its interior. [1:182]

Reminiscent of Wordsworth's "monstrous ant-hill on the plain / Of a too busy world,"[4] the "universe" of London is here presented as a forbidding labyrinth that poses an intricate problem of perspectivism. From a distance the city constitutes a fixed, definable entity, but upon a closer view it tends to spin off into the incalculable and incomprehensible. Distracted by the teeming multiplicity of all that meets his gaze, De Quincey admits to being paralyzed by a "blind sense of mysterious grandeur and Babylonian confusion."

Agoraphobia is by no means a syndrome limited to De Quincey's impressionable adolescence. In one guise or another, usually combined with a pronounced element of existential dread, it crops up later in his comparison of man's life to an unmapped "Hercynian forest" (3:314), in his awed reaction to the granite bust of Memnon in the British Museum (1:41–42; 8:17), in his idiosyncratic habit during the 1850s of leaving a series of rented rooms virtually "snowed up" with crumpled manuscripts (Page, 1:363), and, not least, in his consternation over the "illimitable growths of space" (8:16) disclosed by William Parsons's huge reflecting telescope (see below). Wherever or however encountered, such discoveries of mystifying indeterminacy always reinforce De Quincey's fear that "undesigned equivocation prevails everywhere" (1:77). But in literature and in life alike he attempted to counteract the abhorrent vacuity of space by strategies meant to reclaim its expanses and to convert absence into presence. This impulse is epitomized in his writing by a style of elaborate, self-sustained filigree and in his personal history by an eccentricity symbolically connected to his London experience.

One of De Quincey's many quirks was his inveterate fondness for walking, a mode of exercise which afforded him relief from the waves of depression brought on by his periodic withdrawal from opium. Yet, unlike the legendary "Walking Stewart," to whom he devoted two essays, De Quincey never once set foot beyond England and for a time restricted his compass to a considerably narrower scope. For eighteen months, beginning in the summer of 1843, he confined his rambles to the small garden (only forty-four yards in circuit) at Mavis Bush, near Lasswade, the cottage outside Edinburgh to which his children had moved a few years earlier. There it became his practice, which he recommended to "all persons suffering from nervous irritability" (14:274), to pace the garden's periphery with watch in hand and tally the distances covered—one mile for every forty revolutions—by arranging ten stones on the rungs of a chair as he passed. With the help of this abacus he estimated that he tramped a thousand miles in one period of ninety days (Page, 1:327). While orbiting a circumscribed area, De Quincey presumably managed to ward off the dizzying volatility of space and time that he found so frightful. Moreover, by this regimen *he* became the measure of his environment, the sufficient demiurge of a makeshift cosmos, in much the same way that as a boy he presided over the imaginary island kingdom of Gombroon (1:88–93). Vagrancy, as De Quincey knew intuitively from his survey of London, has its perils, but perhaps they might be held in check, if not overcome, by some offsetting system or process.

Certainly this was De Quincey's ardent hope in his "Introductory Notice" to *Suspiria de Profundis* when, as already discussed in these pages, he decried nineteenth-century technology's "colossal pace of advance" and spoke of the urgent need for "counter forces of corresponding magnitude, forces in the direction of religion or profound philosophy" (*SP*, p. 148). Only the emergence of such compensatory principles could arrest, as he believed, the spiritual attrition and subjugation being caused by applied science. Ironically, De Quincey employs Newton's third law of physics to propound his solution to the gathering crisis: his mind, in other words, cannot abandon faith in the dynamics of complementarity, cannot disavow the Newtonian axiom that every action is (or can be) matched by an equal and opposite reaction. It should not be surprising, therefore, that when De Quincey's attention turns from the juggernaut of technological change overtaking British society to the celestial mechanics of an expanding universe, he should again revert almost unconsciously to the same ingrained way of thinking. Both his instinctive aversions and intellectual accommodations on the latter subject can tell us much about the age. Recently Hans Eichner has argued that "Romanticism is, perhaps predominantly, a desperate rearguard action against the spirit and the implications of modern science," especially as they were defined by dramatic breakthroughs in the field of astronomy.[5] Although Eichner's critical method can be challenged, his thesis is useful for understanding De Quincey's provisional cosmology in "System of the Heavens" with its key postulate of "the loom of *palingenesis*" (8:11).

A curious and uneven piece in which De Quincey describes himself as "one belonging to the laity, and not to the *clerus*, in the science of astronomy" (8:29), his essay of 1846 is ostensibly a review of John Pringle Nichol's *Thoughts on Some Important Points Relating to the System of the World*. However, as invariably occurs in the prose which he produced for the magazines, De Quincey uses the occasion to expatiate on matters of special concern to him—in this case the bewildering optics of the macrocosm unveiled the year before by the enhanced telescope of William Parsons, third Earl of Rosse and later (1849–54) president of the Royal Society.[6] Oddly, De Quincey does not condemn, as might be expected, this marvel of technological ingenuity. He in fact declares that "a new era for the human intellect, upon a path that lies amongst its most aspiring, is promised, is inaugurated, by Lord Rosse's almost awful telescope," which he then likens to the scepter of a modern philosopher-king who sits "enthroned upon the shores of infinity" (8:14, 16). But his approbation rings somewhat hollow, as is betrayed by the qualifying phrase "almost awful," and the remainder of the essay amply documents the speaker's underlying agoraphobia. Surveying "that epoch when ... man's eye is arming itself for looking effectively into the mighty depths of space," he asks what it is that Lord Rosse has accomplished "at a price of incalculable anxiety" and replies that "he has revealed more by far than he found" (8:14, 15). What specifically has been opened to man's vision, though not to his comprehension, is the kaleidoscopic plenitude of the skies and the uncertain geometry of interstellar distances; he thus speaks of "frightful magnitude," "immeasurable worlds," and, recalling the sculptured head of Memnon, an "eternity which baffles and confounds all faculty of computation" (8:18, 23, 17). Paradoxically, the telescope becomes for De Quincey an intimidating symbol of occultation, since in its speculum he finds proof that balance and proportion are merely the vanishing assumptions of individual consciousness.

How, then, is one to account for the mixed, even antithetical, quality of the essay in which "De Quincey's pride in human technology exist[s] side by side with an anxiety about human systems and their close alliance with the powers of chaos"?[7] Several answers can be proposed, the simplest involving the work's journalistic background. As David Masson explains in an editorial footnote (8:7–8n.), the paper originally appeared in *Tait's Edinburgh Magazine* to give congratulatory notice of the book by John Pringle Nichol, professor of astronomy in the University of Glasgow and an intimate friend of De Quincey. In light of their personal relationship, the circumstances of publication (the proprietor of *Tait's* was also the publisher of *Thoughts on Some Important Points*), and the widely respected abilities of Nichol himself in the popular exposition of scientific knowledge, it is unlikely that De Quincey would have felt completely at liberty to voice all his apprehensions on a subject which, by his own admission, lay beyond the pale of his expertise. He therefore takes refuge in the partial disguise of forced humor, particularly at the start of the essay, and in the historical progression of intellect, trying to avoid too naked a display of his misgivings concerning the concept of astronomical infinitude.

A second reason has to do with De Quincey's readiness to embrace what Robert M. Maniquis terms "imperial visions" of collective wholeness.[8] Terrified by the prospect of personal fragmentation, De Quincey characteristically is inclined to exalt various manifestations of communal energy which, he would like to believe, attest to the existence of some immanent design, purpose, or teleology in the world. The result is an author frequently given to proclaiming the Tory gospel of political conservatism and, late in life, capable of prophesying Britain's sublime destiny as wrought by "great mechanic changes":

> Many an imperfect hemisphere of thought, action, desire, that could not heretofore unite with its corresponding hemisphere, ... now moves electrically to its integration, hurries to its complement, realizes its orbicular perfection, spherical completion through that simple series of improvements which to man have given the wings and *talaria* of Gods. [*PW,* 1:166]

Such rhapsodies on the abstract idea of "progress," if placed alongside the alarm registered in the "Introductory Notice" to *Suspiria de Profundis,* sound like mere ranting until one recognizes how deeply divided De Quincey is on the issue and how important it is for him to remain equivocal. Maniquis states the case incisively: "He constantly spiritualizes ambiguity out of the pit of possible nothingness, but his is not the ethics of ambiguity that gambles with nothingness.... De Quincey had little of the French taste for ontological bets."[9] It is thus the fear of his individual "irrelevance," discussed at the outset, that engenders *both* rhetorics—that which indicts and that which extols technological advance. "System of the Heavens" reverberates with strains of each because De Quincey's mythologizing imagination cannot encompass Pascalian "abysses of the heavenly wilderness" (8:18), cannot divine there as in *The English Mail-Coach* the "conscious presence of a central intellect" (13:272). However much he may borrow from astronomy in the above passage to descant upon "orbicular perfection" or "spherical completion," his real confidence always stems from some familiar, terrestrially restricted perspective.

The third and most compelling explanation for De Quincey's inconsistent stance in the essay pertains to his contrapuntal style of writing. Although his celebrated theory of the "literature of power" revolves around the heuristic value of language as an incarnation of thought,[10] his mind shuttles back and forth between dialectical extremes while he seeks the elusive goal of inclusiveness, of harmonized vision. When successful as "a *nisus* both of reflection and of large combination," an author's style demonstrates "metaphysical relations" and can itself become "a mode of existence" (10:262). Hence derives his admiration for the fugal interconnectedness of works by Sir Thomas Browne and Jeremy Taylor; hence springs also his elevation of Edmund Burke over Samuel Johnson as a stylist, for in contrast to Johnson's writings—where "nothing is positively added, everything is simply unveiled"—in Burke's allegedly operates the syncretic principle of *"Epigenesis*, where each stage of the growth becomes a causative impulse to a new stage, . . . in the mysterious process of generation" (5:134). Through the whorled structure of his nondiscursive prose, as his trope of the entwined caduceus (*SP,* pp. 157–59) suggests, De Quincey labors to achieve the same kind of epigenetic coherence. And though he disliked composing for the magazines because their deadlines limited the opportunity for leisurely craftsmanship,[11] he attempts a comparable technique in "System of the Heavens." Again, as in "The Affliction of Childhood" section of *Suspiria,* De Quincey functions as "ruler of the oscillations" controlling the "cloud-scaling swing" of language: "Seated in such a swing, fast as you reach the lowest point of depression, may you rely on racing up to a starry altitude of corresponding ascent. Ups and downs you will see, heights and depths, in our fiery course together, such as will sometimes tempt you to look shyly and suspiciously at me, your guide" (*SP,* p. 222). The immensities of space are not, admittedly, as easily manipulated as the landscape of autobiographical memory. Nevertheless, drawing on the law of flux and reflux whereby "the very extremity of any force is the seed and nucleus of a counter-agency" (6:431), he strives for an architectonics of balanced polarities that will provide him with some measure of spiritual reassurance. If he can carry it off, if he can approximate that law through the pendular sweep of prose, conceivably (or so De Quincey's aesthetic faith implies) there may never arise the threat of a cosmic determinism or vacuum too dreadful to contemplate. Everything instead will adumbrate a superordinate economy of motion; everything, in short, will be perpetually emerging from "the loom of *palingenesis.*"

The metaphor, crucial to understanding the cosmology projected in "System of the Heavens," validates the interpretation I have just sketched by its kinship to a variation found elsewhere. In his essay "Language," already discussed by Frederick Burwick,[12] De Quincey expounds his concept of nexus, that wherein "the true life of composition resides," by speaking of it as "the great loom in which the textile process of the moving intellect reveals itself and prospers" (10:258, 259). The figure clearly delineates all that he means by the *"organology"* versus the *"mechanology"* of style (10:163–64), the thrust of the former being the weaving together of disparate strands of thought. The consummate potential of language, therefore, is homologous with the evolutionary activity of palingenesis, the scientific theory that ontogeny recapitulates phylogeny. Realization of this postulate at work in the universe constitutes a virtual beacon of hope for De Quincey, since it opposes any hint of entropy or geophysical decline; however, to comprehend his logic requires that we trace the texture, the intermeshed warp and woof, of the essay itself.

Roughly the first quarter of "System of the Heavens" is given over to what appears to be a whimsical attack on Kant for trying to ascertain the earth's longevity. Without explicitly saying so, De Quincey is probably alluding to Kant's *Allgemeine Naturgeschichte und Theorie des Himmels,* published in 1755, when he acknowledges that the German philosopher considered "no such barren conundrum" as "how many years the Earth had lived" but rather the riddle of "what proportion ... that amount form[s] of the total career allotted to this planet" (8:8). At this juncture De Quincey launches into a fanciful, seemingly digressive, barrage of conceits regarding the globe's chronological maturity. Thus, after confiding his own opinion that "our mother Tellus, beyond all doubt, is a lovely little thing" who "cannot be superannuated," he proceeds to wonder whether, if an adult, she is a partner better suited for waltzing or the whist table and whether, if a child, she is a playful ingenue or more reserved maiden. Through the reductive, tongue-in-cheek absurdity of these anthropomorphisms De Quincey moves obliquely toward his main criticism: "What Kant understood by his question is something that still remains to be developed. It is this:—Let the earth have lived any number of years that you suggest, still that tells us nothing about the *period* of life, the *stage*, which she may be supposed to have reached" (8:9). The clause "that tells us nothing," it might be noted in passing, echoes one of De Quincey's objections to Johnson's writing style ("nothing is positively added").[13] But the crux of his sally here is that Kant's endeavor is similarly flawed: however interesting it might be to construe the planet's age in human terms, the attempt is inherently vacuous and devoid of meaning because it ignores a quintessential factor. "The first *datum* overlooked by Kant," he avers, "was—the analogy of our whole planetary system" (8:13). If the cosmos defies temporal measurement, then the bankruptcy of any universal history which seeks to determine the earth's relative antiquity lies in its method. Accordingly, De Quincey concludes: "Kant's very problem explodes, as Venetian wine-glasses of old were shivered by any treacherous poison they might contain. For is there, after all, any stationary meaning in the question?" (8:10).

Several impulses combine to produce this arraignment, the most salient being De Quincey's long-standing quarrel with the philosopher. Although the issue of how well he fathomed Kant's ideas has occasioned warm debate,[14] he unarguably came to be disenchanted with the metaphysician who, in the second edition of his *Kritik der reinen Vernunft*, rightly conceived of himself as having effected a Copernican revolution in philosophy. De Quincey indicates the scope of his disillusionment in *Autobiographic Sketches*, where he admits how, during his tenure at Oxford, Kant's transcendental thought initially "had been a pole-star to my hopes, and *in hypothesi,* agreeably to the uncertain plans of uncertain knowledge, the luminous guide to my future life" (2:89). Shortly thereafter, however, the attitude of youthful expectation underwent a decisive reversal:

The philosophy of Kant—so famous, so commanding in Germany from about the period of the French Revolution—already, in 1805, I had found to be a philosophy of destruction, and scarcely in any one chapter so much as *tending* to a philosophy of reconstruction. It destroys by wholesale, and it substitutes nothing. [2:86]

In the last few words of the passage we hear a familiar refrain, but what specifically prompts the accusation? Much of the answer is encapsulated in Shadworth H. Hodgson's observation in 1881 that for someone like De Quincey, whose mind "almost demanded mysteries in so mysterious a system of relations as those which connect us with another world" (2:154), Kant's separation of the noumenal and the phenomenal "sweeps wholly away the old speculative foundations of theology."[15] If one accepts this explanation of De Quincey's antipathy for "the world-shattering Kant" (2:155), he then recognizes that the lampoon with which "System of the Heavens" opens is part of a highly conservative strategy aimed exclusively at rescuing the ideals of permanence and stability.

Two additional concerns, both linked to the contemporary erosion of those values, may have animated the essay's introductory critique. The first centers on the fact that Kant's *Allgemeine Naturgeschichte* rigorously applied the Newtonian laws of inertia and gravity to a historical problem while also assimilating Thomas Wright's proposal in *An Original Theory, or New Hypothesis of the Universe* (1750) concerning the asymmetrical and nonheliocentric distribution of stars. On the one hand, therefore, the treatise "tried to describe the evolution of the present cosmic order from a former undifferentiated and unorganized state of matter"; on the other hand, it "revealed a marked incongruity between the *container*, the Euclidean space—infinite, homogenous, isotropic—and the *content*, the galaxy, this material system—finite, 'local,' and only seemingly regular."[16] The result was a cosmogony over which presided no creator or divine artificer and a cosmography which devolved into endless reaches of void space. Man, from De Quincey's perspective, was doubly dispossessed.

The second concern, though not tied directly to Kant, involves a well-known controversy of the early nineteenth century that undoubtedly influenced, if not sharpened, De Quincey's reaction to the philosopher's inquiries. During its formative years as an independent science, that is, from about 1790 to 1820, geology was dominated by a lively dispute regarding the inferences to be drawn from the evidence of paleontology: one group, the

Neptunists, endorsed a diluvian theory of geophysical change; another faction, the Vulcanists or Plutonists, argued that periodic eruptions of heat from within the earth's core had shaped its strata. Eventually the competing schools came to be known as the Catastrophists because both espoused a cataclysmic model of the earth's history, and it was not until Charles Lyell published the first volume of his *Principles of Geology* (1830) that gradual evolutionary change, then referred to as uniformitarianism, supplanted the older doctrine.[17] These intellectual developments could only have revived for De Quincey that "killing sense of eternity and infinity" (3:443) which brooded over his Oriental dreams, for they ratified the impression of man's ephemerality within a universe governed by vast impersonal forces.

When faced with the menace of vacancy and disconnection, however, De Quincey typically adjusts as a writer by positing a more encompassing synthesis, by converting signs of absence into proof of unappropriated presence.[18] This is precisely his tactic in the next section of "System of the Heavens." After asserting the nullity of the problem investigated by Kant on the grounds that, even "if our dear excellent mother the Earth could be persuaded to tell us her exact age in Julian years, . . . we should still be at a loss to *value* her age" (8:12), he subsumes the divergent possibilities by suggesting that "perhaps, in reality, the Earth is both young and old" (8:10). Her phoenixlike capacity for regeneration, as he imagines it, allows De Quincey to broach his major postulate:

Not otherwise, by secular periods, known to us geologically as facts, though obscure as durations, *Tellus* herself, the planet, as a whole, is for ever working by golden balances of change and compensation of ruin and restoration. She recasts her glorious habitations in decomposing them; she lies down for death, which perhaps a thousand times she has suffered; she rises for a new birth, which perhaps for the thousandth time has glorified her disc. Hers is the wedding-garment, hers is the shroud, that eternally is being woven in the loom of *palingenesis.* [8:11]

Countering the destructive linearity of terrestrial time with the "golden balances" of celestial aeons, the passage articulates a redemptive article of faith for its author, who later, in his "Postscript" of 1854, expands on the tenet. As will be seen shortly, the construct entails an irony which the essay seems deliberately intent upon skirting and leaving unresolved. But the immediate appeal of the premise for De Quincey is that it outlines a hypostatic substitute or transmutation for what he elsewhere terms "the dreadful loom" (*PW*, 1:229) of Chronos.

Another of his essays, a meditation titled "Sir William Hamilton" (1852), offers insight into why De Quincey is quick to embrace the speculative metaphysic presented in "System of the Heavens." "Of all curses," he declares, "that which searches deepest is the violent revelation through infinite darkness . . . of a happiness or a glory which once and for ever has perished" (5:304–305). Hearkening back to the prelapsarian idyll of his childhood at Greenhay before Elizabeth's death, the statement underscores the trauma of his subsequent fall into consciousness. With that event, however, begins also the protracted fall into temporality, a more insidious dislocation because it seems to ensure the irretrievability of primal wholeness. Evanescence, foremost among the "villainies of Time," thus masks errancy and effacement, since in its margin man cannot write "one perpetual iteration of *stet., stet.*" (5:306) whereby he might minimize the ratio of loss. De Quincey attempts something of the kind when he explores Zeno's paradox pitting "the endless divisibility of time against the endless divisibility of space" (5:332), but the futility of the exercise soon becomes glaringly obvious. Tying together all these ruminations is the symbolic clepsydra in the "Savannah-la-Mar" section of *Suspiria de Profundis*, where the Dark Interpreter gives the following lesson in time's fractional declensions: "All is finite in the present; and even that finite is infinite in its velocity of flight towards death" (*SP*, p. 225). From this chronometric standpoint the world indeed assumes the appearance of a vast necropolis. Unwilling to accept so bleak an outlook, De Quincey chooses instead to view the earth sub specie aeternitatis in order to convince himself of its ultimate vitality and perennially self-renewing dynamics.

Behind his effort to salvage the concept of teleological design or purpose from insinuations of universal randomness or accident extends, of course, a philosophical crisis long in the making. Thanks to the research of Alexandre Koyré and others, we are familiar with the complex history of ideas which led to the breakdown of traditional "cosmic syntaxes" like that of the Great Chain of Being and which in demoting God to an abstract First Cause seemed only to promote atomism in league with mechanism.[19] The full repercussions of that crisis came to a head during the Romantic period, as many of its leading spokesmen repeatedly attest. In his *Aids to Reflection* (1825), for example, Coleridge fulminates against the Cartesian-Newtonian episteme for bequeathing to his generation, rather than "a world created and filled with productive forces," the schema of "a lifeless machine whirled about by the dust of its own grinding."[20] De Quincey, to be sure, shared all of Coleridge's anxieties, but in terms of the cosmology which he projects in "System of the Heavens" a droll irony emerges. His mythologem of "the loom of *palingenesis*" is meant to express a theodicean plan within sempiternal process, yet the trope itself connotes the mechanistic determinism of Newtonian physics. The rest of the essay shows that De Quincey was not unaware of his analogue's dichotomous implications; however, in trying to reconcile the empirical findings of astronomy with his own conservative weltanschauung, he was caught on the horns of a linguistic dilemma. Though he never overtly acknowledges the difficulty, it eventually causes him to wrestle with the notion of "the mysterious architect" who "plays at hide-and-seek with his worlds" (8:22).

The anomaly can be explained from another perspective as well. Recently Peter L. Thorslev, Jr., has proposed that "in the Romantic age the problem of identity consisted more often in a threat to one's sense of destiny than in a threat to one's freedom," in support of which claim he notes that according to the *Oxford English Dictionary* modern usage of the word *determinism* did not commence until Sir William Hamilton's edition of 1846 of Thomas Reid's works.[21] The coincidence that "System of the Heavens" was published the same year, on the eve of this semantic shift, is meaningless unless one considers how aptly Thorslev's hypothesis pertains to De Quincey.

As remarked earlier, De Quincey is prone at the start of his essay to encomiums on the millennial promise of scientific discovery, celebrating the "new era for the human intellect" ushered in by Lord Rosse's telescope, because he desperately wants to believe in some overarching power of necessity that guides all things to a harmonious end. But such rhetoric is invariably short-lived, rarely rising above the level of velleity. As soon as he begins to ponder soberly the "mighty depths of space," his agoraphobia returns in spasms of querulous apprehension; once more he becomes the victim of some "eternal spectacle of the infinite" (8:437), comparable to a desert in which "nothing is circumstantiated or differenced" (8:31). What the pattern signifies, I think, is that the divergent tendencies inherent in De Quincey's paradigm of "the loom of *palingenesis*" actually merge in, or are superseded by, his yearning for systemic coherence of any kind. And behind it all, as always, is his constant need for confirmation of the idea of relationship. Thus if he had read another book by Nichol entitled *Views of the Architecture of the Heavens* (1840), he would have been profoundly alarmed by one sentence in particular: "Absolute permanence is visible no where around us, and the fact of change merely intimates, that, in the exhaustless womb of the future, unevolved wonders are in store."[22]

Perhaps to guard against so discomfiting and unnerving a possibility, De Quincey sketches his version of a solution to the cosmological uncertainties blithely accepted by Nichol. The relevant passage, among the most telling in all his writings, deserves to be quoted in its entirety:

Great is the mystery of Space, greater is the mystery of Time. Either mystery grows upon man as man himself grows; and either seems to be a function of the godlike which is in man. In reality, the depths and the heights which are in man, the depths by which he searches, the heights by which he aspires, are but projected and made objective externally in the three dimensions of space which are outside of him. He trembles at the abyss into which his bodily eyes look down, or look up; not knowing that abyss to be, not always consciously suspecting it to be, but by an instinct written in his prophetic heart feeling it to be, boding it to be, fearing it to be, and sometimes hoping it to be, the mirror to a mightier abyss that will one day be expanded in himself. [8:15]

A tour de force of evasionary compensation at first glance, the speech intones a doctrine that transforms the indices of De Quincey's alienation into reflex images of a spiritual fecundity. The basic outlook is one shared by Jorge Luis Borges in "The Mirror of Enigmas," where the Argentine writer approvingly cites a gloss of Saint Paul's assertion in 1 Corinthians 13:12 ("Videmus nunc per speculum in aenigmate"): " 'The terrifying immensity of the firmament's abysses is an illusion, an external reflection of *our own* abysses, perceived "in a mirror".'"[23] But De Quincey is not quite dismissing the asymptotic reaches of the universe as being illusionary or unreal; he rather is delineating a phenomenology whereby the mysteries of the spatiotemporal world progressively unfold from their origin in consciousness. The net result of this internalization, hardly a victory for Romantic organicism, is that the "illimitable growths of space" beyond are matched, or counterbalanced, by correlative "depths" and "heights" within.

In effect, De Quincey wants to convert the cosmos of the new astronomy into the "heaven-created palimpsest" of the mind in which "there are not and cannot be ... incoherencies" (*SP*, p. 233). His justification for doing so hinges on a composite model of the psyche anticipated in the "Introductory Notice" to *Suspiria*. There, immediately after voicing concern over the "dissipation" likely to be precipitated by technology's "colossal pace of advance," he exalts in contrast the "machinery for dreaming" which connects man with a transmundane and noumenal realm of unchanging verities. Such "magnificent apparatus," he maintains, "forces the infinite into the chambers of a human brain, and throws dark reflections from eternities below all life upon the mirrors of the sleeping mind" (*SP*, p. 149). When later appropriated in another context, the phrase was amended to read "upon the mirrors of that mysterious *camera obscura*" (13:335), betokening the irresistible hold of "machinery" on De Quincey's imagination. That fact is even more evident from another comment in both versions which describes the faculty of dreaming as "the one great tube through which man communicates with the shadowy." The metaphor analogically conjures up the telescope, as do also the mirrors irradiated by some hidden and paradoxically tenebrous source. However, De Quincey finally discovers that the attempt to elevate the psyche, nucleus of the endangered self, into an *Urgrund* or Jungian *"eidos* behind the supreme ideas of unity and totality"[24] is a hazardous, highly unpredictable maneuver.

Just how hazardous, of course, is graphically portrayed in the third part of *Confessions of an English Opium-Eater*, where the dreamer is so besieged by primordial nightmares that he wonders whether "some dropsical state or tendency of the brain might thus be making itself (to use a metaphysical word) *objective*" (3:440). The same demonization, only slightly more controlled, occurs in "System of the Heavens." Hailing Lord Rosse as a "philosopher" who has enlarged man's unique "prerogative of perceiving space in its higher extensions as of geometrically constructing the relations of space" (8:16), De Quincey decides to put the legacy to a test. The Orion nebula, famous for "the submission with which it has begun to render up its secrets to the all-conquering telescope," becomes the focus of a fantasia that hypothetically should demonstrate positive sublimity, but what instead it reveals to him is a "detestable phantom" poised with "pomp of malice in the features towards a universe seasoned for its assault" (8:18). All the further traits discerned in this harrowing apparition point to an immutable force of malignancy and destruction, an entelechy forever beyond or apart from the looming process of cosmological palingenesis. Despite intentions to the contrary, therefore, the essay subverts the principle of *concordia discors* which it set out to establish. And all that Lord Rosse and nineteenth-century astronomy have accomplished, we are told, is "like the reversing of some heavenly doom, like the raising one after another of the seals that had been sealed by the Angel in the Revelation" (8:21).

The crowning irony of the work is that, in his eagerness to refute Kant's *Naturwissenschaft*, De Quincey ends up approving the German thinker's more mature epistemology—only to realize afresh how equivocal are the categories of space and time. In the remainder of the essay, less an integrated movement than a series of abortive exercises, he struggles to escape the impasse of perspectivism. Reflecting on the seemingly endless "compression" of nebulas spangling the heavens, he searches for a law of "deeper centralisation" whereby the "effect" of optical relativity "shall be defeated" (8:22) but finds none. Astronomy simply teaches, he concludes, that "magnitude and distance are in collusion with each other to deceive," that "motion subjective is in collusion with motion objective," and that "duplex systems are in collusion with fraudulent stars" (8:26). There follow several pages of incongruous praise for Dr. Nichol and the Glasgow Observatory, intermixed with a resurgence of strained humor, before he brings the whole to a close with his previously published translation of "Traum über das All" from Jean Paul Richter's novel *Der Komet* (1820–22). Significantly titled "Dream-vision of the Infinite as it reveals itself in the Chambers of Space," the recycled bravura transports the dreamer "stripped of gravitating body" through "wildernesses of death that divided the worlds of life" until, wearied out with the architectural "persecutions of the Infinite," he hears his angelic guide exclaim: "'End is there none to the Universe of God? Lo! also *there is no beginning*'" (8:33–34). God is thus confirmed rhetorically as the abiding Alpha and Omega of the material universe, but the illimitability of his celestial temple is "insufferable" and increases De Quincey's fears of his own ontological "irrelevance."

Nothing, however, is ever final for the author who finds a salvation of sorts in the literary art of supplementarity. Eight years after appending his dark epilogue to "System of the Heavens," worried about being classed "with those who use geology, cosmology, &c., for purposes of attack or insinuation against the Mosaic cosmogony," he added a "Postscript" that purports to offer "conclusive" arguments on "the true relations of the Bible to merely human science" (8:35). The defensiveness of his rationale indicates how sympathetically attuned De Quincey was in 1854 to the insecurities of his Victorian audience, one which nervously recognized that it was living in an age of unprecedented transition and doubt. With that audience as much as himself in mind, therefore, he grapples with the question of why the truths of modern astronomy, "a science so nearly allying itself to religion by the loftiness and by the purity of its contemplations," were not imparted during an earlier era of the world's career. His answer, as one might perhaps expect, is that such epiphanic revelation would have contravened "a determinate scheme of divine discipline and training for man" (8:38–39). Although the logic is patently casuistical, it permits De Quincey to believe in the metahistorical reality of a providential destiny being enacted within the aeonic time of God's arrangement. He consequently weaves a putative rapprochement between Scripture and Science that allays his insistent agoraphobia.

In a period like our own, accustomed to discussion of black holes, red shifts, quasars, and the big-bang theory, De Quincey's essay may seem amusingly naïve and anachronistic in the earnestness with which it confronts the aftershocks of the Newtonian displacement. Yet we would do well to remember that, after the founding of the Royal Astronomical Society in 1820, British culture was gradually accommodating the revolutionary advances emerging on various fronts in science and that we ourselves may be undergoing a comparable process of intellectual revision. According to Stephen Toulmin, the present age is witnessing a renaissance of interest in cosmological speculation which marks a return to the theology of nature.[25] Because he stands on the nineteenth-century forefront of such preoccupations, De Quincey can help us appreciate both the courage and the agility required to move toward a more encompassing synthesis of thought. In the end he looms as an undervalued, infinitely complex, but always fascinating progenitor.

Notes

1. Robert Martin Adams, *Nil: Episodes in the Literary Conquest of Void During the Nineteenth Century* (London: Oxford University Press, 1966), pp. 15, 13. Regarding the specifically Romantic phenomenon of *désoeuvrement* see also Georges Poulet, *The Metamorphoses of the Circle*, trans. Carley Dawson and Elliott Coleman (Baltimore, Md.: Johns Hopkins University

Press, 1966), p. 92: "For the first time there clearly appears the consciousness of the non-identity which distinguishes the self-center from the circumferential non-self."

2. J. Hillis Miller, *The Disappearance of God: Five Nineteenth-Century Writers* (1963; reprint, Cambridge: Harvard University Press, Belknap Press, 1975), pp. 67-69. Like all other students of De Quincey and the spiritual rupture of his age, I am deeply indebted to Miller's classic study as will be evident from my critical orientation throughout the essay.

3. Cf. Paul Hamill, "Other People's Faces: The English Romantics and the Paradox of Fraternity," *Studies in Romanticism* 17 (1978): 465-82. Without citing this passage, Hamill discusses comparable scenes in *Confessions of an English Opium-Eater* (pp. 477-78).

4. William Wordsworth, *The Prelude: 1799, 1805, 1850*, ed. Jonathan Wordsworth, M. H. Abrams, and Stephen Gill (New York: Norton, 1979), 7.149-50 (1850).

5. Hans Eichner, "The Rise of Modern Science and the Genesis of Romanticism," *PMLA* 97 (1982): 8.

6. After several years of experiments with casting and polishing a metallic speculum seventy-two inches in diameter, Rosse (1800-67) finished erecting the telescope at his estate in King's County, Ireland, in February 1845. The "leviathan of Parsonstown," as it came to be called, far surpassed in optical resolution and range the telescopes of William Herschel (1738-1822), which were equipped with specula ranging in size from eighteen to forty-eight inches, and enabled Rosse to become the first to discover the spiral structure of nebulas. For further details see Agnes M. Clerke, *A Popular History of Astronomy During the Nineteenth Century*, 3d ed. (London: Adam and Charles Black, 1893), pp. 142-49; Bernard Lovell, *Emerging Cosmology* (New York: Columbia University Press, 1981), pp. 118-19; Colin A. Ronan, *Discovering the Universe: A History of Astronomy* (New York: Basic Books, 1971), pp. 114-15; Pierre Rousseau, *Man's Conquest of the Stars*, trans. Michael Bullock (New York: Norton, 1961), p. 259.

7. V. A. De Luca, *Thomas De Quincey: The Prose of Vision* (Toronto: University of Toronto Press, 1980), p. 96. In the immediately following sentence De Luca concludes that " 'System of the Heavens' thus captures deep ambiguities in De Quincey's thought concerning the relation of God and death, of human power and human destructiveness, of pastoral repose and nightmare, themes which *The English Mail-Coach* develops even more intensely."

8. Robert M. Maniquis, "Lonely Empires: Personal and Public Visions of Thomas De Quincey," in *Literary Monographs*, vol. 8, ed. Eric Rothstein and Joseph Anthony Wittreich, Jr. (Madison: University of Wisconsin Press, 1976), p. 65.

9. Maniquis, "Lonely Empires," p. 71.

10. See my "De Quincey's Literature of Power: A Mythic Paradigm," forthcoming in *Studies in English Literature, 1500-1900* 26 (1986). Other analyses

that approach the subject from a somewhat different angle are Michael E. Holstein, "The Anapestic Triad: A Structural Paradigm in De Quincey's Imaginative Prose," *Études Anglaises* 28 (1975): 398-408; John E. Jordan, *Thomas De Quincey, Literary Critic: His Method and Achievement* (Berkeley and Los Angeles: University of California Press, 1952), pp. 89-119; Sigmund K. Proctor, *Thomas De Quincey's Theory of Literature* (Ann Arbor: University of Michigan Press, 1943; reprint, New York: Octagon, 1966), pp. 107-47; Laurence Stapleton, *The Elected Circle: Studies in the Art of Prose* (Princeton, N.J.: Princeton University Press, 1973), pp. 119-65; and the works listed in notes 11 and 12 below.

11. D. D. Devlin, *De Quincey, Wordsworth and the Art of Prose* (New York: St. Martin's Press, 1983), pp. 3-11.

12. See chap. 13.

13. Even so, it might be argued, does De Quincey's other charge against Johnson's style ("everything is simply unveiled") parallel in imagery and resonance his previously cited reservation about Lord Rosse's telescope: "He has revealed more by far than he found." Such recurrent formulations, I believe, cannot be written off as mere accident. They seem instead to define De Quincey's symptomatic aversions, specifically all that comes under the rubric of agoraphobia, and also his need for epigenetic articulation—no matter whether the field of scrutiny is literature, astronomy, or philosophy.

14. For the opposing sides in this debate see Proctor, *Thomas De Quincey's Theory of Literature*, pp. 28-38, 293-97, and the following discussions by René Wellek: *Immanuel Kant in England, 1793-1838* (Princeton, N.J.: Princeton University Press, 1931), pp. 171-80; "De Quincey's Status in the History of Ideas," *Philological Quarterly* 23 (1944): 248-72 (reprinted in René Wellek, *Confrontations: Studies in the Intellectual and Literary Relations Between Germany, England, and the United States During the Nineteenth Century* [Princeton, N.J.: Princeton University Press, 1965], pp. 114-52). See also Peter Michelsen, "Thomas De Quincey und die Kantische Philosophie," *Revue de Littérature Comparée* 33 (1959): 356-75.

15. Shadworth H. Hodgson, *Outcast Essays and Verse Translations* (London: Longmans, Green, 1881), pp. 36-37.

16. I cite, respectively, Ernst Cassirer, *An Essay on Man: An Introduction to a Philosophy of Human Culture* (New Haven, Conn.: Yale University Press, 1944), p. 176, and Jacques Merleau-Ponty and Bruno Morando, *The Rebirth of Cosmology*, trans. Helen Weaver (New York: Knopf, 1976), p. 87. For an excellent edition of Kant's treatise see *Universal Natural History and Theory of the Heavens*, trans. Stanley L. Jaki (Edinburgh: Scottish Academic Press, 1981). Jaki's introduction to the text and its background (pp. 1-76) is especially helpful.

17. For further details about this geological controversy see Gertrude Himmelfarb, *Darwin and the Darwinian Revolution* (New York: Norton, 1968), pp. 82-93.

18. Cf. Martin Heidegger, *Poetry, Language Thought*, trans. Albert Hof-

stadter (New York: Harper and Row, 1971), p. 184: "The default of God and the divinities is absence. But absence is not nothing; rather it is precisely the presence, which must first be appropriated, of the hidden fullness and wealth of what has been and what, thus gathered, is presencing."

19. See Alexandre Koyré, *From the Closed World to the Infinite Universe* (Baltimore, Md.: Johns Hopkins University Press, 1957); Arthur O. Lovejoy, *The Great Chain of Being: A Study of the History of an Idea* (Cambridge, Mass.: Harvard University Press, 1936); A. D. Nuttall, *A Common Sky: Philosophy and the Literary Imagination* (Berkeley and Los Angeles: University of California Press, 1974); A. N. Whitehead, *Science and the Modern World* (1925; reprint, New York: Macmillan, 1964). I borrow the phrase "cosmic syntaxes" from Earl R. Wasserman, *The Subtler Language: Critical Readings of Neoclassic and Romantic Poems* (Baltimore, Md.: Johns Hopkins University Press, 1959), pp. 10-11.

20. Samuel Taylor Coleridge, *Aids to Reflection*, ed. Henry Nelson Coleridge (New York: Stanford and Swords, 1839), p. 314.

21. Peter L. Thorslev, Jr., *Romantic Contraries: Freedom versus Destiny* (New Haven, Conn.: Yale University Press, 1984), pp. 17, 19.

22. J. P. Nichol, *Views of the Architecture of the Heavens*, 2d ed. (New York: Dayton and Newman, 1842), p. 106. The immediate context of the remark concerns Newton's prediction of the ultimate collapse of the solar system, an eventuality which Nichol manages cheerfully to accept. Urging his readers to "mark the Chrysalis," he then offers a *consolatio* that parallels De Quincey's notion of "aeonic" time: "Nay, what though *all* should pass? . . . Then would our Universe not have failed in its functions, but only been gathered up and rolled away, these functions being complete. That gorgeous material framework, wherewith the Eternal hath adorned and varied the abysses of space, is only an instrument by which the myriads of spirits borne upon its orbs, may be told of their origin, and educated for more exalted being; and a time may come, when the veil can be drawn aside—when spirit shall converse *directly* with spirit, and the creature gaze without hindrance on the effulgent face of its Creator" (pp. 106-107).

23. Jorge Luis Borges, *Labyrinths: Selected Stories and Other Writings*, ed. Donald A. Yates and James E. Irby (New York: New Directions, 1964), p. 210.

24. C. J. Jung, *Aion: Researches into the Phenomenology of the Self*, vol. 9, pt. 2, of *The Collected Works of C. G. Jung*, trans. R. F. C. Hull, ed. Herbert Read, Michael Fordham, and Gerhard Adler, Bollingen Series 20 (New York: Pantheon, 1959), p. 34.

25. Stephen Toulmin, *The Return to Cosmology: Postmodern Science and the Theology of Nature* (Berkeley and Los Angeles: University of California Press, 1982), passim. Toulmin discusses such cosmologically oriented thinkers as Arthur Koestler, Pierre Teilhard de Chardin, Jacques Monod, François Jacob, Carl Sagan, and Gregory Bateson. See also Richard J. Bernstein, *Beyond Objectivism and Relativism: Science, Hermeneutics, and Praxis* (Philadelphia: University of Pennsylvania Press, 1983).

The Contributors

JOHN BEER, Reader in English Literature in Cambridge University and Fellow of Peterhouse, is the author of *Coleridge the Visionary* (1959), *The Achievement of E. M. Forster* (1962), *Blake's Humanism* (1968), *Blake's Visionary Universe* (1969), *Coleridge's Poetic Intelligence* (1977), *Wordsworth and the Human Heart* (1978), and *Wordsworth in Time* (1979). He has also edited and contributed to the bicentenary volume *Coleridge's Variety* (1974), has produced a new edition of Coleridge's *Poems*, and is editing Coleridge's *Aids to Reflection*. In addition to many articles on the Romantic poets, his "The Englishness of De Quincey's Ideas" is forthcoming in *English and German Romanticism: Cross-Currents and Controversies.*

JOEL D. BLACK is Assistant Professor of Comparative Literature in the University of Georgia. His publications include articles on aspects of literary theory, Romantic aesthetics, and the relationship between literary and scientific discourse. His essay on Jean Paul and De Quincey appeared in *Comparative Literature,* and he has recently completed a book manuscript entitled "Romantic Transgressions: Levity, Digression, and Murder in the Age of Thomas De Quincey." He is presently at work on an interdisciplinary study on model theory in art, science, and culture.

MARTIN BOCK, Assistant Professor of English in the University of Minnesota, has published articles on sensationist epistemology and voyages of disorientation in *Conradiana.* With research interests in twentieth-century British and American literature, he is finishing an article entitled "De Quincey, *Rifacimento,* and the Fictionalizing of Malcolm Lowry."

FREDERICK BURWICK is Associate Professor of English and

Comparative Literature in the University of California at Los Angeles. Reflecting his interests in Anglo-German literary relations, literature and science, phenomenological criticism and linguistic theory, and perception theory, his articles have appeared in such journals as *Comparative Literature, Neuphilologische Mitteilungen, Studies in Comparative Literature, Studia Neophilologica,* and *Keats-Shelley Journal.* He is also editor of *Selected Essays on Rhetoric by Thomas De Quincey* (1967) and the author of a forthcoming book entitled *The Damnation of Newton: Goethe's Color Theory and Romantic Perception.*

V. A. DE LUCA, Professor of English in Erindale College, University of Toronto, is well known to students of De Quincey for his book *Thomas De Quincey: The Prose of Vision* (1980). His articles on Blake, De Quincey, and Shelley have been published in such journals as *Studies in Romanticism, Criticism, Texas Studies in Literature and Language, English Language Notes, Blake Studies, Keats-Shelley Journal, University of Toronto Quarterly, Ariel,* and *Blake Illustrated Quarterly.*

JAN B. GORDON is Professor of English in Tokyo University of Foreign Studies, Tokyo, Japan, where he specializes in nineteenth-century British literature with emphasis upon narrative rivalry and replication. His articles on the fiction of this period have appeared in *Criticism, Journal of Aesthetics and Art Criticism, Modern Fiction Studies, Salmagundi, English Literary History,* and *Dickens Studies Annual.* He is currently writing a manuscript on gossip and oral speculation as metalanguage in the Victorian novel and, with Masao Shimura, completing the first English translation of Kawabata's novella "The Dandelions."

JOHN E. JORDAN, Professor of English in the University of California at Berkeley, has been the unofficial dean and chief bibliographer of De Quincey studies for several decades. He is the author of *Thomas De Quincey, Literary Critic: His Method and Achievement* (1952), *Robert Louis Stevenson's Silverado Journal* (1954), *De Quincey to Wordsworth: A Biography of a Relationship* (1962), and *Why the "Lyrical Ballads"? The Background, Writing, and Character of Wordsworth's 1798 "Lyrical Ballads"* (1976). He is also the editor of *De Quincey as Critic* (1973) and, with James V. Logan and Northrop Frye, of *Some British Romantics: A Collection of Essays* (1966). He edited Edward Sackville-West's *A Flame in Sunlight: The Life and Work of Thomas De Quincey* (1936) for its republication in 1974 and *Peter Bell* in the Cornell Wordsworth (1985).

GREVEL LINDOP is Senior Lecturer in English Literature in the University of Manchester and author of *The Opium-Eater: A Life of Thomas De Quincey* (1981). Besides being a widely published poet and scholar, he has edited a volume entitled *Thomas De Quincey: Confessions of an English Opium-Eater and Other Writings* to be issued by Oxford University Press as part of its World's Classics Series in 1985.

ROBERT M. MANIQUIS, Associate Professor of English in the University of California at Los Angeles, where he also teaches in the Comparative Literature Program, has written many articles and reviews on Romantic literature and literary criticism. His "Lonely Empires: Personal and Public Visions of Thomas De Quincey" (1976) was published in the University of Wisconsin's *Literary Monographs,* and he is at work on a forthcoming study of Romantic ideologies.

A. S. PLUMTREE completed his Ph.D. dissertation, "Freedom and the Labyrinth: An Existential Study of Thomas De Quincey," at the University of Nottingham in 1977. He is presently Commissioning Editor for Addison-Wesley Publishers.

CHARLES L. PROUDFIT, Professor of English in the University of Colorado, is a practicing psychotherapist who holds degrees from the Denver Institute for Psychoanalysis and the University of Denver Graduate School of Social Work. General Editor of *English Language Notes* from 1970 to 1981, he has participated in many symposia on psychoanalysis and literature. In addition to scholarly articles and conference papers, he is the editor of *Selected Imaginary Conversations of Literary Men and Statesmen* (1969) and *Landor as Critic* (1979).

ARDEN REED is Associate Professor of English in Pomona College and the author of *Romantic Weather: The Climates of Coleridge and Baudelaire* (1983). His scholarly essays, dealing primarily with English and French literature from 1750 to 1900 and literary theory, have appeared in several journals, and he is also the editor of

Romanticism and Language (1984). He is presently completing research for a study of the relation of narrative and digression.

ROBERT LANCE SNYDER, Associate Professor of English in Seattle Pacific University, has published articles in such journals as *Studies in Romanticism, Bucknell Review, Biography, Essays in Literature, Research Studies, Studies in Short Fiction,* and *Studies in English Literature, 1500-1900.* He is completing a book manuscript on the Romantic aesthetic of expression which reflects his interests in both Romanticism and literary theory.

E. MICHAEL THRON is Professor of English and Humanistic Studies in the University of Wisconsin at Green Bay, where he teaches interdisciplinary courses involving Romanticism and the social function of the arts. In addition to articles on Renaissance literature in *Shakespeare Quarterly, Studies in English Literature, 1500-1900,* and *Renascence,* he has published essays on De Quincey in *Interspace and the Inward Sphere: Essays on Romantic and Victorian Self* (1978) and *Prairie Schooner.*

JOHN C. WHALE, formerly at University College Cardiff, is Lecturer in English in the University of Leeds. He is the author of *Thomas De Quincey's Reluctant Autobiography* (1984) and has published articles on De Quincey in *Durham University Journal, Essays in Criticism,* and *The Explicator.* He has also prepared an annotated edition of Trollope's *Phineas Redux* for the World's Classics Series of Oxford University Press.

MICHAEL COCHISE YOUNG is Assistant Professor of English in Tulane University, where she specializes in nineteenth-century poetry and nonfictional prose, autobiography, and theories of genre. She has published an article in *Blake Illustrated Quarterly* and is working on a book-length study of the confessional mode from Rousseau through the Aesthetes.

Index

Adams, Robert Martin: 338
Andreä, John Valentine: 247-48, 253
Ann of Oxford Street (in *Confessions of an English Opium-Eater*): 14, 103, 141, 170, 173-76, 188, 210, 317, 318-20, 322-25, 329-30
Aristophanes: 204, 313
Aristotle: 276; *Poetics*, 264; *Politics*, 264, 269
Augustine, Saint: 167, 321, 330
Autobiographical theory: 57-63
Axon, William E. A.: 214

Bakhtin, Mikhail: 134
Barthelme, Donald: 202
Baudelaire, Charles: 46, 132, 138n.
Blackwood, William: 6
Blackwood's Edinburgh Magazine: 37-39, 43, 47-50, 94, 143, 148, 154, 208, 295, 307n.
Blake, William: 22, 25-27, 32, 62, 260; *Jerusalem*, 23-24; *The Marriage of Heaven and Hell*, 122
Blanchot, Maurice: 133
Bloom, Harold: 22, 27, 256&n.
Booth, Wayne C.: 199-200
Borges, Jorge Luis: 294, 353
Bostetter, Edward E.: 243
Brawne, Fanny: 183
Brecht, Bertolt: 313
Brill, A. A.: 95
Brontë, Emily: 245
Browne, Sir Thomas: 345
Brun, Frederica: 241

Brunel, Isambard Kingdom: 11
Bruss, Elizabeth W.: 58, 105, 252
Bunyan, John: 109-12, 117, 119, 125, 127, 134, 135
Burke, Edmund: 152, 345
Burke, Thomas: 156, 157
Burnett, James (Lord Monboddo): 267
Burwick, Frederick: 346
Byron, George Gordon, Lord: 55, 62, 67, 200, 208, 332; *Childe Harold's Pilgrimage,* 59, 68; *Don Juan,* 311-12, 314

Carlyle, Thomas: 106, 136n., 140, 148, 165
Chomsky, Noam: 265, 268
Coleridge, Samuel Taylor: 3, 24, 73, 91, 125, 164-65, 167, 169-75, 177-78, 180-81, 183-85, 188, 192, 204, 260, 268, 274, 275, 286, 320; *Aids to Reflection,* 113, 351; "Constancy to an Ideal Object," 113; "Dejection: An Ode," 172; "The Pains of Sleep," 173; "Kubla Kahn," 181, 316; "Hymn Before Sun-rise, in the Vale of Chamouni," 241; *Essays on the Principles of Method,* 264; *Logic,* 265
Collins, Mortimer: 214
Colt, Samuel: 11

Daguerre, Louis Jacques Mandé: 11
Dante Alighieri: 306-307n.
Davies, Hugh Sykes: 46
De Luca, V. A.: 3, 4, 8, 104, 206, 213, 234
De Man, Paul: 75, 148, 253
De Quincey, Thomas:
— life and career of: at Oxford, 6, 217, 253, 266-67, 281, 347; early London experience, 6, 103, 319-20, 322-23, 339-40; editorship of *Westmoreland Gazette,* 6, 146, 208; addiction to opium, 8, 73, 172-74, 241, 244, 255, 259, 320; procrastination, 12, 42, 209; disgust for process of writing, 14&n.; at Manchester Grammar School, 63, 82, 84, 164, 174, 187, 188, 218, 320, 322; physical exercise, 72, 185, 340-41; relationship with Wordsworth, 73, 144, 164, 169-71, 174-85; childhood at Greenhay, 74, 90, 350 (*see also* De Qunicey family); myopia, 77-78; at Shrewsbury hotel, 80-81, 84; death, 88, 195-96, 291; grief over Catherine Wordsworth's death, 104, 170, 179-80 (*see also* Catherine Wordsworth); relationship with John Wilson, 142-44; relationship with Coleridge, 164-65, 169-75, 188; and Mrs. Dashwood Lee, 218-19
— alienated self in works of: determinism, 4, 83, 345, 351 (*see also* special topics in works: technological progress); horror, 35, 46,

INDEX 367

49, 74, 82, 157, 209, 231, 273; neurosis, 60, 186–87; divided self, 62, 75, 122, 126; entropy, 249, 251, 254, 257, 346; agoraphobia, 338–42, 352, 356, 358n. (*see also* on dreams, violence, and the psyche: his obsession with murder)
— on dreams, violence, and the psyche: the sublime, 7, 9, 146, 164–96, 210, 225, 274, 354; the unconscious, 9, 96, 109–35, 136n.; opium as catalyst for dreams, 12, 15, 66, 76, 78, 81, 315–16, 328, 338–39 (*see also* life and career: addiction to opium); the dreaming mind, 72–73, 93, 95–100, 353–54; violence, 111, 114–35, 140–41, 155–60, 234–35; obsession with murder, 140–42, 146–48, 159–61
— special topics in works of: Ricardo's economic theory, 4, 55, 246–47; technological progress, 10–12, 285–86, 341–44, 352–53; language, 32, 64–66, 116–18, 263–76, 279–304, 346; music, 32, 64–66; humor, 35, 41–42, 149, 150, 153–54, 161, 204, 343, 355; memory, 66, 69, 95–96, 130, 303, 345; optics, 72–85, 340, 342, 355; nexus in his theory of language, 263–76, 346; cosmology, 338–56; palingenesis, 342, 345–46, 351–52, 354
— as prose writer and stylist: forgery and plagiarism, 4, 5, 239–44, 255, 262n. (*see also* genres in prose: counterfeit translation); persona of Opium-Eater, 4, 6, 12, 16, 38–39, 58–59, 112, 252, 256; persona of gentleman-scholar and journalist, 6, 35–42, 45, 51; sensationalism in, 6, 38–39, 44, 47, 49; digression in, 8, 12, 14, 15, 37, 40, 46, 75, 204, 280, 283–85, 296, 298–99, 308–34, 346; avoidance of linearity, 12, 283–85, 332, 334, 349–50; footnotes in 14, 36, 96, 203, 210, 211, 260, 302; decadence in, 35, 45; sentimentality in, 35, 252, 332; ambivalence in, 36–37, 40, 49, 146, 157, 188, 202, 226, 228, 297, 320; irony in, 47, 148–54, 199–211, 233, 235, 350, 351, 354; satire in, 47–49; parasitism in, 52, 239–62n.; role of involutes, 74, 79, 83, 207; Wordsworthian phrases in, 175–79, 182–83, 197n.; style, 204, 243, 260, 263–64, 267, 269–71, 276, 279–81, 295, 340, 344–46; rhetoric, 205, 252, 276, 284–85, 344, 352; "law of antagonism," 207, 325; dynamic of supplementarity in, 239–61, 355
— genres in prose of: periodical journalism, 6–8, 35–52; the Gothic, 7, 35, 156, 181, 182, 213, 215, 231, 233, 239, 242–45, 251, 256–60; dream visions, 7–9, 16, 20–22, 24–27, 99, 114, 120, 274, 286, 315–19, 323–28, 334; "literature of power," 9, 193, 251, 263, 276, 344; confessional mode, 35, 37–38, 54–57, 59–63, 70, 308, 312, 315–19, 321–22, 324–28, 334; fantasy, 76, 316–19, 324–28; fiction, 213–36, 256–60; counterfeit translation, 239–43, 248, 251–52, 256 (*see also* as prose writer and stylist: forgery and plagiarism)
— recurring metaphors and motifs in works of: paradigm of jour-

ney, 3, 83-84, 87n.; figure of pariah, 4, 74, 85n., 114, 146, 174, 209-10, 220, 221, 244, 323, 338; guilt motif, 14, 57, 80, 84-85, 105, 141, 146, 236; Spectre of the Brocken, 14, 112-20, 124-25, 134; caduceus metaphor, 15, 283, 292, 321, 332, 333, 345; images of chariot and temple, 20-22, 24-27, 305n., 306n.; vertigo or sensory disorientation, 25, 60, 75-84, 291, 339-40; fugal motif, 32, 201-202, 252, 305n., 345; theme of time, 64, 67-70, 86n., 189-90, 272-73, 349-50, 356; lost paradise, 69, 104, 286-89, 350; childhood motif, 70, 73-75, 77-85, 93, 96-97, 100-106, 286-87; labyrinth, 70, 110, 187-88, 191, 228-29, 257, 340; analogues of intoxication, 72-85; London, 76, 80-82, 339-40; palimpsest metaphor, 78, 95-96, 128-35, 138n., 244-45, 249-50, 259, 301; Whispering Gallery, 82-84, 191, 210, 218; theme of loss and bereavement, 94, 104-105, 221; archetypal Fall, 104, 285-90, 310, 320, 322, 323, 332-34, 350; mirror phenomena, 110-11, 113, 117-19, 123-28, 135, 283, 353-54; Dark Interpreter, 111-28, 131, 133-35, 174, 241, 244, 247, 254, 256, 260, 272, 350; *Doppelgänger* and *dédoublement*, 134, 150-51, 226, 230-31, 257; anxiety, 142, 146, 165, 186, 338, 340; motif of masque, 228, 229, 258; motif of theater, 228-30; motif of letters, 257-60, 281, 287, 288, 294-98; motif of gravitation, 310, 328-34, 339; theme of transgression, 314, 320-22, 324, 327-28
—literary stature and significance of: compared to Romantic contemporaries, 3, 5, 7-9, 22-33, 55-56, 67-69, 72-73, 75, 82-83, 164-65, 169-85, 188, 191-93, 286, 309-10, 332-34; in canon of English Literature, 3, 5-9, 16-17; critical approaches to, 3-9, 16-17, 165-67, 280; compared to Freud, 88-106, 109-11, 117-18, 127, 129-30, 136n., 287; as precursor of modern literature of crime, 140, 155, 161

De Quincey, Thomas, works of:
"Analects from Richter": 274
"Antigone of Sophocles, The": 210
Autobiographic Sketches: 3, 61, 73, 88, 105, 251-53, 255, 304n., 329, 339-40, 347; "Travelling," 11; "Introduction to the World of Strife," 74, 85n.
"The Avenger": 141, 213, 214, 220, 222-24, 233-36
Confessions of an English Opium-Eater: 3, 6, 14, 21, 26, 35, 40-43, 51, 54-70, 73, 80-84, 88, 93-95, 99, 103, 104, 106, 110, 132, 141, 160, 179, 197n., 203, 217, 224, 231, 252, 253, 272, 274, 312; version of 1821-22, 7, 8, 10, 38-39, 44, 57-59, 63, 68-69, 279, 316, 319-23, 325, 329; version of 1856, 7, 63, 67, 70, 187, 210, 218, 279, 281, 315-16; "The Daughter of Lebanon," 69, 316-18, 323; "The Pains of Opium," 173, 211, 319, 324, 354

INDEX

"Conversation": 272
Diary of 1803: 72, 73, 77, 164–65, 267
English Mail-Coach, The: 7, 20–33, 35, 51, 76, 190, 251, 272, 275–76, 279–304, 306–307n., 344; "The Vision of Sudden Death," 14, 42, 141, 276, 284, 287–304; "The Dream-Fugue," 26, 29, 32, 86n., 194, 201–202, 283, 303
"Historico-Critical Inquiry into the Origin of the Rosicrucians and the Free-Masons": 247–48
"Household Wreck, The": 26, 144–45, 186, 213, 218, 220, 226–27, 231–34, 292
Klosterheim: 156, 213, 214, 218, 224, 228–31, 233, 244, 256–60
"Language": 268–69, 346
"Letters to a Young Man Whose Education Has Been Neglected": 200
"Malthus on Population": 247
"Notes from the Pocket-Book of a Late Opium-Eater": 7, 12
"On Christianity as an Organ of Political Movement": 253–54
"On the Knocking at the Gate in *Macbeth*": 7, 12–14, 146–47, 161, 191, 208, 225, 251
"On Murder Considered as One of the Fine Arts": 7, 13, 14, 45–51, 140–61, 190, 203, 208, 314
"On the Supposed Scriptural Expression for Eternity": 189
"Peasant of Portugal, The": 213, 224–25, 228, 233
"Reminiscences": 88, 143, 239
"The Revolt of the Tartars": 14
"Rhetoric": 63
Selections Grave and Gay: 203
"Sir William Hamilton": 279, 350
"The Spanish Military Nun": 21
The Stranger's Grave: 213–24, 226–28
Suspiria de Profundis: 3, 7, 35, 43, 45, 51, 58, 61, 72, 73, 85n., 88, 93–98, 104–106, 111, 123, 132, 224, 252–54, 303, 317, 321, 330, 332; "Introductory Notice," 10, 15–16, 36–37, 98, 174, 280, 315, 341, 344, 353; "The Affliction of Childhood," 14, 77–80, 194, 221–22, 318, 319, 324–29, 332, 338, 345; "The Apparition of the Brocken," 14, 100, 112–20, 318; "The Dark Interpreter," 44; "Levana and Our Ladies of Sorrow," 85n., 222, 318, 323, 329, 330; "Savannah-la-Mar," 121–22, 124, 131, 272, 350
"Style": 60, 270–71, 295, 296, 298, 303, 307n.
"System of the Heavens as Revealed by Lord Rosse's Telescopes": 25, 189, 249, 272–74, 338–56
"Walking Stewart": 180, 341

De Quincey family: Elizabeth (Thomas De Quincey's sister), 14, 77–80, 84, 104, 105, 156, 165, 167–68, 170, 178, 185, 189, 195, 205, 207, 219, 221, 225, 291, 319, 324–28, 330, 332, 338, 350; Margaret (wife), 68, 91, 141, 143–45, 156, 180, 218, 219, 291; William (brother), 76, 89, 142, 158, 219; Mrs. Elizabeth Quincey (mother), 89–90, 165–67, 186, 195–96, 227; Thomas Quincey (father), 89–90; Florence (daughter), 91, 142, 209; Eva (granddaughter), 102–103; William (son), 144, 158; Richard (brother), 214; Emily (daughter), 219

Derrida, Jacques: 133, 136n., 298
Descartes, René: 265, 268, 351
Dickens, Charles: 157
Diderot, Denis: 308, 311, 334
Donoghue, Denis: 202
Dostoevsky, Fyodor: 155
Duckers, J. Scott: 214

Edinburgh Saturday Post: 241
Eicher, Hans: 342
Erickson, Erik H.: 97
Ezekiel, Book of: 22–28, 305n., 306n.

Fichte, Johann Gottlieb: 149
Fielding, Henry: 311
Fliess, Wilhelm: 92
Freud, Anna: 101
Freud, Sigmund: 126, 135, 137n., 287; life of, 88–93; *The Interpretation of Dreams*, 88, 93, 94, 96, 100, 106, 110; *Three Essays on the Theory of Sexuality*, 88, 97, 106; concepts of dreams, childhood, and unconscious, 93–106, 109–11, 117–18, 127, 129–30, 136n.; *Beyond the Pleasure Principle*, 93; *Jokes and Their Relation to the Unconscious*, 94–95; *Five Lectures on Psycho-Analysis*, 98; *Civilization and Its Discontents*, 110
Fruman, Norman: 241
Frye, Northrop: 5, 9
Furst, Lilian R.: 199, 202–203

Gass, William H.: 202
Genette, Gérard: 128, 132, 138n.
Gide, André: 132
Goethe, Johann Wolfgang: 311
Goldman, Albert: 4, 5, 241

INDEX

Gothicism: 7, 35, 156, 181, 182, 213, 215, 231, 233, 239, 242-45, 251, 256-60

Habermas, Jürgen: 137n.
Hamilton, Sir William: 351
Hart, Francis R.: 62
Hayter, Alethea: 83, 173
Hazlitt, William: 5, 177, 183, 184
Hegel, Georg Wilhelm Friedrich: 110
Heraclitus: 267
Herder, Johann Gottfried: 265
Herschel, Sir William: 357n.
Hessey: *see* Taylor and Hessey
Hobbes, Thomas: 153
Hodgson, Shadworth H.: 168-69, 348
Hoffman, E. T. A.: 148
Hogarth, William: 283
Hogg, James: 148
Hogg's Instructor: 279
Hölderlin, Friedrich: 333
Homer: 282, 297
Howarth, William L.: 64
Humboldt, Wilhelm von: 265, 268, 269
Hume, David: 254, 268
Hunt, Leigh: 182
Hutchinson, Sara: 169, 171, 183

Irony: 31, 47, 140, 148-54, 199-211, 233, 235, 350, 351, 354

John Bull Magazine: 143
Johnson, Samuel: 345, 347, 358n.
Jones, Ernest: 90, 94
Jordan, John E.: 144, 180-81

Kafka, Franz: 145-46, 231
Kant, Immanuel: 126, 173, 255, 265, 349, 354; *Kritik der reinen Vernunft*, 269-70&n.; *Allgemeine Naturgeschichte und Theorie des Himmels*, 346-48
Keats, John: 3, 5, 8, 9, 22, 27, 29-32, 183, 184
Kernan, Alvin B.: 5, 12, 17
Kierkegaard, Søren: 146, 148, 149
Koyré, Alexandre: 351

Lacan, Jacques: 126, 136n.
Laing, R. D.: 165, 167
Lake District, England: 15, 217, 222, 291
Lamb, Charles: 5, 160
Lawrence, D. H.: 155
Lawson, Charles: 63
Leyris, Pierre: 145
Lindop, Grevel: 4
Literary Souvenir, The: 224
Lloyd, Charles: 145, 192
London Magazine: 6, 7, 12, 38, 93, 143, 160, 214, 239–40
Longman (publisher): 214, 215, 224
Luther, Martin: 247
Lyell, Charles: 349

McFarland, Thomas: 241
Maginn, William: 143, 158
Mahler, Margaret S.: 101
Malthus, Thomas: 247
Maniquis, Robert M.: 3–4, 9, 343–44
Masson, David: 213, 239, 317, 318, 343
Mellor, Anne K.: 199–200
Miller, J. Hillis: 26, 75, 104, 165, 185, 206, 245, 339
Milton, John: 69, 220, 225, 232, 292, 306n.
Monboddo, Lord: *see* James Burnett
More, Hannah: 153
Moreux, Françoise: 155
Muecke, D. C.: 205

Newton, Sir Isaac: 323, 330, 332, 333, 341, 348, 351, 356, 359n.
Nichol, John Pringle: 342–43, 352, 355, 359n.
Nietzsche, Friedrich: 109, 134
Novalis: 333

Paley, William: 263, 265–67, 272
Palmer, John: 281
Parmenides: 266, 267, 273, 275
Parsons, William (Lord Rosse): 340, 342, 352, 354, 357n., 358n.
Pascal, Blaise: 125, 126, 344
Paul, Saint: 353
Peckham, Morse: 75
Phaedrus: 210

Piranesi, Giambattista: 26, 201, 202, 229, 231, 272, 274–75, 339
Plato: 5, 134; *The Republic*, 253, 264; *Timaeus*, 273; *Phaedrus*, 288
Plumtree, A. S.: 165, 166
Poe, Edgar Allan: 39–40, 155, 307n.
Porter, Roger J.: 8–9
Poser, Michael von: 313, 315, 335n.
Praz, Mario: 52, 243
Proust, Marcel: 128–32, 135, 138n.
Pynchon, Thomas: 251

Radcliffe, Ann: 181–82
Raphael: 235
Reid, Thomas: 351
Renza, Louis A.: 59
Ricardo, David: 4, 55, 246, 254
Richter, Jean Paul Friedrich: 308–10, 312, 314, 315, 333, 334, 355
Ricoeur, Paul: 137n.
Rimbaud, Jean: 78
Rosenmeyer, Thomas G.: 199
Rosse, Lord: *see* William Parsons
Rousseau, Jean Jacques: 55, 56, 63, 69, 286, 312, 321
Ruskin, John: 244
Ryle, Gilbert: 263

Sackville-West, Edward: 4
Sade, Marquis de: 160, 161
Sarte, Jean-Paul: 161
Saussure, Ferdinand de: 109, 117
Schiller, Friedrich von: 271, 292
Schlegel, Friedrich: 149, 331, 334; "Über die Unverständlichkeit," 150; on Romantic irony, 199–200, 202, 209, 310; *Gespräch über die Poesie*, 308–10; on concept of *parekbasis*, 310–15, 319, 335n.; on gravity, 333
Schubert, Franz: 244
Scott, Sir Walter: 239–41
Serres, Michel: 250, 261–62n.
Shakespeare, William: 63, 147, 208, 223, 309
Shelley, Mary: 244
Shelley, Percy Bysshe: 5, 8, 22, 31, 32, 122, 201; *Prometheus Unbound*, 27–28; *The Triumph of Life*, 28–29, 34n., 133
Shrapnel, Henry: 11
Simpson, David: 199

Smith, Adam: 246
Socrates: 264
Sophocles: 223
Spitz, René A.: 101, 103
Stapleton, Laurence: 16–17
Starobinski, Jean: 57, 62
Stephenson, George: 11
Sterne, Laurence: 283, 308–12, 321, 331–32, 334
Stevenson, Robert Louis: 155
Sundelson, David: 280
Swift, Jonathan: 150, 310; *A Modest Proposal*, 7, 154; *A Tale of a Tub*, 312

Tait's Edinburgh Magazine: 239, 241, 343
Taylor, Jeremy: 47, 345
Taylor, John: 143
Taylor and Hessey (publisher): 6, 214
Tennyson, Alfred, Lord: 32
Themistocles: 255
Thorslev, Peter L., Jr.: 351
Tieck, Ludwig: 149
Tooke, John Horne: 267
Toulmin, Stephen: 356

Virgil: 284

Wainewright, Thomas Griffiths: 160–61
Walker, Sarah: 183
Walpole, Horace: 244
Watts, Alaric: 224
Wellek, René: 280
Wilde, Oscar: 161
Williams, John: 13, 145–47, 150–59, 161
Wilson, John: 142–45, 158, 161
Wilt, Judith: 243
Wittgenstein, Ludwig: 110, 137n.
Woodhouse, Richard: 143, 222
Woolf, Virginia: 16, 45
Wordsworth, Catherine: 104, 156, 170, 171, 173, 178–80, 183
Wordsworth, Dorothy: 169, 171, 178, 184; on Coleridge, 172–73; on De Quincey, 209
Wordsworth, Mary: 184

Wordsworth, William: 3, 8, 21, 24, 27, 55, 72–73, 75, 78, 82–84, 91, 143, 144, 151, 152, 158, 164, 169–71, 174–85, 187–88, 190–93, 201, 214, 217, 224, 226, 270, 285, 286, 340; *The Prelude*, 8, 182, 184, 193, 197n., 274, 312; *The Excursion*, 21, 274; *Lyrical Ballads*, 168, 180; "Guilt and Sorrow," 171; "The Old Cumberland Beggar," 171; *The White Doe of Rylstone*, 175; "She Was a Phantom of Delight," 176, 177; "Ode: Intimations of Immortality," 178, 179, 197n.; "There Was a Boy," 183; *The Borderers*, 187; "Elegiac Stanzas Suggested by a Picture of Peele Castle," 191; "Home at Grasmere," 192; "Afterthought," 193; "We Are Seven," 205; "Strange Fits of Passion Have I Known," 223; "'Tis Said That Some Have Died for Love," 223; "A Jewish Family," 235
Wright, Thomas: 348

Yeats, William Butler: 32, 33, 202

Zeno: 272, 273, 275, 350